MW00813959

THE
BIBLE
EXPLAINER

THE BIBLE EXPLAINER

MICHAEL WITTMER

BARBOUR BOOKS
An Imprint of Barbour Publishing, Inc.

ISBN 978-1-64352-081-0

Cover Design: Greg Jackson, Thinkpen Design

Published by Barbour Books, an imprint of Barbour Publishing, Inc., 1810 Barbour Drive, Uhrichsville, Ohio 44683, www.barbourbooks.com

Our mission is to inspire the world with the life-changing message of the Bible.

Printed in China.

CONTENTS

PART 2: Origins—Where Everything Comes From

PART 3: Israel—Why the Old Testament Matters Today

PART 5: The Church—How the New Testament Affects Our World

PART 6: The End—Where Things Are Ultimately Headed

A Final Question

INTRODUCTION: Explaining the Explainer

What is the Bible?

Many people will have a ready reply to that question, but others—even some who attend Christian churches—might struggle to answer. Obviously, the Bible is a book, but its meaning, purpose, and relevance aren't as generally known.

Through much of American history (and European history before that), the Bible was commonly accepted as "the Word of God," the basis of Christian belief and behavior. For generations, even people who didn't adhere to the Christian faith often knew much about the Bible and respected what it had to say.

But today many people view the Bible as dusty, out-of-date, or completely irrelevant to modern life. Worse, some think it's only a weapon for bigots or a refuge for "haters." Why such a change in perception? We believe that's because the Bible has been misunderstood. And it's misunderstood because even many of its supporters have failed to read, study, and apply its message as they should have. If Christians have sometimes taken the Bible for granted, the non-Christian world will certainly care less for it.

The Bible Is Worth Knowing

The Bible may be the least-read bestseller in publishing history. It was the first major book produced on Johannes Gutenberg's revolutionary movable-type press, and millions (if not billions) of copies have been printed since then. The Bible is also available, free of charge, on numerous internet sites. In much of the modern world, it is easily accessible to anyone who wants to read it.

But the Bible can be a daunting book. It contains nearly eight hundred thousand words—six or seven times as many as a typical novel—and much of the text describes people, places, and things that are foreign to us. Depending on the translation you use, there are strange words like *regeneration* and *propitiation*. Many readers are troubled by scenes of violence, by the mention of God's "wrath," and by the exclusive claims made by and for Jesus. These are serious issues deserving real answers, and we will attempt to provide them throughout *The Bible Explainer*.

First, though, let's distill this complex book into three words: *God loves you*. It's true—this is the "gospel," a term that means "good news." Even the dark, difficult parts of the Bible fit into this reality when you understand the overall story of God.

That's what we hope to provide with *The Bible Explainer*—a perspective on the Bible that shows what it purports to be, why that's believable, and how it provides meaning to your life today. Since everybody starts with a particular perspective, here is ours: We believe the Bible is truly "God's Word," a record of exactly what He wants people to know. We believe the historical events in the Bible really happened and that they tell the one big story that makes sense of our own little stories.

How This Book Works

The Bible Explainer provides answers to common questions about the Bible—250 plus one bonus question. You can read the book straight through or digest one entry per day like a devotional. Either way, by the end of your reading, you will have a clearer, fuller understanding of our opening question: *What is the Bible?*

Questions are presented in a logical order, so that the answers build upon each other. The initial questions address very broad matters, such as what the Bible is, who wrote it, and when. As you progress, questions will tackle more specific concerns (such as "What is sin?" and "Who are the Gentiles?") or difficult issues (like "Why would God tell Joshua to kill every man, woman, and child in Canaan?").

Of course, good people can differ on their interpretations of controversial passages, so *The Bible Explainer* respectfully acknowledges the various viewpoints within the Christian world. But most of the Bible is straightforward and not confusing. So our goal is to present it as the coherent, understandable revelation of God to humanity, the ultimate authority on all matters of belief and behavior.

We begin on the next page with the foundational question of how God speaks to us today. We hope that this book will not only interest you but inspire you—to spend more time and energy on the Bible itself.

The Publishers

A Note on Illustrations

This book makes use of many classical paintings to illustrate Bible characters such as Jesus, Paul, and Moses. No one knows for sure how these individuals looked, but they most certainly had darker skin, eyes, and hair than many European artists portrayed them with. Please enjoy the artwork while recognizing its historical limitations.

PART 1: BIBLE BASICS

What It Is, How We Should Read It

1 How does God speak to us today?

This may not be the best question to begin with but not for the reason you'd think. You might suppose our first question shouldn't be "*How* does God speak to us?" but rather "*Does* God speak to us?" The Bible says God "lives in unapproachable light, whom no one has seen or can see" (1 Timothy 6:16). No one can see God and live (Exodus 33:20). So shouldn't we first ask if knowledge of God is even possible?

No. We're skipping that question because everyone (including you, dear reader) already knows God does speak to us. He speaks to everyone in every moment through *nature, history*, and *ourselves* as His image bearers.

Nature. Open your eyes and look around. Every peony, squirrel, and strawberry—every natural thing you see, hear, touch, taste, and smell—tells you something about the God who made it.

***History*.** Look at your last week. Then go back five years. Ten. Now twenty. Your life may not have been easy. You may have suffered agonizing trials. Yet don't you also see God's hand carrying you? You're still here because God has been loving you all this time. Tell God you know it was Him, and also thank Him for routinely meeting your needs through ordinary means, such as work and family.

Ourselves. God also speaks to us from deep inside. He created us in His image, so each of us is hardwired to know Him. We may convince ourselves this idea of God is unconvincing, but deep down we all know something about His "eternal power and divine nature" (Romans 1:20). This is why whenever we're in big trouble, the first thing we'll do is pray.

God speaks to all people, all the time. But *how God speaks to us today* is not the best question to start with because it drastically undersells what God is doing. God doesn't merely speak; He calls. God doesn't chitchat; He summons. His Word beckons us into passionate, everlasting communion with Him.

We may hear rumblings of God's call through other people, a surprising opportunity, or an inner compulsion. Someone says something that grabs our attention, and we sense God is calling us through them. A big break falls into our lap, and we wonder if it might have been heaven sent. Or we feel a strong urge to say or do something. If we suspect this prompting came from God, we might follow it and see what happens.

But the fullest, clearest, most authoritative and saving way that God calls us is through His holy Word, the Bible. You may never hear God's summons through other people, circumstances, or inner impressions. That's okay. You'll still hear God call, in all the important ways, when you read the Bible.

Do you want to hear God speak directly to your heart? Do you want to know what God has done for you, what He has promised to still do, and what He expects from you? Do you want to know God's plan for your life? Get yourself a Bible.

Do you have one? Great. I'm guessing you may have questions about it. The Bible can seem intimidating. That's why I've written *The Bible Explainer,* to help you understand God's Word and hear His voice when you read it. Whether you buy this book or put it back on the shelf, the important thing is to read the Bible, and read it well. There's no better way to hear God's call.

2 What is the Bible?

The Bible is a big book. It's much larger than *The Cool Dads of Teenagers* or *The Wisdom of Daytime Television,* though it's still roughly 30 percent smaller than the Harry Potter series.

The Bible consists of sixty-six sections, which themselves are called "books." These stand-alone books were written by at least forty authors over roughly fifteen hundred years. The books are gathered into two main sections: the "Old Testament," which contains thirty-nine, and the "New Testament," which has twenty-seven.

The Bible was the first major book printed on Johannes Gutenberg's revolutionary movable-type printing press in 1455.

But the Bible is more than simply a book or even a collection of books. It is *God's Word.* The Bible says, "All Scripture is God-breathed and is useful for teaching, rebuking, correcting and training in righteousness, so that the servant of God may be thoroughly equipped for every good work" (2 Timothy 3:16–17). The Bible is God's story about His love for us. It tells how He made us, how we disobeyed Him and got ourselves into the deepest trouble, and how He came to earth to give His life to rescue us.

What is the Bible? It's the defining story of our lives.

3 Where did the Bible get its name?

The word *Bible* means "book." This may seem ironic, because the Bible was written before there were books, at least as we understand them. Let me explain.

The first "books" of the Bible were written on sheets that the Egyptians made from the stalks of papyrus reeds that grew among the marshes of the Nile delta.

Papyrus roll

These papyri were spliced together and rolled onto scrolls rather than bound into books, as we do with paper today.

The Greeks called papyrus *byblos,* so it seemed natural to call a scroll of papyri *biblion* (which meant "little book)" or, if it was larger, *biblos* ("book"). Eventually *biblion* lost its diminutive connotation, and early Greek-speaking Christians began calling the Old and New Testament "the books" (*ta biblia*). In the Middle Ages, Latin-speaking Christians changed the meaning of *biblia* from plural to singular, and so the Bible came to be known as "The Book."[1]

The Bible is so clearly the best in its class that it is named for the entire class. There is no "The Movie" or "The Song," but there is "The Book." Christians are people of The Book. We read, reflect, and savor The Book, for it is how we hear the call of God.

4 What is the point of the Bible?

That's hard to answer only one way. If we were asked about the point of our lives, we might refer to a personal mission statement: *to serve and bring joy to others, to become YouTube famous,* or *to retire at fifty to an island in the Caribbean.*

But even the best mission statements cannot capture the whole point of our lives. If we want others to know us, we must share our story. We must tell them about the people and places that shaped us.

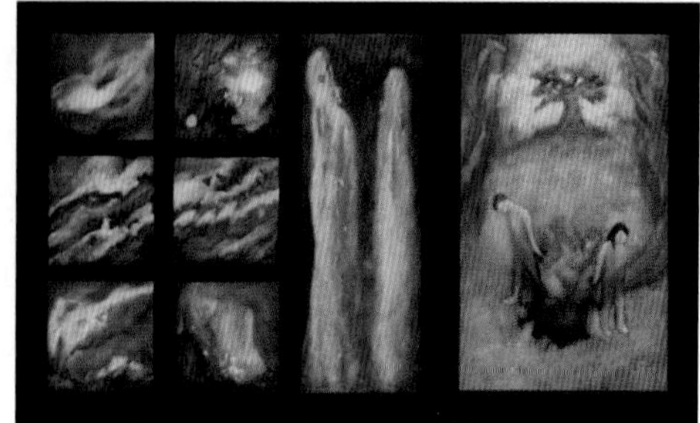

Similarly, the Bible's "mission statement" gives us an understanding of its overall point: "God so loved the world that he gave his one and only Son, that whoever believes in him shall not perish but have eternal life" (John 3:16).

Our personal salvation is for the sake of the church, which God says is the "Bride of Christ." Since the Bible calls Satan a dragon (Revelation 12:9), the point of the Bible may be as familiar as a children's story: *Slay the dragon, get the girl.* [2]

To understand this mission, we must know the rest of the Bible's story—the greatest story ever told.

5 What is the story of the Bible?

Like any good book, the Bible has a plot. In simple terms, it goes like this:

CREATION	FALL	REDEMPTION	CONSUMMATION
Genesis 1–2	Genesis 3–11	Genesis 12–Revelation 22	Revelation 21–22

The Bible opens with *Creation*, which explains how God made the world and then Adam and Eve to run it on His behalf. Everything was exactly as it should be. But paradise didn't last long.

In the Bible's third chapter, we learn about the *Fall,* when Adam and Eve rebelled against God and delivered His good world to the devil. Genesis 3–11 describes how sin shattered human beings and the rest of our world. Adam blamed Eve for blowing it, and she turned on the serpent for tempting her. The humans now must die and suffer on the way. The earth sprouted thorns and thistles. Humanity's first son murdered his brother. The world became so violent that God sent a flood to

This panorama of the biblical story was painted by Bette Dickinson and is used with her permission. Bette's paintings can be found at www.bettedickinson.life/.

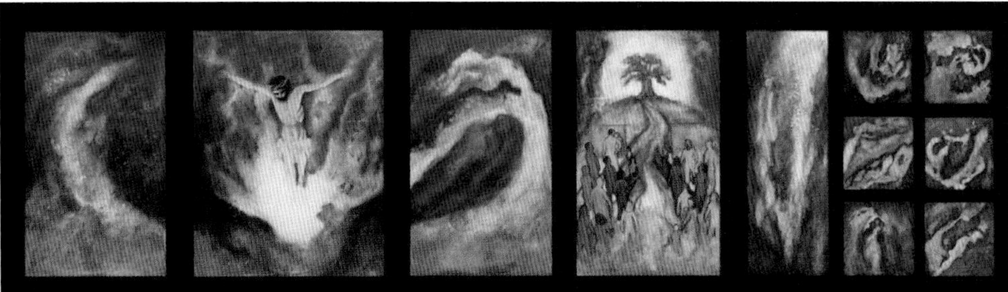

wipe out everything—except Noah's family and a starter set for each animal—and begin again.

The Bible's third and longest act is God's ambitious plan to take back His world from Satan, restore creation, and set things right. *Redemption* takes up nearly the entire Bible, starting in Genesis 12 and continuing right through to the end. It's so long, it requires an intermission between the Old and New Testaments.

Redemption is a big job, one that unfolds slowly in four movements.

First, God established a foothold in enemy territory when He selected Abraham as forefather of His special people. They would become the nation of Israel, God's light to the nations. They would show the world how God blessed the people who faithfully served Him.

But Israel rebelled as Adam had. So God decided He would accomplish redemption by Himself—which had been His plan all along. In Redemption's second movement, God sent His only Son, Jesus, to be the faithful Israelite and Last Adam who obeyed perfectly and then died as a sacrifice for our sin.

When Jesus arose from the dead and returned to heaven, He sent His Spirit to unite His followers in the church. This is Redemption's third phase, the period we live in today. Christians now gather to celebrate what Jesus has done, then scatter into our communities to tell others the good news.

We will continue this mission until Jesus returns and restores all things. This fourth movement of Redemption blends into God's final act, the culmination of world history. *Consummation* is Redemption-plus. Jesus doesn't merely restore creation to its original goodness—He is coming back to make it better than ever. The end of God's story returns us to the beginning but at a much higher level. (For details, see "How is the end better than the beginning?" on page 458.)

6 Who are the Bible's key characters?

Sports commentators often play the "Mount Rushmore game." As Mount Rushmore portrays the heads of America's four greatest presidents—can you name them all?—these talking heads debate who are the four greatest players in the history of football, baseball, or basketball. Hint: the last category contains Jordan and LeBron then lots of arguing. That's why it's fun to play.

Who belongs on the Mount Rushmore of the Old Testament? The New Testament? Of the whole Bible? I'll list some candidates. You grab a couple of friends and see if you can amicably argue your way to consensus.

Here are the contenders from the Old Testament:

Adam. Head of the human race, though he isn't mentioned much in the Bible until the apostle Paul justly blames him for all the sin in the world (Romans 5:12–21).

Noah. Built a floating zoo that gave the world its one redo. Appears on the cover of every children's Bible.

Abraham. Father of our faith and the Jewish people. Not bad for a man who begot his first son when he was eighty-six years old. His willingness to sacrifice his second, promised, son on the site of Israel's future temple foreshadowed what God would do to save us from our sin.

Jacob. Mr. Jew. God changed his name to "Israel." His sons are the heads of Israel's twelve tribes. He deceived his family his entire life, so it was tragically fitting that his sons deceived him into believing his favorite son was dead.

Joseph. Jacob's favorite, and good, son. Sold into slavery in Egypt, he rose to power and provided refuge for his family, which eventually led to their enslavement in Egypt.

Moses. Redeemer who led Israel out of bondage in Egypt. He is the Old Testament picture of Jesus, and his name is shorthand for the Law. Given the miserable task of leading a nation of whiners across the desert, he finally lost his temper and consequently was prohibited from entering the Promised Land.

Joshua. Moses' protégé who led Israel into the Promised Land. Last seen as a cucumber in the VeggieTales story of Jericho, "Josh and the Big Wall."

Samuel. Prophet who told the newly settled nation of Israel what God thought of their sin and to knock it off.

David. Israel's greatest king and ancestor of Jesus, who is called the "Son of David." Perhaps made of Teflon, he committed adultery and murdered a man and yet is still remembered as "a man after God's own heart."

Solomon. David's son and king of Israel during its golden age. His reign started well, but by the end he was worshiping the false gods of his seven hundred wives and three hundred concubines. His homelife is a cautionary answer to the question, what if *The Bachelor* marries them all?

Elijah. Greatest prophet sent to warn Israel and her kings to repent or God would take them into captivity. Famous for his throwdown on Mount Carmel, which though it sounds delicious, did not end sweetly for the prophets of Baal.

Elisha. Successor to Elijah. An important figure in his own right, but there probably isn't space on Mount Rushmore for more than one prophet. And I already said Elijah was the greatest.

Job. Suffered the worst twenty-four hours ever because of a bet God made with the devil. If that makes you angry, that's why Job is in the Bible.

Isaiah. The prophet with the most beautiful prose, but he wrote so much that too

Two of the Bible's great prophets—Elijah and Elisha—appear in a nineteenth-century fresco. Elisha is watching his mentor ascend to heaven in a "chariot of fire" (2 Kings 2:11).

few Christians bother to read him. You're different, though. Start reading the book of Isaiah. You won't be disappointed.

These next five names are from the New Testament.

Jesus. Son of God and Savior of the world. Jesus is obviously the most important Person, so consider taking him out of consideration for the purposes of this game. Who is on the Mount Rushmore of those who are merely human?

Mary. Mother of our Lord, praised a little too much by some. Mary is the one woman on our list, proving the events of the Bible occurred before the rise of feminism.

Peter. Lead disciple. Roman Catholics say his person, and Protestants say his teaching, supplied the foundation for the church. Always the first to jump and to get in trouble.

John. The disciple whom Jesus loved most. Lived longest of any of the disciples, long enough to write the last book of the Bible.

Paul. Missionary to the Gentiles. Preached the Gospel and planted churches throughout the Roman world, wrote more books of the Bible than anyone else, including the ones that are read the most. His letters supply the foundation for what Christians believe.

Notice the New Testament has barely enough people to populate its Mount Rushmore. Or maybe I left off someone who should be here? Let the argument begin.

7 Where did Bible events take place?

Because Europe and America have enjoyed a long history of Christian influence, many mistakenly assume Christianity is a Western religion and the Bible a Western book. In truth, the Christian faith and its Scriptures arose in the Middle East.

The events of the Bible began in what is modern Iraq. The Garden of Eden may well have been in Iraq, and Noah also may have lived there. Mount Ararat, where Noah's Ark came to rest, lies in eastern Turkey, an easy float from Iraq during the great flood.

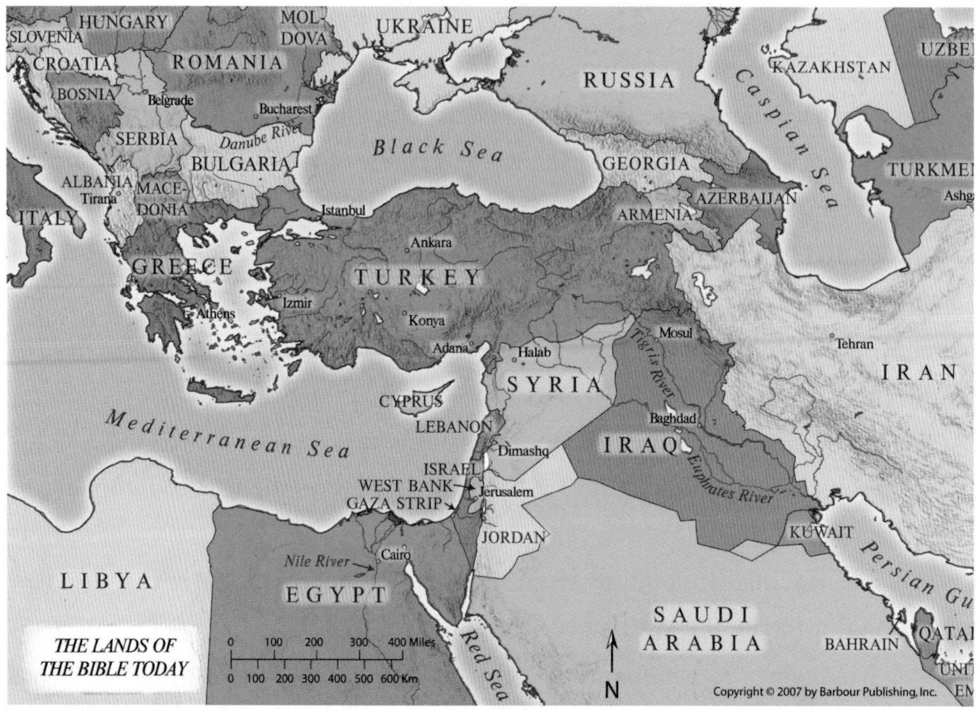

While we cannot be sure about Eden and Noah, we do know that redemptive history began in Iraq. Abram was living near the Persian Gulf, in the city of Ur, when God called him to go west, crossing what is now Iraq, Syria, and Lebanon and settling in Israel, on the eastern coast of the Mediterranean Sea.

The Bible, and Christian history, has headed west ever since. The events of the Old Testament occurred mostly in the center of the world—Israel is a land bridge that connects Asia, Africa, and Europe (Ezekiel 5:5)—with various forays and exiles into Egypt, Assyria (northern Iraq and southeastern Turkey), Babylon (Iraq), and Persia (Iran). The New Testament starts in Jerusalem, the capital of Israel, then follows Jesus' disciples obeying His command to take His good news through Judea, Samaria, and to the ends of the earth (Acts 1:8).

The apostle Paul was the greatest missionary of the early church. Since he was a Roman citizen, he traveled easily throughout the Roman Empire. This empire stretched west from Israel, so Paul spent the latter half of the book of Acts walking across modern Syria and Turkey and sailing around the Mediterranean Sea. We're not sure if he made it all the way to Spain, but he did visit Greece more than once and finally came to Rome.

This westward expansion of Christianity continued when the Roman Empire adopted the Christian faith in the fourth century. Europe remained Christian throughout the Middle Ages, then brought its faith to America when Christopher Columbus and other explorers "discovered" the New World. American Christians sent thousands of missionaries to Asia during the nineteenth and twentieth centuries, and now Chinese Christians aim to complete the circle: their "Back to Jerusalem" movement intends to build churches in the primarily Muslim countries that lie between China and Israel. They are prepared to sacrifice their lives for Jesus, fulfilling His command to take the Gospel from Jerusalem to the ends of the earth. Because the world is round, the ends of the earth meet back in the middle, where it all began.

The Bible is rightly popular in the West, but it remains a Middle Eastern book. That is where it started and by God's grace where it will finish.

This theater in Ephesus was the site of a riot against Paul and the Gospel (Acts 19:23–41).

8 Why are there "Old" and "New" Testaments?

The word *testament* means "covenant," which is God's promise to rescue His people and be their God. There are Old and New Testaments because there are Old and New Covenants—two phases of God's plan to save the world. The Old Covenant unfolds in God's mounting promises to Noah, Abraham, Moses, and David, while the New Covenant makes them all come true through the saving acts of Jesus and the Holy Spirit.

The New Testament may be when the decisive battle between Jesus and Satan occurs, but it seems rude to call the earlier covenant the "Old" Testament. After all, it's the foundational section, taking up well over half the Bible. We could call it the "Senior" or "First" Testament, but to avoid confusion we'll use the standard "Old Testament," though we really mean "Original."

Jewish people particularly disagree with the name "Old" Testament, since they don't believe Jesus is Part Two of God's rescue plan. But Christians believe Jesus is the turning point of the Bible and of all history. As He indicated during the Last Supper: "This cup is the new covenant in my blood, which is poured out for you" (Luke 22:20). This story of Jesus and His new covenant is told in the New Testament, which is the smaller, climactic half of the Bible.

Jesus announces the "new covenant" during the Last Supper. His life, death, and resurrection marked the breaking point between the Old and New Testaments.

9 What's in the Old Testament?

The Old Testament is the only Bible of Judaism and the first, larger part of the Christian Bible. It contains thirty-nine books gathered into three sections: the *Law*, the *Prophets*, and the *Writings*. Jesus referred to all three when He told His disciples, "Everything must be fulfilled that is written about me in the Law of Moses, the Prophets and the Psalms" (Luke 24:44). Psalms is the most important of the writings, so Jesus was alluding here to the entire Bible. (In His time, of course, only the Old Testament had been written.)

The Jews call this testament the *Tanakh,* which is a Hebrew acronym spelled with the first letter of each part: T for *Torah* (law), N for *Nevi'im* (prophets), K for *Ketuvim* (writings). There's a final H because it's in Hebrew, and each word is required to end in the back of your throat.

The *Law* consists of five books: Genesis, Exodus, Leviticus, Numbers, and Deuteronomy. Christians unimaginatively call these five books the *Pentateuch*, an intimidating Greek word that only means "five books." Jewish people, though, use a more descriptive term, calling these books the Torah—a Hebrew word that means "instruction," "teaching," or "law." (Jews also use *Torah* to refer to the entire Old Testament and sometimes even to their entire religious tradition, so you may have to ask what they mean when they use the term.) Whatever it's called, the Law is foundational for the entire Bible. These books tell about creation, Adam's fall, and how God founded His people, the nation of Israel, by delivering them from bondage in Egypt and giving them His law to live by.

The *Prophets* contain two subsections. The "Former Prophets" (Joshua, Judges, 1–2 Samuel, and 1–2 Kings) are historical books that guided future generations by describing Israel's successes and failures. The "Latter Prophets" include the large books of Isaiah, Jeremiah, and Ezekiel, as well as twelve "minor" (meaning briefer) prophecies from men such as Hosea, Joel, Amos, and Obadiah. The prophets are God's police force, sent to arrest Israel's disobedience and warn of dire consequences if they continued to serve idols and abuse each other.

The *Writings* contain three subsections. The "Poetic Books" include the large books of Job, Psalms, and Proverbs. They are full of exquisite speeches, prayers, and wise sayings. The "Five Scrolls" are much smaller and include the historical books of Ruth and Esther along with the lyrical yearnings of Ecclesiastes, Song of Songs, and Lamentations. The "Historical Books" are included in the Writings because they were among the last books to be written. First and Second Chronicles describe how stubborn Israel was led into exile by Assyria and Babylon, and Daniel, Ezra, and Nehemiah tell how the Jews survived in captivity and were finally allowed to return home.

The First Testament ends with the Israelites back in their Promised Land yet still under the thumb of foreign powers. They needed God to send a deliverer, but God had gone silent. He would not break His silence for more than four hundred years. When He did speak, His first word was Jesus.

A scroll of the Torah—the first five books of the Christian Old Testament—is read during the Sukkot holiday near Jerusalem's Western Wall.

10 What's the story of the Old Testament?

There are many riveting stories in the Tanakh, such as Abraham preparing to sacrifice his son, Joseph turning the tables on his brothers, David killing Goliath, Delilah sapping Samson's strength, Esther outwitting the despicable Haman, and Elijah challenging priests of Baal to a sudden-death, can-your-god-top-this competition. These stories will be more meaningful when you understand how they advance the Bible's main plot.

The story of the Old Testament is the nation of Israel and how God established her to save the world. Here's the thumbnail plot: *Origins→Exodus→Kingdom→Exile.* And here's a longer explanation:

Origins. The Old Testament begins by briefly explaining how God's good creation came to be broken then jumps quickly into God's plan for redemption. God called Abram, a man from the polytheistic land of Ur, changing his name to Abraham, and saying this "father of many" would become a "great nation" to bless the world (Genesis 12:1–3; 17:1–8). Abraham and his wife were elderly and childless, but God miraculously enabled ninety-year-old Sarah to conceive and give birth to Isaac. This child of promise fathered Jacob, whose name God changed to Israel. Jacob had twelve sons, who—except for Joseph, whose lineage was divided between his sons, Ephraim and Manasseh—became the heads of the "twelve tribes of Israel." Remember the names Abraham, Isaac, and Jacob. They are the revered founding fathers of the Jewish nation.

Exodus. Jacob's sons detested their younger brother Joseph. He was their dad's favorite, and he rubbed their noses in it. So the older sons sold Joseph into slavery in Egypt, which oddly enough turned out to be their salvation. By God's miraculous intervention, Joseph climbed Egyptian society until he was second only to Pharaoh. When famine forced his brothers to seek refuge in Egypt, they found a tough but forgiving Joseph to take them in. Read the story in Genesis 37–50, and try not to cry.

Jacob's descendants lived in Egypt for a couple hundred years. Initially they

The Old Testament is all about origins, including the beginnings of time and space: "In the beginning God created the heavens and the earth" (Genesis 1:1).

flourished, which made the Egyptians jealous. So they enslaved the Jews, drove them without mercy, and even killed their infant sons. God heard Israel's cries and sent Moses to deliver them. But Pharaoh refused to cooperate, saying, "Who is the LORD, that I should obey him and let Israel go?" (Exodus 5:2). Ten plagues later, Pharaoh had a pretty good idea. God afflicted the Egyptians with boils, frogs, locusts, hail, and perpetual darkness. He turned the Nile into blood and slew their firstborn sons. Pharaoh finally gave in and said Israel could go. He quickly changed his mind, but Israel had already gone. God opened the Red Sea so Israel could pass through then closed the waters in time to drown Pharaoh's pursuing army.

Moses led Israel to Mount Sinai, where God claimed them as His people and gave them Ten Commandments to follow. But Israel was already breaking many of the rules as Moses was receiving them. They started their relationship with God by worshiping a golden calf and apparently participating in indiscriminate sex, omens of what was to come. (It usually spells trouble when your wife has an affair on your wedding night.)

Still, God hung in there with His people. He held them accountable for their rebellion yet also forgave, giving them repeated chances to return to Him. God made Israel wander in the desert for forty years when they refused to believe He would defeat the giants in the Promised Land. He used the next generation, led by Moses' former assistant, Joshua, to claim the territory that is basically where the nation of Israel is today.

Kingdom. Israel never did claim all the land God had promised, but they settled on enough ground to become a great nation. When Israel grumbled for a king, God said *He* was their king. When they said they wanted a tangible, human king like the other nations, God relented and gave them Saul. His insecurities and sin caused his reign to end badly, but he was succeeded by David, a man after God's own heart. The reigns of David and his son Solomon are the golden age for Israel. Life was never better, before or since.

Exile. Later kings were less devout than David and Solomon (at least in his early years), and the nation suffered for it. The ten tribes in the north (Israel) soon split from the two tribes in the south (Judah), and both nations continued their slide into oblivion. God sent a parade of prophets to warn both kingdoms to stop worshiping other gods and wounding their neighbors, but they would not listen for long. God finally had enough of their idolatry and injustice, and He sent the Assyrians to capture Israel and the Babylonians to enslave Judah. The best and brightest of God's children were taken into captivity.

The ten northern tribes never made it back home, dissolving into Assyria and the surrounding nations. Only the two southern tribes were given a final chance. The Old Testament concludes with a king of Persia (contemporary Iran) decreeing that Judah, after languishing in exile for seventy years, could return home. Stragglers came back to Jerusalem, rebuilt a scaled-back version of the temple and the city's walls, and wept for the glory of the city they once knew. They had thrown away their privilege and become a shell of their former selves. They needed help.

God did not respond for more than four hundred years. When He finally appeared, He came to win.

Jesus is the focus of the entire New Testament, though the four Gospels are the specific record of His life and ministry. He is shown here in a 16th-century fresco, healing the crowds.

11 What's in the New Testament?

The New Testament contains five parts: *Gospels* that describe the life and work of Jesus; *the Acts of the Apostles*, which presents the early history of the church; *Paul's Epistles* to individuals and churches; *General Epistles* written by John, Peter, James, and Jude; and the concluding *Revelation of St. John.*

The four *Gospels* are Matthew, Mark, Luke, and John. Why several? Because Jesus is the most important Person who has ever lived. He's the most important Person for your life. So we'd want more than just one of His followers to write about Him. The more faithful perspectives, the better!

We think Mark was the first one to write and that he got much of his material from Peter, the lead disciple. Peter seemed to suffer from a kind of ADHD, blurting out words, swinging swords, and generally acting before he thought through his next move. He's the guy who loses his queen by the fifth turn but has a blast capturing a couple of your pawns. Peter's Gospel, as channeled through Mark, is a ready-made script for an action movie.

The other Gospels have their own unique flavors. Matthew emphasized that

Jesus came to take back this world from Satan; Luke centered his Gospel around Jerusalem, where the climactic battle would occur; and John wrote to prove that "Jesus is the Messiah, the Son of God" (20:31). Seven times in John's Gospel, Jesus refers to Himself as "I am," the holy name of Israel's God. The Jews got the point and demanded His death because He had blasphemously "claimed to be the Son of God" (John 19:7).

The Acts of the Apostles, often called simply "Acts," tells the story of the early church. The book opens with Jesus ascending to heaven then sending the promised Holy Spirit to believers on the Day of Pentecost. The Spirit filled the disciples, who spread the good news about Jesus from Jerusalem through the rest of the known world (Acts 1:8). Acts concludes with the apostle Paul, having preached the Gospel across what is modern-day Syria, Turkey, and Greece, finally making it to the capital city of Rome.

Paul's Epistles are thirteen letters written to encourage leaders and churches in Rome, Corinth, Ephesus, and elsewhere. Because these letters were also correcting errors in belief and practice, they are a gold mine for Christian thought. Some people include the Epistle to the Hebrews in Paul's writings, but we don't actually know who wrote this anonymous, richly theological book.

The *General Epistles* are sometimes called the "catholic" (meaning universal) epistles and include James, 1–2 Peter, 1–3 John, and Jude. These small books are read somewhat less than Paul's, in part because they contain less doctrinal material. While still inspired scripture, their lesser status shoves them toward the end of the Bible.

The New Testament's final book is the *Revelation of St. John.* Exiled to the island of Patmos by the indomitable power of Rome, John received encouragement from Jesus Himself. Jesus invited John on a tour of heaven, giving him a message for the persecuted church: Jesus remains Lord over every king, and He and His followers will ultimately triumph (Revelation 1:5; 11:15).

That is a message for us today too. Don't fear. Faithfully serve Jesus, and you will receive the "victor's crown" (Revelation 2:10).

12 What's the story of the New Testament?

The plot of the New Testament has two main parts: *Jesus* and *the Church.*

Jesus. The Jews needed a Savior. They wanted someone who would march on Jerusalem, defeat the powers of evil, and free them from perpetual bondage. This is precisely what they got. But because they were looking for a different kind of Savior, they missed who Jesus was. They missed so badly that they killed Him. And by killing Him, they made their salvation possible.

The Jews yearned for a king who would overthrow the occupying Romans and cleanse the corrupt religion in their temple. Jesus came to do both, but only after rescuing the people from their own sin. He knew the first-century Jews' deepest need was the same as ours today—reconciliation with God. Our primary problem isn't political or social. It's personal. We have rebelled against our Creator and are justly bound for hell unless Someone intervenes. This is why Jesus came.

Jesus invested three years around the Sea of Galilee in northern Israel, mentoring His disciples, healing the sick, and proclaiming that, with His arrival, the kingdom of God had come. When the time was right, Jesus and His small band of disciples marched south to Jerusalem. He triumphantly rode into the city, drove the corrupt moneychangers from the temple, denounced the self-righteous religious leaders, and announced that Israel's king had finally arrived.

The Jewish leaders were jealous of Jesus' popularity, angry at His personal attacks, and sure He had committed blasphemy by claiming to be equal with God. They pressured the Romans to arrest and crucify Him.

Game over.

Except this had been Jesus' plan all along. He had come to die, the innocent Last Adam bearing the guilt of the first Adam and his children. Jesus suffered in our place. He absorbed the wrath of God that we deserved.

And Jesus did not stay dead. Three days later, God the Father raised Him to life, releasing Him from the guilt He had shouldered for us. Now all who turn from sin and put their faith in Jesus will be forgiven and counted as clean as He is. We may be sinners in ourselves, but in Jesus we are saints.

The word *church* may describe a building, but the New Testament idea is that of Jesus' "body"—every true believer, everywhere, from all time.

The Church. For forty days after His resurrection, Jesus appeared periodically to His disciples then ascended to heaven, where He now sits at His Father's right hand. Ten days after His ascension, the Holy Spirit came to fill the disciples and empower the church to spread the good news about Jesus around the world. The first Christians went to the synagogues and excitedly told the Jews that Jesus was the Savior they had long sought. Many Jews believed, while others said the Christians should die for supporting a blasphemer like Jesus.

Saul was one of the angry Jews. He traveled from town to town searching for Christians to imprison. But on one such trip, Jesus appeared to Saul in a bright light that knocked him to the ground. This experience changed Saul forever.

Initially, he tried to convert his fellow Jews, but when they repeatedly tried to kill him, Saul shook off the dust from his feet and said he would take the Gospel to the Gentiles. He now used his Greek name, Paul, and traveled the Roman Empire declaring that Jesus—not Caesar—is Lord. Paul finally reached Rome itself, where in Caesar's capital "he proclaimed the kingdom of God and taught about the Lord Jesus Christ" (Acts 28:31).

So Jesus did come to free His people from the powers of Rome—just what the Jews wanted. But in the process He provided what they (and we) need most: not a rescue from the evil that lies outside but salvation from the evil that lurks in every human heart. Jesus came to reconcile us with God (2 Corinthians 5:21).

13 What's the most important part of the Bible?

This is a dangerous question. I don't really want to answer it, but it seems fair, so let's try.

In a Slovakian church icon, Jesus embraces His best friend on earth, the apostle John. John's account of Jesus' life could be considered the best starting point for Bible reading.

If you could only take one book of the Bible with you to a deserted island, which would it be? The Psalms, because they'll teach you how to cry for help? Maybe Genesis, because its story of Noah building a boat from scratch might give you some ideas?

I know what I'd take and why. Let me explain:

When Jesus met some men confused by reports of His resurrection, He rebuked them for not understanding what the Old Testament said about Him. "And beginning with Moses and all the Prophets, he explained to them what was said in all the Scriptures concerning himself" (Luke 24:27). Jesus believed the payoff of the whole Bible—and any part of the Bible—is what it says about *Him*.

If that's true, then I would take the

book of the Bible that says the most about Jesus. That would be one of the four Gospels, and probably John's, because it was written "that you may believe that Jesus is the Messiah, the Son of God, and that by believing you may have life in his name" (20:31).

My answer, then, to our dangerous question is that the most important part of the Bible must be the part that most explicitly teaches about Jesus—who He is and what He did. The most important book would be John, and its most important verse would be this one: "For God so loved the world that he gave his one and only Son, that whoever believes in him shall not perish but have eternal life" (3:16).

If I could take a second book, it would be Romans, because the apostle Paul explains the salvation Jesus won for me and how it transforms my identity, thoughts, and interactions with others. That last part won't be important if I'm alone on the island, but it's necessary now!

14 Why are some letters red?

Many Bibles use red letters to highlight the words of Jesus. The first red-letter New Testament was published in 1899 by Louis Klopsch, who was a close friend of the evangelist D. L. Moody. Klopsch wanted to emphasize the centrality of Christ in the Bible, and he chose red because it was the color of Jesus' blood.[3]

I appreciate how the red letters draw my attention to Jesus, though it's important to remember the red letters do not carry more authority than the black type. I often hear Christians comment, "I'm glad Jesus did not say anything about ______," and they fill the blank with some controversial issue that the Bible clearly addresses. They forget that whatever the Bible says about something is Jesus' view on the subject. For instance, Jesus isn't recorded to have said anything about bestiality, but you can be sure He agrees with the black letters that do (Leviticus 18:23; Exodus 22:19; Deuteronomy 27:21).

We treasure everything that Jesus said, but the Bible's red letters do not count more. Black letters matter just the same. *All* the letters are God's Word. And all of God's Word belongs to Jesus.

Red-letter editions of the Bible have only been around since the turn of the twentieth century. The chapter-and-verse divisions go back to the Middle Ages.

15 Why does the Bible have chapters and verses?

Throughout history, various Jews and Christians suggested ways to divide the Bible into manageable chunks, but the divisions that stuck occurred during the Middle and Early Modern Ages. Stephen Langton, the archbishop of Canterbury, proposed our current chapters in the early thirteenth century. Robert Stephanus, Genevan printer for John Calvin's books, further divided these chapters into verses in the middle of the sixteenth century.

Legend says Stephanus selected his verses while riding horseback from Paris to Lyons. It seems possible, as sometimes there seems little reason why the breaks fall where they do. Maybe the trot was bumpy? (If you grew up in church, you know the shortest verse in the King James Bible has only two words, and you know this because it was the easiest way to win candy for memorizing a verse of Scripture.

You smiled and said, "John 11:35—Jesus wept. Lollipop, please!" The shortest verse in contemporary versions is Job 3:2, "He said." Really, Stephanus? If you're up for a larger challenge, the longest verse is Esther 8:9.)

Chapter and verse numbers make it easier to cite and memorize passages, but these divisions are not inspired by God—so while they are often helpful, they also sometimes break the text in the wrong place, interfering with the line of thought. For a fresh reading experience, try reading a Bible that doesn't have chapter and verse designations. You will make connections you hadn't seen before.

16 Who wrote the Bible?

God did. He wrote every last word of the Bible, though not all by Himself.

Some parts of the Bible did come directly from God. At times, He told prophets exactly what to say, and God himself wrote the Ten Commandments on tablets of stone. (He actually had to write these twice, after Moses came down the mountain from his meeting with God, saw the Israelites' idolatry, and smashed the tablets on the ground. God wrote them again, perhaps telling Moses not to take His Word for granite. Get it?)

While some of the Bible came directly from God, without any human input, most of it was written by God through and with human authors. The Bible is a lot like Jesus—just as He is different from any other man, so the Bible is different from any other book. Jesus is both fully divine and fully human, and the Bible is a fully divine, fully human book.

The human element is obvious when you read the Bible in its original languages. The apostle John was a humble fisherman, and he used simple words in his Gospel (an account of Jesus' life and teaching) and epistles (instructive letters to individuals or churches). Beginning Greek students always start with John's writings because his baby Greek is much easier to read than that of the highly educated apostle Paul or Luke. Luke was a physician, and his words in the Gospel of Luke and the Acts of the Apostles are more technical. If you're reading these in Greek, you'll need a *lexicon*—a smarty-pants word for dictionary.

The Bible was clearly written by humans. Its individual books reflect the knowledge, personalities, and quirks of its human authors. But as the human nature of Jesus both conceals and reveals the divine Son, so the humanity of the Bible both conceals and reveals its original and primary author. God wrote a book, and He used the full participation of humans to do it.

17 How did God write the Bible with humans?

We can't say exactly how God wrote the Bible *because we're not Him*. His ways far exceed anything we can comprehend, so we can't explain how He wrote the Bible through human authors while preserving their freedom and unique personalities. But the same infinite power that prevents us from saying precisely how God did it does explain how it was possible.

Paul says "All Scripture is God-breathed" (2 Timothy 3:16). The Greek term for breath means "spirit," so this verse teaches the *inspiration* of Scripture. God "breathed out" the Bible. He didn't merely inspire the human authors, planting ideas in their heads that they expressed in their own words. The words themselves originated in God.

This does not reduce the human authors to note takers or passive keyboards on which God typed. They remained full coauthors of what they wrote. The Psalms are active prayers of human supplicants. Luke actively conducted research for his Gospel and Acts (Luke 1:1–4; Acts 1:1–2). Paul actively wrote letters to the people and churches he loved. He concluded his letter to the Romans by greeting nearly thirty individuals by name (Romans 16). The words these human authors wrote belonged to them.

The human authors wrote with a human level of intention. The Psalms are prayers, Luke researched history, and Paul gave pastoral advice in his letters. Without minimizing this human intent, God wrote in, with, and through the human authors with a higher level of intention. We call this the *superintendence* of the Holy Spirit. He superintended the human authors so that, without violating their minds or wills, they freely wrote the exact words that God wanted.

God is able to do this because He is God. We cannot explain how He did this because we are not.

The Dutch master Rembrandt's painting of a meditative apostle Paul, writing from a prison cell.

18 How did humans write the Bible?

Most books of the Bible were not written all at once. The authors of Scripture didn't sit at their desks, raise their pens, and ask God to write as He wished. Many of the books were composed over a long time, as prophets received new messages from God or historians sorted through stories, records, and documents. The process often seemed very human because God used a *fully*, though not *merely*, human process to write His Word.

The stories in Genesis—of creation, the fall, Noah, and the patriarchs—were first passed through oral tradition. Parents told children who told their children until someone finally wrote the stories down. This person may have been Moses, or perhaps he pulled together stories that others had written. The authors of the historical books interviewed witnesses, examined writings, and gathered family histories, then pieced the stories together in a compelling narrative.

An image from a Jerusalem church depicts Luke, author of the third Gospel and the book of Acts. He opened the former by saying he had "carefully investigated" the life of Jesus to create an "orderly account" (Luke 1:3).

Some books, such as Psalms and Proverbs, are collections of writings that already existed. The compilers didn't write all these prayers and wise sayings—they gathered and perhaps edited what others had done. Sometimes they used material from surprising sources. Proverbs 31 begins with the pithy advice of a pagan king's mom: "The sayings of King Lemuel—an inspired utterance his mother taught him" (31:1). While this mom's words may have been "inspired" in some sense, Christians reserve the "inspiration of Scripture" for the process, especially that final moment when her words were collected and edited into their Proverbs 31 form.

The Bible's books were written in a variety of ways. Sometimes, as with the prophets, the authors sensed they were expressly writing God's words. At other times, the authors were doing more common activities of research, collecting, and editing. The Holy Spirit directed both processes so that however it was achieved, the final, canonical form of each book is the inspired, authoritative, and true Word of God.

19 What does divine and human authorship mean to me?

Because the Bible was written by humans, we must study their original historical-cultural context to understand what their words mean. What were the human authors trying to say? How would their first readers have understood them? This essential emphasis on the human element is why Christians often say "James wrote," "David prayed," or "Paul argued."

We must keep this focus on the human element while remembering the Bible is much more than a human book. The Bible's primary author is God, which means it carries divine authority. When we say "James wrote" or "Paul argued," we ultimately mean "God said." We should periodically say "As God wrote in His letter to the Galatians" or "God says right here in James chapter 3" to remind ourselves the Bible is first and foremost God's book.

This does not mean every line in the Bible expresses God's thoughts. The Bible includes the words of God's enemies, such as Pharaoh, the Pharisees, even Satan. Obviously the mob's shouts to crucify Jesus were not what God thought His Son deserved. But the Bible's entire story, including its bad parts, is God's Word to us.

If God is the primary author of the Bible, there may be passages where He intends more than the human author understood. This is somewhat controversial. The first rule that beginning Bible students learn is that God's Word cannot mean to them what it did not mean to its original audience. I appreciate this and even teach it.

And yet, this rule may be an overly modern, naturalistic way of reading the Bible.

Before the sixteenth century, Christians started with the literal, human intent of the biblical passage, but they did not stop there. They remembered God is the primary author, so they expected to find higher, spiritual meanings in the text. This seems subjective, because it's hard to confidently discern what these spiritual meanings might be. It seems safer to stick to the literal, human meaning.

Except there are examples *in the Bible* that emphasize a higher, spiritual meaning. Deuteronomy 25:4 says, "Do not muzzle an ox while it is treading out the grain." Paul quotes this verse in the New Testament and asks, "Is it about oxen that God is concerned? Surely he says this for us, doesn't he? Yes, this was written for us, because whoever plows and threshes should be able to do so in the hope of sharing in the harvest." Paul says the point of this text, which could not have been what the original human author intended, is pay your preacher! (1 Corinthians 9:9–12; compare with 1 Timothy 5:18).

There also are examples where God wrote through human authors more than they could have understood. Isaiah 53 gives specific, horrifying details of Jesus' crucifixion centuries before the Romans had invented this form of execution. Psalm 22 is David's lament for being rejected by both God and men. While the details describe his experience, they were filled up yet again as the Son of David hung on the cross. So we read Psalm 22 on two levels: what the human author meant about his suffering and what the divine author prophesied about Jesus.

Every intersection of God and humanity must produce inexplicable tension. We read the Bible as a *fully* human book, but not as an *only* human book. The Bible is primarily and originally God's. As such, it carries an authority that far exceeds any human power. And it may also convey a meaning that exceeds what the human authors intended. Sometimes they wrote more than they knew.

20 Is the Bible written to me?

Read most any book on how to study the Bible, and you'll likely learn the Bible is not written *to* you but only *for* you. The Bible is written *to* its first hearers living in Judea, Corinth, or Ephesus. If you want to know what the Bible means, you must

How should we approach the Bible? Is it written *to* us or simply *for* us?

put yourselves in their ancient sandals. The more you understand their world and the issues they confronted, the better you will understand what the Bible meant *to* them. You must then translate this meaning into your contemporary, somewhat different context to understand what the Bible means *for* you.

I agree that we must understand the original historical-cultural context. But throughout this process we must remember we're not reading someone else's mail. The Bible truly is addressed *to* us. If God is the primary author of Scripture, then He had you and me in mind just as much as the first recipients. God not only wrote *for* us; He also wrote *to* us.

He says so in the Bible. Paul explained, "Everything that was written in the past was written to teach us" (Romans 15:4). And he gave examples. After describing Israel's rebellion in the wilderness, Paul said, "These things happened to them as examples and were written down as warnings for us" (1 Corinthians 10:11). Noting what God said about not muzzling the ox, Paul said, "Surely he says this for us, doesn't he?" (1 Corinthians 9:10).

continued on p. 49

What are BCE and CE?

What year is it? Maybe it's 2020, the year every organization, including the Optometrists of America, feel morally obligated to publish their "vision statement." I'm sorry. But I digress.

Have you wondered what 2020 means? *What are we counting from?* The Romans counted from the founding of their city. That was year one. One thousand two hundred seventy-eight years later, a Christian monk named Dionysius Exiguus decided to number his calendar from something infinitely more important, the birth of Jesus. Jesus was born in year one, and every subsequent year was *anno domini* ("in the year of our Lord"), or AD for short. Every year before Jesus' birth was BC, or "before Christ." Counting backward, this made the founding of Rome, year one in the Roman calendar, 753 BC for the Christians.

Exiguus's Christian calendar gradually took over and became the accepted European system by the middle of the eighth century. Everyone, even those who did not claim to be Christians, told time by how many years since Jesus was born. What a powerful reminder of the centrality of Christ!

There was a problem though. Exiguus was slightly off on the year of Jesus' birth. Most scholars think Jesus was born between 6 and 4 BC, not quite in AD 1. Many people also worry whether it's fair to impose the Jesus calendar upon those who are not Christians. So in a gesture of goodwill, they have softened BC to BCE, "before the common era," and AD to CE, the "common era."

I am one of those people. I much prefer BC and AD because they announce the supremacy of Jesus. He is Lord. All history revolves around Him. And yet, I'd rather offend people with Jesus than with His calendar. I want people to freely confess Jesus is Lord, and that may be hard to do if they feel I'm imposing my will upon them. Compelled speech is not free. And it's not loving.

The once-common "A.D.," an abbreviation of anno domini, Latin for "in the year of our Lord," is often replaced by the more generic CE, or "common era."

So I will use BCE and CE in this book, not because I am removing Jesus from history, but because I want to respect others and lead them to Jesus. If they freely repent and trust Jesus, every year will be *anno domini*, "the year of our Lord," no matter what it's called.

Similarly, Jesus quoted Exodus 3:6, which was written centuries before, and asked his opponents, "Have you not read what *God said to you?*" (Matthew 22:31, emphasis added). Hebrews 3:7 applies Psalm 95's warning about rebellion and states, "So, as the Holy Spirit says." This verse does not say, "as the Holy Spirit *said*" but instead uses the present tense, "as the Holy Spirit *says*." Psalm 95 was not merely written *for* you. It was written *to* you and is speaking to you right now. So Hebrews 4:7 concludes, "Today, if you hear his voice, do not harden your hearts."

The better we understand the historical-cultural context of the original audience, the better we will understand what the Bible means *for* us. But never forget the Bible is more than written *for* you. God had you in mind when He inspired the Bible, and He wrote the whole thing *to* you.

21 When was the Bible written?

When I was a child, the Bible seemed like ancient history. Moses, David, and Paul lived an unimaginably long time ago. But now I've lived half a century. Put a few of my lifetimes end-to-end and I'm back to the American Revolution. Stack a few more on top and I've reached the age of knights and castles. There's still some way to go until the time of Jesus, but the older I get, the less distant that seems. The world has changed dramatically since Bible times, but humans remain much the same. The Bible understands us because it contains stories of people who are just like us.

The first books of the Bible were written after the Exodus they describe. Depending on where you date the Exodus, either 1446 or 1260 BCE, determines whether you think Moses wrote the Pentateuch in the late fifteenth or thirteenth century BCE.

The Pentateuch describes events that happened centuries earlier, such as the story of Abraham (either 2166–1991 or 2000–1825 BCE), but it wasn't written until roughly a millennium and a half before the time of Christ. There may be one book older than the Pentateuch: Job tells the trials of a man who may have lived before Abraham, but we don't know exactly when his book was composed.

The last Old Testament book to be written was either Nehemiah or Malachi.

They were contemporaries who led the rebuilding of Jerusalem after the exile and wrote sometime around 430 BCE. Old Testament revelation stopped after Nehemiah and Malachi. The Jews were back in their land, still waiting for the full salvation God had promised.

God answered their prayers with the arrival of Jesus. He finished His work and ascended to heaven approximately 30–33 CE. The four Gospels were probably written in the fifties and sixties, and perhaps some as late as the seventies. James wrote his epistle in the late forties, while Paul wrote his letters between the forties and midsixties, when he was martyred. The last book is John's Revelation, written in the midnineties in response to Roman persecution of Christians.

That was nearly forty lifetimes ago for me. That's a lot, but less than I first thought. The Bible is like my car's side mirror: its images are closer than they appear.

22 What language was the Bible written in?

Hebrew:

ץראה תאו םימשה תא םיהלא ארב תישארב

(Genesis 1:1)

Greek:

Ἐν ἀρχῇ ἦν ὁ λόγος, καὶ ὁ λόγος ἦν πρὸς τὸν θεόν, καὶ θεὸς ἦν ὁ λόγος

(John 1:1)

The Bible was written in two main languages whose modern forms are still used. The Old Testament was written almost entirely in Hebrew, and the New Testament was written in Greek. Travel to Israel and Greece today, and you will see signs in these languages and hear people speaking them. If you have studied Scripture in these original languages, you might imagine you've stepped inside the Bible. It's exciting and a bit surreal.

A couple parts of the Old Testament were written in Aramaic, a sister language to Hebrew that became the language of diplomacy when Assyria ruled the Ancient Near East (eighth–seventh centuries BCE) and the official language of Persia after that (sixth century BCE). The Jews learned Aramaic when they were in exile, and it remained their common, everyday language in Jesus' time. Aramaic was Jesus' heart language, as expressed in his cry from the cross, *"Eloi, Eloi, lema sabachthani"* ("My God, my God, why have you forsaken me?" Mark 15:34).

Three long Aramaic sections of the Old Testament are Ezra 4:8–6:18, 7:12–26, and Daniel 2:4–7:28. The Ezra passages record verbatim the letters and decrees written by Ancient Near Eastern rulers, so it makes sense that these appear in Aramaic. Scholars aren't sure why the middle of Daniel was written in Aramaic while its beginning and end are in Hebrew. Perhaps Aramaic seemed appropriate because these middle chapters describe Daniel's and his friends' experience in a foreign court. Aramaic also appears in Genesis 31:47, when a non-Jew calls a place by its Aramaic name; and Jeremiah 10:11, when God apparently wanted to make sure that Jews who couldn't understand Hebrew still got His point.

After the Old Testament was completed, Alexander the Great (356–323 BCE) left the idyllic beauty of Greece to conquer most of the Middle East. While we might question Alexander's life choices, his military conquests did instill Greek culture and language on the Middle Eastern world. The Romans followed two centuries later. They left the idyllic beauty of Tuscany—seriously, *what is wrong with these people?*—to conquer the western edge of Alexander's former empire (modern Egypt, Israel, Syria, and Turkey) plus the North African coast and Europe to the Rhine and Danube Rivers. The Roman Empire circled the Mediterranean Sea and included much of modern Europe.

Roman culture at this time was less advanced than the Greeks', so the Greek language remained the empire's international language for business. The Romans used Latin in their military and government and allowed Greek for most everything else. And so the New Testament, which was written during the first century of the Roman Empire, came to be written in Greek. Jesus' Jewish disciples preferred

Aramaic, but when they wrote Gospels and epistles for the widest possible audience, they used Greek. The widespread use of Greek meant the New Testament could spread throughout the empire without language barriers, and the precise, expressive nature of Greek made it the perfect vehicle.

The existence of Greek culture wrapped inside the peaceful stability of the Roman Empire made this period the perfect time for Jesus to come. And so, "when the set time had fully come, God sent his Son, born of a woman, born under the law, to redeem those under the law, that we might receive adoption to sonship" (Galatians 4:4–5).

23 What was the Bible written on?

The apostle Paul shivered in a Roman cell, enduring a lonely imprisonment that would end with his execution. But he continued to study. He wrote his close associate, Timothy, urging him to come before winter. And "when you come, bring the cloak that I left with Carpus at Troas, and my scrolls, especially the parchments" (2 Timothy 4:13). Paul's scrolls were probably made of papyrus—the origin of our word *paper*—while the parchments were more expensive sheets of animal skin.

The Egyptians developed papyrus from reeds that grew in the marshy Nile River delta. They cut the papyrus into strips, laid them in alternating vertical and horizontal directions, then dried them on a hard, flat surface. The sugars in the plant bonded the two layers together, producing a smooth, front side for writing. (The back was usually too rough.) Papyrus was the most economical way to make paper, though it became brittle and crumbled over time. Scribes dutifully and repeatedly copied the books of the Bible so we could have them today. Ironically, ancient people used shards of pottery to scribble notes and shopping lists. Many of these still survive, while pages of far more important writings have disintegrated from centuries of sun and humidity.

Biblical authors and scribes also wrote on leather, which though initially stronger than papyrus, also deteriorated over time. Leather was replaced in the second century BCE by parchment, which was made from sheep, calf, or goat skins that had been soaked in lime to turn white. Parchment was smoother, brighter, and more

This "Dead Sea Scroll" discovered in the Judean desert at Qumran demonstrates both one of the biblical languages (Hebrew) and the material used to capture it.

durable than papyrus and leather and allowed writing on both sides. A Christian leader such as Paul would have owned a quality copy of the Scriptures, so it's likely the parchments he requested included a Greek translation of the Old Testament (called the Septuagint).

Whether papyrus, leather, or parchment, the sheets were spliced together into scrolls. When Jesus read the Scriptures in His hometown synagogue, He was handed "the scroll of the prophet Isaiah. . . . Unrolling it, he found the place where it is written: 'The Spirit of the Lord is on me. . . .' Then he rolled up the scroll, gave it back to the attendant and sat down" (Luke 4:17–18, 20). The biblical scrolls were grouped together into the three Old Testament sections of the Law, Prophets, and Writings. Their canonical order was ultimately fixed when the book was invented in the century after Christ. The books of Scripture were then bound in place by a single binding, so their order did not change.

24 How much did writing the Bible cost?

The Bible is the most valuable book ever written, so it's fitting that it was expensive to write. Some biblical authors sought wealthy patrons for their work, the ancient equivalent of a GoFundMe page.

Consider Paul's epistle to the Romans. Paul used a scribe named Tertius (Romans 16:22), who either volunteered his time or was paid by a patron, perhaps the wealthy Erastus (Romans 16:23). Paul would have written more than one copy of this important letter, in case his courier, Phoebe, was mugged or lost the letter on her voyage to Rome (Romans 16:1).

Each copy of Romans would have taken a couple days to write out, and scholars estimate this epistle would have cost Paul at least $2,275 in today's dollars. Books such as Luke and Acts are twice as long and would have cost at least $7,000 each, not counting Luke's research expenses. Perhaps Luke dedicated both books to Theophilus because he was the patron who covered his costs (Luke 1:1–4; Acts 1:1–3).[4]

God spared no expense in giving us His Word. Let's express our appreciation by taking it into our heart.

25 Why do some Bibles have more than sixty-six books?

Roman Catholics have more books in their Old Testament because they include the fourteen or fifteen books of what is called the Apocrypha. (The exact number depends on whether the Letter of Jeremiah is combined with Baruch.) The main apocryphal books are 1 and 2 Maccabees, which describe Israel's fight for independence from 167 to 134 BCE; and 1 Esdras, which covers the same ground as Ezra and Nehemiah, telling how Judah returned to the Promised Land after their Babylonian captivity. Other significant books include Tobit, Judith, Baruch, Ecclesiasticus, and the Wisdom of Solomon.

continued on p. 59

Roman Catholic Church, Protestant Church

The Western church officially split from the Eastern church in 1054 then split again during the Reformation of the sixteenth century. The Western church was known as the Roman Catholic Church. "Roman" because its leader was the bishop of Rome and "Catholic" because, despite its challenge from the East, the Roman Church claimed to be the one, true, universal church.

By the late Middle Ages, money and power had corrupted the Western church. Popes raised armies to defend their lands. Celibate priests somehow fathered children. The church sold indulgences that promised salvation to desperate sinners. Monks messed around with nuns and grew fat from their incessant begging. Everyone knew the church had big problems. Something had to be done.

A German monk named Martin Luther thought these moral lapses were symptoms of a deeper problem. In 1517 he wrote ninety-five "theses" that questioned the church's sale of indulgences, including whether or not priests had the power to remove penalties from the dead. Luther believed the church had turned the free salvation of Christ into a lucrative business in which people who could not earn their salvation were made to pay for it. The pope told Luther to back down. When he refused, he was kicked out of the church.

One quickly apparent difference between the Roman Catholic and Protestant churches is the leadership structure. Catholics look to a single figure, the pope, while Protestant churches and their leadership are widely varied.

The pope persuaded the Catholic Holy Roman Emperor to take his side, and together they pressured German princes to side against Luther. A few princes protested the Roman Catholics at the Diet of Speyer (1529), and the name *Protestant* was born.

The largest initial Protestant groups include Lutherans, who began in Germany and then spread to Scandinavia; the Reformed, who began in Switzerland and spread to the Netherlands, England, and Scotland (where they became known as Presbyterians); and the Anabaptists, who started in Switzerland then scattered to escape persecution. They are the ancestors of the Mennonites and some Brethren groups.

Seventeenth-century England gave rise to the Baptists, eighteenth-century America produced the Methodists, and twentieth-century America gave birth to the Pentecostals, the largest Protestant denomination today. We recently have seen the rise of nondenominational churches, which though technically independent tend to reflect one of the denominations mentioned above. (They are usually stealth Baptists or Pentecostals.)

Protestants and Roman Catholics agree on much, such as the Trinity and two natures of Christ. We disagree mainly on three important issues:

1. *Authority*—Is our final authority the Bible or the church?
2. *Salvation*—Are we saved by faith alone in Jesus or by faith and works?
3. *Church*—How many sacraments and how do they work? Are ordinary laypeople an essential part of the church or is the church ultimately defined by its clergy?

If you belong to the Western church and you are not Roman Catholic, you are some type of Protestant. If your church emphasizes the final authority of Scripture, long sermons that explain that Scripture, your need to express faith in Christ, salvation as God's gracious gift, and the right of each believer to approach God directly without a priest, you are definitely in a Protestant church. If your church asks for your Social Security number, encourages adult sleepovers, and prays to Lord Krypton, then you have overshot and are obviously in a cult. Leave immediately.

Remember that Roman Catholics didn't evict Protestants until the sixteenth century. If you and I had lived in the West during the fifteenth century, we would all have attended a Roman Catholic church. Our differences are important, but we have a shared history that is much longer than our time apart.

Western Church, Eastern Church

The previous sidebar mentioned Protestants, Roman Catholics, and various Orthodox churches, so it might help to explain the main wings of the Christian world. Individual churches have always identified with their location. The apostle Paul wrote to churches in Ephesus, Corinth, and Philippi, for example, and today we have the Archdiocese of Boston and the First Baptist Church of Atlanta. So when Emperor Diocletian divided the sprawling Roman Empire into East and West in 285 CE—his roughly vertical line runs through the Balkans, just east of Italy's boot—it was only a matter of time before the church followed suit.

East and West never did get along. The East spoke Greek and loved philosophy. Their half of the empire gave us Socrates, his student Plato, and his student Aristotle. It's no accident that the first seven church councils met in the East, and all focused on philosophical doctrines of the Trinity and the two natures of Christ. The Eastern church loves to celebrate the mystery of God. *Come worship with us,* they say, *and you won't need to solve all of your doctrinal questions.*

The West spoke Latin and was much more practical. The West didn't produce many great thinkers, but just got the job done. The West built Roman roads, which exist to this day, and Roman law, which undergirds America's legal system. Westerners tend to be shallow and pragmatic but highly efficient people. The Western church rarely teaches on mystical doctrines like the Trinity because there isn't much to apply to our lives. *What's the cash value?* Instead we prefer practical sermons on marriage, parenting, and managing conflict.

The division between East and West solidified when Emperor Constantine moved his eastern capital to Byzantium (330 CE) and renamed it after himself. Because Constantinople (now called Istanbul) was capital in the East and Rome was usually the capital in the West, church leaders of both cities jockeyed for ecclesiastical influence. The bishop of Rome always came in first, since his church was founded by Jesus' lead disciple Peter, while the church in Constantinople was started by a politician. However, the First Council of Constantinople (AD 381) called its city the "new Rome." The patriarch of Constantinople might come in second, but he was closing fast.

The East and West churches continued to vie for power until they officially split in 1054. The Western church attempted to defend the deity of Christ by inserting a single word into the Nicene Creed; they said the Holy Spirit proceeds not only from the Father but also *filioque,* or "and the Son." The Eastern church said the creed was sacred and should not be tampered with; they argued the Spirit may proceed *by* the Son or *through* the Son but not *from* the Son. So they excommunicated the Western church. (If you're wondering *what's the big deal,* congratulations, you're a Westerner. That's exactly what the Eastern church thought your shallow heart might say! The fact that you don't appreciate the problem is most of the problem!)

The divide between East and West continues to this day. The Eastern church signals it is the one true church by calling itself "the Orthodox church" (a confederation of national churches, such as Greek, Russian, and Serbian). The West signals it is the one true church by calling itself "the Catholic church." *Orthodox* means "right belief" and *Catholic* means "universal," so both names stake high claims.

Leaders of the East and West are now on friendly terms, but reunification won't occur until we resolve the *filioque* conflict. And we won't solve that problem unless people in the West understand why the East considers it a problem.

Onion-shaped church domes—often in gleaming gold—are characteristic of Russian Orthodox churches, part of the Eastern branch of Christianity.

None of the apocryphal books appear in the original, Jewish Bible, what Christians call the Old Testament. All were written after 400 BCE, when Jews believed divine revelation had ceased. However, some of the books were included as an addendum to the Old Testament when Greek-speaking Jews translated their Hebrew Scriptures into Greek, between 250 and 100 BCE.

This version of the Old Testament, called the Septuagint, was used by the first Greek-speaking Christians. When later generations in the West wanted a Bible in their own language, Latin, they followed the order of books in the Old Testament that Christians were used to. So the Latin Vulgate, translated by Jerome into the "vulgar" (common) language of the people, contains the Apocrypha. Translated in the late fourth century, the Vulgate became the standard Bible of the Western Church by the eighth and ninth centuries and is now the official Bible of the Roman Catholic Church.

But not for Protestants. The sixteenth-century Reformation arose with the Renaissance, an intellectual movement that, among other things, emphasized returning to original sources. No longer content to read Latin translations of Plato and Aristotle, humanist scholars said they should read these philosophers in their original Greek. When Renaissance scholars turned their attention to the Bible, they similarly said it must be read in its original language and form. This meant returning to the Hebrew Old Testament, which does not include the Apocrypha. And so Protestant Bibles, because they follow the original Old Testament, do not contain the Apocrypha.

"The Martyrdom of the Maccabees," a nineteenth-century painting by Antonio Ciseri, draws upon information from the Apocrypha, a collection of books not included in Protestant Bibles.

The Roman Catholics doubled down at their sixteenth-century Council of Trent, declaring against the Protestants that the Vulgate—with its apocryphal books—is the official Bible of the church. Since the statements of councils are irrevocable, Roman Catholics are forever committed to regarding the Apocrypha as Scripture. Yet even they distinguish between *protocanonical* books, which were originally recognized by the entire church, and *deuterocanonical* books that were accepted later (the Apocrypha).

Elsewhere, opinions are mixed. The Russian Orthodox Church does not include the Apocrypha in its Bible, while the Eastern Orthodox and Anglican Churches do. However, Anglicans distinguish the Apocrypha from the rest of Scripture. When they read an Old or New Testament passage during worship, they say "The Word of the Lord" when they finish. They do not say this after reading from the Apocrypha.

The Protestant Reformer Martin Luther conceded the Apocrypha was "profitable and good to read." Besides a passage that alludes to purgatory (2 Maccabees 12:40–46), the Apocrypha is generally not going to hurt you—it simply does not rise to the level of inspired Scripture. The early Christians wrote commentaries on every book of the Old Testament, but they did not write any on an apocryphal book. This indicates that, though their Septuagint did contain the Apocrypha, they considered it to be less authoritative than the rest of their Bible.

26 How did Israel decide which books belong in the Old Testament?

We don't know much about this, as neither the Old Testament nor national history say how the Jews determined which books were divinely inspired. First-century historian Josephus does not tell us how the final list was decided, but he does say his Jewish people believed they had the right and complete books. He wrote, "Although such long ages have now passed, no one has ventured either to add, or to remove, or to alter a syllable; and it is an instinct with every Jew, from the day of his birth, to regard them as the decrees of God, to abide by them, and, if need be, cheerfully to die for them."[5]

We know the process of creating Israel's Scriptures began with Moses, Israel's first prophet. On Mount Sinai, he received the Ten Commandments, which the Jews immediately understood to be God's inspired Word. They put the two stone tablets inside the Ark of the Covenant and the rest of the Law alongside it. They publicly read and promised to obey everything the Law said, adding and subtracting nothing (Deuteronomy 10:5; 31:9–13, 24–26).

Moses not only gave Israel the Law, he also served as the template for future prophets. He promised that after his death "the LORD your God will raise up for you a prophet like me from among you, from your fellow Israelites. You must listen to him" (Deuteronomy 18:15). God had told Moses, "I will raise up for them a prophet like you. . .and I will put my words in his mouth. He will tell them everything I command him. I myself will call to account anyone who does not listen to

Orthodox Jews in prayer shawls surround a scroll of the Torah, their scriptures, in Jerusalem.

my words that the prophet speaks in my name" (vv. 18–19).

Israel expected God to send prophets after Moses, but they still had to sort the true from the false. God told His people to look for two criteria: a true prophet must urge Israel to return to the Lord and keep His law, and any predictions he made must come true (Deuteronomy 13:1–5). Any prophet who checked both boxes was considered sent by God, and his writings were considered to have divine authority.

Isaiah may have been the first prophet to write down his prophecies from the Lord. God told him to "bind up this testimony of warning and seal up God's instruction among my disciples" (Isaiah 8:16), so that future generations could read God's Word and take it to heart (compare Isaiah 30:8). Similarly, God told Jeremiah, "Take a scroll and write on it all the words I have spoken to you concerning Israel, Judah and all the other nations. . . . Perhaps when the people of Judah hear about every disaster I plan to inflict on them, they will each turn from their wicked ways; then I will forgive their wickedness and their sin" (Jeremiah 36:2–3).

The Jews believed these prophetic writings were divinely inspired Scripture. The books themselves refer to the "word of the Lord," "vision," or "oracle" that the prophets received from God. And they would cross-check each other. Jeremiah quoted Micah's writing as God's Word, and Daniel called Jeremiah's book "the Scriptures" (Jeremiah 26:18; Daniel 9:2). When a wicked king threw the scroll of Jeremiah into a fire, God announced He would punish the king and his family because "they have not listened" to the Word of the Lord. God told Jeremiah to write out the words again and—to register His annoyance—add some more (Jeremiah 36:20–32).

We have less information about the compilation of the Writings, though we know some were in dispute. The Song of Songs was questioned because of its erotica, Esther because it does not mention God, and Ecclesiastes because its hand-wringing over the futility of life seemed bleak, even for longsuffering Jews. However the process transpired, the Law, the Prophets, and the Writings were set by the time of Christ.

The New Testament quotes from nearly every Old Testament book, and Jesus assumed its canon was complete. Jesus told His murderous enemies they would be charged with the deaths of every Old Testament martyr, "from the blood of righteous Abel to the blood of Zechariah" (Matthew 23:35)—Abel is the first martyr in Genesis and Zechariah is the last martyr in 2 Chronicles, the final scroll of the Hebrew canon. So Jesus was implicitly saying "from A to Z," or as Christians might say about our Bibles, "from Genesis to Revelation."

Jesus confirmed the entire Old Testament canon, from beginning to end. If He believes our Old Testament contains the right books, that's good enough for me.

27 When did Israel decide which books belong in the Old Testament?

We don't know how early the Jews determined their canon, but they had almost certainly done so by 300 BCE. Israel had three types of leaders: prophets, priests, and kings. Prophets delivered God's Word, priests obtained God's forgiveness, and kings kept God's civil order. When Babylon toppled the nation and burned the temple, the Israelites lost their king and priests. So they doubled down on the one office that was left. No longer a free nation that could offer sacrifices in the temple, they nevertheless could collect their sacred Scriptures and continue to hear from God.

The Jews met in synagogues to hear a teacher read and expound the Scriptures, much like future generations of Christians would do in churches. Of course, to use the Bible you must first have the Bible, so the Jews urgently gathered and affirmed their Scriptures. The Greek translation of the Old Testament (the Septuagint) proves the Jews had a canon by 250 to 100 BCE, though it's unclear whether their Hebrew Bible included some apocryphal books. One of those, Ecclesiasticus, also affirms the completion of the Old Testament canon. Written in the late second century BCE, its prologue refers to "the Law and the Prophets and the others that have followed in their steps" (that is, the Writings).

When they returned from captivity, the Jews rebuilt their temple, and King Herod built an even better one during the time of Christ. The Jews could sacrifice again in Jerusalem, yet they continued to meet weekly in their synagogues. That was wise, because the Romans destroyed the temple one last time in 70 CE.

This final loss of their temple prompted the Jews to tie up any loose ends with their canon. Sometime around 90 CE, either a council or a group of scholars working in Jamnia resolved all outstanding questions. They affirmed Esther, even though it does not mention God's name; Proverbs, despite its surface contradictions (for example, Proverbs 26:4–5, which for different reasons says to answer and not answer "a fool according to his folly"); Ecclesiastes, despite its unrelenting pessimism; and Song of Songs, even though its racy language made it unfit for children.

The Old Testament was fixed by the time of Christ because the Jews resolved

Ruins of a third century CE synagogue at Capernaum, built on the site of an earlier synagogue in which Jesus taught (Mark 1:21–28).

never to waste a crisis. At their lowest point, when their nation was invaded and their temple destroyed, they knew they needed to hear from God. It would be a long road, and the Jewish nation has not yet made it all the way back. But they got one important thing right: they affirmed which books belong in their Bible. And so they may confidently hear God's voice. They are not without hope.

28 Why were some books rejected from the Old Testament?

They weren't. There is not one shred of evidence that any book written during Old Testament times was considered and then rejected from the Jewish canon. We know of no close calls.

Many religious writings did appear after 400 BCE, when Israel believed divine revelation had ceased until the coming of their Messiah. The Jews had returned to their land, waiting for the prophecies already made to be fulfilled. They suffered terribly when their land became a battleground between the Seleucids in the north (Syria) and the Ptolemies in the south (Egypt), and even more when the Romans swept in and took over. Where was the deliverance that God had promised?

Apocalyptic literature began appearing around 200 BCE to explain the delay. These heavily symbolic and cryptic texts encouraged Israel to hang tough. She was the center of a cosmic struggle between good and evil. If she continued to resist, she would ultimately be rescued. Just wait.

Some of these writings, such as 2 Esdras, belong in the Apocrypha (see "Why do some Bibles have more than sixty-six books?"), while many others are found in the Old Testament *Pseudepigrapha*. This term means "false inscriptions" and describes books attributed to ancient patriarchs or key Jewish figures who had lived long before. While the New Testament book of Jude cites two pseudepigraphal works (1 Enoch and the Assumption of Moses), there is little reason to think Jude believed these works were divinely inspired. Nor is there reason to think the Jews did, either. They knew revelation had ceased until the age of the Messiah. Tragically, they missed Him when He came, and they're still waiting.

29 How did the church decide which books belong in the New Testament?

The first Christians did not confer authority on the books in the New Testament. They merely recognized the divine authority these books already had. The twenty-seven books are not authoritative because they are in the New Testament; rather they are in the New Testament because the church realized they were inspired by God.

Christians felt the Holy Spirit moving in their hearts when certain books were read. They could tell they were hearing the voice of God. But they also had objective tests that guided them as they gathered the books God had written. They asked three key questions: Who wrote the book, how was the book received, and what does the book teach?

1. ***Who wrote the book?*** The night before Jesus died, He promised the disciples He would send the Holy Spirit to "guide [them] into all the truth" (John 16:13). The disciples understood later that Jesus had deputized them to authoritatively pass down His teaching and way of life.

   The apostle Paul, a latecomer to the band of disciples, claimed he was passing on the Gospel he had received from Jesus (1 Corinthians 15:1–8; 11:23). The Latin term translated "passing on" is *traditiones,* and Paul believed his traditions carried God's authority. He wrote, "I praise you for remembering me in everything and for holding to the *traditions* just as I *passed them on* to you" (1 Corinthians 11:2). "So then, brothers and sisters, stand firm and hold fast to the *teachings we passed on* to you" (2 Thessalonians 2:15). "In the name of the Lord Jesus Christ, we command you, brothers and sisters, to keep away from every believer who is idle and disruptive and does not live according to the *teaching you received* from us" (2 Thessalonians 3:6; all emphases added).

   The importance of the disciples' role in passing on the Christian tradition led the early church to check for a writing's *apostolicity.* Was the book written by an apostle, someone who had been in Jesus' inner circle and received unique authority from Him? Most New Testament books easily pass this test, and those that have questions are readily explained. The Gospel of Mark was not written by an apostle, but Mark was writing for Peter, the lead disciple. Luke and Acts were written by Luke, who, though not an apostle, was a companion of Paul. James and Jude may have been brothers of Jesus, and the author of Hebrews, unknown to us but not to the original recipients (the slip bearing his or her name may have fallen off the scroll), was likely a close associate of Paul.

The "four evangelists" are depicted in a seventeenth-century painting. As original apostles of Jesus, Matthew and John wrote books that were readily accepted as scripture. Mark and Luke, though not apostles themselves, worked closely with Peter and Paul, respectively.

2. ***How was the book received?*** The first Christians paid attention to how the book was used in church. Did churches in various locales read it during worship and regard it as inspired by God? The same Spirit who inspired the book would help Christians to receive it as such, so the universal acceptance of a book was strong, objective evidence of its authority. Every New Testament book was widely accepted, receiving many more "votes" than even the most popular books that were ultimately rejected.

3. ***What does the book teach?*** A book written by an apostle and welcomed by the church still had to teach orthodoxy, so Christians dutifully examined the contents of each book. The church had to have some idea of what orthodoxy was in order to judge whether a given book was orthodox. For this the church turned to its baptismal creeds. Let me explain.

   The word *canon* did not originally mean "list of books" but "rule of faith." It described the content that the church believed. The church expressed this content in the baptismal creeds that every person recited when they were baptized and joined the church. We have records of baptismal creeds from various early churches, and they are similar to each other and to the Apostles Creed, which arose from the baptismal creed used in Rome. When we recite the Apostles Creed ("I believe in God the Father Almighty, Creator of heaven and earth; I believe in Jesus Christ, his only Son, our Lord. . ."), we stand with the earliest Christians and confess what they regularly declared in church.

   The church used its rule of faith to fend off heresy. The first threat to the young church were Gnostics, who believed God would not create this icky physical world or allow His Son to take an earthly body then physically suffer and bodily rise from the dead. The creed responds by saying God is the Creator of all things and Jesus was "born of the virgin Mary," "suffered under Pontius Pilate, was crucified, died, and was buried," and "the third day he rose again from the dead." Also and importantly, our physical bodies will rise too! When a church in Syria used the Gnostic *Gospel of Peter*, the bishop of Antioch told them to stop because this false Gospel's low view of Jesus' humanity violated their rule of faith.

The church used its canon, or rule of faith, to determine which books belonged in its canon, or list of authoritative books. The church then used these books to develop and expound its faith. Right teaching recognizes right teaching, which then produces more right teaching. The process is circular, but how else could it go? The same Spirit who inspired the books guided the church through objective tests to recognize which books were from Him.

Evidence of His work exists within the New Testament, whose authors twice recognized others who had written inspired Scripture. Peter said Paul's letters "contain some things that are hard to understand, which ignorant and unstable people distort, as they do *the other Scriptures*" (2 Peter 3:16, emphasis added). And when Paul wrote, "*Scripture says*. . . 'The worker deserves his wages'" (1 Timothy 5:18, emphasis added), he was citing what his friend Luke wrote in his Gospel (Luke 10:7), calling it Scripture. These examples confirm what Christians already know: we hear God's voice when we read the Bible because the Bible is God's authoritative Word.

30 When did the church decide which books belong in the New Testament?

The process began almost immediately. Peter recognized Paul was writing Scripture and Paul recognized Luke, though each had written only a few years before. By the end of the second century, the church had settled on twenty-three of the New Testament's twenty-seven books. We know this because the earliest list of New Testament books, called the Muratorian Canon (c. 180), contains all four Gospels, Acts, Paul's thirteen epistles, Jude, 1 John, 2 John, Revelation, and probably 3 John (the Canon lists "two epistles of John," which likely refers to 2 and 3 John, 1 John having been mentioned already with the Gospel of John).

This canon proves the majority of the New Testament was accepted right away. Consider the four Gospels: second-century church father Irenaeus declared "since there are four zones of the world. . .and four principal winds. . .it is fitting that [the church] should have four pillars," Matthew, Mark, Luke, and John.[6] This is not

Peter (holding a key that represents Jesus' words in Matthew 16:19) wrote that he considered as scripture the letters of Paul (shown holding a sword that represents his martyrdom).

the most persuasive argument, but the fact that Irenaeus could get away with it shows the early church agreed on the Gospels soon after they were written.

Still, the first lists of New Testament books that are identical to ours appeared in the mid to late fourth century: Canons of the Synod of Laodicea (AD 360), Bishop Athanasius's letter that set the date of Easter (AD 367), Synod of Hippo (AD 393), and the Synod of Carthage (AD 397). Why did it take more than 270 years—longer than America has been a country—to finally determine all the books that belong in the New Testament?

For starters, the divinely inspired books were not sent to the same place. It took a while to copy the epistles and send them on foot or by ship to other churches across the empire. There were also heretical letters that taught false doctrine and spurious letters that were not written by their alleged authors. These books had to be weeded out, and that took some time.

There was also some disagreement regarding what kind of Gospels would be best. An early bishop named Papias wanted to collect the sayings of Jesus—sort of "The Best of Jesus"—while others wanted narrated versions of Jesus' life. The narrative view won, as our four Gospels intersperse Jesus' words with events from His life. Still, the New Testament contains a trace of the existence of Jesus quotes. Paul told the Ephesian elders to remember "the words the Lord Jesus himself said: 'It is more blessed to give than to receive' " (Acts 20:35). These words do not appear in our Gospels, so Paul was probably drawing upon a collection of Jesus' sayings.

Nevertheless, the church settled quickly on our four Gospels and most of the rest of the New Testament. Only a few books were ever in dispute. We'll examine them next.

31 Why were some books rejected from the New Testament?

Dan Brown's book *The DaVinci Code* is an exciting piece of fiction. Despite what his story says, there is no evidence the Council of Nicea (CE 325) discussed which books belong in the New Testament. There *is* evidence that Saint Nicholas, bishop of Myra, marched across the great hall and slapped the heretic Arius. (This has inspired my favorite Christmas meme, a picture of the original Santa Claus and the words, "I've come to give presents to children and punch heretics in the face, and I've just run out of presents.") As the story of Santa shows, the bishops met at the Council of Nicea to discuss Arius's heresy and the right understanding of the Trinity. They did not debate the biblical canon.

Eusebius of Caesarea was an important bishop who attended Nicea, and he said the church had divided the various canonical candidates into four groups:

First, everyone agreed that the four Gospels, Acts, Paul's epistles, Hebrews, 1 John, 1 Peter, and Revelation belong in the Bible.

Second, there was some debate about a few books: James and Jude, because their proximity to Jesus is not clear, they have slim doctrinal content, and James's emphasis on works seems to collide with Paul's celebration of grace; 2 and 3 John, because they are brief, personal, and lacking in doctrinal content; and 2 Peter, because its vocabulary and style seem different from 1 Peter. These books appear near the back of our Bible, perhaps indicating their longer road to full acceptance. They ultimately were affirmed by the church, receiving much more support than the books in the following categories.

Third, Eusebius said the church rejected spurious books, such as the Shepherd of Hermas, Acts of Paul, Apocalypse of Peter, and the Epistle of Barnabas, which were not written by their alleged authors.

Fourth, the church also swiftly and assuredly rejected heretical books, such as the Gnostic Gospels of Peter, Matthias, and Thomas.

This is an important point. Many today are suspicious of authority, and some allege the early church stifled the Gnostic Gospels' stories of Jesus so its preferred narrative would win. It's true the church rejected the Gnostic Gospels, but only because these false Gospels denied basic Christian teaching, such as the goodness of creation, the full deity and humanity of Jesus, and His and our bodily resurrection. The true church has always known about the Gnostic Gospels and has always dismissed them because they opposed the church's rule of faith.

Those who suggest we open our minds to the Gnostic Gospels should be careful what they wish for. For instance, the Gospel of Thomas presents a misogynistic Jesus. After Peter said Mary should go away "because women are not worthy of the Life," Jesus replied, "See, I shall lead her, so that I will make her male, that she too may become a living spirit, resembling you males. For every woman who will make herself male will enter the Kingdom of Heaven."[7] Oops.

The church rejected only a handful of the books it seriously considered, though always for good reason. The Shepherd of Hermas is the noncanonical book that came closest to making it, but it taught a binity rather than trinity (it merged the Son and Spirit into the same divine person), said baptism was necessary for salvation, and claimed there was only one repentance after baptism. The shepherd also criticized his wife for talking too much. As with the Gospel of Thomas, let's be glad this book is not in our Bible!

There is a vast difference between the books that were recognized as God's Word and their closest competitors. The books that made it into the canon were written first (the noncanonical works don't appear until the second century), came from an apostle or someone nearby, and expounded the churches' beliefs as expressed in their baptismal creeds. The gap is so wide that you or I could have made this call. If we could have done it, we can trust the early church, empowered by the Spirit of God, was able to do it too.

32 How were the original Bible writings preserved?

They weren't. The original writings, probably made on papyrus or leather, eventually disintegrated. But they probably existed a long time, perhaps one hundred fifty to five hundred years. This was more than enough time to make hundreds of copies. In fact, our second- and third-century New Testament manuscripts may themselves be copies of the originals!

The distance between the original and our copies is wider for the Old Testament because these writings are older, were written in less literate times, and may have

Jewish scribes today use techniques similar to those of Bible times, ensuring that copies of the scripture are as accurate as possible.

been destroyed when first Babylon and then Rome burned Jerusalem. The Greek Septuagint sometimes differs from our Hebrew Bibles, which suggests it was translated from Hebrew manuscripts we no longer have. These mostly minor differences were resolved in the first century CE, when the Jews established a standard text of their Scriptures.

Ancient scribes carefully copied the sacred Scriptures by hand. The Latin word *manuscript* means to "write by hand," and the Hebrew word for scribe means "to count." The copyists were called scribes because they checked their work by carefully counting all the letters in their Hebrew manuscripts. The Masoretic scribes, who worked from 500 to 1,000 CE, also counted the middle letter of each book. If this was off, they knew they had made a mistake somewhere and would go back until they found it. The scribes were so accurate that one group in Spain continued to copy and sell manuscripts a century after the printing press was stamping out perfect copies with machinelike consistency.

Scribes conducted their work in reverence, especially when it came to the name of God. They would not write the name of God (Yahweh) with a newly dipped brush nor give their attention to anyone, even a king, until they had finished the name.[8] Because these sacred writings contained the name of God, scribes ritually buried old and worn manuscripts lest they fall into abusive hands. This practice may explain what happened to the originals and testifies to the scribes' confidence in the accuracy of their work.

33 How can we know our English Bibles say what the original writings said?

The Bible is the most accurately preserved ancient book, and it's not even close. We have more than fifty-seven hundred Greek manuscripts of the New Testament, some dating only one hundred years after the original. We also have more than ten thousand Latin translations, plus more than a million quotations in the church fathers. Compare this with our seventy-five copies of the ancient historian

Herodotus (fifth century BCE), twenty copies of his contemporary Thucydides, and twenty-seven copies of the Roman historian Livy (first century BCE to first century CE), none closer than four centuries after the original. Or compare with the newly popular Gospel of Thomas, which exists in only one complete fourth-century copy and fragments of three second-century texts.

The closest any ancient books come to the Bible are Homer's *Iliad* and *Odyssey*. Impressively, these have nearly twenty-five hundred extant copies, though the earliest is a whole five hundred years after Homer. Anyone who doubts we have a well-preserved Bible must also doubt the text of every ancient book. He must doubt the text of everything written before the fifteenth century, when the printing press made perfect copying as easy as pulling a lever.[9]

We know we have accurate Bibles because of the scholarly discipline of textual criticism. Scholars continue to weigh ancient copies to fine-tune our biblical text. We are not missing words. If anything we have a little too much. Scribes were extraordinarily careful, but inevitably one might miscopy a word here or there. The

Ancient copies of biblical texts, found in the 1940s and 50s in these caves at Qumran, Israel, confirm the accuracy of the scriptures we read today.

next scribe would copy the new, wrong word, and an errant manuscript tradition would begin. Textual critics examine the various traditions to determine which mistakes were more likely and which words are found in the most reliable manuscripts. We may not know exactly which word is correct, but in most cases we know it's one of only a couple choices. None of the extra words affect essential Christian beliefs. They tend to be relatively unimportant—should John be spelled with one *n* or two, should a particular word be "in" or "on"—and they are less than one half of 1 percent of the entire New Testament. We have no doubts about 99.5 percent of the New Testament. And our confidence in the Old Testament has only been confirmed since the discovery of the Dead Sea Scrolls.

In 1947 a shepherd boy was throwing rocks into a cave near the Dead Sea when he heard what sounded like pots breaking. He climbed into the cave and discovered jars containing ancient texts. Many of them were fragments of the Old Testament, and every book except Esther was represented. Before this discovery our oldest Old Testament manuscripts came from the Masoretic scribes and dated no earlier than 1008 CE. The Dead Sea Scrolls date to a community called the Essenes that lived between 250 BCE and 50 CE. When scholars compared our medieval Masoretic text with these writings from more than a millennium earlier, they found mostly only minor differences. For example, the Dead Sea Scrolls include the entire book of Isaiah, and it is nearly identical to our Masoretic text. These scrolls prove the scribes did well, carefully preserving God's Word to pass on to us.

34 Did Moses write the Pentateuch?

Jesus seemed to think so. He called the Pentateuch "the Law of Moses" or simply "Moses" (Luke 24:44; 16:29) and said the Exodus story of the burning bush was in "the Book of Moses" (Mark 12:26). And His fellow Jews agreed. After Philip met Jesus, he told Nathanael, "We have found the one Moses wrote about in the Law" (John 1:45). The Pentateuch itself says Moses wrote large sections, including the "Book of the Covenant" (Exodus 20:22–23:33) and the "Book of the Law" (Deuteronomy 5–26). Until the eighteenth century, Jews and Christians alike

Michelangelo's famed 1515 sculpture of Moses.

assumed Moses was the author.

This consensus was shattered by modern scholars who assumed that religion, like other aspects of nature and culture, must slowly advance from simple to complex forms. Rather than believe Moses wrote the entire Pentateuch at the beginning of Israel's story, these scholars looked for hints that other, later authors contributed to these books. They noticed that Genesis uses two different names for God and concluded these sections must have been written by two different authors—one who favored *Elohim* and one who preferred *Yahweh*. A third writer, they speculated, added exhortations (Deuteronomy) and a fourth contributed laws about holiness and temple sacrifice. These four authors, the Yahwist (c. 840 BCE), Elohist (c. 700 BCE), Deuteronomist (c. 620 BCE), and the Priestly Writer (c. 500–450 BCE), were assumed to have lived nearly a millennium after Moses. In this view, the Jewish religion didn't start with Moses but much later, with prophets writing before and after the Assyrian and Babylonian exiles.

This "Documentary Hypothesis" was popular in the nineteenth and twentieth centuries, but it failed to produce external evidence for its claims—and is now largely discredited as unsubstantiated speculation. But one lingering benefit is the spotlight it shines on the various kinds of material that comprise the Pentateuch. It seems plausible that Moses did not write each genealogy, story, law, and poem, but that he wrote some while also compiling and perhaps editing other existing material. Divine inspiration does not require us to believe Moses wrote every word; it only requires us to believe the writing and editing process was controlled by God, so that the final version of the Pentateuch is precisely what He wanted to say.

It's also plausible that later authors updated or added inspired sentences to the Pentateuch. For instance, would Moses have written the nearly self-refuting line, "Now Moses was a very humble man, more humble than anyone else on the face of the earth" (Numbers 12:3)? Or what about the description of his death and burial (Deuteronomy 34:1–12)? Unless God had Moses script his impending death before it happened, someone else finished this final chapter.

Moses may not have written every word of the Pentateuch, but he seems to have written or edited most of it. Enough to agree with generations of Jews and Christians—and Jesus Himself—that the Pentateuch is "the Book of Moses."

35 Who wrote Isaiah?

Isaiah says he did, and in the very first verse. "The vision concerning Judah and Jerusalem that Isaiah son of Amoz saw during the reigns of Uzziah, Jotham, Ahaz and Hezekiah, kings of Judah" (Isaiah 1:1). He says it's still him in chapters two and thirteen (2:1; 13:1).

But chapters 40 through 66 describe Judah's future exile and return, including the specific name of the Persian king who will allow the people to come home (Isaiah 44:28; 45:1). Since Isaiah lived 150 years before these events, modern skeptics assume he could not have known Cyrus's name—a later prophet must have added these sections after they happened. These scholars conclude a "Second Isaiah" wrote chapters 40 through 66, or perhaps only 40 through 55, while an even later "Third Isaiah" wrote chapters 56 through 66.

However, predictions that come true are no problem for Christians who believe God ultimately wrote the book of Isaiah. We aren't surprised when God's prophets make predictions that come to pass—that's in their job description. We read Isaiah 53's description of the Suffering Servant and realize God through Isaiah foretold the agony of Jesus' crucifixion centuries before it happened. Prophecy is not a reason to search for a later writer; it's a reminder that God is Scripture's primary author.

As with last question's analysis of the Documentary Hypothesis, there is no external or historical evidence for a Second or Third Isaiah. Skeptics ask us to believe this alleged person or persons delivered some of the most compelling oracles in the Old Testament and then faded back into obscurity, never to be heard from again. Possible but unlikely.

Before modern times, no one questioned the unity of Isaiah. An Isaiah scroll

In a stained-glass window from Brussels, Belgium, an angel uses a hot coal to purify the lips of God's chosen prophet, Isaiah (6:6–7).

was found in the Dead Sea collection, and it has no break between chapter 39 and 40. The Jewish historian Josephus and the apocryphal book Ecclesiasticus both say Isaiah wrote the entire book. So did God: the Gospel of John quotes from Isaiah 6 and 53—supposedly First and Second Isaiah—then attributes both citations to a single "Isaiah [who] said this because he saw Jesus' glory and spoke about him" (see John 12:38–41). The New Testament cites the book of Isaiah nineteen more times and always credits the same individual.

When you hear challenges to Scripture, remember to do three things: insist on evidence (as we have seen, critics often make things up), check for naturalistic assumptions (critics often make things up because they don't believe God wrote the Bible), and then side with God.

36 Is the Bible true?

God wrote the Bible, so it must be true. Jesus assumed as much when He said the Scriptures, because they are "the word of God," "cannot be set aside" (John 10:35). He used the veracity of the Old Testament against Satan, three times telling the devil, "It is written" (Matthew 4:4, 7, 10). Jesus was so certain that every word of the Bible is true that He grounded one argument in a verb tense. When He quoted Exodus 3:6, in which God tells Moses, "I am. . .the God of Abraham, the God of Isaac and the God of Jacob," Jesus noted that *am* is present tense—meaning Abraham, Isaac, and Jacob are still alive. Death is not the end for us.

Despite Jesus' complete confidence in Scripture, some people believe the Bible contains errors. It says God answered Joshua's prayer for a longer day by making the sun stop in the sky, but we know the sun doesn't actually move (Joshua 10:12–13). The Bible quotes Jesus saying the mustard seed is "the smallest of all seeds" (Matthew 13:32), when certain orchid seeds are even smaller. The Bible says the metal "sea" (a large basin for water) inside the tabernacle was ten cubits in diameter and thirty cubits in circumference (2 Chronicles 4:2). But that can't be right, as the ratio between this diameter and circumference would be three, when we know it's actually *pi*, or 3.14159265. . . .

Such worries arise from an overly wooden understanding of words. When we say the Bible is true, we're saying the *meaning* of the words is true. Whatever the Bible *intends* to say is true. Granted, Scripture isn't always as precise as we might write today. Modern historians typically aim to produce an objective photograph of people or events, giving blow-by-blow accounts of who said and did what, in precise order. We put words in quotation marks, quoting people verbatim. But the Bible was written two to three thousand years ago with a Middle Eastern, commonsense view of the world. It wasn't trying to meet our modern standard of sterile objectivity.

For example, the Gospels paraphrased people's words and sometimes even rearranged the order of events. In describing the time Jesus asked the disciples who they thought He was, three Gospels give slightly different answers. In Mark, Peter said "You are the Messiah" (8:29); in Luke, "God's Messiah" (9:20); and in Matthew, "You are the Messiah, the Son of the living God" (16:16). This does not mean Jesus asked the same question on three different occasions, receiving marginally different responses each time. Instead, each Gospel writer freely paraphrased Peter's response to highlight a different aspect of it. Note that Scripture's paraphrases may more accurately convey the speaker's intent than our direct citations. We can take someone's exact words out of context and twist them into saying something the person never meant. Paraphrases, while not exact, may better communicate the gist.

Similarly, the order of Satan's temptations of Jesus differs in Matthew and Luke. Luke has the last temptation as Satan's dare for Jesus to jump off the temple, while Matthew says it was Satan's offer to give Jesus the world if He bowed and worshiped him. Matthew and Luke rearranged the order to suit their literary and theological purposes. The Gospel of Matthew emphasized Jesus' authority over the world, so it made sense for him to put Satan's offer of the world last. Luke structured his Gospel around Jesus' journey to Jerusalem, so it's understandable that he would place the final temptation on the temple there.

The Bible's intent is particularly important when reading prophecy. For example, what did God mean when He promised to bless Israel if they obeyed Him and curse them when they disobeyed? He promised specific things: obedience would lead to large, healthy families and abundant crops; disobedience would result in famine, disease, and early death (Deuteronomy 28). If one faithful Jew had a small harvest or an idolatrous Israelite had a good year, would that mean God's Word had failed? No—God was using stock prophetic warnings. *In general,* those who obeyed would be blessed and those who disobeyed would be cursed. Exceptions may test or "prove the rule," but they don't break it.

Returning to the examples in the second paragraph, the Bible is speaking generally and with common sense when it describes the sun stopping, the smallest seed, and the dimensions of the metal sea—it does not mean to speak with the precision of a scientist or mathematician. The ratio of the sea is roughly three, the mustard seed is the smallest seed Jesus' audience knew, and the sun—from Joshua's perspective—did appear to stand still. We moderns know the sun does not move around the earth, yet we still refer to "sunrise" and "sunset." When the TV weatherman says the sun will rise tomorrow at 7:00 a.m., few of us yell, "Liar!" We understand what he *means,* and we understand he's *right.* That's what we mean when we say the Bible is true.

37 Is everything in the Bible true?

Whatever the Bible *means* must be true, but to some Christians, this allows some of its details to be wrong. One scholar compared reading the Bible to a doctor's visit. Attempting to explain your immune system, the doctor might compare your body's defenses to a baseball team. "You follow the Detroit Tigers?" he asks. "They have Babe Ruth pitching, Lou Gehrig at first base, Derek Jeter playing shortstop, Mickey Mantle in center field. . ."

You cut him off. "Wait, doc! That's not the Tigers. You're describing the New York Yankees' all-time greats."

"Whatever," he says, shrugging. "I wasn't trying to get the names right. The point is, your immune system is like a baseball team."

Similarly, some say the Bible isn't concerned about insignificant details, that God wasn't trying to get those right. He only cares about the Bible's main points, like who Jesus is, what He did, and why we need Him. This view is called *limited inerrancy.* The Bible is inerrant (without error), but this is limited to the big stuff. Incidental details may be wrong.

But I ask, if we can't trust God to get the small details right, why would we believe Him on the big points? If we know He messed up on claims we can check out, why would we trust Him for what we can't see? If your doctor confuses today's Tigers with the old-time Yankees, he may not be that bright. I'd question his advice on anything.

Jesus said God cares about the details in His Word: "not the smallest letter, not the least stroke of a pen, will by any means disappear from the Law until everything is accomplished" (Matthew 5:18). Think about it: God is all-wise and powerful, so He could easily get every detail right. He wouldn't even break a sweat. And since He is entirely loving and true, wouldn't He want to?

The Valley of Elah, where the Bible says David slew Goliath and routed the Philistines (1 Samuel 17).

It's better to believe in *full inerrancy.* Whatever the Bible intends to say is true, and it intends to get the little facts right. We can trust the Bible whenever it speaks to lesser, checkable items in geology, botany, biology, and history. And we can trust the Bible when it tells us about large, imperceptible truths like who Jesus is and how He died for our sins. The whole Bible is true, from start to finish, top to bottom, large to small.

38 Is everything in the Bible right?

The Bible may be true, but some people worry it may not be right. They have moral objections to the great flood that drowned everyone except Noah's family, the ten plagues that culminated in the death of the eldest sons in Egyptian families, the Israelite invasion and conquest of Canaan, David's killing of Goliath, and Elijah slaying hundreds of false prophets. According to the Bible, these violent episodes were divinely approved and—in some cases—divinely commanded. Has the Good Book gone bad?

Pharaoh and his wife sit in the dark, grieving the death of their firstborn son. Many people question biblical stories that offend modern sensibilities.

Readers may also worry about Scripture's commands for wives to submit to their husbands and slaves to obey their masters. Does the Bible endorse patriarchy and slavery? Future questions will address the problems of genocide, slavery, and husband-wife relationships. For now, though, I want to establish two ground rules for reading Scripture:

1. ***Interpretation:*** We must not jump to quick conclusions from a superficial reading of the text. The culture of biblical times differs significantly from our day, and we must take that into account. Before we become outraged by the Bible, let's make sure we know *what* the passage means and *why* God said it.

2. ***Application:*** Once we are reasonably sure we know what the Bible means, we must agree it is right. If God's Word can be wrong, there is no telling what is right. How would we discern right from wrong if we could not ground morality in the Word of God? Each of us would be left to decide for ourselves. But eight billion people doing what is right in their own eyes is bound to cause trouble, don't you think?

If we dismiss some biblical teaching because it does not meet our own moral standard, we really indicate that we don't believe we need the Bible—we already know what's right and wrong. Rather than come to the Bible with our minds made up, let's allow God's Word to tell us the right and best way to live. As the apostle Paul declared, "Let God be true, and every human being a liar. As it is written: 'So that you may be proved right when you speak and prevail when you judge' " (Romans 3:4).

39 Did the ancient authors of Scripture write things we now know are wrong?

Consider how many times the Holy Spirit must have blocked the false beliefs of the human authors from making it into the Bible. Scripture's human authors likely held many wrong views about nature, astronomy, history, and medicine. Remember, it wasn't that long ago that our best doctors recommended "bloodletting" to remove "bad humors" from an ailing body. That's how George Washington died. He woke up with a sore throat, called for the doctors, and soon passed away when they drained out 40 percent of his blood.

Moses, David, Jeremiah, John, and Paul likely held similarly mistaken views about many things. But none of these errors appear in the Bible. The Holy Spirit directed their words so only their correct beliefs made it into the text. This is amazing evidence for the inspiration of Scripture!

"Not so fast," say some people. What about Psalm 93:1—"the world is established, firm and secure"? Isn't this saying the earth does not move? The sixteenth-century

Nicolaus Copernicus holds a model of the solar system, in this statue from Warsaw, Poland. Does the Bible oppose his discovery of the heliocentric (sun-centered) solar system?

reformer Martin Luther thought so. He believed the young astronomer Copernicus was trying to prove his own brilliance by proposing a new view that the earth revolves around the sun.

We now know that Copernicus was right and Luther's reading of Psalm 93:1 was wrong. This verse is not giving a scientific description of the world. The psalmist may have believed the earth was the immovable center of the universe, but that is not the point he was making here. He was merely affirming God's providential care for us. When tragedy strikes, remember that "the LORD reigns, he is robed in majesty" (Psalm 93:1). He remains in complete control of our lives; "indeed, the world is established, firm and secure." God's got you.

What about Philippians 2:10, which says "at the name of Jesus every knee should bow, in heaven and on earth and under the earth"? Isn't this teaching the ancient view of a three-tiered universe—heaven above, earth beneath, and an underworld below the ground? And don't we now know this is wrong?

No, on both counts. Some scholars argue the ancients didn't literally believe in a three-tiered universe any more than they believed there were literal "floodgates" in heaven that released rain (Genesis 7:11). Their descriptions of heaven above and Sheol below (a sleepy place where the dead, especially the wicked, went to await their resurrection) were phenomenological—how each appeared to them. Others notice that Philippians 2 is a poetic hymn rather than a scientific description. The hymn writer's point isn't about the location of the underworld but that everyone—the living and the dead, the saved and the damned—will bow their knee to King Jesus. We cannot tell from this hymn what the writer thought about the universe and the location of the dead. As literature professor C. S. Lewis explains about medieval peasants, the average person probably didn't think much about such questions at all—they were more concerned about daily life, like how their crops were faring and whether there was food for dinner.

But even if Philippians 2:10 were teaching a three-tiered universe, this would not be an obvious error. Do we know for sure that Sheol was not located underground? When the witch of Endor summoned the dead Samuel, his spirit came up "out of the earth" from Sheol (1 Samuel 28:13). When God punished the family of

Korah, He opened the ground and swallowed them alive down to Sheol (Numbers 16:30–34). We should be careful not to dismiss the idea of an underworld. As God said to Job, "Have you journeyed to the springs of the sea or walked in the recesses of the deep? Have the gates of death been shown to you? Have you seen the gates of the deepest darkness?" (Job 38:16–17). A little humility is in order.

Despite what some critics say, the Bible makes no false claims. The Holy Spirit wholly governed the human authors so that everything they intended to say is wholly true.

40 Does the Bible ever contradict itself?

While reading the Bible, you may occasionally think you've stumbled upon an obvious contradiction. Why does the Gospel of John say Mary Magdalene went to the tomb on Easter morning; the Gospel of Matthew say it was Mary Magdalene along with Mary, the mother of James; and the Gospel of Mark say it was those two plus Salome? Which was it?

Why does the Gospel of Mark say Jesus healed a blind man as He was *leaving* the city of Jericho (10:46), while the Gospel of Luke says He healed a blind man as He *approached* Jericho (18:35)? Did the healing occur when Jesus was coming or when He was going?

What about Luke's story of the apostle Paul's conversion? In Luke's first telling, he says men traveling with Paul "heard the sound" of Jesus speaking but "did not see anyone" (Acts 9:7). In his second telling, the fellow travelers "saw the light, but they did not understand the voice of him who was speaking" (Acts 22:9). Did they hear and not see, or did they see and not hear?

These questions, though perhaps initially disturbing, are easily resolved. They may be resolved *factually*. The various Gospels highlight different women who came to the tomb, but no account contradicts the others. If all three women went to the tomb, then John is correct to say Mary Magdalene traveled there. He does not need to mention the others, especially if he intends to single out Mary for her pivotal conversation with the risen Christ (John 20:11–18).

Regarding the blind man at Jericho, there was an old, deserted city on the path to Jerusalem and a new, populated city a bit off the beaten path. If the beggar was sitting between old and new Jericho, Jesus would have encountered the man as He was leaving one Jericho and entering the other.

Regarding Paul's conversion, the two stories do not contradict each other. The second telling does not say Paul's companions did not *hear* a sound, only that they did not *understand* the sound. Likewise, the first telling does not say the travelers did not see a *light*, only that they did not see *Jesus*. Both accounts say Paul alone saw Jesus and understood what He was saying. His companions knew something was happening but not what.

Some apparent contradictions may also be resolved *literarily* or *theologically*. The Gospel writers freely rearranged certain details to serve their literary purposes. Besides the last temptation of Christ mentioned in an earlier question, the Gospels differ on when Jesus threw the money changers out of the temple. John says it happened at the start of His ministry (2:13–22) while the other Gospels say it came near the end (Matthew 21:12–13; Mark 11:15–18; Luke 19:45–48). This discrepancy may be resolved factually, as it's quite possible Jesus cleansed the temple twice. Or perhaps John put the incident early for theological reasons: to demonstrate Jesus' divine authority at the outset of His ministry—that He was taking the fight to the religious leaders.

Similarly, the Gospels may have literary or theological reasons for singling out who came to the tomb and whether the blind man was healed coming or going from Jericho. Luke seemed to have such a purpose when he mentioned Paul's companions hearing the voice of Christ: he may have said first that they heard and second that they did not understand to artfully show the men's distance from Christ's call to Paul. Their progressive ignorance demonstrates Jesus was specifically targeting Paul to be an apostle. His friends could only look on, baffled.

The Bible does not contradict itself. But what should you do when you think you've found an error? I'll answer that next.

41 What should I do if I think I've found an error?

When I think I've found an error in the Bible, I remember I'm probably not the first person who has noticed it. The Bible is the most scrutinized book ever, so someone else must also have seen the problem and commented on it.

First, I open my study Bibles and read their notes on that verse. If they don't mention the problem or if their explanations aren't satisfying, I look for a commentary on that book of the Bible. Commentaries are verse-by-verse expositions of biblical books. Because they are large, they have room to discuss every issue the writers deem important. Some commentaries are more reliable than others, so ask your pastor for advice or read online comments before you buy or borrow one. As a rough guide, remember that reputable Christian publishers have congregated in Grand Rapids, Nashville, and Dallas. Commentaries published in these cities tend to be pretty good.

If my problem is not addressed in my study Bibles or commentaries, I might do an online search. (I might do this first, especially if I'm in a hurry.) If I still come up empty, I'll ask my pastor and friends, either in person or through social media. Of course, I'll also check popular Bible reference books like this one!

Let me demonstrate my process by using a problem that's bothering me now.

A reputable scholar says he doesn't believe the Bible is entirely true because he has found an error. Paul writes in 1 Corinthians 10:8, "We should not commit sexual immorality, as some of them did—and in one day *twenty-three thousand* of them died." The scholar said Paul was referring to a story in Numbers 25:1–9, in which God sent a plague that killed twenty-*four* thousand promiscuous Israelites. Paul remembered the gist of the story but got the number wrong. He was off by a thousand.

I agree this sounds like an error, so I opened the *NIV Biblical Theology Study Bible* to see if it has noticed the discrepancy. Its notes on 1 Corinthians 10:8 say Paul may have combined Numbers 25 with Exodus 32, another story of immoral and idolatrous Israelites. Exodus 32:28 says three thousand Israelites died, and Numbers 25:9 in the Septuagint—the Greek Old Testament that Paul would have used—says that "four thousand and twenty thousand" died. Perhaps Paul combined the three thousand of Exodus 32 with the twenty thousand of Numbers 25 to show he meant both stories.

I like this, but I'm not entirely convinced, so I looked up 1 Corinthians 10:8 in the *ESV Study Bible.* Its notes say Paul was referring to Numbers 25, and that both twenty-three thousand and twenty-four thousand are fair approximations, and probably all that either author intended. This seems right, though I understand why someone might use this as evidence for limited inerrancy—the Bible sometimes gets details wrong even though its main points are true. In response, I note that one person's error is another person's round, imprecise number. Paul may have been recalling Numbers 25 from memory and didn't care if he was off by one digit. Of course, Paul wasn't actually wrong—if twenty-four thousand Israelites died then twenty-three thousand died too. If anything, Paul undershot. (I understand if this solution seems a little too cute!)

How many women went to Jesus' tomb on Easter morning? Different Gospel writers provided different numbers—are these contradictions that call Scripture into question?

Please notice the kind of alleged errors we're debating: they are not important, and they are not many. And there are various solutions for resolving them (I haven't mentioned the possibility of scribal error in our copies of the biblical manuscripts). I believe it's important to use a solution that preserves the full truthfulness of the Bible, down to the smallest, insignificant detail. But even if someone believes Paul was slightly wrong about how many Israelites died, this worst-case scenario is still very good. Nothing we believe about Jesus or our salvation is at risk.

42 What's a study Bible?

A study Bible is the Walmart of Bibles: one-stop shopping that meets most of your Bible-reading needs. If you are serious about learning the Bible, you need to get one. They make great Christmas or birthday gifts. Study Bibles typically have the following features, listed here in descending order of importance:

1. ***Commentary:*** A study Bible gives running footnotes that explain the biblical text on that page. These notes differ according to the theme of the Bible. I'd start with a general study Bible, such as the *NIV Biblical Theology Study Bible*, the *ESV Study Bible*, or the *NLT Christian Basics Bible*. One of these is usually enough, but if you want to add something more specific, consider the *NIV Cultural Background Study Bible*, the *CSB Apologetics Study Bible*, the *NIV Faith and Work Bible*, or the *ESV Archaeological Study Bible*. Famous teachers sometimes publish study Bibles with their notes as commentary too. You're only getting one person's thoughts, so watch out for idiosyncrasies—but if you enjoy someone's teaching, you'll probably like their study Bible.

2. ***Cross-References:*** Have you read a verse and wondered where else a particular word or concept appears in Scripture? A cross-reference study Bible will tell you. It puts superscript letters beside key words, then in the margins lists what other passages contain that word or idea. Look these up, and their superscript letters may give you even more references to check. In no time you'll have a good handle on what the whole Bible says about any given concept.

3. ***Book Introductions:*** Study Bibles introduce each biblical book with a few pages that explain the who, what, when, where, and why. The introduction typically closes with a summary of the book's themes and an outline of its contents.

4. ***Concordance:*** These were more valuable before the internet made it easy to simply put a word or phrase in quotes in an online search box. But if your device is down or if you want to see in one glance the most important verses that contain a specific word, look up that word in the concordance at the back of your study Bible.

5. ***Maps:*** Behind the concordance are usually color maps of the Ancient Near East, Israel during the time of the Old Testament, Israel during the time of Jesus, Paul's missionary journeys, and so forth.

6. ***Charts, Pictures, and Articles:*** Study Bibles contain a varying assortment of helpful charts, essays, and pictures of biblical sites or items. You won't set out looking for these, as you would the features above, but they can be fun and fascinating to stumble upon. Right now, I'm looking at a photo of a hand holding a widow's mite. Understanding its size adds color to the story of Jesus praising a widow who gave her last penny (Mark 12:41–44).

43 What outside evidence supports the Bible's accounts?

It is impossible to definitively prove a miracle for the simple fact that it's a miracle. Skeptics can always claim they need more proof that a miracle occurred—but if they get enough proof, it would eliminate the miracle. If you can explain *how* something happened, it wasn't a miracle.

So we are unable to prove the miraculous stories of the Bible, and that's a good thing. But do we have evidence to corroborate the Bible's most important accounts?

Here's a little thought experiment: consider the churches in your town. Where did they come from? The Bible says the church—the worldwide assembly of everyone who trusts Jesus for salvation—began on the day of Pentecost, ten days after Jesus returned to heaven. The Holy Spirit fell upon the small group of disciples, Peter proclaimed the good news in Jerusalem, and some three thousand people believed and were baptized (Acts 2). The church has steadily grown ever since. Christianity has survived intense persecution, internal divisions, and self-inflicted wounds to become the leading religion of the world. The individual churches in your neighborhood are evidence that *something* happened in the first century, as the Bible says.

The Roman historian Tacitus, no friend of Christianity, agrees. Writing between 115–117 CE, he said Christians got their name from Christ, "who had been executed in Tiberius' reign by the governor of Judaea, Pontius Pilatus. But in spite of this temporary setback the deadly superstition had broken out afresh, not only in Judaea (where the mischief started) but even in Rome. All degraded and shameful practices collect and flourish in the capital."[10]

Another ancient historian, Flavius Josephus (37–101 CE), was a Jew who nevertheless confirmed many references in the New Testament, such as Jericho, Herod, and Pilate. Here's what he wrote about Jesus and the church:

> About this time there lived Jesus, a wise man. For he was one who wrought surprising feats and was a teacher of such people as accept the truth gladly. He won over many Jews and many of the Greeks. When Pilate, upon hearing him accused by men of the highest standing amongst us, had condemned him to be crucified, those who had in the first place come to love him did not give up their affection for him. And the tribe of the Christians, so called after him, has still to this day not disappeared.[11]

It's not only the church that has survived. How to explain the persistence of the nation of Israel? This beleaguered people has suffered more than any nation ever has. The term *holocaust* was capitalized and applied to their mass murder under

The existence of the nation of Israel is an argument for the trustworthiness of the Bible.

Hitler. Their nation has been conquered and scattered twice, the last time for nearly two thousand years. And yet they doggedly retain their identity. Other nations have come and gone, with their descendants melting into the people of their new homes. Not Israel. You have never heard of a Canadian Midianite or Russian Philistine, but to this day Jews are found all over the world. And since 1948, they have their nation again.

Israel has outlasted every empire that once soundly defeated it. The Babylonian, Assyrian, Roman, and Nazi Empires have all been swept away, yet somehow Israel remains. How else to explain the survival of this long-suffering people other than to say that God is keeping His Word? He promised to make Abraham into a great nation that would occupy the entire land of Palestine: "Look around from where you are, to the north and south, to the east and west. All the land that you see I will give to you and your offspring forever. I will make your offspring like the dust of the earth, so that if anyone could count the dust, then your offspring could be counted" (Genesis 13:14–16).

History, from the ancient writings of Tacitus and Josephus to our own day, continually confirms the biblical story. The evidence persists in Palestine and in your town.

44 Does archaeology support the Bible?

Archaeology is a relatively new science that attempts to make sense of the pottery, glass, mosaics, statues, coins, inscriptions, walls, bones, and other "material culture" that it painstakingly unearths around the world. So far we've only found a tiny fraction of what we know is there. Whole cities, such as Colossae, lie buried beneath two millennia of dirt and debris, waiting for someone with time and money to start digging. What little we have found must be interpreted by scholars, who often have various theories about what any given artifact means. Often, no one knows for sure.

Despite these limitations, archaeologists working in the Middle East regularly make discoveries that confirm the biblical record. For instance, many scholars used to suggest King David was merely legend—no more real than King Arthur—as

To the untrained eye, the Tel Dan Stele may not look like much. But it's a big archaeological confirmation of the Bible's King David.

there was no mention of him outside the Bible. Until 1993, when an archaeologist working at the ancient city of Dan in northern Israel found a basalt fragment used as fill in a wall. As Gila Cook set her equipment down, she noticed what appeared to be random scratches on a nearby stone. She investigated and discovered the etchings were an ancient inscription from a victory stele, a commemorative column that had been smashed and used as building material (two other fragments were found nearby the following year). The broken stone contained an Aramaic inscription of the king of Damascus boasting that he had defeated both the "king of Israel" and "the king of the House of David." These words, written by the Jews' enemy, confirmed the biblical account that David existed and had founded the royal line of Judah.

Notice how random this important discovery was. What other evidence is still buried or, like this Tel Dan Stele, lies hiding in plain sight, waiting for the low angle of the afternoon sun to catch the eye of a passerby?

We've already found the Cyrus Cylinder, which confirms the Bible's story of how God moved Cyrus, king of Persia, to permit the Jews to return from exile and rebuild their city and temple in Jerusalem (Ezra 1:2–4; 2 Chronicles 36:22–23). Found in Iraq and now located in the British Museum, this clay cylinder dates to Cyrus's time (539 BCE) and contains his boasting of victory and subsequent order that all conquered peoples could return home to rebuild their cities and temples.

Other significant discoveries include the Dead Sea Scrolls, which include fragments of 190 biblical scrolls; Hezekiah's tunnel, a long shaft that supplied water to Jerusalem and through which David's soldiers furtively entered the city (2 Samuel 5:6–8); the Epic of Gilgamesh, an Assyrian origin story written on stone tablets that mirrors several aspects of Noah's Flood (Genesis 6–9); the Moabite Stone, which describes battles with Israel from Moab's perspective (2 Kings 3); and the Lachish Letters, notes written on pottery sherds that corroborate Judah's battle with Babylon (Jeremiah 34:6–7).

We've also uncovered a Galilean fishing boat; a nail through the heel of a crucified man; the ossuary box of the high priest Caiaphas, who presided over Jesus' trial; various coins such as shekels, denarii, and widow's mites; water pipes leading into Laodicea (Revelation 3:15–16); and the agora and magnificent theater in Ephesus (Acts 19). And we're finding more all the time. If you like this sort of thing, and you should, consider purchasing the *ESV Archaeological Study Bible*.

Every now and then, of course, someone claims to find something that casts doubt on the Bible. Here's a scrap of papyrus that might be read to imply Jesus had a wife! Here's an ossuary box that may have held Jesus' bones! When you hear such sensational stories, take a breath and remember that archaeology is a young, inexact science and that archaeologists usually disagree. Look around a little, and you'll easily find competing, often better interpretations of the discovery.

The hysteria surrounding Jesus' alleged wife and ossuary box died away when the

The ossuary that contained the bones of Caiaphas, the Jewish high priest who handed Jesus over to Pilate to be crucified (Matthew 26:57–27:10).

evidence was weighed. And so it will the next time. Don't throw away your faith on the whimsical claims of an archaeologist. Believe the Bible, and enjoy the subterranean treasures yet to come.

45 Is the Bible more than true?

It's important to say the Bible is true. It's also important to remember that that's not the most important thing to say. The Bible is so much *more* than true. It's the authoritative Word of God. Many books are true—I've written five (out of seven total!). But only one book—the Bible—is God's inspired Word.

God isn't satisfied merely to tell us things that are true. He yearns to draw us higher into vibrant fellowship with Him. So the Bible aims for goals that are higher than true. It includes *worship*: "Praise the Lord!"; *passions*: "I will awaken the dawn!"; *commands*: "Do everything for the Lord Jesus Christ"; *pleas*: "Lord, save me!"; *commitments*: "As for me and my house, we will serve the Lord"; and *questions*: "Who do you say that I am?"

None of these statements are "true." What would that even mean? A command isn't true or false. Neither are expressions of devotion, passion, or purpose. That's the wrong question to ask. Truthfulness does not apply to the highest aims of Scripture.

And yet, truthfulness is foundational for these higher aims. If the Lord is not God then "Praise the Lord" misfires. If Jesus is not the Lord then doing everything for His glory is pointless. If Jesus is not God, it is futile to ask Him to save us. The highest goals of Scripture may transcend the category of truth, but they depend on foundational facts that must be true. The truthfulness of Scripture is not everything, but it's an essential something. It may not be the goal, but it is necessary for reaching our goal of knowing and loving God.

46 What about translations?

When my friend graduated from seminary, his grandfather called to offer congratulations. Before they hung up, the man asked his grandson, "Did your seminary teach you how to read the Bible's original languages?"

"Yes, Grandpa. I can read Hebrew and Greek."

"Then can you tell me, our English Bibles, are they, you know, accurate?"

My friend's heart sank. His grandfather had faithfully read his Bible for decades. He had relied on it for his relationship with God. It was how he heard from his Lord. Yet all this time, in the back of his mind, he wondered, *Is what I'm reading correct? Is it faithful to the original?*

My friend assured his grandfather, as I assure you, that our mainstream English Bibles are excellent translations of God's Word. Some depth and color is always lost in translation, so our English Bibles are equivalent to watching television in black and white. But what they depict is really there in the original Hebrew, Aramaic, and Greek.

Teams of our brightest scholars translated the New International Version, English Standard Version, Christian Standard Bible, New English Translation, New American Standard Bible, New Revised Standard Version, New King James Version, and more. We have an embarrassing amount of excellent English translations. You may read any of them with confidence that you are reading the Word of God.

There are dozens of English translations of the Bible—the website BibleGateway.com makes nearly sixty separate translations and variations available to anyone with an internet connection.

47 Which Bible translation should I use?

Use whichever translation you most enjoy. Because if you enjoy it, you will use it.

Still, it wouldn't hurt to have more than one version on hand because of translation issues. If you've learned a foreign language, you know that some words and phrases don't easily translate into English.

Imagine you're trying to explain to your mother what a German man is saying—you can either translate each word as it comes or wait and translate the entire sentence in one chunk.

Going word by word produces a more literal translation (called *formal* or *verbal equivalence*), but it rarely sounds good in English. German puts its verbs at the end of phrases and sentences, so translating word for word will make the speaker sound like Yoda. Woodenly literal translations can also be unclear or wrong. Anyone who has used an online translator knows that accurate translation requires more than saying what each word means.

Skilled translators opt instead to interpret larger chunks (called *dynamic equivalence*), giving an easily understandable sense of what the foreign sentence means. But these translators must be careful lest their expansive interpretations become untethered from the individual words. The fullest way to communicate what the German man means is to provide two complementary translations: a formal translation that gives a sense of each individual word and a dynamic translation that gives the larger sense.

The same is true for Scripture. Some translations are more literally word for word, such as the English Standard Version, New American Standard, New King James, and New Revised Standard Version. Read these for the most precise rendering of the Hebrew and Greek words. But these translations can be harder to read and sometimes may obscure the text's fuller meaning. So you can also read more dynamic translations, such as the New International Version and Christian Standard Bible. Using both word for word and dynamic translations will give you a good sense both of the original words and their larger meaning.

I also enjoy the New Living Translation, which is a full-on dynamic translation.

It does not try to render each individual word precisely but strives to communicate the meaning of larger phrases in today's English. As long as you remember this translation is an interpretation and should be checked with word-for-word translations, you will learn much from it.

Some translations are so dynamic they're not actually translations but paraphrases. The Message is one popular example. It too can be read profitably as long as you remember it is not trying to give a literal translation.

48 What about the King James Version?

The King James Version is a fine translation. It was the only Bible many of us had as children, and we memorized our verses from it. Even today, when I attempt to recall a passage from the Bible, it often comes to me in words from the KJV. It's my heart language for God.

But the KJV is old. Originally authorized by King James of England, it was translated in 1611 and revised in 1769, so it feels a bit like reading Shakespeare. This is eloquently poetic in the Psalms, though often we aren't sure what the words mean. They no longer clearly communicate, or they communicate something entirely different. Read the story of Balaam's dumb ass in Numbers 22:21–38, and you'll realize that terms have changed meaning over the centuries. Never read this story in a class of junior high boys! The New King James Version fixed these problems when it came out in 1982, and if you prefer the KJV, I highly recommend it.

The latter half of the twentieth century produced many new English translations, which unsettled many KJV devotees. They worried that other translations were too progressive, too Roman Catholic, or too influenced by modern scholarship, and they feared they were losing something precious. Some overreacted by claiming the KJV was the only true Bible, at least in English. Some said it was the only true Bible period, which raises questions about the plight of non-English-speaking Christians. Do they have God's Word in their language?

KJV-only advocates argue their New Testament was translated from better,

King James I ruled England from 1603 to 1625. The Bible he commissioned was published in 1611.

more reliable Greek manuscripts than the newer translations used. (KJV-only supporters focus almost entirely on the New Testament.) But they are wrong.

Greek manuscripts can be sorted by similarities into four different regions: Alexandria, Caesarea, Rome, and Byzantium. The KJV was translated from the Byzantium family. This family contains the largest number of Greek texts—80 percent of all the Greek texts we have—but they are quite late. The earliest dates only from the tenth century. This means the KJV was translated from Greek manuscripts that were only six to seven centuries older than itself. Most scholars believe the Alexandrian family, though fewer because these texts are older, is closer to the original writings.

The accuracy of our Greek New Testament, already exceedingly high, is continually improving. As we discover new manuscripts, we weigh them with the ones we already have. The result is a highly reliable Greek text, a significant upgrade over what was available in 1611. The original KJV was translated from Greek texts that relied on Erasmus's third edition of his *Novum Instrumentum* (1522), which synthesized only a half dozen Greek manuscripts. KJV-only people claim this small stream of Greek texts produced a flawless Textus Receptus, or "Received Text," but there is no evidence for this. No one has found the Textus Receptus. Our best evidence suggests the KJV relied on a small number of Greek texts, none of which were identical to the others.

The KJV is an excellent translation of God's Word. But so are several of our recent English translations. They may even be superior, as they are translated from more and better vetted Greek manuscripts than existed in 1611. Rather than argue over which translation is best, let's use the Bibles we enjoy and thank God for the rest.

49 How should I read the Bible?

The Scriptures are God's tended garden of spiritual fruit and flowers to nourish our souls. A garden can be enjoyed in two complementary ways. First, we can gaze from a balcony and appreciate its orderly lines of roses, lilies, and lavender—there's nothing like an overview to understand how the gardener plotted his treasures. But when we look down on a beautiful garden, we won't be satisfied until we actually walk among its flowers, soaking in their beauty and fragrance.

Similarly, we should savor the Bible both in large, sweeping glances and in slow, leisurely strolls. We should read the Bible both fast and slow, covering much ground in one sitting and also meditating on a single verse or phrase. We're all different, and each of us will usually read in the way that benefits us the most. But we'd all grow from changing things up from time to time.

When you skim an entire book in one sitting, you will make connections you didn't see before. The big picture of Romans or John will emerge, and you'll see where the individual flowers go. When instead you ponder an individual verse or phrase, your mind will slow down to inhale its fragrance. One sure way to do this is to write out the verse by hand. This forces you to think about each word and how it relates to the other words in the sentence. What beauty you will discover!

Of course, pondering a single verse or skimming an entire book are not your only options. I often fall somewhere in the middle, reading a single chapter of the Bible and then meditating on the one or two lines that stood out to me.

I also find it helpful to read passages out loud. God's Word is alive, so it's meant to be heard now, in the moment. This is why we read the Bible aloud when we gather as the church. When someone speaks the Word of God in the assembly of the people of God, the Spirit of God uses that Word to penetrate and change

Schoolchildren read the Bible in Harare, Zimbabwe.

our hearts. The power of God resides in His Word, and that power is unleashed whenever His Word is spoken. So let's continue to read the Scriptures and *hear* them.

50 What should I read in the Bible?

The whole thing! Do an online search for "reading the Bible in one year," and you will find various plans that intersperse Old and New Testament readings in three to four chapters per day. This is a wise approach, as it keeps us balanced and reading the entire Word of God.

But if we're honest, most of us spend the most time reading those parts of Scripture that seem most directly applicable to us. We read the four Gospels to learn about Jesus, Acts to learn about the church, and the ensuing Epistles to discover how we must live in this church. In the Old Testament, we ponder the wisdom of Proverbs and pray the Psalms to jump-start our hearts and loosen our tongues. Unfortunately, this is where many of us stop.

We should venture out more and reflect on the melancholy of Ecclesiastes, the tortured suffering of Job, the powerful display of God's providence in Ruth and Esther, and the soaring beauty of the prophecies of Isaiah. We shouldn't let Isaiah's large size frighten us from dipping our toes into its refreshing stream. We also should regularly read the stories of Israel: how God chose the patriarchs (Genesis); delivered His people from Egypt (Exodus); brought them kicking and screaming into the Promised Land (Numbers, Deuteronomy, and Joshua); sent judges, prophets, and kings to deliver them (Judges, 1–2 Samuel); drove their rebellious nation into captivity (1–2 Kings); and finally began calling them home (Ezra, Nehemiah).

There are many more books than I have mentioned, and we need a plan to regularly read them all. It's okay to have favorites, such as the Gospel of Mark or Philippians, so long as we remain balanced in our reading schedule. If it's been a while since you've read Leviticus, Ezekiel, or Zephaniah, why not do it today? The part you've been avoiding may be the part you need most. As you read His Word, ask God to speak to your heart—then write down the parts that do.

51 When should I read the Bible?

You can read the Bible anytime, but most people who are striving to cultivate friendship with God start their day with Scripture and prayer. Beginning each morning with God signals that He is our most important relationship and orients our day in His direction. We are better prepared to meet the challenges of each day when we dedicate that day to Him.

Many Christians also enjoy reading a passage of Scripture at lunch or dinner. They remember Jesus' words that "Man shall not live on bread alone," and they feed their bodies and souls at the same meal (Matthew 4:4).

A few wise Christians also recognize the benefits of reading Scripture before bed. Not only can it calm our minds for a quiet night's sleep, but since the Bible is the last thing on our minds, we may subconsciously meditate on it while we sleep. When we read Scripture before falling asleep, we'll often wake up with that passage, and perhaps an insight or two, on the top of our minds.

Read Scripture whenever you want, but do set aside regular time each day for just you and God. There is no better way to know Him and to tell Him that you love Him.

52 How does the Bible read me?

In their classic text *How to Read a Book,* Mortimer Adler and Charles Van Doren rank the various kinds of books. They say most books are not worth reading carefully. "Skimming will do."

Other books, perhaps "no more than a few thousand," are the good books that are worth reading once. You may return to check certain points, but you got everything you're going to get out of them in one reading. You're grateful for what you learned, "but you know [they have] no more to give."

Of these good books "there is a much smaller number—here the number is probably less than a hundred—that cannot be exhausted by even the very best reading you can manage." You sense the book contains more truth than you picked up, so you return to it often. And every time you do, you find this great book "*seems to have grown with you.* You see new things in it—whole sets of new things—that you did not see before."[12]

Of course, the book didn't really grow, because books don't change. The book was simply so far above you that you appreciated its heights as you grew tall enough to reach them.

The Bible is one of these great books that grows with us. We grow when we apply what we learn there to our lives, then we return to discover new truths to apply. We never outgrow the Bible because, unlike all the other great books, it alone is alive with the power of God.

The Bible is not merely static words on a page. Its words are inspired by the Spirit of God, who presses those words upon our hearts while we read. This explains why we sense we're not reading Scripture as much as Scripture is reading us. God's Word "is alive and active. Sharper than any double-edged sword, it penetrates even to dividing soul and spirit, joints and marrow; it judges the thoughts and attitudes of the heart" (Hebrews 4:12).

The Bible probes beneath our felt needs and diagnoses the deepest yearnings and fears of our hearts. It lays us bare before the holy love of God, whose Word binds our wounds and kicks us in the pants, as needed. To read the Bible is to make ourselves vulnerable to the jealous grace of God. We may open and close the Bible, but we realize we are not in control. He is.

53 What's the best way to understand the Bible?

Start by asking the Holy Spirit to help you understand what He has written. This won't magically guarantee that you will comprehend everything, as God's Word always exceeds our grasp. It won't even guarantee that you won't get something wrong. But if you want to understand the Bible, why not ask its Author for help?

One essential help that He's already given is the early church's baptismal creeds, now summarized in the Apostles Creed. The church has long used this rule of faith to read Scripture. Any interpretation that disagrees with this Creed must be wrong.

The Apostles Creed declares:

> I believe in God, the Father Almighty, creator of heaven and earth.
>
> I believe in Jesus Christ, his only Son, our Lord, who was conceived by the Holy Spirit and born of the virgin Mary. He suffered under Pontius Pilate, was crucified, died, and was buried; he descended into hell. The third day he arose again from the dead. He ascended to heaven and is seated at the right hand of God the Father almighty. From there he will come to judge the living and the dead.
>
> I believe in the Holy Spirit, the holy catholic church, the communion of saints, the forgiveness of sins, the resurrection of the body, and the life everlasting. Amen.

A stained glass window depicts the doctrine of the Trinity, a key teaching of the Apostles Creed.

The Apostles Creed teaches that God is sovereign and Triune, creation is good, Jesus is God who died for our sins and rose again, and one day we too will rise from our graves. If your interpretation of Scripture disagrees with any of this, you're reading it wrong.

Do not read Scripture alone. Invite the Holy Spirit to read with you, and read with the church and our rule of faith.

54 What's the best way to understand a specific Bible passage?

Question 73 explains how to explore a biblical text from the inside. We'll do that job better if we learn to look at our passage in the following ways and ask these questions:

Understanding historical and cultural references outside the Bible can help us to grasp the truth that's in the Bible.

1. ***Look up: Where are you in the larger story?*** Are you reading from the Old or New Testament? If the New Testament, is your passage before or after the start of the church (Acts 2)? Everything in the Bible is written to us, but not everything applies in the same way. The first step of biblical interpretation is to gain your bearings.

2. ***Look beside: What is the biblical context?*** Once you have a sense of the big picture, look around your immediate vicinity. Take a large enough chunk, at least a whole chapter, to grasp the context of your passage. If you pull a single

verse and look at it by itself, you're apt to misunderstand what it's really saying.

Have you noticed how some athletes write "Phil. 4:13" in eye black before a big game? This verse says, "I can do all things through him who strengthens me" (ESV). Quarterbacks use this as motivation to throw touchdown passes and lead their teams to victory. But if they had read the verse immediately before Philippians 4:13, they would realize the "all things" that the apostle Paul is speaking of includes winning and losing, having a lot and having a little. Paul says he has "learned the secret of being content in any and every situation." So by writing "Phil. 4:13" on their cheekbones, these quarterbacks are saying they're okay with losing. Not exactly the inspirational message they were going for!

3. ***Look outside: What is the historical-cultural context?*** The immediate biblical context is generally sufficient to understand the basic meaning of your passage. But the Bible was not written in a vacuum, so knowing something about its time and place can add depth and color.

For example, when you know that kings in the Ancient Near East were believed to be images of their god, you understand the countercultural punch of Genesis 1. God says every human bears His image, not only those at the top of the food chain. We humans don't exist merely to serve the king and his god; the true God serves us by creating a vast world for us to enjoy.

Similarly, knowing that women's hair was a turn-on for men in the ancient world helps us understand Paul's command for Christian women to cover their hair (1 Corinthians 11:2–16). Understanding the history between the Jews and their Roman overlords adds insight to Jesus' testy interactions with the Pharisees, just as knowing something about the Roman imperial cult helps us to better interpret John's apocalyptic visions in Revelation.

You can grasp the general point of any passage with the Bible alone. You don't need to be an expert in Middle Eastern studies. But knowing something about your passage's historical-cultural context will help you get more out of it. This is the number one reason to own a study Bible.

*4. **Look appropriately: What is the genre?*** We don't read history, letters, parables, and poetry in the same way, so the final question to ask is *What kind of writing is this?* Each genre has its own set of rules, so I'll give each its own entry on the following pages.

You might find it helpful to approach the biblical narrative from the perspective of a movie director.

55 How should I read the stories of the Bible?

If you enjoy a good story, you'll love the Bible—because it's full of them. Nearly half the Bible is narrative. You'll enjoy Scripture's stories even more if you think like a movie director and consider a few key elements.

*1. **What is the setting?*** How many scenes would you shoot for this story? Where would they be located?

*2. **Who are the characters?*** Who is the hero? Who is the opponent? Who fills the supporting roles? How would you film scenes so the audience knows who to root for?

3. ***What is the plot?*** What problem does the hero need to solve? How is the problem resolved? What do the other characters want? What is blocking them? How do they overcome it? How might the outcome have changed if the hero or another character had chosen differently? How would you film the key moment of decision?

4. ***What dialogue seems important?*** Is there a single line or two that captures the point of the story? What spoken words must you keep for the story to make sense? How should the characters read their lines?

5. ***Whose perspective is expressed?*** Is the story written in an objective, matter-of-fact way or through the eyes of one character? Whose point of view does the story want you to take?

The Bible was written within an oral culture. Its stories are meant to be heard not just silently read. . .so you'll get more from an account if you read it out loud. Listen for repeated words and phrases. And try reading dialogue with different inflections. For example, when the prophet Nathan confronts King David for murdering Uriah, he says "You are the man!" (2 Samuel 12:7); try reading the words with accusatory denunciation. Then anguish. Then pity. Perhaps a sigh. Which one seems to fit the story, and what difference does it make?

You'll remember stories better (and gain new insights) if you read them out loud and then retell them in your own words. You may forget certain details, but what you include is a sign of what you think is most important. Try it with friends, each of you contributing what you remember, and together you'll discover a story's main point.

56 How should I apply the stories of the Bible?

This is a tricky question for two reasons. First, stories are ambiguous. If you've ever discussed a movie with friends, you know that the moral of the story often depends on each person's perspective. Stories show rather than tell, so they leave room for various interpretations. (That's a big reason we like them.) Stories aren't preachy, but that also makes their points easier to miss.

Second, stories in the Bible are not primarily about moral guidance anyway. When we read them looking only for lessons or lifehacks, we may miss what they are actually trying to say.

In light of these limitations, here are two corresponding tips for taking away what God most wants you to get.

1. ***Remember that stories are descriptive not necessarily prescriptive.*** The stories of the Bible describe what happened; they do not necessarily set examples for us to follow. Consider how Gideon tested God to certify His command (Judges 6:36–40). Gideon told God that if the morning dew made his fleece wet and the surrounding ground dry, he would believe what God had said. When everything happened just that way, Gideon changed it up, asking God to keep the fleece dry and make the ground wet the next morning. God graciously answered both requests—but this does not mean He wants us to follow Gideon's example in discerning His will. When God tells us to do something, He expects us to obey right away rather than putting out a fleece.

   God is so great that He can use any human action—even sin—to accomplish His will. He used Joseph's bragging to his brothers and Esther's sleeping with a Gentile king to rescue His own people. But just because the "hero of the story" does a particular thing does not mean God approves of it. Biblical stories often illustrate the moral teaching but not always. Sometimes the writers simply said what happened, expecting knowledgeable Bible readers to understand what God thinks about that. In sum, God more definitively instructs us through Scripture's direct commands than through stories that describe people more or less obeying those commands.

2. ***Ask what the story teaches about God and how He saves His people.*** This is the main point of every Bible story. For example, the thrilling stories of Joseph (Genesis 37–50) are primarily about God's protection of His people and the preparation for their redemption from slavery in Egypt. We easily lose this big picture if, for example, we turn these stories into lessons for leadership. We can

learn life lessons from Joseph—say, to run from Potiphar's wife and keep your integrity, even when it hurts—but we must remember the primary reason for these stories: to tell us how God saves His people.

God is the ultimate hero both of the Bible and all history. If you determine what a Bible story tells you about God, you will get everything you need to know. Then, once you articulate that, ask how you should live in response. That is your moral lesson, the main takeaway God wants you to apply.

Joseph resists the advances of Potiphar's wife—a good lesson for us today, but not the main point of the Joseph story.

Why did God forbid pork chops and bacon to the Israelites? How does Old Testament law relate to Christians today?

57 How should I read the law?

The Old Testament law is perhaps the most difficult part of the Bible. Few Christians read the second half of Exodus or the book of Leviticus for their morning devotions. Why should I care about eating kosher or rules for offering animal sacrifices?

The New Testament church is not the same as Old Testament Israel, so not all of Israel's commands apply to us. The law has three different kinds of rules: *civil* laws that governed life in ancient Israel, *cultic* laws that described how priests should dress and offer sacrifices, and *moral* laws that instructed Israelites how to serve God and neighbor. The civil laws do not apply to Christians, as we are not a political nation. Nor do the cultic laws, since we do not sacrifice animals to cover our sin now that Jesus, the perfect and final sacrifice, has come. But many of the moral laws, particularly those repeated in the New Testament, do apply to us. These moral laws are distilled in the Ten Commandments, which God delivered to Israel on the day He agreed to be their God.

And that is the point of the law. Every enduring relationship has rules. Marriages have vows, countries have constitutions, and God and His people must have their expectations. When God delivered Israel from bondage in Egypt, He brought them to Mount Sinai and declared they were His people by making a covenant with them and giving Ten Commandments to govern their relationship. Many years later, Jesus said the entire law could be summarized in two commands: "Love the Lord your God" and "Love your neighbor as yourself" (see Matthew 22:37–40).

Our human relationship with God has matured since Old Testament times. Jesus' perfect sacrifice eliminated our need to slay animals to cover our sin. And rather than remain apart as a separate nation, Jesus sends His church into all nations. But every Old Testament law still tells us something about God and how He wants us to live in the world. Think of it this way: few of us worry about keeping the rules our parents laid down when we were children. *Don't throw food! No hitting! Pants must be worn at all times!* We have matured beyond our need for such instructions, yet these rules still tell us something important about our parents and how they wanted us to treat others.

You'll learn a lot from the law when you ask two questions: What does this command tell me about God, and how does it teach me to love others? The answers may not be obvious, given that we live in a different time and place, but a study Bible will usually help. Here are a few examples to whet your appetite:

1. ***Why did God tell Israel not to eat pork?*** *(Leviticus 11:7).* Pigs ate garbage, sewage, and even corpses, so people eating their meat risked catching various parasites. Besides these possible health risks of disease-carrying pigs, God wanted Israel to avoid mingling with surrounding nations who would entice them to worship idols. Since these people loved bacon—and who doesn't?—God told His people they couldn't have any. In this way, the Israelites wouldn't eat in pagan homes and become seduced by their false gods. The Lord welcomed the nations to join His people, but He warned His people not to join the nations. Israel was to remain separate, a holy nation through which the Messiah would come.

2. ***Why did God say to "not cook a young goat in its mother's milk"?*** *(Deuteronomy 14:21).* God probably thinks it cruel to use a mother's life-giving milk to prepare her offspring for dinner. He also may have wanted to prevent His people

from participating in the fertility cult of the Canaanites, whose symbolic magic often "married" things that should not be mixed to influence their gods to bestow more offspring. God was protecting His people from idolatry, so He warned against the pagan practices of mating different kinds of animals, planting with two different kinds of seeds, and wearing clothes with two different kinds of material (Leviticus 19:19).

3. ***Why did God say a man must marry his dead brother's widow?*** *(Deuteronomy 25:5–10).* This strange command would not work in modern society, but in these early years it was a sign of love. A man who loved his brother would not see the latter's death as an opportunity to take his land. Rather, the surviving brother would beget a son who would "carry on the name of the dead brother so that his name will not be blotted out from Israel" (Deuteronomy 25:6).

None of the Old Testament laws are arbitrary, pointless rules. Every one teaches God's people how to love Him and serve their neighbors in their particular cultural moment. Read the law with this in mind, and you will learn much about how to live for God and others today.

58 How should I read prophecy?

The Old Testament prophetic books are probably the least read part of the Bible. Ezekiel, Isaiah, and Jeremiah are too large, and the twelve minor prophets describe unfamiliar people and places. What do Edom, Tyre, and Moab have to do with me? Well, more than you might think. The people and places have come and gone, but the God who gave these prophecies remains the same.

The prophets are God's covenant cops. They appear near the end of the Old Testament (760–460 BCE) to police the law that God had given centuries earlier. God wrote the law to govern Israel's covenantal relationship with Him, and He sent the prophets to arrest Israel when she broke their covenant. The prophets warned of dire consequences should the Israelites continue to disobey and promised that God ultimately would send His Messiah to save the day. These warnings and promises foretold the future, and that is why prophecy is often identified with predictions.

But at its core, prophecy is so much more. The prophets consistently convicted Israel of two big sins. The law was about loving God and loving neighbor, so when Israel broke the law, they were always guilty of both *idolatry* against God and *injustice* against their neighbors. These sins are not mutually exclusive, because those who only look out for themselves will inevitably reject God and hurt others. God noticed the connection and declared He would reject worshipers who unjustly trampled the poor. He was weary of sacrifices offered by hands that dripped with other people's blood (see Isaiah 1:10–23).

A fresco of the prophet Isaiah from a Viennese church. What do Isaiah and other Old Testament prophecies mean to us today?

This is why the prophets remain relevant today. Christians (and even many non-Christians) agree that our largest problems, both individually and as a society, are idolatry and injustice. We don't love God or others as we ought. Reading the prophets reminds us that our problem is not new and that it doesn't necessarily have a happy ending, at least in the short term. The prophets warned people who did not listen and were swept away into the dustbin of history. If it happened to them, it can happen to us.

Christ and His kingdom will win with or without you, so make sure it's with you. As you read the prophets—preferably with a study Bible that can supply historical and cultural context—ask how you might be repeating the same sins. How do we cheat the poor and defenseless? How do we add to their pain? How do we hedge our bets and give God less than the full, exclusive devotion He deserves?

Don't merely ask what you should stop doing. Flip it around and ask what you must start doing. How can we give voice to the voiceless so that everyone gets a fair shake? What can we do to protect the orphan and widow? How can we make sure we have no other gods but Jesus? Fighting injustice and idolatry are two sides of the same coin. The Bible explains, "Whoever claims to love God yet hates a brother or sister is a liar. For whoever does not love their brother and sister, whom they have seen, cannot love God, whom they have not seen. And he has given us this command: Anyone who loves God must also love their brother and sister" (1 John 4:20–21).

59 How should I read poetry?

God is a poet. He filled one-third of His Bible with poetry, putting it in the Prophecy books, Ecclesiastes, and Revelation, and most of Psalms, Proverbs, Job, and the Song of Solomon.

God loves poetry, perhaps because poems wrap their truth in beautiful verse and arresting images. Poems are a concentrated form of writing. They are usually short, which invites us to read slowly, pondering their meaning and feeling their emotions. Here are a few tips for reading them well.

1. ***Focus on the images.*** Biblical poetry sometimes speaks directly but often makes its point by speaking about something else. For example, the Psalms explicitly say, "the LORD protects and preserves" His people (41:2), but often they communicate this idea by talking about rocks, fortresses, and shields. Psalm 18:2 says, "The LORD is my rock, my fortress and my deliverer. . .my shield and the horn of my salvation, my stronghold." No one thinks God is a literal rock, fortress, or shield. But these concrete images evoke powerful emotions that seal the truth of His protection deep in our hearts. It is one thing to say God cares for us. It is a whole new experience to read, "The LORD is my shepherd, I lack nothing. He makes me lie down in green pastures, he leads me beside quiet waters, he refreshes my soul" (Psalm 23:1–3).

2. ***Feel the images.*** When you find an image, close your eyes and imagine it. Let its colors, smells, and sounds wash over you. What do you feel? This is not "extra," something you can take or leave. It's the point. If God didn't want the image to move you, He wouldn't have written poetry.

3. ***Describe the comparison.*** To understand the meaning of an image, ask how its concrete form expresses the abstract truth it represents. How is God like a rock, a shield, or a shepherd? Why did God choose these images to represent Himself? While we must not reduce a poem to this abstract content, we will better understand its point when we grasp the logic of its images.

The familiar imagery of Psalm 23—the Lord as a shepherd—is depicted in a stained glass church window.

4. ***Find the big idea.*** Poems are not logically structured essays, but they are trying to say something. You will better understand a poem if you can state what it's about and then explain how its sections, though loosely, advance this theme. For example, the big idea of Psalm 23 is God's care for His children in normal times (verses 1–3), in peril (verses 4–5), and forever (verse 6). This is only one possible way to outline this psalm—try your own, and you will discover the many shades of meaning in this poem.

5. ***Look for figures of speech.*** Because poems are not literal, they typically use non-literal figures of speech. Look out for these:

    - ***Hyperbole:*** Poetry often grabs our attention and stirs our heart through exaggeration. For example, "You are altogether beautiful, my darling; there is no flaw in you" (Song of Solomon 4:7). The beloved isn't literally flawless, but every lover gets the point. No Valentine cards read, "You're smokin' hot despite a few obvious flaws." We'd rather our lovers lie!

    - ***Personification:*** Poetry brings the world to life by assigning human qualities to nonhuman things. For example, "the mountains and hills will burst into song before you, and all the trees of the field will clap their hands" (Isaiah 55:12).

    - ***Anthropomorphism:*** Biblical poetry often makes God intelligible to us by describing Him with human characteristics. David said his cry for help came to God's ears. Then, "Smoke rose from his nostrils; consuming fire came from his mouth. . . . He parted the heavens and came down; dark clouds were under his feet" (Psalm 18:6–9). God is spirit, so He doesn't possess a physical mouth, nose, and feet. But these vivid, concrete images better communicate His urgent, passionate response than simply saying, "God answered my cry."

6. ***See the parallels.*** Biblical poetry often thinks in pairs.

A second line may repeat the first line:

God is our refuge and strength,
an ever-present help in trouble.
PSALM 46:1

or make a contrasting point:

Trouble pursues the sinner,
but the righteous are rewarded with good things.
PROVERBS 13:21

or finish the thought:

Sing to the LORD a new song;
sing to the LORD, all the earth.
PSALM 96:1

These parallels will not help you understand the meaning of the poem, as the meaning lies in the images—but they will move your heart with the poem's beauty and make its lines impossible to forget.

60 Should I pray every psalm?

The psalms are God's inspired prayer book, so He wants us to pray them. Even when they make us uncomfortable.

Consider the lament psalms, which outnumber all the rest. Lament psalms often yell at God for not keeping His promises. *We've been faithful. Why won't you save us from our enemies?* "Awake, Lord! Why do you sleep? Rouse yourself! Do not reject us forever. Why do you hide your face and forget our misery and oppression?" (Psalm 44:23–24).

This sounds disrespectful, so lament psalms typically end by expressing confidence in God's goodness. But not always. Psalm 88 bitterly wonders why God refuses to respond and ends in despair: "darkness is my closest friend" (verse 18).

Why would the Bible include such irreverent gloom? Because God knows that's how we often feel. He doesn't want us to stuff our emotions. He knows what we're thinking, so we might as well say it. He's got broad shoulders, and He can take it.

When you feel that God has forsaken you, follow the example of Jesus. Find a lament psalm and scream it to Him: "My God, my God, why have you forsaken me? Why are you so far from saving me, so far from my cries of anguish?" (Psalm 22:1).

What about those ferocious psalms of lament, called "imprecatory psalms," that not only cry out for deliverance but also call down God's wrath on those who hurt us? Are we really supposed to pray Psalm 137:9, which says about God's enemies, "Happy is the one who seizes your infants and dashes them against the rocks"?

I have never felt low enough to pray this, but I commiserate with the Jews whose babies *had* been killed and so wanted God to do the same to their enemies (verse 8). God knows our hearts, so if we're thinking something awful, we might as well tell Him. We're not just venting, we are channeling our anger to and through God. We cry out to our just Lord, leaving all vengeance in His hands. We also remember that He is merciful, so our ultimate wish is for our enemies to repent and receive forgiveness. This desire is implicit, though unsaid, in the psalms' agonizing cries for justice.

Bottom line: there is a psalm for whatever you are feeling right now. Leaf through the psalms to find your emotion. Speak or shout the psalm to God until its words morph into your own.

61 Can I claim every proverb?

We all seek wisdom for life's decisions, both big and small: *Which job should I take? Who should I date? Should I dress up or down? How should I spend my time? My money? Should I speak now, and if so, what should I say?*

Sometimes we have wise sayings that inform our decisions: *A stitch in time saves nine. A man is known by the company he keeps. Fortune favors the bold. Good things come to those who wait.*

We understand these brief maxims are guidelines rather than guarantees. They are general principles that help us make wise choices; they are not fool-proof promises. And we often need wisdom to know which one to apply. When considering a risky investment, should we go for it because "fortune favors the bold" or pass because "good things come to those who wait"? Both proverbs are generally true, though only one can be followed in each situation.

The book of Proverbs is God's inspired collection of wise sayings. These pithy maxims are wiser than anything a mere human could come up with, but they are not guarantees. Proverbs 22:6 says, "Start children off on the way they should go, and even when they are old they will not turn from it." This is not a promise from God that every child raised in a godly home will one day return to the Lord. If this were the case, Proverbs wouldn't devote its early chapters urging children to heed their father's advice. People make their own choices, and some obstinately and tragically refuse to listen. Proverbs 22:6 is a principle that encourages parents to teach their children the faith, and having done that, to never lose hope. It is *generally* true that adults remain formed by their upbringing and often return to their childhood faith. So wise parents never stop imploring God to save their children.

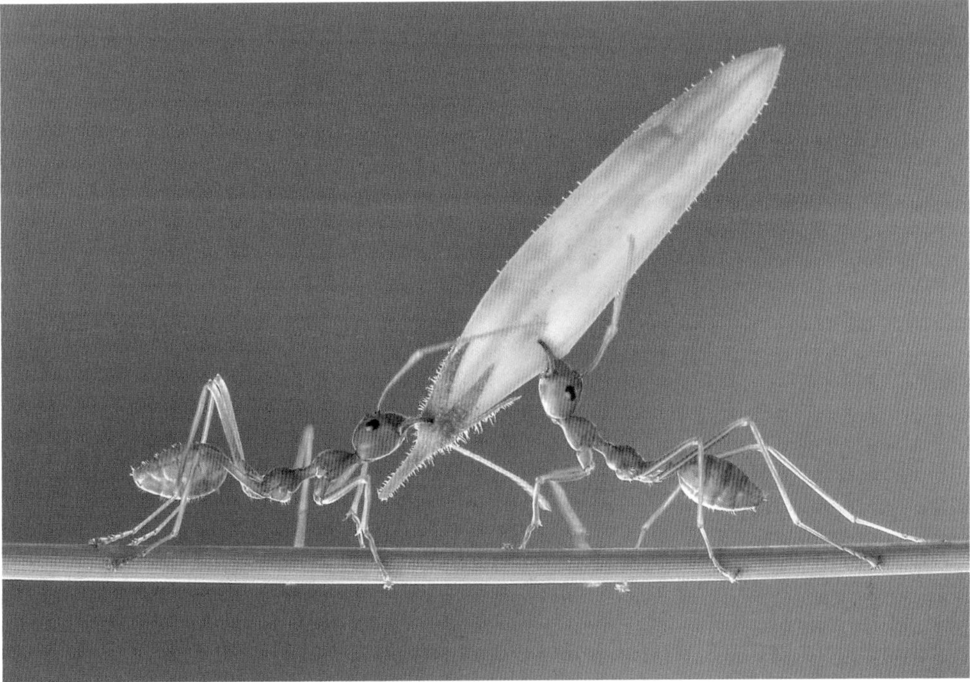

Proverbs 6:6—"Go to the ant, you sluggard; consider its ways and be wise!"—seems applicable to everyone. But is every biblical proverb?

Similarly, Proverbs 16:3 ("Commit to the LORD whatever you do, and he will establish your plans") is not an ironclad promise. Wise people do submit their plans to God, but this is no guarantee they will reach their goals. This proverb reminds us that our best ideas need God's blessing and that His idea of success may look different than ours.

God's wise maxims also require wisdom to know how and when to apply them. Proverbs 26:4–5 says, "Do not answer a fool according to his folly, or you yourself will be just like him. Answer a fool according to his folly, or he will be wise in his own eyes." Which is it? Well, it depends. There is risk in both answering and not answering a fool, and we need wisdom to know when to do which. Fortunately, God promises to give His wisdom whenever we ask (James 1:5–6).

He's already given us a great start. Think of it: unlike the ancient Greeks who trekked to the oracle of Delphi, you have direct access to the wisdom of God! Savor God's proverbs—read them by the fistfuls—and let their insights guide your daily choices. No guarantees, except one: you will become a wise person who wisely makes wise decisions.

62 What's up with Job?

The book of Proverbs is thirty-one chapters of wisdom for winning at life. The book of Job is proof that things don't always work out. Job is God's inspired story for anyone personally grappling with the problem of evil. That's all of us at one time or another.

Job was "the greatest man among all the people of the East." He "was blameless and upright; he feared God and shunned evil" (Job 1:1–3). God rewarded Job's faithfulness by blessing him with a large family and great wealth. He was so proud of the man that He mentioned Job to Satan. "Have you considered my servant Job? There is no one on earth like him" (1:8).

Satan said God had bought Job's obedience with His blessings. Take the goodies away "and he will surely curse you to your face" (1:11). God said, essentially, "You're on," and Satan went to work, killing Job's children, ruining his health, and destroying his wealth. The only thing Job didn't lose was the one thing he may have wanted to. Satan let Job keep his wife, who in exasperation told her husband, "Curse God and die!" (2:9). But Job never would.

Most of the book is a series of poetically poignant conversations between Job and his three friends. They were sure Job had sinned terribly, for they agreed with what Proverbs would later suggest, that God blesses the righteous and destroys the wicked (see, for example, Proverbs 10:9–11, 24–30; 11:2–11, 19–23). They could only guess at what evil Job had committed. They begged him to repent and be reconciled to God.

Three "friends" accuse the suffering Job of causing his own trouble. Much of the book is frustrating and depressing.

But Job knew he was innocent. He grew increasingly angry with their pious platitudes and with God for permitting him to suffer. Job even demanded that God appear and explain Himself! God finally came down, cloaked in a powerful storm, and thundered that both Job and his friends were wrong. The friends had misrepresented God and maligned Job, and Job had mistakenly thought he could out-debate God. (This is important to remember when reading the speeches in this book: the story truly presents what Job and his friends said, but that does not mean what they all said was true.)

God basically took Job on a tour of his local zoo. Look at those mountain goats, oxen, and ostriches (39:1–18)! God pointed out His vast creation, saying that if Job was unable to run the physical world, what made him think he could govern the moral universe? Job was overwhelmed by God's presence and words, agreeing that he didn't know what he was talking about: "Surely I spoke of things I did not understand, things too wonderful for me to know. . . . Therefore I despise myself and repent in dust and ashes" (42:3, 6).

God forgave Job and restored his wealth. He even gave Job new children, though the first ten were never to return. Not everything is restored to Job, which makes his story one of the most bracing tales for the problem of evil. Centuries of Christians have pondered Job's anguished cries, his friends' judgmental counsel, and God's seemingly tone-deaf speeches at the end. Remarkably, something God said or did calmed Job, who made peace with God and the evil he had endured. *What was it?* Read the story and see for yourself. Then you'll be prepared for whatever comes your way.

63 What's up with Ecclesiastes?

The book of Proverbs is thirty-one chapters of wisdom for winning at life. The book of Ecclesiastes wonders if that's even possible. Everyone dies, so who really wins in the end?

Fun fact: Ecclesiastes is my favorite book. Not because it's fun. It's not. But it's brutally honest about life and its futility.

Ecclesiastes begins and ends the same way, " 'Meaningless! Meaningless!' says the Teacher. 'Everything is meaningless!' " (1:2; 12:8). The Hebrew term translated "meaningless" is *hebel,* which literally means "breath." The Teacher might mean that life is empty like breath (how much would you pay for a jar of air?) or that life is futile, like trying to catch the wind (1:14). Perhaps he means both.

Any book on the meaning of life is bound to generate controversy and various interpretations. Read Ecclesiastes for yourself, keeping these clues in mind:

1. ***The rest of Scripture interprets this book.*** The Teacher often complains about the futility of life "under the sun" (1:3; 2:11, 17–22; 4:1–3; 5:13; 6:1, 12; 8:14–15; 9:1–12). How might these issues be resolved in the Bible's larger story of God's Son?

2. ***The book has small bursts of pleasure.*** It's not all doom and gloom. The Teacher also praises the joys of life, though often these are situated within despair. I'm not sure if I should laugh or cry after reading this: "Go, eat your food with gladness, and drink your wine with a joyful heart, for God has already approved what you do. Always be clothed in white, and always anoint your head with oil. Enjoy life with your wife, whom you love, all the days of this meaningless life that God has given you under the sun—all your meaningless days" (9:7–9).

3. ***The key is in the conclusion.*** The Teacher's final word is this: "Fear God and keep his commandments, for this is the duty of all mankind. For God will bring every deed into judgment, including every hidden thing, whether it is good or evil" (12:13–14). At first blush this could scarcely seem worse. My life is meaningless, and then I'm judged for it too? Woe is me!

Think again. What if divine judgment is the only thing that could give life meaning? Your life may seem small and insignificant, but if God cares enough to hold you accountable, then you count! The Last Judgment is terrifying and necessary. Thank God for judging you and for Jesus, who bore the punishment we all deserve.

I'm telling you, you need to read this book! Go to your favorite thinking spot, open Ecclesiastes, and ponder away.

When the Song of Solomon mentions pomegranates in bloom, what exactly does it mean?

64 What's up with the Song of Solomon?

"Your stature is like that of the palm, and your breasts like clusters of fruit. I said, 'I will climb the palm tree; I will take hold of its fruit.' May your breasts be like clusters of grapes on the vine, the fragrance of your breath like apples, and your mouth like the best wine" (7:7–9).

Are these lines from a Harlequin romance? A risqué movie?

Would you believe the Holy Bible? If teenage boys knew the Song of Solomon was in the Bible, they would never be bored in church!

The Song of Solomon is God's racy love poem. It's difficult to interpret because we can't always tell what is real and what is make-believe. Are the lovers rising early to visit vineyards "to see if the vines have budded, if their blossoms have opened, and if the pomegranates are in bloom," or are these euphemisms for what they are doing in bed (7:12)? Has the lover really searched throughout the city for her beloved, or is she merely describing how she yearns for him when he is away (3:1–3)? Lovers tend to let the world go by and focus entirely on each other, so we shouldn't be surprised when they blend reality and fantasy. The fantasy is their reality!

Medieval Christians were embarrassed by the Song's sexuality, and they read the book as an allegory for their relationship with Jesus. This isn't necessarily wrong, as the apostle Paul says marriage between a husband and wife is a picture of "Christ and the church" (Ephesians 5:32). But we should first take the Song on its own terms, as God's celebration of marital love and sexual pleasure. Sex was His idea, and He is all for it. Our Father takes pleasure from our pleasure in His good gifts.

The God who invented sex knows how best to enjoy it, and He commands that we have sex only within the covenant of male-female marriage (Genesis 2:24). The lovers in this Song are exclusive. They only have eyes for each other, which heightens their pleasure. "I am my beloved's and my beloved is mine; he browses among the lilies" (6:3).

Read this Song to fuel your passion for your spouse. Pledge that your "love is as strong as death. . . . It burns like blazing fire, like a mighty flame. Many waters cannot quench love; rivers cannot sweep it away" (8:6–7). Give your whole self to your beloved. You will enjoy the highest intimacy without regret.

If you're single, read the Song of Solomon as a prayer, asking God to give you someone to love. Until then, direct your passion to Christ—and after reading the Song, take a cold shower.

65 How should I read the Gospels?

The four Gospels—Matthew, Mark, Luke, and John—are complementary perspectives on the one Gospel—the good news that Jesus has brought salvation and the kingdom of God through His life, death, resurrection, and ascension to heaven. Here are some thoughts on how best to approach them:

1. ***Read the Gospels as real history.*** You can visit Israel and see where Jesus taught and performed miracles and the likely spots where He was born, crucified, and rose from the dead. The Christian faith is historical. It depends entirely on what Jesus did in our time and space. The Gospels describe what He did and how He saves us.

2. ***Read the Gospels with an eye on the end.*** The most important thing Jesus did was die on the cross for our sins and then rise again, so the Gospels understandably slow down when they reach the climax of Jesus' earthly life. A quarter of Luke, a third of Matthew and Mark, and half of John cover just one week—the most important week since the days of creation in Genesis 1. The Gospels are essentially passion narratives (stories of Jesus' redemptive suffering) with long introductions. Read Jesus' words and actions with His goal in mind.

3. ***Read the Gospels as different yet harmonizing stories.*** Each Gospel highlights a slightly different angle on the story of Jesus. Matthew emphasizes that Jesus is the Jewish Messiah who brought God's kingdom to earth. Mark focuses on Jesus' suffering and Luke on Jesus' love for both Jews and Gentiles, especially the poor and oppressed. These three are called the "synoptic Gospels," because they have much in common. *Synoptic* means "seeing together," from the roots *syn* ("together with") and *optic* ("seeing"). John, though, is unique. He skips the Christmas story and jumps straight into his purpose: proving that Jesus is the divine Son of God (20:30–31).

   There are various theories on which Gospel was written first and who borrowed from whom. No one knows for sure. But the cross-fertilization means there is some overlap. A study Bible will say if the story you're reading in one Gospel is repeated in the others. Compare what each Gospel adds or omits. You'll often find that Mark, though the shortest Gospel, includes more details.

4. ***Read the Gospels as transitional between the Old and New Testaments.*** The stories in the Gospels occur in the era of the old covenant. Israel is still sacrificing animals in the temple, striving to keep the law, and waiting for her Messiah. Jesus is that Messiah who will deliver His people by fulfilling the law and making the ultimate, unrepeatable sacrifice. But those climactic moments on the cross and in the tomb haven't yet happened during Jesus' earthly ministry. He came to deliver the new covenant, but He lived under Israel's old covenant. This truth helps us interpret Jesus' practice of observing the Sabbath, His command to offer sacrifices (Mark 1:44), and His challenging words to a Gentile woman

(Mark 7:24–30). Not everything Jesus did applies directly to us today, because of what He would later do in His death and resurrection. When reading the Gospels, remember the time and where these events fall in the Bible's big story.

Matthew, Mark, Luke, and John are the only inspired, authoritative accounts of the life of Christ. Do you want to know Jesus? Read the Gospels!

The four Gospels—Matthew, Mark, Luke, and John—together comprise the biography of Jesus' life on earth.

66 How should I read Jesus' parables?

Jesus didn't invent the parable, but He perfected it. This tends to happen when you are the Son of God!

As long as there have been parents trying to guide children, teachers trying to shape students, and debaters trying to get opponents to see their side, there have been invented stories—parables—to make a point. Teaching financial stewardship? Tell a story about the squirrel storing acorns for winter. Hard work? Tell a story about the ant. Perseverance? The tortoise and the hare.

Parables are not only memorable. They can also slip past people's front line of defense and detonate deep inside their heart. When the prophet Nathan confronted David's sin of murder and adultery, he told a parable about a rich man who slaughtered a poor man's baby lamb. David "burned with anger" and said the man must die. Nathan turned on David and said, "You are the man!" (2 Samuel 12:1–14). What could David do but repent? He knew he was caught.

Jesus also told pointed parables that caught His listeners by surprise. He didn't merely tell the Pharisees they were proud and spiteful; He told the story of the Prodigal Son, which ended with the elder son furious that everyone was celebrating his younger brother's return. Jesus didn't explicitly accuse a teacher of the law of racism; He told the story of the Good Samaritan in which the hero was not the priest or Levite but a hated Samaritan.

The story of the "Good Samaritan" is one of the best-known parables of Jesus.

Parables are a lot like jokes. You either get them or you don't. If you have to explain the parable, it loses its punch. We're two thousand years and a couple continents away from the culture of Jesus' day, so we may not get the point as quickly as His original listeners. It will help us to pay attention to the parable's immediate context.

Ask yourself, *What prompted this parable?*, and you will better grasp the story's point. For instance, Jesus told the story of the Prodigal Son when the Pharisees and teachers of the law muttered that he was dining with "sinners" (Luke 15:1–2). He told the story of the Good Samaritan to answer a lawyer's question, "Who is my neighbor?" Jesus turned the question around and asked, "Who *was* a neighbor?" Turns out it was the last person anyone in His audience expected (Luke 10:25–37).

Parables generally have one main point, though they may also make other, lesser points. The main point of the Prodigal Son is the jealous reaction of the elder brother—but the story may also be told through the eyes of the father and the prodigal. The Good Samaritan is about racism, but it also challenges us to serve all others, even if they happen to look like us. Margaret Thatcher, prime minister of Great Britain from 1979 to 1990, slyly noted the story may also warn about the poverty of socialism: "No one would remember the Good Samaritan if he'd only had good intentions; he had money too."

If parables are like jokes, it may sharpen their point by retelling them with contemporary figures. Make the Good Samaritan into someone your audience would despise. Update the sins of the Prodigal Son until your audience begins to loathe him. Many of us haven't worked as shepherds, slaves, or hired hands, so consider retelling the parables of the Good Shepherd (Luke 15:3–7), the Lazy Servant (Matthew 25:14–30), and the Workers in the Vineyard (Matthew 20:1–16). Read the parable as Jesus told it, then see if you can capture His point with people and places from our world. If Jesus was telling this story today, what might He say? Do this right, and there will be no need to say more. The parable will do its work on your heart.

67 How should I read Acts?

The Acts of the Apostles is Luke's thrilling sequel to his Gospel. If you like adventure, you'll love Acts' stories of shipwreck, stoning, imprisonment, and dramatic rescues.

Acts records the exploits of Peter and Paul, but it's really about Jesus. The book recounts "all that Jesus began to do and to teach until the day he was taken up to heaven" (Acts 1:1–2). Acts is Jesus' second act, what the ascended Christ continued to do through His church that remained on earth.

The theme of Acts appears in Jesus' final words to His disciples: "But you will receive power when the Holy Spirit comes on you; and you will be my witnesses in

Jerusalem, and in all Judea and Samaria, and to the ends of the earth" (Acts 1:8). The first part of Acts describes how Peter led the church in Jerusalem, Judea, and Samaria (chapters 1–11), and the second half tells how Paul's missionary travels took the Gospel to the ends of the earth (chapters 12–28).

Acts is a book of transitions. The church began among Jews in Jerusalem and spread to the Gentiles throughout the world. The Holy Spirit marked each new people group by falling upon the converts, allowing them to speak in languages they had not studied. This supernatural "speaking in tongues" certified the church at its start (Acts 2:1–41), then as it expanded to the Gentiles (10:1–48), and finally some Ephesian disciples of John who came late to the party (19:1–7).

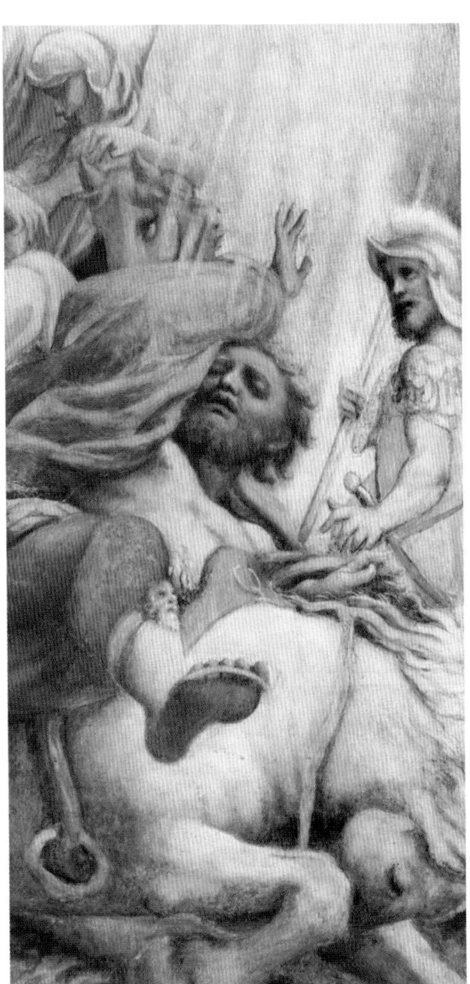

The book of Acts introduces the apostle Paul, shown here in the midst of his conversion.

Christians understand this speaking in tongues in different ways. Pentecostal and charismatic Christians note these first Christians spoke in unknown languages and say if we are filled with the Spirit then we will too. Other Christians counter that the Spirit used tongues to authenticate the church with each new advance. Now that the church has reached the Gentiles and the ends of the earth, there is no need for further authentication.

As you read Acts, ask which parts of the story are transitional, meant only to apply to first-century Christians, and which parts God would still want us to follow. Besides the issue of tongues, consider how the earliest Christians "were together and had everything in common. They sold property and possessions to give to anyone who had need" (Acts 2:44–45). Some say this means the first Christians were socialists. Others reply their giving was voluntary, and since these Christians were still selling land later (Acts 5), they hadn't immediately pooled all their resources. Still, the unity of this initial church is something we all want.

Acts is an exciting history of the church's beginning. Read Luke's inspired account to learn where we came from and what we may need to recover.

68 How should I read the New Testament Letters?

These are the easiest books of the Bible to read because we've all received letters. At least we used to, before the internet. If you haven't received a letter lately, think of the New Testament epistles as a string of social media posts. Only far more important than a picture of your lasagna and less angry than your uncle's political rant.

The New Testament letters were meant to be read out loud, in one sitting, often to an entire church. If you want to experience each letter's full effect, read it aloud all at once. Of course, you may also read the letters silently—after several times, themes and patterns emerge and you begin to see how the pieces fit. Pay special attention to transitional terms, such as "Therefore" or "Now about." These indicate the author is moving to a new point.

If you have time, try stating the letter's theme—its one big idea—and outlining how its various sections either advance the theme or supply parenthetical asides. There is usually more than one possible way to outline a letter, so don't worry about "getting it right." If you're a visual learner, turn your outline into a chart or diagram. Either way, you will learn more if you try your own summary before checking how your study Bible maps the letter.

Do consult your study Bible, though, when you begin to examine each section. Its notes will provide important historical-cultural background for understanding what prompted Paul, Peter, James, or John to say what they said. Reading their letters is like listening to one side of a phone conversation. We know what they

The apostle Peter may be receiving divine inspiration in this painting from Parma, Italy. The leader of Jesus' disciples wrote two letters that became books of the New Testament and was likely the source for Mark's Gospel.

are saying, but we can't always hear what they are responding to. We have their answers, but we don't always know the precise problem they were trying to solve. A study Bible will help.

As with letters today, these biblical letters (also called "epistles") were written in a specific time and place for a specific people and purpose. The more you know about the ancient church in Rome and Corinth, for example, the better you'll understand Paul's letters to them. And the more clearly you'll hear God's Word through Paul to you.

69 What's up with Revelation?

John's Revelation is the last book of the Bible, and it is the last book anyone should say they entirely understand. Martin Luther chuckled that Revelation was a funny name for a book that reveals so few of its secrets, and John Calvin, who wrote commentaries on most books of the Bible, took one look and put his pen away.

Revelation is a challenge to interpret because it is chock full of apocalyptic images. "Apocalypse" is a distinct brand of writing that was common between 200 BCE and 200 CE. The Jews had been beaten down by the Egyptians, Syrians, and finally Rome. It seemed God was not keeping the promises He'd made in the Old Testament. The Jews, apparently, were cursed to perpetually lose.

Some defied this despair by writing apocalyptic works. They didn't use their real names—perhaps from fear or to give an aura of higher authority—and they drew upon the mysterious symbols of Old Testament prophecies to inspire their fellow patriots to hang tough and resist the foreign powers. God was about to fulfill His prophecies in a climactic, cosmic battle between good and evil, these writers insisted. Those Jews who persevered to the end would be saved.

The first Christians arose from within Judaism, and they faced a similarly hopeless situation. The Roman imperial cult demanded every citizen pinch a bit of incense and say, "Caesar is Lord." Devout Christians refused to say anything but "Jesus is Lord," and they were punished and sometimes killed for not being loyal citizens. What could they do? They couldn't run from the long arm of Rome. How would the Christians survive?

While the apostle John was mulling these questions, he was given a series of apocalyptic visions from Jesus Himself. Like other apocalyptic literature, John's visions are full of fantasy creatures—a dragon, a beast with seven heads and ten horns, locusts with scorpion tails and human heads—but the message is real. Despite how things seem, Jesus is still "the ruler of the kings of the earth" (Revelation 1:5). Roman soldiers, governors, and Caesar himself may not realize it, but they all report to King Jesus. He remains in charge, and soon He will appear in the sky, riding a white stallion and leading the armies of heaven. Jesus will annihilate

The last book of the Bible is full of frightening imagery. . .but ends with Jesus as king over a restored, perfect world.

His enemies and restore justice and peace to His renewed creation. All will be right with the world; you'll see (Revelation 19–22).

Christians disagree on how to interpret details of John's visions—and whether these visions were fulfilled in John's day, fulfilled between his time and our own, or are still to come. This makes for interesting and important conversations, but if we're not careful, we may miss the main point.

Do you feel unsafe in this world? Do you worry for your children and grandchildren? Then read Revelation! This is Jesus' promise to you. Don't trust your eyes, but let His Word tell you what is really going on. Jesus is reigning at the right hand of His Father. He is in complete control over whatever happens on earth and in your life. In the end, He wins. And if you're with Him, so will you.

70 Are we supposed to take the Bible literally?

As you can tell by the recent questions on genre, not everything in the Bible is meant to be read literally. No one thinks the dragon in Revelation 12 is literal or that the lover in the Song of Solomon has goats for hair, sheep for teeth, or deer for breasts (4:1–5). Rather than read the Bible literally, we must read it *literarily*, taking each genre on its own terms. Apocalyptic literature, poetry, proverbs, parables, and even some prophecies may contain metaphors, symbols, and images that should not be taken literally.

But we must be careful. While we can make a mess by mistakenly reading nonliteral images as literal, we will do more damage by taking Scripture's literal events as nonliteral metaphors. The Christian faith is a historical faith. Our salvation depends entirely on what God has done in time and space. Jesus is literally God and man. He literally died for our sin and literally arose from the dead. If any of this is merely "spiritual," "metaphorical," or in some sense less than actual, there is no reason to be a Christian.

Given this fundamental importance of history, Christians should read the Bible with a bias toward the factual. Our default position should be literal. We rightly read much of the Bible as nonliteral, but only when we have contextual or genre reasons for doing so. If the passage could go either way, we are usually wise to lean toward a literal interpretation, all the while acknowledging that we could be wrong and giving other Christians room to disagree.

The cliff in Nazareth that Jesus' townspeople attempted to throw Him from (Luke 4:14–30).

71 How can we know for sure what the Bible means?

Protestants have always said the Bible is generally clear. We don't need educated professionals or the teaching office of the church to explain the central story of Scripture. Simply translate the Bible into the language of the people and let them read it for themselves.

But the Bible isn't entirely clear about everything. It says so itself. The apostle Peter commended "our dear brother Paul," whose "letters contain some things that are hard to understand" (2 Peter 3:15–16).

The Bible is clear enough for any literate person to read and get the gist. The Bible is also deep enough that accomplished scholars can spend a lifetime exploring a passage and not reach bottom.

Our strength of conviction should match the Bible's varying degrees of clarity. We should ask two questions of each passage: How *important* is our interpretation and how *certain* are we that we're right? When the text is clear and the interpretation matters a lot (for example, it touches on God and salvation), we should say "The Word of God declares. . . ." When the topic is less important and good Christians disagree, we should appropriately hedge: "I think the Bible indicates. . ." or "The Bible seems to say. . . ." Examples of these issues include questions like, "Will Jesus rapture the church, and if so, will He take us away before, during, or after the tribulation?"

Bottom line: we won't be sure about all of our interpretations, and that's probably a good thing. People who think they know precisely what God thinks about everything tend to act like the devil.

Double bottom line: we will gain more confidence in our interpretation when we read the Bible with the church. Biblical interpretation is not a solo activity, so consult the Apostles' and Nicene Creeds, trusted theologians, mature Christians, and the leaders of your local church. We may not resolve every question, but we'll discover the Bible is clear enough.

Triple bottom line: watch out for arguments that muddy the water, making the

Bible seem more complicated than it is. Nineteenth-century philosopher Søren Kierkegaard wisely cautioned, "The New Testament is very easy to understand. But we human beings are really a bunch of scheming swindlers; we pretend to be unable to understand it because we understand very well that the minute we understand we are obliged to act accordingly at once."[13]

It's okay to be confused about a passage, as long as we're not using our questions as a smokescreen to hide from the text.

72 What is the Holy Spirit's role in helping me read the Bible?

I often pray while reading the Bible, inviting God to help me concentrate and understand what I'm reading. But praying for the Holy Spirit's help is not a shortcut to diligent reading and study. God hasn't promised to fill in the gaps and tell us what we could have seen if we had been more careful or less tired. He hasn't even promised that good readers will always get it right. It's entirely possible that two Spirit-filled and attentive readers will study the same passage and draw contrary conclusions. Both asked God for help, but at least one of them is wrong. What's going on?

The Holy Spirit (depicted as a dove) falls like fire upon Jesus' followers on the Day of Pentecost (Acts 2:1–4).

Our experience, background, biases, stress, influence of family and friends, ignorance of a text's historical-cultural background, and simple human error are a few of the reasons we might misinterpret a Bible passage. These mistakes are on us. They are never God's fault.

The Spirit's main job is not to help us understand what a biblical passage means. *We* must study the text carefully for that. Once we understand a passage, though, we do need the Holy Spirit to open our eyes to its beauty and bow our knees to what it says. If the Spirit does not do this work of illumination, we may correctly explain what the text means and yet remain unmoved.

Have you noticed? People who lack the Spirit can still understand the Bible. They just don't think it's glorious. They're unimpressed. The apostle Paul says, "The god of this age has blinded the minds of unbelievers, so that they cannot see the light of the gospel that displays the glory of Christ, who is the image of God" (2 Corinthians 4:4).

Satan and sin dull our hearts to the glorious beauty of the Gospel. Jesus solves this problem by giving us His Spirit, not primarily to explain the Bible but to change our hearts so we love God's Word and want to do what it says. This is what we cannot do on our own. Knowledgeable and careful readers can rightly interpret the Bible, but only those who depend on the Spirit of God will be forever changed by it.

73 How should I study a Bible passage?

I hope these questions on reading Scripture and its various genres have inspired you to study the Bible. If so, great! Take what you've learned and follow this three-step process: observe, interpret, and apply.

1. ***Observe.*** Begin by looking at the text. Then look some more. Dr. Howard Hendricks, a renowned Bible teacher, gave our class the assignment of making fifty observations from a single verse. This was overkill, as to reach fifty we had to note the person, number, tense, and voice of each verb, then comment on pronouns and prepositions. It was tedious, but we discovered important details hiding in plain sight.

   If you're reading a biblical story, list its context, characters, setting, and plot. If you're reading poetry, look for its images, parallelism, and figures of speech. If you're reading Paul's densely packed epistles, diagram his sentences to see clearly what he's saying.

This is a good time to note that God's revelation comes in the form of a book, so the better we are at reading books, the more we will hear from God! Digital technology reduces our attention spans and ability to focus, so many of us read less and less well than we used to. We're good at clicking and skimming, but we struggle to examine the deep architecture of a sentence or story. We must sharpen our reading skills, for the better we can diagram sentences, interpret poetry, and map the plot of stories, the better we will know God's Word. And the more we know, the more we can trust and obey. Reading well raises the ceiling for our relationship with God!

The observation stage is the time for collecting all pertinent data, so don't merely look inside the passage. Scan the notes in your study Bible for any helpful historical or cultural background. Check the cross-references for significant words. Where else do these themes appear in Scripture? As you look deeper in and around your passage, questions will pop into your mind. They will lead you to step two.

A London statue of the famed Sherlock Holmes. Students of the Bible should approach the text with the same attention to detail that Sir Arthur Conan Doyle's fictional detective demonstrated.

2. ***Interpret.*** This stage strives to understand a passage by bombarding it with questions. Think like an investigative journalist, and ask *who? what? where? when? why?* and *how?* Who does the author have in mind? Where do they come from? What does the writer think they should do? How does his argument solve their problem? Where does he ground his argument? Why does he think they should obey?

   If you're reading a story, ask "What do the characters want? What is blocking them? What is the problem they are trying to solve? How does it get resolved? Why was it resolved in this way? What were other possible options? How might the story have turned out differently? Why is this story in the Bible? What is God trying to tell us?"

   Ask and answer every relevant question, and you'll understand what the passage means. Now you're ready for the final step, the payoff.

3. ***Apply.*** The point of reading the Bible is to be changed by it. We don't merely want to know what the Bible means; we need to know what the Bible means *to us*. How should we live its truth today? This is such an important question, it deserves its own entries, next.

74 How can I tell how the Bible applies to me?

Once we interpret a biblical story, poem, or letter, we're left with either something to believe or something to do. Every application of Scripture comes down to a promise to claim or a command to obey. But how can we tell if the promise or command is for us? Obviously not every command in the Bible still applies, as none of us refuse bacon on religious grounds or consider it our duty to marry our brother's widow.

How does the Bible apply to me? This is the million-dollar question. We'll have the answer when we solve this more precise question: *How can we distinguish what is universally applicable in Scripture from what is culturally relative?*

God gave the promises and commands of Scripture to people living in a specific time and place. How can we tell which parts applied only then and there and which parts carry on to us? Christians may disagree on the details—this is why churches have differing views on worship, the role of women, speaking in tongues, and so on—but we should agree on the general method. Here are five questions to ask when determining which aspects of a biblical passage apply directly to us and which are confined to its day. I'll give the first half here and the second half in the next question.

1. ***Consider the whole Bible.*** How consistently does Scripture give this promise or command? Is this a unique instance or does it appear in both testaments?

   For example, the Bible repeatedly promises that our sovereign, loving God watches over us. Moses promised the Israelites that God would go with them when they entered enemy land, for "he will never leave you nor forsake you" (Deuteronomy 31:6). Although we are not members of the Israelite army, Hebrews 13:5 quotes this promise of divine protection and says it still applies to us.

   Conversely, God promised King Solomon, "If my people, who are called by my name, will humble themselves and pray and seek my face and turn from their wicked ways, then I will hear from heaven, and I will forgive their sin and will heal their land" (2 Chronicles 7:14). This is a specific promise made to the nation of Israel living in the land of Palestine. God does not make this promise in the New Testament because the church is not an ethnic nation and His plans for us are not focused on one land. So Christians should be careful when applying this today. God does want us to humbly pray and repent of sin, but He has not promised that if enough Christians band together, He will bless their country.

   As with promises, so with commands. Some commands, such as abstaining from sexual immorality, are repeated throughout the Bible. Leviticus 18 is a long chapter that tells Israelite men all the people they must not have sex with—not your mom, not your aunt, not your sister. (How dumb were these guys?) The New Testament reinforces these commands. Jesus spoke against *porneia,* or "sexual immoralities" (Matthew 15:19). This plural Greek term included every sexual sin of the Jewish Bible, including adultery, bestiality, and homosexual practice. So despite what you may have heard, Jesus did speak about homosexual acts. Paul also warned against sexual immorality, most vociferously in Romans 1:24–27 and 1 Corinthians 6:9–20. The Bible speaks with one voice: all sex outside of male-female marriage is sin.

Other commands, such as the Old Testament's Sabbath rest, are explicitly fulfilled in Jesus (Hebrews 4:1–11; Colossians 2:16–17). The Sabbath was not an end in itself but pointed to the ultimate rest we have in Jesus. Now that Jesus has come, we are no longer commanded to religiously observe the Sabbath—though we might still enjoy taking a holiday every seven days!

In sum, if a promise or command is repeated often, and especially if it appears in the New Testament, we should believe it directly applies to us, unless we have some compelling reason to think it doesn't.

2. ***Consider the specific passage.*** Does the promise or command apply to everyone, or is it merely a cultural application of some higher universal principle?

For instance, the Bible gives specific commands to women. They should cover their heads when praying (1 Corinthians 11:2–16), "dress modestly," not wearing "elaborate hairstyles or gold or pearls or expensive clothes," and they should not presume "to teach or to assume authority over a man" (1 Timothy 2:9–12). Some Christians follow all these commands to the letter. Others say these commands are merely a first-century application of a higher, universal principle, so they no longer apply. Still others say the higher principle is male headship and propriety, both of which go all the way back to God's original creation order. Since creation is a universal category that applies to everyone, we must not quickly dismiss these commands.

The discussion regarding women will not be resolved soon, but every side agrees on the fundamental question. If we think the biblical commands are specific to their ancient cultural context, we'll believe they no longer apply. If we think the commands are grounded in a universal principle, and if there is no other plausible way to honor the principle, then we'll believe we must follow them today.

75 How else can I tell how the Bible applies to me?

Here's part two for distinguishing Scripture's universal truths from their limited, cultural application.

3. Consider your situation. How similar is your cultural context to the text? The more similar your situation, the more directly you may apply the divine promise or command. Conversely, the more dissimilar your situation, the higher you must climb "the ladder of abstraction" to find the universal principle that you may then apply to your cultural context.

For example, the Corinthians disagreed about whether it was okay to participate in pagan banquets or eat meat that had been offered to idols. The apostle Paul's counsel on this question might easily transfer to Asia, where Christians must negotiate questions surrounding ancestor worship and Hindu and Buddhist sacrifices (1 Corinthians 8–11). Western Christians aren't normally invited to pagan banquets or served hamburgers prepared in the name of Aphrodite, so Paul's advice about idols isn't immediately applicable to us at ground level. So we must climb the ladder of abstraction to reach the general, universal truths Paul was applying to the situation in Corinth. Once we understand his points about Christian freedom and the demons that animated pagan practices, we may then climb

The Amish take literally the Bible's teaching on women's head coverings, while most other Christians think this command does not apply directly today (1 Corinthians 11:3–16).

back down and apply these principles to the specific issues of our day. We may never visit a pagan temple, but we are pressured to participate in various sinful activities. What would Paul say to us?

4. ***Use common sense.*** If the human author of the passage appeared today, would he be more surprised that we *are* or *are not* claiming his promise or following his command?

For instance, Paul commands husbands to sacrificially love their wives and wives to submit to their husbands, "as the church submits to Christ" (see Ephesians 5:21–33). As you might guess, Paul's word about submission is hard to accept in our modern world. Some Christians try to solve the problem by saying Paul's command was limited to the wives in Ephesus, whose unruly behavior was causing trouble both inside and outside the church. Others suggest Paul was merely being culturally sensitive in his patriarchal world. He took the world as he found it and told Christian spouses to love each other well, within their male-dominated system. If Paul had lived in a matriarchal culture, he may have flipped his advice and told husbands to submit to their wives.

I realize this is controversial and I may be tipping my hand, but when trying to decide which promises and commands still apply now as they did then, it's clarifying to ask what the human author would expect from us. Is Paul more likely to agree that his commands to husbands and wives were limited to that ancient culture, or would he wonder why we're evading what he said? Someday we will give account to Jesus for how we read and applied His Word. However you decide which commands to apply, aim for an argument you believe the Lord will accept. When in doubt, lean toward a more literal, direct application. I'd rather have Jesus wonder why I naively took His commands at face value than chasten me for creatively avoiding what He told me to do.

5. ***Stay appropriately humble and confident.*** Our understanding of Scripture is not identical to Scripture, so we must humbly listen to other perspectives and be prepared to change our minds. But we must not be so humble that we mumble. The Bible is clear enough for us to live with confidence.

As we consider how to apply God's Word, we need both personal conviction and interpersonal communication. We declare what we believe God is saying, then check our answers with trusted others. There are no guarantees we'll get everything right, but we'll be listening attentively to God's Word with our brothers and sisters. Isn't this what matters most?

Young children instinctively trust their parents. Shouldn't we have a similar confidence in the Word of God?

76 Why should we trust the Bible?

You had no say in being born, but now that you're here, you've got a say in whom you trust. And you will trust someone.

We begin life trusting other people, usually our parents. We trust them to keep us safe and warm, and we obey their bedtimes and house rules. This is the wisest way to start life, and really, what else could we do? Babies have no choice but to trust the person who's holding them. Soon enough though, we realize our parents are finite and fallen, and like other mistake-prone sinners, they inevitably let us down. We may continue to trust them anyway, or we may find other, more reliable people to take their place. But these replacements, though perhaps wiser, smarter, or more something, will ultimately disappoint us too.

We're now at a crossroads, and the decision we make here will determine the course of our lives—and our everlasting destiny. We may decide our mistake was trusting others in the first place and choose from now on only to trust ourselves. *We* will be the final authority on everything pertaining to us. This initially invigorates—we're taking back our lives!—but it cannot end well. We know that. We're as finite and fallen as the next guy, and our biased eyes will distort the world until we eventually and certainly die. Rats.

There is one other way, though. What if we concluded our initial problem wasn't that we trusted others, but that we didn't go far enough? Rather than trust a finite, nearby other, what if we trusted the infinite Other who made and loves us? This is obviously the only way to go, but how can we know Him? The Bible claims to be the Word of this compassionate Creator, so an essential question we must answer is whether that's credible. *Is the Bible God's Word?* That's next.

77 Can I prove the Bible is God's Word?

The Bible is a uniquely special book. No other writing has such rigorously verified manuscript tradition, archaeological support, fulfilled prophecy, wisdom, or influence upon the world. The Bible obviously deserves our full and unparalleled attention.

We can prove the Bible stands alone above all books, but we can't prove it's the Word of God. How would we do that? No list of criteria could prove this book or that is God's inspired revelation. We might say any book God writes must be true, wise, life-changing, and so on, but many books check these boxes (you're reading one now!) and still aren't God's Word.

We can't prove God from below, and neither can we prove His Word. It's a good thing too, because if we could prove the Bible is God's Word, then we, not the Bible, would be our final authority. Whatever we use to prove the Bible would have authority over the Bible. So if we think we've proved the Bible is God's authoritative Word, we've actually proved it's not.

Can the Bible be "proven" in the sense of a scientific experiment? Does it need to be?

We finite people cannot *prove* God or His Word, but we can still *know* both of them. Our modern, scientific age insists we can only know what we can prove. Hogwash. Everyone, including scientists, knows many things they cannot prove. We know this world is real and not merely software in some supercomputer, even though as the movie *The Matrix* showed, it's impossible to prove. If you're inside the computer program, how would you show you're not? We know other people have minds, even though we can't see this immaterial aspect of their brains. And we know what we ate for breakfast, even though that and all of our memories are impossible to prove.

Contrary to what many assume, we don't have to prove what we believe to claim we know it. Philosophers explain that knowledge amounts to a justified, true belief. If we claim we know something, (a) we must believe what we're claiming, (b) what we believe must be true, and (c) we must have good reasons for our claim. We can't just get lucky and call it knowledge. I can say I know it's raining because I look outside and see that it's raining. I can't say I know it's raining because I just washed my car, and it always rains after I wash my car. It may actually be raining, but I can't say I *know* so if that's my reason. My belief may be true, but it remains unjustified.

We don't have to prove the Bible, but we do need justification, some reason that turns our true belief into knowledge. If no amount of evidence will do the trick, what ultimately will tip the scales so we can claim we know the Bible is God's Word? What justifying reason can we give? That's next.

78 How can I know the Bible is God's Word?

A sixteenth-century French pastor named John Calvin answered this question best. He said those who demand proof for the Bible will "be perpetually beset by the instability of doubt."[14] They must continually hold their breath at every archaeological discovery or sensationalist book. *What if Dan Brown is right? Did Jesus have a wife? Are there secrets the first Christians didn't want you to know?* Such Christians will never fully rest in Jesus and His Word.

But what if we don't have to prove the Bible? What if we can simply let the Bible prove itself? Calvin said God's Word is *self-authenticated.* When we read the Bible, we hear the voice of God. We know God is speaking to us, and that's all the proof we need.

We rely on self-authentication with everyone we know well. When we hear our spouse or parent on the phone, we don't ask a series of verification questions. *If it's really you, who's your favorite teacher? Worst movie? Last four digits of your social security number?* We immediately know our loved ones, unless they have an identical twin that sounds like them! God is one of a kind, though, so we don't need to be suspicious. When we read the Bible, we know we're hearing Him.

But what about people who read the Bible and *don't* hear God's voice? Calvin said that would be all of us if God had left us to ourselves. Sin blinds our eyes and puts noise-canceling headphones on our ears so that we miss what is right in front of us (2 Corinthians 4:4). We need the Holy Spirit to override our sin, opening our eyes and ears so we can see the Bible for what it is. Calvin concluded, "The same Spirit, therefore, who has spoken through the mouths of the prophets must penetrate into our hearts to persuade us that they faithfully proclaimed what had been divinely commanded." Only the Spirit of God can supply "that certainty which piety requires," giving us the confidence to eagerly throw all our weight on the promises of God's Word.

So here's our justifying reason for knowing the Bible is God's Word: God's voice in the Bible is self-authenticating (it proves itself), and we realize this as the Holy Spirit overrides our sin and enables us to see what has been there all along.

We can't prove the Bible either to ourselves or others, and *we don't have to*. If you aren't sure the Bible is God's Word, ask Him to show you. Then read a passage out loud, perhaps a psalm or a passage in John, and see if you don't sense God speaking to your heart. If you still aren't sure, keep reading until you are. Tell God you won't give up until His Word gets through and grabs you.

If you have friends who don't yet believe, invite them to read the Bible. Better yet, read it out loud together. Ask God to speak to them so they too can know His Word and be saved. You might also share some of the evidence for the Bible being unique and trustworthy, as long as you explain that evidence alone is not the reason you believe. Calvin said evidences are "very useful aids" that confirm Scripture—if the Bible is God's Word, we should expect some remarkable support within and around it—but they don't prove Scripture. We wouldn't want our friend's faith to rest in evidence or arguments but wholly in the self-authenticating Word of God.

John Calvin (1509–64) said God's Spirit confirms His Word in the hearts and minds of believers.

The witness of the Spirit to the self-authenticating Scripture takes the pressure off us. It's not our job to argue our friends into the kingdom. (When has that ever worked?) Don't fret that you couldn't do more. You've brought your friend to meet Jesus. She is reading Scripture, so she is in God's hands now. There is no better place to be.

79 Why should we obey the Bible?

When my children were young, we lived on a busy, five-lane road where tractor-trailers rumbled past, shaking our house. I told my toddlers they must play in the backyard, and I built a fence to keep them in. I showed them a crack on the driveway and said if they ever crossed it for any reason, they would be disciplined. If a ball bounced past the line, they must let it go. We could buy another ball. We couldn't replace the kids.

My boys couldn't comprehend the reason for my rule. They didn't understand the possibility of death, and sure enough, the youngest—without a care in the world—once rode his tricycle down the sidewalk. He quickly learned I was serious about my rule.

I didn't expect my sons to grasp the gravity of what was at stake. But I did need them to trust me. Their mother and I loved them more than anyone else in the world. We wouldn't make rules for the fun of it.

Is our heavenly Father any different? He created us and sent His Son to die on the cross for us. No one loves us more than He does. So we know His rules are not arbitrary. He doesn't give us random commands to test our resolve or steal our fun. Every command in His Bible, properly interpreted and applied, is for our good. Our Father wants only the best for us. If we believe that, we'll have no trouble doing anything He says, even when we're not sure why.

God's love includes rules and warnings to keep us safe. . .a key reason we should obey the Bible.

We'll be proud of our Dad and of His Word. We will never apologize or make excuses for anything in the Bible. If it's in the Bible, and we're reading it correctly, we'll assume it's for our good. So we'll submit our entire selves to the Bible. Not just our hands, not just our minds, but our hearts too. We won't say,

"If I were God, I wouldn't have said that. But He did, so I guess we have to go with it." We'll assume our heavenly Father knows more and loves more than we will ever grasp. We'll cling to His promises and cherish His commands. We'll hide His Word in our heart, that we might not sin against Him (Psalm 119:11).

Why obey the Bible? Because your Father loves you more than you'll ever know.

80 Are there parts of the Bible I won't like?

I hope so. Since God's thoughts are higher than ours (see Isaiah 55:9), there should be many truths in the Bible that rub us the wrong way. That's good—it's a sign that humans didn't ultimately write it. If we instinctively knew and agreed with everything in the Bible, we wouldn't need the Bible. We would already know what's best for us and how we should live.

Though I'm a theologian and a seminary professor, I'm also a sinner who struggles to do everything the Bible says. I don't particularly like the passages that tell me to forgive those who hurt me, generously share with others, swallow the gossip I'm burning to spill, or admit I deserve the punishment Jesus bore for me. I don't like these texts at all, which probably means they are the passages I need most.

Other people protest the violence of Noah's flood, David slaying Goliath, or the Jewish conquest of Canaan. These stories offend their sense of right and wrong. Did God really drown everyone who didn't believe in Him? Did He really tell His children to kill their enemies?

We'll address these hard questions later in the book. For now, let's settle for a little perspective.

Anselm was the greatest theologian of the eleventh century. He lived in a hard-nosed medieval context of knights and feudal lords. So the biblical stories of war didn't bother him. That was the world he knew. If God slew His enemies, Anselm assumed they had it coming.

You know which parts of the Bible did trouble him? The passages that spoke of God's mercy. Anselm reasoned that mercy is a negative emotion, so a God who feels mercy would not be entirely happy. That kind of God would have allowed the suffering of our world to get to Him; He would not be as high above us as He should be. Anselm concluded the Bible says God is merciful because we feel the effects of His mercy, but God Himself does "not experience any feeling of compassion for misery."[15]

What? *We* feel God's mercy but *He* doesn't? Who today would worship a God who only seems to have compassion?

Here's the point: one generation's problem passages are the next generation's prized passages. Anselm didn't blink at Old Testament battles, yet he stumbled over the mercy of God. Today, we memorize the passages that speak of God's compassion and worry about the wars.

It's not wrong to wonder about the Bible's war stories—we will address them later—but I am saying that what bothers us about the Bible may say more about us than God's Word. If you read something in the Bible you don't like, just wait—generations change. The passage that offends you might be cherished by your great-grandchildren. And the verses you cross-stitch and hang on your wall might be the ones they try to explain away.

Are there parts of the Bible you won't like? Of course. Take it as a sign the book is from God. He knows what we need to hear most.

PART 2: ORIGINS

Where Everything Comes From

The famed "Earthrise" photo from the Apollo moon mission of the late 1960s.

81 Why is there anything?

Sometime soon, find a quiet spot and ponder the question of existence. Think of the many things you take for granted: air, water, trees, friendship, puppies, and sweet corn. All of these come with our world. But where did our world come from? Why is there something rather than nothing?

(Did a wave of nausea just wash over you, buckling your knees? Good. Then you're doing this right.)

Why is there anything? There are only five options.

1. ***The world is eternal.*** Someone could say the world just is, and has always been, without offering an explanation. But this seems like a cop-out. Our intricately beautiful world appears to have been designed on purpose, which implies some Mind mapped it out and executed the plan. Is it plausible that our intelligent, structured world of symbiotic systems and creatures has always existed for no reason at all?

2. ***The world is eternally emerging from God.*** Another option was proposed by some ancient philosophers called the Neoplatonists (250–650 CE). (You don't need to remember their name—I only mention it because that's what they're called and you can look them up if you're interested.) They taught the world was continually emanating from the being of the One, their name for God. But if our world is part of God, then the One is divided. The world is a threat to God's sovereignty, something the One must clean up to recover its unity. And a god who isn't fully in control is no God at all.

3. ***The world is eternal yet separate from and dependent on God.*** The ancient philosopher Aristotle believed the world was eternal yet continually attracted to the Unmoved Mover, his name for God. While it's impossible to prove the world isn't eternal, this view does raise questions about the God who supposedly rules over it. Can God remain fully sovereign if something besides Himself has always existed? It's no accident that Aristotle didn't think his Unmoved Mover was real. He was merely a hypothetical idea that Aristotle needed to explain the world.

Bottom line: it's impossible to believe the world is eternal, as these three options do, and still believe in a sovereign, all-powerful God. That leaves two remaining options, which go in opposite directions.

4. ***The first elements of our world spontaneously appeared.*** Acclaimed physicist Stephen Hawking agreed that our world must have had a beginning. Hawking did not believe in God, so he argued the beginning of our world spontaneously emerged, similar to the way bubbles suddenly appear on the surface of boiling water. Most bubbles popped and disappeared, but some grew larger and became ever-expanding universes. Our lucky bubble is one that survived, so here we are. Of course, Hawking's theory doesn't explain where the conditions for life came from. Who made the water and brought it to boil? That seems to require the next and final option.

5. ***God created the world.*** The difficulties with the preceding views indicate there must be something, or better yet, *Someone*, behind and beyond our world. The Bible claims everyone knows this Being is God. Romans 1:20 declares, "For since the creation of the world God's invisible qualities—his eternal power and divine nature—have been clearly seen, being understood from what has been made, so that people are without excuse."

   Someone may object: *But who made God?* If the world needs a Creator, why doesn't God? Why is He allowed to be uncaused? We cannot comprehend this because our finite minds are limited. We can't wrap our minds around existence, so we shouldn't be surprised that we can't comprehend the God who made it. It's enough to say that unlike our world, which obviously was made and designed by Someone, God is necessarily uncaused. Being eternal and uncreated are essential aspects of what it means to be God. The Bible says everyone knows this—"his eternal power and divine nature"—and anyone who claims otherwise is "without excuse."

So find your quiet place and ponder existence. *Why is there anything?* You already know the answer, and God knows that you do.

If God seems distant and hard to understand, Jesus provides the human touch: "In Christ all the fullness of the Deity lives in bodily form" (Colossians 2:9).

82 Can anyone really know God?

You may agree you know there's a God, but how can you know which religion has the right one? If God is as high and holy as the Bible says, how can anyone really know Him? His infinite majesty lies beyond our comprehension, and His glory must consume any creature that gets too close.

God solves both problems by clothing Himself in creaturely forms. He stoops to our level and reveals Himself in the words of Scripture and the Word who is Jesus. John begins his Gospel by saying, "In the beginning was the Word, and the Word was with God, and the Word was God" (John 1:1). This "Word" is the Son of God, whose "life was the light of all mankind. The light shines in the darkness, and the darkness has not overcome it" (John 1:4–5).

As God accommodates Himself to us, there's an inevitable slippage—we simply can't grasp the entirety of anything about Him. But the truth of God still gets through. It's like how you talk to an infant. You make a funny face, talk sweetly, and make lots of noises: *Goo Goo Gai Pan.* That actually sounds like a Chinese stir-fry, but you get the point. There are many things about yourself that you cannot communicate to a baby—but what the infant does pick up about you is true. It may only be the tip of the iceberg, but the baby is assured that you love and care for her.

So it is with God. He cannot unveil His essence without killing us, since no one can see God and live (Exodus 33:20). We can't look directly into the sun, so how could we perceive the One who made the sun? If God were to give us a direct glimpse into His blazing glory, we would be vaporized on the spot. We wouldn't leave a trace. Not even a puddle. That's why God cloaks Himself in the human nature of Jesus, who both reveals and conceals God.

Jesus fully reveals God. He told Philip, "Anyone who has seen me has seen the Father" (John 14:9). But Jesus also conceals God's glory for our own protection. When Jesus pulled open His human nature even a little, allowing just the edges of His divine glory to shine through, His closest friend, John, fell at His feet as if he were dead (Revelation 1:17).

We will never fully comprehend God because He is God. But because He is God, He is able to truly reveal Himself. Jesus is God's full and final Word, so we never have to worry that God is anything other than what we see in Jesus. We who love Jesus will live forever with Him, sinking deeper into His bottomless love.

God is not other or different than what we see in Jesus, but Jesus is more than we will ever fathom. We meet God in Jesus, and we discover more each time we meet.

83 Don't all religions lead to God?

Whenever the topic of religion comes up, someone usually shrugs and says there is more than one path up the mountain, and any of the main religions can get you to the top. Religions may seem superficially different—with various practices and names for God—but essentially they're all the same. Strive to be a good person, and God will accept you and let you into heaven.

This popular religious pluralism is not as impartial as it sounds. It's actually textbook Hinduism. Hindus worship many and all gods, including yours, so a vote for every religion is essentially a vote for Hinduism. As *Newsweek* magazine once said on its cover story of American religion, "We're all Hindus now."

Jesus was not Hindu, and He explicitly rejected all competitors. He declared, "I am the way and the truth and the life. No one comes to the Father except through me" (John 14:6). There is only one path up the mountain, only one Person who will keep you safe when you get there. How will any of us survive being judged by God? We won't—unless He views us in the righteousness of His perfect Son. God will not reject Jesus, and He will love and accept everyone who by faith is united to Him.

We may feel tempted to embrace other religions, to allow that their path to salvation might work. But Jesus is exclusive. He does not share His worship with anyone else. We cannot bring other gods in without pushing Jesus out. And if Jesus is the only Savior, then pushing Him out makes it impossible for any person to be saved.

Think about it: if other religions could save, then Jesus didn't have to suffer His excruciating death on the cross. A religious pluralist might say the cross was nice—because it shows God's love—but he can't say it was necessary. He actually can't say either, because if the cross wasn't necessary then it wasn't even nice. What kind of monster would sacrifice His Son if our sin could be forgiven some other way? We know our heavenly Father believes the death of Jesus was necessary, because when Jesus asked if there was any other way, the answer He received was a resounding silence (Luke 22:41–44).

Christians don't believe other religions are wrong about everything. Being kind to others and practicing self-control are taught by most world religions. Hindus, Buddhists, Muslims, and religious Jews make great neighbors. We love them and thank God for their friendship. But every religion except Jesus is wrong about the most important things: who God is and how sinners like us can be accepted by Him.

You might think religions are superficially different and essentially the same, but you've got it backwards. Religions are superficially the same—they each teach varieties of the Golden Rule—but they are essentially different. Especially the unique religion of Jesus.

An idol of the Hindu god Ganesha.

84 How is Christianity different from other religions?

The Christian faith dramatically differs from every other religion on the most important question: How can we be saved? And it differs on this most important question because it differs on something even more foundational: Who is God?

How can we be saved? Christianity is the only religion that says we are accepted by God solely and entirely on the basis of His grace. Every other religion says we avoid damnation at least partially on the basis of our works.

Consider Islam, which claims Allah will weigh our good and bad works on his scale of justice. Because Allah is merciful, he may place his thumb on the scale so our good works outweigh the bad—but we can't say for sure. All we can do is try hard to please him and pray it's enough. Notice how Islam emphasizes a high view of God while also retaining room for human pride. We do something, however small, to contribute to our salvation.

I heard a Muslim leader say the final judgment gives reason for both hope and fear. Hope because we pray Allah will show mercy, and fear because our good works might not be enough. I waited until we were alone, then I asked whether he had more hope or fear. "Would you be more surprised if you failed God's judgment or more surprised if you passed?" He said that was a good question, one he hadn't considered. He guessed he'd be more surprised if he failed.

That's a key difference between Islam and Christianity. The Bible teaches that each of us is born guilty and corrupted by Adam's sin (more on this in subsequent questions) and that left to ourselves we would certainly fail God's holy judgment. But God has not left us to ourselves. He sent His only Son, Jesus, to live the perfect life for us and then die on the cross in our place. Jesus bore our guilt when He died, and He was released from that guilt when His Father raised Him from the dead (Romans 4:25; 1 Corinthians 15:17). Now, anyone who repents of their sin and puts their faith in Jesus is united to Him. His righteousness is counted to us, and God accepts us just as He accepts His pure and obedient Son.

Christianity does teach us to do good works. But we do good not to earn our acceptance but because we already are accepted. Good works are the fruit of our acceptance; they are never the basis, ground, or reason for that acceptance. We do good works from gratitude: we are so thankful for God's gift of salvation that we yearn to please Him. We do good works freely, confident that our heavenly Father will reward our imperfect efforts for Jesus' sake.

Our salvation, from start to finish, is entirely of grace. There's a reason why Christianity's most beloved hymn is "Amazing Grace." The first stanza reads, "Amazing Grace, how sweet the sound, that saved a wretch like me. I once was lost, but now am found, 'twas blind but now I see."

God's saving grace arises from His infinite love, and God's love is rooted in who He is. This is the second foundational difference between Christianity and other religions, and we'll discuss it next.

85 Who is God?

We are saved by grace, which God showers upon us because He is love. God does not merely *have* love; God *is* love (1 John 4:8). And God is love because He is triune: Father, Son, and Holy Spirit, three persons existing together in one divine essence.

If God were only a single person, He would not be love. Not really. God can only love when there is someone else to love. If there is no one else, He'd have to create someone just so He could love them. But then He'd be creating them because He's needy, a lonely deity who longs for someone to talk with. And needy people don't fully love. They demand too much from others to completely give themselves to them.

The Trinity is an incomprehensible mystery—how can God be three persons yet only one God?—but it is absolutely necessary for God to be love. *Why is God love?* Because He is three persons eternally existing in self-giving community. As the great theologian Augustine explained, the Father is the lover, the Son is the beloved, and the Spirit is the bond of love that unites them.

We finite creatures cannot explain the mystery of the Trinity, but the Trinity is the mystery that explains us. *Why do we thrive only in relationships?* Because God, who is ultimate reality, is inherently relational. Our triune God made us in His image and declared it isn't good for us to be alone (Genesis 1:26; 2:18). Some of us may be more introverted than others, but we all need others to love and be loved by.

Why do we thrive when we love sacrificially? Because the God who made us in His image is a community of self-giving lovers. The Father, Son, and Spirit all seek each other's good. The Father exalts the Son and Spirit. The Son obeys the Father and praises the Spirit. The Spirit brings glory to the Father and Son. Each divine person honors the others, setting aside what might be in His own best interest to serve the others. The Son agreed to come to earth and die. The Father agreed to let Him do it. (Every parent knows the crucifixion was at least as hard on the Father as it was for the Son.) And the Spirit left heaven to dwell within us, directing our attention to the Father and Son.

This triune God of self-giving love is life itself, so we never feel more alive than when we imitate God and serve others. Aren't your happiest days the ones you give away? You put down your work to listen to a friend who was struggling. You painted someone else's house, brought them dinner, or drove them to an appointment. You made their day and you went to bed with a wide smile. Why? Because on this day you lived like the self-giving God who made you in His image.

Don't worry that you can't fully understand the Trinity. We shouldn't be able to comprehend the infinite God. Believe in the Trinity because of Scripture and the teaching of the church, and because it's the only possible ground for love. *Do you believe in love?* Then you must believe in the Father, Son, and Holy Spirit.

86 What is the Trinity?

Our triune God is the Father, Son, and Holy Spirit, mutually indwelling one divine essence. This is a mouthful, but what did you expect? We're talking about the nature of God. Stay with me, and you'll learn important truths about Him.

The mystery of the Trinity raises the question of both numbers and persons.

1. ***Trinitarian Numbers.*** When Christians say God is both one and three, it's tempting to think we're bad at math. The Trinity would be nonsense if we said God is one and three in the same way. But we don't. We say God is one *essence* and three *persons*. These are not the same thing. We can't explain how God is fully both one and three, but this is not a contradiction. It's a mystery, which is exactly what we should expect when we talk about God.

   The sixth-century Athanasian Creed declares "we worship one God in Trinity, and Trinity in Unity." The creed repeats itself, in reverse, to underline that we must emphasize equally both God's oneness and His three-ness. God is one in three; three in one.

   Those who soften God's oneness fall into the heresy of "tritheism." They worship three separate deities that are no longer one. Tritheists emphasize the persons but lose their unifying divine essence. Those who lessen God's three-ness commit the heresy of "modalism." They believe God is just one person who appears in three successive modes, playing the role of Father, then Son, and finally the Spirit. Modalists emphasize the unity of the divine essence but lose the reality of the persons.

We must not soften God's oneness to make room for His three-ness or weaken His three-ness to make room for His oneness. We must say as strongly as we can that God is one and as strongly as we can that God is three. . .and live with the mystery. The Athanasian Creed says it best: "So the Father is God, the Son is God, and the Holy Spirit is God. And yet they are not three Gods, but one God." Our incomprehensible Lord!

Rubliov painted this "Holy Trinity Icon" in the early 1400s in Russia.

The mystery of the Trinity means no earthly example can illustrate it. You may have heard the Trinity is like water, ice, and steam. This analogy nails God's oneness but ruins His three-ness. It's a perfect illustration for the heresy of modalism: God is one substance (water) that assumes three different modes (liquid, ice, and steam). You may have heard the Trinity is like an egg, apple, or watermelon. These analogies emphasize God's three-ness (yolk, white, and egg; core, pulp, and peel; seeds, flesh, and rind) but lose His oneness. God's three persons cannot be separated like the three parts of an egg or elements of a fruit.

Here's the point: Christians worship one God but not one Person. Our God is three persons yet only one God. We fully embrace both the one and the three and bow before His mystery. Are you ready for a brain teaser? If God was coming for dinner, how many place settings would you put out?

2. ***Trinitarian Persons.*** When we speak about God, we must get the numbers right. Just as important, we must call the Persons by the right names. The three divine Persons are known by their eternal relations: the Father is the Father because He is unbegotten; the Son is the Son because He is begotten of the

Father; and the Spirit is the Spirit because He proceeds (or "spirates") from the Father and the Son.[16]

The Son is not less than the Father because He is begotten. He is eternal, uncreated, and all powerful, just like the Father. The Spirit is not less than the Father and the Son because He proceeds from them. He is eternal, uncreated, and all powerful, just like the Father and Son. The Nicene Creed of 325 CE declares the Son is "God from God, Light from Light, true God from true God, begotten, not made, of the same essence as the Father." The revised Creed of 381 adds the Spirit is to be worshipped and glorified with the Father and Son.

These three divine persons are fully equal in every way. Yet they function in a distinct order. All things come *from* the Father, *through* the Son, and *by* the Spirit. Creation comes from the Father, through the Word He spoke (John 1:1–4 says this Word is the Son), by the Spirit hovering over the waters (Genesis 1:2). Salvation comes from the Father, through the work of the Son, applied by the Spirit to our lives. And the Bible comes from the Father, through the Word, inspired by the Spirit.

Jesus taught us to pray by working our way up the chain. It's okay to pray to the Son and Spirit, as both are God. "Lord Jesus, save me!" is a fine prayer when you're in trouble. But the most appropriate, fully trinitarian prayers are offered *to* the Father, *through* the Son (in Jesus' name), *by* or *in* the power of the Spirit.

We cannot comprehend the inner workings of the Trinity, but

Heresy

Heresy is any belief that contradicts the core tenets of a system of thought. For example, free enterprise is a heresy to socialism, just as redistribution of wealth is a heresy to capitalism. The church has historically monitored the rise of heresies in three main areas: the Trinity, Jesus, and salvation. Errors here may be important enough to put someone's salvation at risk. Someone who believes a heresy has left the true faith.

once again we discover that each Person supplies what we desperately need. We need a Father to give us a home and a family; a Brother who dies for us and represents us in the Godhead; and a Spirit to empower us to live as we should. We can't solve the mystery of our triune God, but He is the mystery that solves our needs!

87 Where is the Trinity taught in the Bible?

The word *trinity* does not appear in the Bible, but its concept of one God in three persons is certainly taught. God did not explain His three-ness all at once but progressively revealed more of His fullness as the biblical story unfolded.

God used the Old Testament to clarify and reinforce His oneness. Deuteronomy 6:4 proclaims, "Hear, O Israel: The LORD our God, the LORD is one." God told Israel that He had no competitors. He alone was God, and He would destroy anyone who turned away from Him to serve idols. Israel did, so God sent the Babylonians to capture the people and lead them into exile. The Jews returned some seventy years later, having learned their lesson. To this day, religious Jews adamantly say the Lord alone is God—which ironically and tragically contributes to their misunderstanding of Jesus.

Two New Testament events lead Christians to believe in the Trinity: the Incarnation and Pentecost. At the Incarnation, when the Son of God became human, His followers discerned that God must at least be two persons. If Jesus is God, and the Father He is praying to is God, then the Lord must be both Father and Son. At Pentecost, when the Spirit of God came from heaven and empowered the disciples to proclaim the good news about Jesus (Acts 2), the church determined God must be three persons: Father, Son, and Holy Spirit.

Subsequent church councils at Nicea (325 CE), Constantinople (381), Ephesus (431), and Chalcedon (451) elaborated the Trinity from what they read in Scripture. They understood the Bible *assumes* the Father is God—Scripture does not argue for God's existence but simply starts with the assertion, "In the beginning God created the heavens and the earth" (Genesis 1:1). They understood the Bible *proves* the Son is God. John wrote his Gospel so "you may believe that Jesus is the Messiah, the Son of God, and that by believing you may have life in his name" (John 20:31). And they understood the Bible *strongly implies* the Spirit is God.

The Spirit:

- is called God (Acts 5:3–4, 9; 1 Corinthians 3:16–17);
- is listed with the Father and Son (Matthew 3:16–17; 1 Corinthians 12:4–6; 2 Corinthians 13:14; 1 Peter 1:2);
- possesses the perfections of God (omniscience—1 Corinthians 2:10–11; John 16:13; omnipotence—Luke 1:35; Romans 15:19; and eternality—Hebrews 9:14);
- does the works of God (regenerates sinners—John 3:5–8; 16:8–11, Titus 3:5; inspires Scripture—2 Timothy 3:16; 2 Peter 1:21).

The church realized that if Jesus told us to baptize converts "in the name of the Father and of the Son and of the Holy Spirit" (Matthew 28:19), then all three Persons must be fully and equally God. In the fourth century, Basil the Great concluded we are baptized in the threefold name, and "as we are baptized, so we believe."[17]

88 What is God made of?

This isn't the right question, because God is not "made." He's always been. A better question is *What does God consist of?* To answer this, I must distinguish between the divine Godhead and the divine essence.

As the last two questions explained, the *Godhead* consists of three persons: Father, Son, and Holy Spirit. Each person is the *divine essence*. But what is this?

Deity can be described in two distinct ways: by its immaterial nature and its perfections.

Sitting by a well, Jesus tells a Samaritan woman, "God is spirit" (John 4:24).

- ***Spirit.*** Jesus told a questioning woman that "God is spirit, and his worshipers must worship in the Spirit and in truth" (John 4:24). Jesus didn't mean that God is merely a larger version of our spirit. The relationship actually goes the other way. God is the original spirit; we are the copies. Our spirits reflect God's spirit like a puddle on the beach conveys the vastness of the ocean. We're like God in some ways, but the gap is infinitely more than we can comprehend. God's spirit, as with everything about God, exists in a whole other dimension.

- ***Perfections.*** God consists of His perfections. He doesn't merely *have* love, holiness, and power over all things; He *is* love, holiness, and power. The church, both East and West, has long held that God is simple. This means that He does not have parts. God is not the sum of His attributes, like a bundle of sticks. Rather He is like a multifaceted diamond, a singularly simple being that sparkles in fresh ways when seen in different light. From this angle, we are struck by God's love. From that angle, we notice His holiness. But since God is simple, His love is identical to His holiness. We may distinguish between them, but they turn out to be the exact same thing.

These truths about God yield at least three important reflections:

1. If God is simple, then we encounter the whole God the whole time. He does not sometimes act in love and other times in holiness. Everything the simple God does is entirely loving, holy, powerful, and everything else God is. We never deal with only one or two aspects of God. We always engage all that is in God.

2. If God is simple, then His divine persons are identical with His perfections. God personifies His perfections. Love has a name: Jesus!

3. The divine essence is simple and cannot change, but the Godhead has. At the first Christmas, when the Son of God was born of Mary, the Son retained His full deity and added a full humanity. From that moment on, the divine Son is not merely divine. He is also fully human, like you and me.

How much does God love you? The Son of God became human so He could die on the cross and save you. He didn't become temporarily human. He permanently changed, becoming human forever. Never doubt that God is committed to you. He became all that you are so you could be holy like Him.

89 Why did God create the world?

We can't give a necessary reason for why God made the world, but we can say that creation is a fitting act for our triune God. He is perfectly contented in His triune community of love, so He did not create us to fill some void in His life. God did not need to create the world, but given who God is—a community of self-giving lovers—it is not surprising that He would. It is just like our triune God to allow His love to overflow His borders and create others to love. Why do you and I exist? Because the God who is love can't stop being who He is. His love is fertile, and He instinctively creates new people to envelop in His fellowship of love.

But we creatures rejected God's love. We rebelled against His commands and refused to have Him rule over us. God would have been completely right to leave us to the hell we deserved. The hell we chose. But He didn't.

Why did God decide to save all who believe in His Son? He didn't have to redeem the world, but given who God is—a community of self-giving lovers—it is not surprising that He would. It is just like our triune God of love to do whatever it takes to win us back. He went to the furthest extreme, becoming a mere man, who was ultimately condemned as a despised criminal. Then Jesus died the most excruciating and painful death on the cross, cursed by His Father. Why can you and I be saved? Because the God who is love can't stop being who He is. His love is redemptive, and He instinctively sacrifices Himself to bring more lost sinners into His fellowship of life.

We can't say exactly why God chose to make and then save the world. But given who God is, neither should come as a shock. Creation? Redemption? They sound like things our triune God would do.

90 When did God create the world?

The Bible doesn't say. If you count the names in the genealogies of Genesis, you might conclude the world is only six to twelve thousand years old. However, the genealogies may have large gaps, and no Bible verse gives the date when time began.

This raises a question that makes my brain cramp: if God is eternal, He exists forever into the distant past. So what was God doing all that time before He made our world? Augustine said the joke going around in his day was that God was creating hell for people who ask such questions!

A better, more serious answer is that if God is eternal, He exists outside of time.

He is able to enter time, yet He also lives beyond time in a never-ending now. So what was God doing all that time before He created the world? Time didn't yet exist, so it's a bad question.

You and I are bound by time, so I gladly concede I am saying more than we can understand. Whenever I read someone's writing about time and eternity, I have no idea what they're talking about. Neither do they. Perhaps if marijuana is legalized in your state, you'll be able to spout confidently about eternity, though you'll know less than before!

Suffice it to say that God has had forever to make an infinite number of worlds, worlds that we may never know about because they exist in some other dimension. They're not our business. It's enough for us to study the Bible to learn about *our* world: how we got here, what went wrong, and God's plan to set us right.

91 How did God create the world?

The Bible opens with two complementary takes on the same event of creation. Genesis 1:1–2:3 supplies an introductory overview ("In the beginning God created the heavens and the earth") and then explains how God created our entire world over a span of six days. Genesis 2:4–25 describes God's same act of creation, with an emphasis on humans and our home in Eden.

Why do we know these two stories cover the same period? Because Jesus cited texts from each and said they address the beginning. When asked about marriage and divorce, Jesus said, "the Creator 'made them male and female' " and declared "a man will leave his father and mother and be united to his wife" (Matthew 19:4–5, quoting Genesis 1:27 and 2:24). Jesus brought the stories of creation together, but He didn't tell us precisely how to read them.

Many Christians interpret Genesis 1–2 literally. They believe these chapters give an exact, blow-by-blow account of how God made our world. He gradually spoke creation into existence over six, twenty-four-hour days, formed Adam from the dust of the ground, and made Eve from one of Adam's ribs. These Christians support their interpretation by saying this straightforward reading was the

Detail of the iconic Michelangelo painting of the creation of man.

dominant view until the eighteenth century; the Hebrew word for day (*yôm*) usually means a twenty-four-hour period; and such normal days are implied when God commanded Israel to follow His example by resting every seventh day (Exodus 20:8–11).

Other Christians believe Genesis 1 is "exalted prose narrative" that may not intend everything to be taken literally. The Hebrew text of Genesis 1:2 says the earth was *tōhû wābōhû*, or "unformed and unfilled." This alliterative heading seems to outline the six days of creation. On the first three days God made forms: (1) light, (2) heavens, (3) land and sea; and on the last three days He filled those forms with their corresponding objects: (4) sun, moon, and stars, (5) birds and sea creatures, and (6) land animals and humans. This literary structure is not perfect, as sea creatures (day 5) don't inhabit the heavens (day 2)—but it does explain why light is mentioned (day 1) before the sun (day 4). Perhaps Genesis 1 is not giving a strictly chronological account but saying that God created spaces and then put each element roughly in the space it belonged.

Another reason to take Genesis 1 nonliterally is that it is the opening chapter of the entire Bible. It would make sense for this chapter to lay out important themes, with the straightforward history beginning in Genesis 2:4, which says, "This is the account of the heavens and the earth. . . ." Whenever you read "this is the account of" in Genesis, you know the book is transitioning to a new historical section. For example, "this is the account of" Noah (6:9), Isaac (25:19), and Jacob (37:2). So Genesis 2:4–25 wants to be read as a historical account.

I prefer to read the Bible literally, unless there are good reasons not to. Genesis 1 has good reasons on both sides, so I'm keeping my options open as I read helpful books on the subject.[18] Ultimately, I don't think it matters if God took an entire week to create the world or if, as Augustine wrote, He made everything in a single moment. There are problems with believing creation slowly evolved over millions of years, though, because if mainstream science is correct, the world that God declared "good" would have contained lots of blood, agony, and death. I'll examine that next.

92 How do Christians explain creation?

Christians have more than one way to explain how God made the world. We may have our favorite theories, but it's important to remember they are exactly that. Only the Bible is inspired. Our interpretations are only theories, with various strengths and weaknesses. We hold firmly to Scripture and gladly revise our theories as we learn more.

Here are our most popular theories, with the strengths and weaknesses of each. I'll start with the most conservative and move left, concluding with a view that defies left-right categorization.

1. ***Young Earth Creationism.*** This view (YEC) reads Genesis 1 as a literal, rigorously historical account. God created the world in six, twenty-four-hour days and stopped working on the seventh. YEC takes the genealogies of Genesis at face value, and depending on how many gaps its adherents allow, posits the

world is between six and twelve thousand years old. YEC believes Adam's fall ravaged creation and Noah's flood covered the whole earth, which accounts for much of the fossil record. (I'll examine "the fall" in subsequent questions.) As one YEC supporter claims, a universal flood explains why we find "billions of dead things, buried in rock layers, laid down by water, all over the earth."[19]

The strength of YEC is theological: it defends the essentials of the Christian faith—a God who intervenes in His world, a good creation, and Adam's cataclysmic fall. Another strength is biblical: it seems to read Scripture in a normal, commonsense way, though some scholars warn its interpretations may be simplistic. YEC is opposed by the claims of mainstream science. This does not mean YEC is wrong, only that it is often dismissed because it denies evolution. YEC doesn't worry much about this, as it doubts macro-evolution's theories of common descent, random mutations, and natural selection. It doesn't believe that humans evolved from fish.

2. ***Old Earth (Progressive) Creationism.*** This view (OEC) agrees the world is generally as old as evolutionary science says but denies that humans and other species evolved from lower life forms. Instead, God intervened at various stages in the earth's development to create ever more advanced creatures, culminating in the creation of humans, between 12,000 and 135,000 years ago. OEC has more than one way to find time for an old earth in Genesis 1. Its favorite options include reading days as merely a literary framework (see "unformed and unfilled" from the previous question); claiming each day represents an extended age; or positing a long gap between God's initial creation (Genesis 1:1) and his subsequent acts of the six days (Genesis 1:3 and following).

OEC falls between YEC and evolutionary creationists, and it is criticized by each. YEC gives primarily theological arguments against OEC: it doesn't take Genesis 1 literally enough and its long ages require a lot of animal suffering and death before humans came on the scene. This implicates God, who declared His created world was very good. Evolutionary creationists give primarily scientific arguments: OEC is right on the age of the earth but wrong to deny macro-evolution and common descent. According to this view, OEC mistakenly believes the Bible speaks scientifically, and it cannot square its more literal interpretations with the reigning scientific consensus.

3. ***Evolutionary Creationism.*** This view (EC) used to be known as theistic evolution, but recently it swapped its noun and adjective so its emphasis would fall on theism/creationism rather than evolution. EC declares God made the world, and evolution is how He did it. EC believes in common descent—that all life evolved from a single, primordial ancestor—though many evolutionary creationists claim God intervened in the evolutionary process to either directly create humans or at least bestow His image on a highly developed hominim (this is the current term, replacing "hominid").

   EC has the opposite problem of YEC. EC fits snugly with mainstream science but faces significant biblical and theological issues. Critics charge EC with functional deism: it believes in God but doesn't believe He intervenes in creation in any noticeable way. If God's activity is undetectable, how is this view functionally different from evolution that doesn't believe in God? EC also struggles to explain how creation was originally good, death is bad, Adam's fall was real, and humans are uniquely special. How is any of this true if we evolved from lower life forms in one long, continuous slog of incremental development?

4. ***Intelligent Design.*** This view (ID) does not easily map onto our right-to-left spectrum. ID offers support to creationists because it argues scientifically and philosophically that evolution doesn't work unless some intelligence is guiding the process. But ID disappoints creationists because it doesn't argue from Scripture, try to prove the Christian God, or challenge common descent and macro-evolution. ID has a limited goal: to prove that some cosmic intelligence lies behind our existence. EC agrees with ID that God is involved with the evolutionary process but disagrees that His presence is detectable. There may be entirely naturalistic explanations for everything. EC says that's okay, as long as we say God did the thing we can't see Him do.

Which one of these theories do you like best? It depends how you put the Bible and science together. That's next.

A common depiction of "the ascent of man," the idea that humanity evolved from lower forms of life.

93 Does science disprove the Bible?

Many of the largest challenges to Christian faith arise from science. We hear science has "proved" that there never was a good creation, Adam and Eve, or a historical fall of humanity, and that animal predation, parasites, death, and decay are just things that have always been. We can be intimidated by scientists who speak so authoritatively, and we wonder what a thinking Christian is allowed to believe. Most of us are not scientists, and we don't know how to begin to respond.

When you feel overwhelmed, remember that it's impossible for God's world to contradict God's Word. There is no conflict between nature and Scripture God is the author of both, and His "two books" cannot be wrong. But our interpretation of each can be and often is. Theology interprets Scripture and science interprets

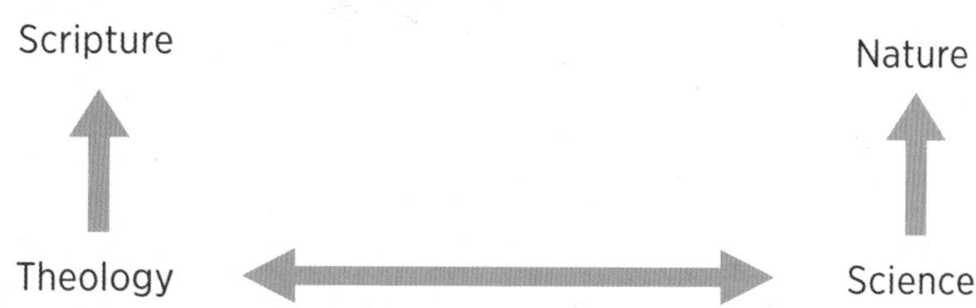

nature—and because either or both interpretations can be wrong, they often seem to conflict.

When you discover a conflict between theologians and scientists, test their interpretations as best you can. If your own expertise is limited, look for teachers or experts you trust to learn how they weigh the evidence. Play out the various scenarios: If your theology is correct, how should that influence the way you interpret the evidence in nature? If the science is right, how would that change the way you read Scripture? You'll often find (as we learned in the last section) that there is more than one plausible way to put theology and science together. You may also find that some options are impossible to hold, either for scientific or theological reasons. Humbly yet confidently push back on controversial claims, explaining why you cannot believe them.

It's important to model the virtues of faith and humility throughout this process. Christians have non-negotiable convictions about God, Jesus, Scripture, humanity, sin, and salvation. We cannot give these up without losing our Christian faith. But perhaps there is more room for adjustment than we sometimes think. So we'll humbly enter hard conversations, firmly holding our beliefs while weighing new interpretations.

We must avoid two extremes: allowing theology to erect unnecessary barriers to faith or allowing science to soften our beliefs into a nebulous, squishy faith. We erect barriers to faith when we draw our lines too tightly, claiming there is only one possible way to reconcile theology and science. Our children may feel forced to choose between Christianity and science, and they may prematurely give up their faith. On the other hand, we may loosen our doctrinal lines so much that we effectively lose our faith. If we allow science to gut our core beliefs, we may discover there's nothing left of the faith to give up.

What an exciting time to be a Christian! Theologians and scientists continually discover new insights from God's Word and God's world. Don't unquestionably accept any interpretation, but test each against the others as you slowly grow in your understanding of nature and Scripture. Growth can be painful, but it's the only path to maturity.

94 How does the Bible improve science?

The discoveries of science can help us interpret Scripture. Many Christians used to think Psalm 93:1 ("the world is established, firm and secure") was a proof text for geocentricity. The sun must revolve around a stationary earth because the Bible says so. When Copernicus suggested instead that the earth goes around the sun, the theologian Martin Luther said he was merely an upstart seeking attention. We now know Copernicus was right, and we use his theory to better understand Psalm 93:1. This verse doesn't prove the earth is stationary, but rather is a poetic promise of God's providence. No matter what happens in life, we need not fear: God holds us and the universe in His hand. We shall not be moved.

The better we understand God's world, the better we'll understand His Word, and vice versa. But God's world and God's Word are not equal authorities. We give priority to Scripture for the following ascending reasons.

1. ***Words clarify what we see.*** This is why we enjoy charades. The game's challenge is to see if we can get others to guess a word or phrase without using words. If we blurt out the answer, the game is over because words instantly clarify.

   Like a person playing charades, nature does not speak. We see birds nesting, clouds gathering, and foxes chasing rabbits, but we don't intuitively know what any of this means. We make informed guesses, but wouldn't it help to have words that interpret what we see?

2. ***Nature is broken.*** Nature isn't merely silent. Its situation is much worse. What we see in God's world has been ravaged by Adam's fall. If we didn't know this, we would think blossom-end rot, oak wilt, tsunamis, tornadoes, and coyotes stalking deer are normal. But Scripture says our world is fallen, and there's no corner of creation unaffected by the consequences of human rebellion. Romans 8:22 says "the whole creation has been groaning," waiting for the Lord Jesus to return and redeem it from corruption. Until then, nothing in our world is exactly as it's supposed to be.

3. ***Scripture is God's perfect, inspired, and authoritative Word.*** We need words to interpret what we see, and we're in luck—because we happen to have the best possible Word! John Calvin compared Scripture to eyeglasses that we wear to make sense of the world.

Mainstream science says nine billion years passed from the Big Bang until earth became inhabitable, and another four billion years passed from the first forms of life until the evolution of humans. Under this scenario, if the entire history of our universe was packed into a twenty-four-hour day, we humans didn't arrive until the last second or two! This means most of our world's history was full of carnage, hundreds of millions of years before humans came on the scene. The good creation, if it ever existed, is a millisecond blip in our otherwise severely suffering world. Christians who are persuaded by evolution marvel at the patience of God, while others wonder how this story can be reconciled with Scripture, which says God made our world good, up to and including the creation of humans.

This may be Scripture's most important contribution to science. The Bible says there has been a cataclysmic fall, so we live on the other side of a catastrophe. Dutch theologian Abraham Kuyper said there are two kinds of scientists, Normalists and Abnormalists. Normalists assume this world has evolved uniformly across billions of years, so what we see is consistent with what has always been. Abnormalists believe there's been a fall and that predation, parasites, and human death are unnatural.

Abnormalists use the insights of God's Word to interpret God's world. We may disagree about all the ways Adam's fall has broken the world, but we know that it must be taken into account when interpreting nature. Those who don't factor the fall into their calculations are bound to get important things wrong. They are like drivers who come upon a twenty-car pileup. Bumpers and bodies are strewn across the median, and they assume this is normal. Without the glasses of Scripture, we wouldn't understand what we're seeing. Without the words of Scripture, our world would be an indecipherable round of charades.

95 Do ancient origin stories disprove the Bible?

The Bible isn't the only origin story from the Ancient Near East. The Babylonians and other Mesopotamians passed down such tales as *Enuma Elish*, the *Gilgamesh Epic*, and the *Sumerian Flood Story*. Similar to Genesis 1, *Enuma Elish* said the world began from a watery chaos and primeval darkness, from which the gods created light, the heavens, and humanity. Similar to Genesis 2–8, the *Gilgamesh Epic* describes a beautiful garden, a plant of immortality, a dishonest serpent, and a great flood.

The flood story of *Gilgamesh* is strikingly similar to what we read in Genesis 6–8. The gods command a man to build a boat and fill it with family and animals. After torrential rains destroy everything else, the boat comes to rest on a mountain. The man sends out birds to see if it is safe to come out, and when his ordeal is finished, he offers a sacrifice of thanksgiving to the gods.

Since *Enuma Elish* and *Gilgamesh* are fantastic stories of gods who kill each other (and in the case of Marduk, fashion heaven and earth from the carcass of his dead victim), many scholars assume the stories in Genesis 1–11 also are myths. But this confuses who influenced whom. Rather than assume Genesis copied Mesopotamian myths, why not believe that both Genesis and the other Ancient Near Eastern stories describe a common origin?

A fragment of the Gilgamesh Epic, on display at the Sulaymaniyah Museum in Iraq.

Adam and Eve would have shared their experience in Eden with their children, who would pass it down to their children, and so on. As happens with oral traditions, the story often changes in the retelling. This was especially true after the Tower of Babel, when God confused people's languages and scattered them throughout Mesopotamia. Each group continued to pass down their version of the origin story, without the checks provided by the others. Some, such as the Babylonian *Enuma Elish,* inserted Marduk into the story to honor the role of their god.

So the world really did begin with the creation of light, the heavens and the earth, the land and the sea, and then the animals and humanity. There was a Garden of Eden, a tree of life, a conniving serpent, and a great flood. Genesis 1–11 provides a true and divinely inspired account of this beginning. The Mesopotamian myths are incomplete, corrupted, and religiously motivated memories of the same thing, but these tales are close enough to corroborate the biblical story.

Something happened in the beginning. If you want to read the vivid imagination of ancient Mesopotamian religion, check out *Enuma Elish,* the *Gilgamesh Epic,* and the *Sumerian Flood Story.* If you want a reliable, authorized account, read Genesis.

96 What must all Christians believe about creation?

As you can see, there is more than one plausible way to read Scripture's opening chapters. Christians may disagree on various points, but we all must believe the following non-negotiables.

1. God created the world from nothing. Genesis does not explicitly say God made the world from nothing, but it is assumed in its very first words. "In the beginning God created the heavens and the earth" implies that neither the heavens and the earth nor their materials existed before God made them. Hebrews 11:3 concurs: "By faith we understand that the universe was formed at God's command, so that what is seen was not made out of what was visible."

Unlike various forms of ancient Greek thought, which said the world emanates from God's being, Christians believe God absolutely originates the stuff of our world. Otherwise He wouldn't be sovereign. God rules over all because everything—all the way down—depends on His Word for its existence. So every creature in heaven praises our glorious God: "You are worthy, our Lord and God, to receive glory and honor and power, for you created all things, and by your will they were created and have their being" (Revelation 4:11).

2. ***The original creation was good.*** God stopped after most of the days of creation, looked at what He had made, and said it was good. When He was all done, He "saw all that he had made, and it was *very* good" (Genesis 1:31, emphasis added). God has the highest possible standards, so you can be sure this world was fantastic. The goodness of creation means that evil and suffering are not God's fault. He created a good world, so the blame for evil must lie somewhere else (I'll explain in a later question, "How could God's good creatures go bad?").

   The goodness of creation also means the physical world is good. Unlike various forms of Greek thought, our problem is not that we are living in a material world. Our bodies are not prisons that have trapped our souls; they are God's gift to us. Our problem is not that we're embodied but that we have rebelled against God. Our problem is sin not physical stuff.

3. ***God created humans as male and female.*** God declared His whole world good, except for one thing. He saw Adam and said, "It is not good for the man to be alone. I will make a helper suitable for him" (Genesis 2:18). God created Eve to complement Adam so that together they might be the image of God (Genesis 1:27).

   God is a fruitful, productive Creator, and His world is full of fruitful, productive difference. God created light and dark, day and night, heavens and earth, land and sea, male and female. These differences play off one another to make an extravagantly creative environment. Imagine art that couldn't use contrasting colors or light and shadow. Or an idea that couldn't be contrasted with something else. Would thought even be possible?

   God created men and women to unite their bodies in marital love so that together their difference might create new others to love. Our sexual union is a creaturely pointer to the triune God, whose personal love is also powerfully fertile and creative.

*4. **God created humans in His image.*** We humans are qualitatively different than the highest functioning animals because, unlike them, we alone bear the image of God (Genesis 1:26–28). This means we *resemble* God: we have intellect, will, conscience, and language fluency. Our erect bodies display a nobility that points to God. Even more, it means we *represent* God. He put us on earth to mediate His presence to the rest of creation. We are the voice of God to our pets, the hands of God to our gardens, and the creativity of God in our development of culture. God placed us on earth to steward this world on His behalf. We are God's representatives on earth. As we go, so goes the planet.

97 Was creation perfect?

It depends on what you mean by "perfect." If you mean that creation could not improve in any way, then no—God made the world with room to grow. He put Adam and Eve in a garden and told them to develop it (Genesis 2:15). They and their descendants obeyed God's command, and the human race eventually produced sweaters, violins, and computers. Human culture continues to advance, as we take the raw materials of the planet and make something out of them.

But if by perfect you mean flawless, then yes—there were neither errors nor evil in God's original creation. Everything was exactly as our perfect and loving Lord wanted it to be.

Since *perfect* can mean "can't get better," it might seem best to say God's original creation was good, and the consummation—when Jesus returns and restores all things—will be perfect. However, life with Jesus on the new earth will always be improving, as there will always be some new poem to write, new game to play, or new technology to create. So the world will never be perfect in that sense. That's a good thing, as there will always be some new delight to explore.

How about this? Let's say our world was *perfect* when God made it, will be *perfected* when Jesus consummates it, and will be continually *perfecting* as each day on the new earth adds a bit more to savor and enjoy.

A botanical garden in Hawaii inspires nostalgia for Eden.

98 Why did God make humans?

The Garden of Eden was God's temple on earth. Like other temples, Eden was on a mountain (major rivers flowed downhill from it, Genesis 2:10–14), facing east (toward the rising sun), and was where God came down to walk with Adam and Eve (Genesis 3:8).

Every temple has an image of its god. Who is the image in this temple? *It's us!* God said, "Let us make mankind in our image, in our likeness, so that they may rule over the fish in the sea and the birds in the sky, over the livestock and all the wild animals, and over all the creatures that move along the ground" (Genesis 1:26).

God placed Adam and Eve as His image bearers "in the Garden of Eden to work it and take care of it" (Genesis 2:15). The Hebrew verbs in this verse are often used together in relation to Old Testament priests, who served in the temple and guarded it from unclean things. God's plan was for Adam and Eve and their children to expand the borders of Eden until the entire world became God's temple. They were to methodically cultivate, arrange, and direct the rest of creation to bring praise to the Lord.

As the meme says, *they had one job*—and they failed. Adam and Eve listened to the unclean serpent. Rather than hurl him out of the garden, they took his advice and ate from the one tree God said they shouldn't. So God evicted them from Eden, placing cherubim (guardian angels) at the entrance of His garden temple to prevent them from returning (Genesis 3:24).

But not forever. Human history is the story of God's plan to restore the sons and daughters of Adam. God ultimately will succeed through the sacrifice of His Son, Jesus, who is the Last Adam, the image of God, and the true temple (Romans 5:12–21; Colossians 1:15; John 2:19–21). In Jesus, and only in Him, do we recover the meaning of our existence.

An angel expels Adam and Eve from the Garden of Eden after they disobey God. Sin ruined their lives, but God had a plan to save them and us.

99 Why are you here?

The first-person version of this question—*Why am I here?*—is the biggest question you could ever ask. Until you know the answer, you're not prepared to live. The good news is that the God who made you knows exactly why you're here. This is what He said:

> *"Let us make mankind in our image, in our likeness, so that they may rule over the fish in the sea and the birds in the sky, over the livestock and all the wild animals, and over all the creatures that move along the ground."*
>
> *So God created mankind in his own image, in the image of God he created them; male and female he created them.*
>
> *God blessed them and said to them, "Be fruitful and increase in number; fill the earth and subdue it. Rule over the fish in the sea and the birds in the sky and over every living creature that moves on the ground."*
>
> GENESIS 1:26–28

God's first words about humans say we are here for four reasons:

1. ***To love God.*** God made us in His image to know and love Him. We are natural creatures with a supernatural end. No person and no success in this life will ever fill the hole in our hearts. The church father Augustine (354–430 CE) said it best in a prayer to God: "You have made us for yourself, and our heart is restless until it finds its rest in You."

2. ***To serve others.*** People cannot take the place of God, but God has wired us to serve and be loved by people. As God is a self-giving community of three persons, so He created us in His image as male and female so that we would need each other to thrive. Even introverts need a community to belong to. We find our place among family and friends, but our number one community should be the church. If you aren't a member of a local church, find one near you and join it. These people are the body of Christ. They are a primary reason God put you on earth.

The early church leader Augustine wrote that our highest purpose is to know and love God.

3. To responsibly cultivate creation. God told the first humans to rule over the earth. He elaborated on this in Genesis 2:15, when He told Adam to guard and develop the Garden of Eden. This is the first command God ever gave us, and it's the basis of culture. We develop culture in our various callings, both paid and unpaid. Whether you're on the job or in your home, ask how what you do serves others and orders creation. You're not just making dinner—you're taking the raw materials of this world and arranging a tasty meal for the ones you love. You're not just plotting numbers on a spreadsheet—you're helping your company wisely manage its resources to better serve its clients. This is why you're here.

4. ***To rest every seven days.*** This purpose of life appears a few verses later, when God stopped creating and rested on the seventh day. He will later tell Israel to follow His example (Exodus 20:8–11). Since Adam and Eve were created late on the sixth day, their first day on the planet was a day of rest. Life must be more than work, work, work. God wants us to take a break every seven days to enjoy what we've done and simply *be*. Life cannot be measured by output alone. Its main goal is rest, and we can only do that when we know why we're here.

100 What is the purpose of marriage?

This may come as a surprise: marriage is not primarily for our sake. If we marry someone in order to become whole (or because we tingle when we're around them), we will soon become disillusioned and divorced.

We're not masochists, so we should marry someone we admire and are romantically attracted to. Marriage gives us someone to share life with, and it's best to choose someone we enjoy. We marry the person because we love them, then we love them because we married them.

When God created Adam and Eve, they immediately saw their bodies were made for each other. Adam said,

> *"This is now bone of my bones*
> *and flesh of my flesh;*
> *she shall be called 'woman,'*
> *for she was taken out of man."*
>
> Genesis 2:23

God added, "That is why a man leaves his father and mother and is united to his wife, and they become one flesh. Adam and his wife were both naked, and they felt no shame" (Genesis 2:24–25).

We marry because we are made in the image of our personal, triune God, and we hunger to love and matter to another person. Our marital love is fruitful, and the consummation of our love produces children. We wisely limit our marital love to our spouse so our marriage creates a stable home that raises and socializes these children.

Nothing is more private than marriage, and nothing does more for the public. When we leave our parents and cleave to our spouse, we create a home that sustains the human race, instills virtue, and orders society. More than anything else we do, our marriage serves the common good. We marry for ourselves, our spouses, our families, and the world.

Marriage cuts across every time and culture, deriving from the original union of Adam and Eve.

The human body is composed of chemicals that break down after death. . .though the soul lives on.

101 What are you made of?

You are 99 percent oxygen, carbon, hydrogen, nitrogen, calcium, and phosphorus. And since the oxygen and hydrogen mix, you are up to 60 percent water! But that's just your body. You also have an immaterial side that is called a soul or spirit.

Some people think the soul and spirit are different, that our soul relates to others and our spirit relates to God. But the Bible uses these two terms as synonyms for the same, invisible aspect. When Paul says, "May your whole spirit, soul and body be kept blameless" (1 Thessalonians 5:23), he isn't dividing us into three separate parts but is merely saying our entire self must be holy. Similarly, when Jesus says to "love the Lord your God with all your heart and with all your soul and with all your mind and with all your strength," He isn't saying we have *four* different parts but simply that we must love God with all that we are (Mark 12:30). And when Hebrews 4:12 says God's Word is a "double-edged sword" that "penetrates even to dividing soul and spirit, joints and marrow," the author's rhetorical point is the Bible is so powerful it can figuratively separate what is literally inseparable.

We are made of a material and immaterial part, but they mesh together so well we can scarcely tell them apart. Philosophers, physicians, and scientists ponder where the body ends and the soul begins and how each affects the other. We know our body can influence our soul and vice versa. There's a reason athletes pump themselves up with music for a peak performance.

We can't neatly divide our body and soul because they were never meant to be apart. The only reason we know we have two separable parts is because of death. At death our bodies and souls are unnaturally ripped apart. Our bodies remain here to be buried or cremated, and our souls go either to heaven or hell until our resurrection. But we were never supposed to die, so we were never supposed to know this was even possible. We only die because of sin, and we only sin because of Adam's fall. That's next.

102 Were Adam and Eve real?

The opening chapters of the Bible may sound like a fairy tale. There's an idyllic garden, magical trees, poisoned fruit, and a talking snake. Perhaps Genesis 1–3 is a religious myth rather than a factual, historical account—but it's still true because it imaginatively describes the goodness and evil we encounter in our world.

This reading of Genesis meshes easily with mainstream science. Since Darwin, science has scoffed at the idea that God created an actual Adam and Eve to live in an actual Garden of Eden. Geneticists have recently sharpened the argument, claiming the rate and amount of diversity in the human genome proves we evolved from several thousand hominims. There were, according to this viewpoint, no original Adam and Eve.

I understand why many prefer a nonliteral reading of Genesis, and it's possible to take parts of the story as symbols without losing the overall meaning. For instance, someone could say there wasn't a literal talking snake and yet believe Adam and Eve's temptation was real. But this raises the problem of the slippery slope: Once we say some parts of the story aren't factual, where do we stop, and on what basis? If there was no snake, perhaps there was no tree of life or tree of the knowledge of good and evil. If there were no trees, perhaps there was no Garden of Eden. . .and, finally, no Adam and Eve.

But the Bible clearly indicates Adam was real and the head of the human race. Luke's Gospel traces Jesus' genealogy from Joseph through seventy-four generations until it reaches all the way back to "Adam, the son of God" (Luke 3:23–38). Paul says we all die because Adam sinned and broke the human race, and we all will live if we put our faith in Jesus, the "Last Adam" who came to fix our race (Romans 5:12–21; 1 Corinthians 15:21–22). Adam is not a marginal character in Scripture—he is the first and foundational figure, the one who explains both our created goodness and our fallen rebellion.

If Adam is merely a mythic symbol, we may use his story to describe our sinful condition but not explain how it came to be. Symbols can illustrate *what* is true, but they can't explain *why*. If you believe something is wrong with us and with our world, if you believe this is not the way things are supposed to be, then you must believe in a real, historical Adam and Eve. There is no other way to account for the brokenness of our world. If there is no Adam, then evil, injustice, predation, and death are not problems. They all are natural. And that's a problem!

Mainstream science may not believe in Adam, but God does. Believe God.

103 What is "the fall"?

God put Adam and Eve in a beautiful garden of delight and gave them one prohibition to test their love for Him. The first humans could enjoy every tree except one, the tree of the knowledge of good and evil. If they ate from that tree, they would die (Genesis 2:15–17).

Satan entered the body of a serpent and deceived Eve into eating the forbidden fruit. The serpent asked if it was true that God had told the couple not to eat from any of the trees. He knew that wasn't close to the truth, but if Eve caught on, he would simply shrug and say he heard wrong. *Don't get upset! I'm just asking a question! Sheesh!*

But Eve didn't get upset. She calmly told the serpent he was wrong. God said they could eat from all the trees except one. They must stay away from it, or they'd die (Genesis 3:1–3).

The serpent's eyes widened. Eve's response was spot on, but she made a crucial mistake: she was talking to a snake. So the serpent brushed aside Eve's response and got to the point. "You will not certainly die," he hissed, implying that God had only given this command because He's small and insecure. "God knows that when you eat from it your eyes will be opened, and you will be like God, knowing good and evil" (Genesis 3:4–5).

Eve should have picked up a stick and beat the serpent's brains in. *How dare you? God made me and every tree in the garden. He clearly is on my side. What have you ever done for me?* At least she could have picked up the snake by the tail and hurled it from Eden.

Eve tastes the forbidden fruit and Adam will soon follow in what is called "the fall of humanity."

But she didn't. Eve pondered Satan's words and looked again at the tree. Its fruit was beautiful and probably delicious. What if she *was* missing out? Wouldn't she always wonder how it tasted? Perhaps it *would* make her like God. Anyway, how could it hurt to have the knowledge of good and evil? Isn't all knowledge good?

She reached out, plucked a fruit, and took a bite.

(By the way, the fruit is commonly described as an apple because the Latin word for apple, *malum,* is the same word for evil. Medieval monks reading their Latin Bibles punned, "When Eve ate *malum,* she got *malum.* Ha!" If you don't think that's funny, try living in a monastery. After a couple weeks, you'll be laughing too.)

Eve "also gave some to her husband, who was with her, and he ate it. Then the eyes of both of them were opened, and they realized they were naked" (Genesis 3:6–7).

This event is what Christians call "the fall." It is the source of all evil, violence, war, and injustice in our world. This is surprising, because what could be more mundane than eating a piece of fruit? But the fruit was forbidden, and eating it was an act of rebellion against God. Mere humans cannot do anything more momentous, or worse, than what Adam and Eve did here. They blew it, and the history of humanity ever since has been God's efforts to put us and His world back together again.

104 What is sin?

Sin has become a word that makes us snicker. Dessert menus offer "decadent" chocolate cake that is "sinfully" delicious. Las Vegas is called "Sin City" because it encourages people to come and luxuriate in booze, illicit sex, and gambling. Despite what the brochures promise, "What happens in Vegas does *not* stay in Vegas." Sin travels. It always has.

So we'd better know what sin is and how to avoid it. Here is my definition: *sin is treasonous rebellion against God that ravages me and my world.* Sin is not an innocent mistake, an oopsie to be fixed with a do-over or better effort next time. Sin could only be forgiven by the crucifixion of Jesus Christ, so it has to be bad—much worse than any of us can fully appreciate.

Our world uses sin as a marketing ploy. The Bible treats it much more seriously.

Sin disguises itself as curiosity, ambition, pleasure, or some other normal desire, even as it aggressively undermines all that is good in the world. Eve knew what God had commanded about the tree of the knowledge of good and evil. She repeated it to the serpent, so she couldn't plead ignorance. Her sin, and what all sin amounts to, is elevating herself above God's Word. That's why I call it treasonous rebellion.

Rather than submit to her loving Creator, the One responsible for everything good in her life, Eve put herself above both God's Word and the serpent's. They had disagreed about the tree, and Eve decided *she* would judge who was right. She used her empirical abilities (she "saw that the fruit of the tree was good for food and pleasing to the eye") and she used her reasoning skills (that the fruit was "also desirable for gaining wisdom") and she concluded she had to have a taste (Genesis 3:6).

Eve's sin began before her first bite. She sinned when she used her mind and eyes to stand in judgment over God's Word. All sin comes down to our need to play God, to be the judge who determines right and wrong, good and evil. I never sin from ignorance. I know what God commands me to do. I sin when I just don't care. I want to do what I want to do because I want to do it. I don't want anyone, especially God, cramping my style.

This is why God told Adam and Eve not to eat from the tree of the knowledge of good and evil. They gained experiential knowledge of good and evil, but who decides what goes in which category? Before the fall, Adam and Eve agreed it was God. But now we too often think it's us. What is good for me might be bad for you, so we fight. And what happens when eight billion people believe they have the right to judge right from wrong? Just look around—we're finding out!

Do you see why God said Adam and Eve must not eat from that tree? He was serious. Sin is treasonous rebellion that ravages us and our world. We'll discuss that next.

If you type "couple arguing" into the photo supplier Shutterstock, you get nearly 26,000 image options. Clearly, Adam's fall has ravaged our relationships.

105 How does Adam's fall damage me?

This question may imply I'm a victim. I'm not. I endorse Adam's fall every time I sin, which happens at least twice a day. That number may seem low because it is. Just ask my wife and kids. (Seriously, don't. Please.)

I sin a whole lot more than twice a day, because Adam passed on to me (and to you) both his guilt and corruption. We call this "original sin," and it's the least popular thing that Christians believe. Original sin seems so unfair, yet every parent knows it's true. Our babies are not as innocent as they appear. What's the first word every child learns? *No!* We don't teach our kids to stomp and scream. They come with attitude, as does every child of Adam.

Adam's fall guarantees we're all born sinners, which causes social strife. When they felt shame, Adam and Eve immediately tried to cover and blame someone else. "Who told you that you were naked?" God asked Adam, and the man pointed at his wife—and indirectly at God Himself. "The woman you put here with me—she gave me some fruit from the tree, and I ate it" (Genesis 3:11–12). Sinners like us have been ducking and shooting ever since. We hide behind threadbare excuses and fire arrows at others.

Especially those we love the most. The suffering of sin is clearest in our closest relationships. God told Eve that from that point on, "Your desire will be for your husband, and he will rule over you" (Genesis 3:16). What God intended to be a complementary marriage of mutual support among equals would now degenerate into abusive parodies of their gender roles. Eve's natural desire for Adam's strength would allow him to dominate and subdue her, while Adam's natural desire for Eve's beauty would allow her to manipulate and control him. Eve would now suffer severe pains in childbirth, and Adam would discover the cursed soil would no longer joyfully yield its fruit (Genesis 3:16–19). We will continually toil in our fallen world, scratching out a hard-scrabble life, until eventually we die and "return to the ground. . .for dust you are and to dust you will return" (Genesis 3:19).

Sin, strife, suffering, and death—these are the main ways that Adam's fall has damaged us. Get mad at him, but don't let yourself off the hook. We endorse these evils every time we disobey God and do what He says is wrong. Do you hate sin's fruit? Then pull it out by the root.

Only one Man can do this. When Jesus arose from the dead, Mary Magdalene mistook Him for the gardener (John 20:15). She wasn't entirely wrong. Jesus died and rose again to yank out our sin and replace it with Himself. We were born in the sin of Adam; we can be born again through faith in Jesus, the true and final Adam.

106 Why is it called "Adam's fall" if Eve sinned first?

Genesis 3 describes at length Eve's temptation and fall, only mentioning Adam at the end. Eve "also gave some to her husband, who was with her, and he ate it" (Genesis 3:6). Yet the rest of Scripture blames Adam for the fall. Paul says "sin entered the world through one man. . . . Death reigned from the time of Adam. . . even over those who did not sin by breaking a command, as did Adam. . . . By the trespass of the one man, death reigned through that one man. . . . Through the disobedience of the one man the many were made sinners" (Romans 5:12, 14, 17, 19). If Eve sinned first, why does the Bible say Adam is responsible for our sin and death?

Because of male headship. This is unpopular in Western culture today, so let me explain what male headship does *not* mean: male headship does not mean men are better than, worth more than, or in any way superior to women. Men and women both fully image God. Male headship simply means God has structured His world so that men bear a special responsibility. God calls men to lead in their homes and to sacrificially love their wives as Jesus loves His church, for "the husband is the head of the wife as Christ is the head of the church" (Ephesians 5:23). God also calls men to lead in the church, for "the head of every man is Christ, and the head of the woman is man, and the head of Christ is God" (1 Corinthians 11:3). The Bible says godly men should authoritatively teach in the church, because "Adam was formed first, then Eve. And Adam was not the one deceived; it was the woman who was deceived and became a sinner" (1 Timothy 2:13–14). Male headship does not mean every man is the head of every woman, but that husbands are heads of their wives and male elders are heads of the church.

Male headship explains why it's Adam's sin rather than Eve's that is passed on to us. It's why God told Israel the sign of their covenant would be to circumcise the males. Nothing was done to the women, as they were covered by the representation of the men. It's why Jesus was born of Mary but not of Joseph. Original sin is passed from Adam to us, so it's fitting that Jesus not have a human father. God could have specially protected his Son from Adam's guilt and corruption anyway, but Jesus' virgin birth underlines the point that

God commands husbands to lovingly lead and protect their families.

the Last Adam was born innocent. Male headship is why Jesus was born a man. If the first man was responsible for passing on sin, then a perfect Man must be the one who removes it.

Male headship is controversial in our world, but it's assumed throughout Scripture. We cannot fully understand the main movements of the biblical story without it. At any rate, this is why the Bible speaks of Adam's fall rather than Eve's.

(This is a hypothetical, but what do you guess would have happened if Adam had not eaten the fruit that Eve offered him? What if only Eve had sinned but not Adam?)

107 How does Adam's fall damage our world?

Adam and Eve bore the image of God; they represented Him on this planet. As goes the head, so goes the body. So when Adam and Eve rebelled against God, they took everything else down with them. Like a massive volcano that erupted in paradise, Adam's fall spewed lava and ash that blanketed every corner of creation. Adam's fall ravaged us, as we learned in the last question, and also damaged human society, animals, and the earth itself.

1. ***Society.*** Adam's fall ruined relationships between people. Adam and Eve not only fought each other, they also birthed one son who killed another. How did eating the forbidden fruit lead to murder and in one generation? Because both sins had the same root. Those who want to play God will do whatever it takes to stay on top. For Adam and Eve, that meant eating a piece of fruit. For Cain, that meant jealously slaying his brother, Abel.

   The fighting has never stopped. Every war that has ever been fought began without a first shot. No one ever says their side started it—they are merely hitting back for what was done to them. The poor steal from the rich because they are oppressed; the rich oppress the poor because of their theft. Employers yell at workers for being lazy; workers slow down because of the yelling. Men and women; East and West; white and black and brown. All have legitimate beefs against the others, grievances that too often fuel a cycle of violence.

   Three short chapters after Adam's fall, the earth had become "corrupt in

God's sight and. . .full of violence. God saw how corrupt the earth had become, for all the people on earth had corrupted their ways" (Genesis 6:11–12). God had seen enough and sent a flood to cleanse the earth and start over.

Are you dismayed by the vitriol spewed online or between former friends? Do you wonder why it's so hard for us all to get along? The volcano of Adam's fall still smolders.

2. ***Animals.*** When God created the world, He gave the animals "every green plant for food" (Genesis 1:30). When Jesus returns to redeem the world, "the wolf and the lamb will feed together, and the lion will eat straw like the ox" (Isaiah 65:25). So it seems that animals prey upon other animals because of the fall. A pack of wolves taking down a lumbering elk appears to be one way "the whole creation has been groaning," longing for the shalom (peace and prosperity) that Jesus will bring when He returns and restores all things (Romans 8:22).

3. ***Nature.*** The wreckage of Adam's fall extends even to inanimate objects. God cursed the ground when Adam sinned, so that it would "produce thorns and thistles" and force Adam to sweat for his daily bread (Genesis 3:18). Natural

The damage caused by volcanic eruptions is evidence of sin's curse upon the earth.

evils, such as tornadoes, hurricanes, earthquakes, tsunamis, and, yes, volcanoes are the things we should expect to see in a world that has been broken by sin.

The volcanic eruption of Adam's sin destroyed everything in its path. This is terribly depressing until we remember this is precisely why Jesus came to earth. As the Christmas carol says, "He came to make His blessings flow, far as the curse is found." *Far as the curse is found?* Yes, far as the curse is found. *Joy to the world!*

Don't let the sunshine and bright flowers fool you, death stinks—thanks to Adam's fall, the cemetery is everyone's destination.

108 Is death natural?

Evolutionary science says death is not only natural, it's the mechanism that makes the whole system go. Nature selects the organisms whose mutations enable them to survive, then kills the rest. If death didn't happen regularly to most creatures, our current world wouldn't have evolved to our present stage. Death isn't a bug in the system, it's a necessary feature.

This view is popular, but it's hard to square with Scripture and our sensibilities. God declared His original creation was very good, which seems to imply it didn't contain death—at least and especially for humans. If you think about it, creation must have contained vegetative death. Any fruit that Eve ate would have died and been digested. Any roses that Adam cut for Eve would eventually die. Everyone assumes this is okay.

Neither would most people have a problem if Adam swatted a fly or stepped on a bug. We don't lose sleep over death of nonsentient creatures. But the higher up the food chain we go, the more difficult it is to think that animal suffering and bloodshed is what God wants for the world. If animal death was no big deal, then why did God use animal sacrifice to impress upon His people the horror of their sin? God isn't cavalier about the killing of animals (Zechariah 11:4–7).

I believe carnivorousness is a consequence of the fall, yet I concede this question has been controversial throughout church history. Not so when it comes to humans. Paul declares, "Therefore, just as sin entered the world through one man, and death through sin, and in this way death came to all people, because all sinned. . . . Consequently, just as one trespass resulted in condemnation for all people, so also one righteous act resulted in justification and life for all people" (Romans 5:12, 18). Paul is contrasting the First Adam, whose sin brought death upon all humans, and Jesus, the Last Adam, whose obedience presented the gift of life to all people.

We die because we are children of Adam, whose sin brought death upon us. *Death is not natural.* Unless Jesus returns first, everyone you know will die—but this does not make death normal. Death is the abnormal intruder into God's good world, the last enemy that Jesus came to destroy (1 Corinthians 15:26).

If death was natural, nothing could be done about it. If death was natural, nothing should be done about it. If death was natural, we could only try to get used to it.

You and I both know that's wrong. When we sit beside loved ones who are dying, we don't believe this is natural or good. We know it's not the way life is supposed to be, and we'd give anything to restore their health and make them whole once more.

The good news is that Jesus has given what was needed! He died on the cross and rose again to defeat our enemy of sin and death. Death is the first enemy to be mentioned in Scripture (Genesis 2:17), and it's the last enemy to go. In Revelation 20:10, Jesus throws Satan into the lake of burning sulfur. Four verses later He throws in death. Death is literally our last enemy, the final opponent that Jesus destroys.

Let's not minimize death by saying it's a natural part of the circle of life. If death is no big deal, then neither is Jesus for beating it. Let's make much of death so we can make much of Jesus.

Unless Jesus returns, we all will die. But death does not have the last word. Jesus may return at any moment, and when He comes, He will raise the dead for judgment. We who have put our faith in Jesus will live forever with Him on this restored earth, fully human and fully alive. And so we shout the closing prayer of Scripture, "Come, Lord Jesus" (Revelation 22:20).

109 Do you have a guardian angel?

Popular music and movies suggest we each have our very own angel who watches over us while we sleep, applies our brakes on snowy roads, and steers us away from the lettuce laced with E. coli. However, the Bible doesn't say we each have a guardian angel assigned to us. Because we have so much more.

The common conception of guardian angels: a winged protector watching over a child.

When an army surrounded the city where the prophet Elisha was staying, his servant panicked: "Oh no, my lord! What shall we do?" Elisha answered, "Don't be afraid. . . . Those who are with us are more than those who are with them." Then Elisha prayed, "Open his eyes, LORD, so that he may see." When the servant looked again, he saw more than the enemy army. He saw "the hills full of horses and chariots of fire all around Elisha." An angel army was defending them! (See 2 Kings 6:15–17).

John Calvin draws the right conclusion. He writes, "But whether individual angels have been assigned to individual believers for their protection, I dare not affirm with confidence." But "we ought to hold as a fact that the care of each one of us is not the task of one angel only, but all with one consent watch over our salvation. . . . For if the fact that all the heavenly host are keeping watch for his safety will not satisfy a man, I do not see what benefit he could derive from knowing that one angel has been given to him as his especial guardian."[20]

It's okay if you don't have a guardian angel. You are protected by all the angels!

110 Who is Satan?

Satan is not a cartoonish red devil with a pitchfork, tormenting hapless souls in hell. Satan has never been to hell.

Hell is not his headquarters; it is his final punishment. When Jesus returns to defeat His enemies, He will throw Satan "into the lake of burning sulfur," where he "will be tormented day and night for ever and ever" (Revelation 20:10). Until then, Satan is somewhere in our world, "the ruler of the kingdom of the air" (Ephesians 2:2), leading his spiteful army of demons against our Lord Jesus.

The Bible does not tell us a lot about Satan because he is a fallen angel, and angels are not the focus of Scripture. Angels appear on the edges of the action. They rarely stay in the frame for long, so we never get a clean look.

We do know Satan, whose name means "accuser," was originally the angel Lucifer, perhaps the highest creature that God ever made. We can't say for sure how or when Lucifer rebelled. Some Christians think the stories in Isaiah 14:12–15 and Ezekiel 28:11–19 describe his fall. Maybe, but these passages are probably only talking about the kings of Babylon and Tyre. Revelation 12:7–17 describes a war in heaven between Satan and his followers and Michael and the good angels. Satan and his demons lost and were hurled to earth, where they led the whole earth astray. Revelation is apocalyptic, so not everything is meant to be literal—but this passage seems to be imaginatively describing a real event.

Having challenged God for supremacy, the angel Lucifer is cast out of heaven. He will trouble the earth as the accuser, Satan.

Lucifer appears to have fallen because of pride, for Paul warns that new Christians who suddenly become elders "may become conceited and fall under the same judgment as the devil" (1 Timothy 3:6). Similarly, James says "bitter envy and selfish ambition" come from demons (James 3:14–15). These passages shaped the traditional view, explained by medieval theologian Anselm in *On the Fall of the Devil,* that Lucifer fell because he "inordinately willed to be like God." Rather than praise God for his talents and beauty, perhaps Lucifer wanted credit for his accomplishments or to bask in some of the glory that only God should receive. He overstepped his creaturely limits when he sought to share the stage with God and was justly cast from heaven.

God declares, "I am the LORD; that is my name! I will not yield my glory to another or my praise to idols" (Isaiah 42:8). Learn from Lucifer's life: If someone so glorious will be thrown into hell, what does our pride deserve? Let's give God all the glory and submit to His authority. There can only be one God, and we are not Him.

111 Can angels switch sides?

At this point, it doesn't seem so. Revelation 12:7–9 describes the fall of Lucifer and his followers, and there is no indication that subsequent falls have occurred or are even possible. As Adam and Eve's wills likely would have been confirmed in righteousness had they passed their probationary period and not eaten the forbidden fruit, so it seems the good angels who refused to side with Lucifer have been locked in to joyful obedience.

From the other side, there is no hint that demons can repent and be forgiven. The church father Origen got into trouble with his church for optimistically implying that everyone could be saved—even the devil! We know this isn't true, because the Bible ends with the devil "thrown into the lake of burning sulfur," where he "will be tormented day and night for ever and ever" (Revelation 20:10). The Bible also teaches that some demons are right now chained in the darkness of hell, awaiting their final judgment. There is no hope for them (2 Peter 2:4; Jude 6).

While the Bible doesn't say enough about angels to give us a slam dunk proof text, it seems both good and bad angels are locked in to their original response to Lucifer's fall. Choices have consequences, and some last forever.

112 What is Satan's role in God's story?

We don't need to fear or be intimidated by Satan. He is much stronger than we are, but he is no match for our Lord Jesus. Satan and his demons cower before the name and power of Jesus. To paraphrase Martin Luther, Satan is "God's devil." He can only do what God allows, and God always protects His children.

Someday God will throw Satan into hell. We don't know why God hasn't done that yet, but His patient permission is the plotline that drives history. You and I are role players in a drama that is as large and long as the story of the world: Who has the right to rule this place? God and Satan are fighting for our allegiance.

The apostle Paul suggests the history of the world is, at least to some extent, God demonstrating his "manifold wisdom. . .to the rulers and authorities in the heavenly realms" (Ephesians 3:10). God wants to prove something to the angels, but what? When Satan was cast out of heaven, he probably charged God with being unloving and intolerant. *You claim to be the epitome of grace, but I make one mistake and you slap me down? You're a phony, insecure tyrant!* There's a reason the serpent told Eve that God was afraid she'd become like Him: he may have been talking from experience.

Michael, Gabriel, and the good angels rejected Satan's accusation, but they couldn't point to a counterexample. The one time an angel had challenged God,

A sculpture called *The Genius of Evil* shows Satan's leg chained—he can only do what God allows him to do.

he had been condemned to everlasting damnation. Perhaps this is why God created our world and a new race that bore His image. This new race fell too, but this time God didn't damn them—He sacrificed Himself to forgive their sin and is methodically uniting forgiven sinners of every ethnicity to Himself and to each other in the church. This is the mystery that God is revealing to the angels, "that through the gospel the Gentiles are heirs together with Israel, members together of one body, and sharers together in the promise in Christ Jesus" (Ephesians 3:6; compare to Revelation 7:9).

God is proving that He is unifying love, which may be why Satan fights against grace and strives to keep people apart. There's probably nothing Satan hates more than grace. It can't seem fair that he was booted immediately while humans, who are much less impressive, continually receive multiple opportunities to be reconciled to God. So "the devil prowls around like a roaring lion looking for someone to devour" (1 Peter 5:8). He blinds "the minds of unbelievers, so that they cannot see the light of the gospel that displays the glory of Christ" (2 Corinthians 4:4). And he tempts Christians to commit ugly sins and tempts others to think they're better. Paul answers by commanding Christians to forgive and reconcile with their repentant brother or sister "in order that Satan might not outwit us. For we are not unaware of his schemes" (2 Corinthians 2:11).

We know how the story ends. The only question is whether God will win with or without you. You are living in an unseen war between God and the devil. Adam's fall delivered this world to the rule of Satan. Jesus wrestled it back when as the Last Adam He died for our sins and rose again. He ascended to heaven, where He sits enthroned as the rightful ruler of our world. Victory is assured, but Satan and his demons are fighting until the bitter end.

Who is Lord? Is God love? You cast your vote for Jesus and kick Satan in the teeth when you submit to God's Word, joyfully bask in His forgiveness, forgive those who have wounded you, and join other reconciled sinners in your local church. Satan cannot win. Will you?

113 How could God's good creatures go bad?

There are two areas of religious belief that will always end in mystery, and this question involves both. We will never entirely understand God, and we will never entirely understand the problem of evil. We won't comprehend God because He is infinite, and we won't comprehend evil because it's irrational. Evil is not supposed to make sense. If we could wrap our minds around evil and explain it, then it wouldn't be so bad. The fall is an event we'll never understand.

Sin is dumb. It shouldn't be possible, especially for creatures that were created good. Think about it: we always choose what we perceive to be the greater good. We eat one thing because it will bring us pleasure or another thing because it will make us healthy. If we didn't think one choice was better than another, we wouldn't do it.

Our choices are always aimed at the good, yet we know that sin is something we'll come to regret. I've never met anyone who said, "My affair was the best decision I ever made." No, they usually say, *"What was I thinking? I threw my family away for that?"* We know the sin we're about to do is going to bite us, yet in the moment we convince ourselves it's worth it—that, somehow, it's for our good.

Sin is dumb, and sin makes us dumb. When we choose an act we know isn't for our good, it becomes easier to make the same decision the next time. But what about good creatures, such as Adam and Eve, who had never sinned? Or back up one step: What about Lucifer, who not only was an exquisitely beautiful and talented angel but also served in the presence of God? How could these good wills go bad?

We will never fully solve this mystery, though it seems important to recognize that humanity's first sin began with deception. This does not excuse Eve, but it does begin to explain her choice. She was deceived into thinking the forbidden fruit would make her like God.

Eve was deceived, but she was not innocent. The serpent appealed to pride and selfishness that she hadn't possessed until that moment.

Where did such pride come from? We can't say, for such is the mystery of evil. But notice that pride can pop up anywhere, even in the paradise of Eden and the throne room of heaven. If the good Lucifer could fall, then *we* are never safe from pride, not even in church. (Perhaps especially there.) When we are diligently worshiping, praying, or serving God, we may start to think that we're doing special works because we are special ourselves. We may think more highly of ourselves than we should and become angry when we don't receive the *attaboys* we think we deserve. Just like the devil.

We're never closer to committing evil than when we think we're doing good. Eve sinned in the moment she was talking about God. The fall of humanity occurred during a theological conversation! Sin is inexplicably dumb and tempts most when we assume we're safe. Stay alert.

114 Why did God allow His good creatures to go bad?

The mystery continues. This question is called "the problem of evil." If God is all powerful, He should be able to stop evil. If God is all good, He should want to. So if God is all good and all powerful, there should not be evil. But there *is* evil, so God must either not be all good or all powerful. In other words, there is no God.

Philosophers attempt to solve this problem by saying either that evil is not as bad as you think—that somehow it's necessary to improve us and our world—or that God's power is not as dominant as you might think. They say God rolled the dice when He gave us freedom, for He couldn't guarantee what free creatures freely choose. God hoped that we'd choose to love and obey Him, but having given us freedom, He had to let us make up our own minds. If He stopped us from making a bad choice, He would essentially remove our freedom. And if we aren't free, then we can't truly love. So God took a chance for love.

These attempted explanations say something important: we are free, evil is our fault, and yes, the suffering that comes from evil often does make us stronger. But these arguments do not solve the problem of evil. There is so much unnecessary evil that doesn't seem to benefit anyone, and why can't a sovereign God guarantee what free creatures choose? All Christians believe God will prevent us from sinning *in the future*, when we'll live with Him on this restored earth. If God will see to it then that we will always choose Him, He could have kept Adam and Eve from sinning without violating their freedom.

We won't solve the problem of evil, because evil is not a problem that's meant to be solved. It's evil, so it's irrational for a reason! But Christians can say more about evil than anyone else. In fact, evil is the best reason I know to be a Christian. I can't explain why a loving and strong God would allow evil, but I can explain why evil is the best possible reason to follow Jesus. That's next.

115 Why is evil a bad reason to not believe in God?

It is logically impossible to use evil to disprove God, because evil cannot exist in a world without Him. Evil is a powerful word, and it requires the strongest possible grounding. When you declare some act is evil, you are saying more than that you strongly dislike it. You are saying more than that your community opposes it. You are assuming there is some Being who transcends every person and community and is offended by that action. That's why it's evil.

If there is no God, our highest court of appeals would be the United Nations. But the peoples of the world don't always agree—and even when they do, they still might be wrong. Regardless, when you say this murder or that war is "evil," you mean to say more than most nations of the world oppose it. You mean to appeal to the highest possible standard, and that standard can only be God.

Do you believe in evil? Then you must believe in God. Evil makes no sense without Him.

Besides this logical argument, there is a psychological reason why evil compels us to believe in God. Consider the horror of believing in evil but no God to protect you from it. We hear daily stories of natural evil, such as cancer, accidents, and storms; and moral evil, such as theft, rape, and murder. If we truly believed there was no God, would we have the courage to leave our house?

Are you able to go about your day without worry that you might be evil's next victim? Then despite what you might think, deep down you really do believe in a

Devastation in New York City in the aftermath of the September 11, 2001, terrorist attacks. The concept of evil only makes sense if you believe there is a God.

God who's got you. A God who keeps you safe.

Do you believe in evil? Then you already believe in God.

116 Why is evil the best reason to believe in Jesus?

When you suffer from excruciating evil, what do you most need to be true? You need to know there is a God who cares, a God who understands your anguish and is strong enough to do something about it. Only one God offers both. His name is Jesus.

Other religions ponder why their god allowed evil into the world. Only the Christian God allowed evil to get to Him. Evil is not on the edges of the Christian faith. It's smack dab in the center. Other religions ask, *Why do bad things happen to good people?* Christianity asks—and answers—*Why did the worst possible thing happen to the very best Person?* This question lies at the heart of our religion. Our faith makes no sense without it.

Consider, no one could suffer more from evil than Jesus already has. The cross is history's greatest evil. Nothing could be more unjust and nothing could inflict more pain. The innocent Son of God bore the guilt of the world as He suffered horrific physical and spiritual agony. Crucifixion is the most barbaric, painful, and shameful way to die. That was the point.

Infinitely worse was the apparent rejection of Jesus by His Father. Jesus knew this moment was coming, and He sweat blood as He braced Himself for it. But the despair still crushed His soul to hell. He screamed, "My God, my God, why have you forsaken me?" (Matthew 27:46).

No one can comprehend what happened in that shattering, precarious moment. The Trinity has always existed in self-giving love, so what happened on the cross shouldn't even be possible. Perhaps the Spirit, who is the bond of love between the Father and Son, fiercely clutched both Persons to keep the Godhead together. If the Spirit's grip had slipped, the Godhead would have split apart and the entire creation would have exploded like a galactic atomic bomb. The moment passed, and God and our world survived.[21]

Why did God put Himself through such agony? Because of love. Jesus' sacrificial

History's worst evil dealt the death blow to evil.

death was the only way to conquer evil at the source. Jesus paid the price for our sin, and when He arose from the dead, He defeated evil forever. Jesus loves you so much that He literally went through hell to save you.

Are you suffering from intense pain? You have a God who knows exactly how you feel. Cry out to Him—He's been there, and He gets it. But He not only suffers with you; through His suffering, He has done something about it. Jesus' cross and resurrection have conquered evil, so evil will not—it cannot—have the last word. When you're in pain, call on God. He's right here, and He's got you.

117 Why did Cain murder Abel?

Think your family has issues? The world's first son murdered his brother.

Cain was a farmer, and his younger brother, Abel, a shepherd. In gratitude for their lives and prosperity, both brought an offering to the Lord. Abel gave God his best, "fat portions from some of the firstborn of his flock," while Cain halfheartedly threw in "some of the fruits of the soil." God was delighted with Abel's sacrifice, but "he did not look with favor" on Cain's effort. "So Cain was very angry," and he pouted (Genesis 4:3–5).

God confronted Cain. "Why are you angry?" the Lord asked. "Why is your face downcast?" *What did you expect?* "If you do what is right, will you not be accepted? But if you do not do what is right, sin is crouching at your door; it desires to have you, but you must rule over it" (Genesis 4:6–7).

Cain rejected God's counsel, and rather than wrestle his anger to the ground, he allowed his jealousy to blossom into envy. Jealousy says, "I want what you have." Envy is worse—it says, "If I can't have what you have, then I don't want you to have it." So Cain "attacked his brother Abel and killed him" (Genesis 4:8).

What? How did Adam's sin of eating a forbidden fruit lead to murder and in one generation? The answer is that both sins had the same root. When we act selfishly, we will do whatever we need to stay on top. We might even kill.

God confronted Cain again: "Where is your brother Abel?" Cain got snippy in reply. "I don't know. . . . Am I my brother's keeper?" Now it was God's turn to become angry. "What have you done? Listen! Your brother's blood cries out to me from the ground. Now you are under a curse and driven from the ground, which opened its mouth to receive your brother's blood from your hand. When you work the ground, it will no longer yield its crops for you. You will be a restless wanderer on the earth" (Genesis 4:9–12).

The world's first murder—by the world's first child—as envisioned by the 19th-century engraver Gustave Doré.

Cain's coldhearted pride inspired violence that led to a life on the lam. He would forever be a fugitive, scratching out an existence in an unfriendly world that resisted his efforts. Such is life without God: Look out for yourself. Strike first. And watch your back. (Do you see now why God warned Adam not to eat the forbidden fruit?)

It's too late to undo Adam's sin, but God's warning to Cain still hangs in the air. Sin stalks your heart. It is crouching, poised to leap and devour you. You must master it. But none of us can do this on our own—that's why Jesus came. The rest of the Bible tells God's plan, culminating in Jesus, to free us from sin and restore us to life.

The regretful and fearful Cain, a sculpture in Paris, France.

118 Who was Cain afraid of?

Cain was a cold-blooded killer. He slew his brother and didn't look back until God sentenced him to a life on the run. That got his attention. "Cain said to the LORD, 'My punishment is more than I can bear. Today you are driving me from the land, and I will be hidden from your presence; I will be a restless wanderer on the earth, and whoever finds me will kill me'" (Genesis 4:13–14).

Cain's cry raises an interesting question: If the only other people on earth are his parents and perhaps a sister or two, who is he afraid of?

The Bible doesn't answer all of our questions. It selects the most important details of a story but leaves a lot to our imagination. So we can't say for sure who these others are.

Some Christians take Cain's fear as evidence that Adam and Eve were not the only first humans. There must have been others nearby who, perhaps like Adam and Eve, evolved at roughly the same time from lower hominims. Others suggest the author of Genesis is being anachronistic, reading back into Cain's day something that would have been true of the author's world.

Others assume Cain feared revenge from his family, from siblings who had not yet been born. Who would have the most interest in killing Cain? Abel's family, who might want to avenge their brother's and uncle's blood. These younger brothers and nephews had not yet arrived, but Cain realized they were on the way. The day would soon come when an aging Cain would not be able to fend off younger, and more numerous family. To be safe, Cain moved away from family to "the land of Nod, east of Eden," and God put a mark on him "so that no one who found him would kill him" (Genesis 4:15–16).

119 Who did Cain marry?

After Cain moved to the land of Nod, he had sex with his wife and fathered a son (Genesis 4:17). This raises another interesting question: Where did Cain get a wife?

Some Christians take this as evidence that more people than just Cain's parents and sisters were alive at this time. Adam and Eve weren't the only first humans. They evolved with many, perhaps thousands of others, at about the same time.

Others say Cain's wife was his sister. This wouldn't have been a big deal then. If there was only one family, it wouldn't have seemed odd to marry your sister. And it wouldn't be an issue for some time. Much later in the biblical story, Abraham married his half sister, Sarah (Genesis 20:12). If Abraham married his half sister, why couldn't Cain marry his full sister?

Once again, the Bible doesn't include every detail or answer every question we might have. It tells us what God most wants us to know, leaving the rest for stimulating, late-night conversation.

A biblically inspired work by Daniel Chester French, the American sculptor who created the sitting figure of Abraham Lincoln in Washington DC's Lincoln Memorial.

120 Did angels have sex with humans?

No, this is not an idea for an HBO miniseries. The question actually arises from Scripture. The period immediately before the great flood was a legendary time. Genesis 6:4 says, "The Nephilim were on the earth in those days—and also afterward—when the sons of God went to the daughters of humans and had children by them. They were the heroes of old, men of renown."

The Hebrew term *Nephilim* means "fallen ones." In Numbers 13:33, the Israelite spies believed they could not conquer the Promised Land because the giant Nephilim lived there. "We seemed like grasshoppers in our own eyes, and we looked the same to them." These Nephilim seem to be descendants of "the sons of God," who "saw that the daughters of humans were beautiful, and they married any of them they chose" (Genesis 6:2).

Who were these "sons of God"? They might be sons of Seth—Adam and Eve's third son—or perhaps sons of Cain or some unknown kings. But "sons of God" means "angels" elsewhere in the Old Testament (Job 1:6; 2:1; 38:7), and Jewish tradition believed these angels assumed bodily form so they could have sex with women (1 Enoch 6–19).

The New Testament seems to agree. Peter seems to have this episode in mind when he writes, "God did not spare angels when they sinned, but sent them to hell, putting them in chains of darkness to be held for judgment" (2 Peter 2:4). Jude compares the angels' sin to Sodom and Gomorrah's sexual perversion, and says "the angels who did not keep their positions of authority but abandoned their proper dwelling—these he has kept in darkness, bound with everlasting chains for judgment on the great Day" (Jude 6).

This strange story implies important truths, such as the necessity of following God's rules for sex, and the interconnection between spiritual and physical powers and pleasures. It's included here to explain the unimaginable wickedness engulfing the earth. God decided to shorten the human lifespan to lessen the damage sinful giants could inflict. When that didn't help, He sent an epic flood and drowned everyone except one family.

121 Why would God destroy the world?

Because God is unfathomably patient. He put up with Adam's rebellion, Cain's homicide, Lamech's boast that he "killed a man for wounding me, a young man for injuring me" (Genesis 4:23), and angels sleeping with humans. Finally, "the LORD saw how great the wickedness of the human race had become on the earth, and

The detail in this 1827 painting *Scene of Deluge* is disturbing—as was the sin that brought on the flood.

that every inclination of the thoughts of the human heart was only evil all the time" (Genesis 6:5). There was nothing left to do but wipe the earth clean and start over. God would have to destroy the world in order to save it.

God sent a great flood because His patience had run out but also because He still had plenty left. He didn't annihilate the world and walk away. His floodwaters cleansed the earth, washing away its sin and corruption, so His plan for our planet could begin anew. The great flood meant God had not given up on this world.

He has remained patient ever since. Angels no longer have sex with humans, but many parts of the world reject God's created norms of sex and gender, attack peaceful neighbors, and brazenly murder those too weak to defend themselves. If God deemed it necessary to flood the earth in Noah's day, what must He think of us today?

Peter warns us not to get comfortable. As God cleansed the world with water, so one day He will purify the earth with fire (2 Peter 3:6–10). Patience must have a limit, or it's just a pushover. God is no pushover, and those who presume on His patience are bound to get burned. Noah's wicked neighbors probably laughed at him for building a big boat—until they felt a raindrop. Our wicked world scoffs at the notion of Jesus' fiery return. But if you're paying attention, you can already see the sparks.

Ponder Peter's question: "Since everything will be destroyed in this way, what kind of people ought you to be? You ought to live holy and godly lives as you look forward to the day of God and speed its coming" (2 Peter 3:11–12).

122 How could God "regret" making humans?

When God saw how wicked His world had become, He "regretted that he had made human beings on the earth, and his heart was deeply troubled" (Genesis 6:6). How should we understand this?

The Bible teaches that God is fully transcendent and fully immanent. That means He is both high above us and here with us; sovereignly unchanging yet involved with our lives. The Bible teaches both at different times, but it doesn't say both all the time.

The *statements* of Scripture emphasize God's transcendence. For instance, "I the LORD do not change" (Malachi 3:6); "God is. . .not a human being, that he should change his mind" (Numbers 23:19); "I make known the end from the beginning, from ancient times, what is still to come" (Isaiah 46:10).

The *stories* of Scripture emphasize God's immanence. He bartered with Abraham, agreeing to spare Sodom for the sake of fifty righteous people. Then forty-five, forty, thirty, twenty, and finally ten (Genesis 18:16–33). When He saw Abraham was willing to sacrifice his son, Isaac, He said, "Now I know that you fear God" (Genesis 22:12). *What?* How can the God who knows "the end from the beginning" also learn something new about Abraham?

The statements and stories of Scripture are two rails that keep our faith train on track. If we minimize the statements, we'll miss God's sovereign power. If we minimize the stories, we'll miss God's interaction in our lives. Both Scripture's statements and stories are anthropomorphic—they describe God in human terms so we can understand. We know God is infinitely more than anything we can say; we just can't say what that is.

When we read that God learned something about Abraham or that God was so troubled by the violence on earth that he regretted making human beings, we must remember that learning and regretting are both similar and different for God. They are similar enough to tell us something about God, but they are different enough to give us pause. God already knows everything, so He doesn't exactly learn; and He cannot change His mind, so He doesn't regret like us either.

God's regret was real. It was more real than any regret we can feel. God's heart was deeply troubled. More troubled than you or I ever could be. Yet unlike us, God remained in full control of His sorrow. His emotions did not overwhelm Him. He stooped to our level and chose to feel the agony of injustice and wickedness with us. All the while He remained fully sovereign, powerfully working through every event to accomplish His indomitable plan. Part of that plan was His feeling of regret.

Because we are mere creatures, we cannot comprehend how this works—but the Bible assures us that both things are true. God is fully transcendent and immanent, high above us and here with us. This doesn't explain how our sovereign God feels regret, but it shows us what to do with ours. When your heart is deeply troubled, unload your burden on the One who knows exactly how you feel. He cares, and He will carry you.

123 Did Noah's flood cover the whole world?

"Enlightened" modern folks often scoff at the idea that God flooded the entire world with water. The story seems too miraculous, too epic, to be taken seriously. But now some of those same people warn that climate change may raise sea levels and trigger a global flood. Which raises an interesting question: If a global flood may be in our future, why couldn't it also be in our past?

The Bible says God opened the springs beneath the earth and the floodgates above, and it rained for forty days and nights. The water "rose greatly on the earth, and all the high mountains under the entire heavens were covered" (Genesis 7:19). The ark eventually came to rest on "the mountains of Ararat" (Genesis 8:4), whose tallest peak is nearly 17,000 feet above sea level—so that would be a lot of water! This certainly sounds like a universal flood, which is how other biblical authors apparently understood it. Peter says God "did not spare the ancient world when he brought the flood on its ungodly people," adding that "the world of that time was deluged and destroyed" by water (2 Peter 2:5; 3:6).

Marine fossils are often found in places far from the sea—an indication, according to some, that Noah's flood covered the entire earth.

Despite this natural reading, other Christians note that a large regional flood would have been sufficient to drown the human race, which had not yet scattered far from Eden. From the perspective of ancient people living in Mesopotamia, the flooding of their land would have seemed like the whole world was underwater. They didn't know continents such as North and South America existed, so we shouldn't read too much into their claim that "all the high mountains under the entire heavens were covered."

Christians who believe in a worldwide flood point to fossils of sea creatures found on the tops of mountains. *How did they get there?* Other Christians say these fossils could have risen with the mountains that were pushed up as continental tectonic plates collided in an ancient sea. This difference of opinion is not surprising, as most evidence for anything can be interpreted in more than one way.

When it comes to the Bible and Christian thought, it's wise to side with the traditional view unless there is good reason not to. As in baseball, where a tie always goes to the runner, so in Christian faith the tie should go to the tradition. I don't have a compelling reason to disbelieve in a worldwide flood, though I leave room for Christians who think it's unlikely. (As long as their reasoning isn't because it's too epic or of "biblical" proportions.)

The story is in the Bible, so of course it's going to be Bible-sized! And given that scientists now warn a global flood is possible, the traditional view seems entirely plausible.

The rainbow is a sign of God's promise never again to destroy the earth with a flood (Genesis 9:8–16).

124 What is the Noahic Covenant?

When you love someone and want to commit to her (or him, if you're a woman), you enter into a covenant that promises what you will do for and what you can expect from her. Throughout the Bible, the God who loves His children makes and keeps covenants with them. His main covenants are the Abrahamic, Mosaic, Davidic, and the New Covenants (more on these later). His first is the Noahic Covenant.[22]

When the great flood had receded, God was so pleased with the righteous Noah and his family that He promised to restart His creation with them. As He had commanded Adam and Eve, God told Noah, "Be fruitful and increase in number and fill the earth" (Genesis 9:1). Remembering how quickly Cain had turned on Abel, God underscored the sanctity of human life, warning, "Whoever sheds human blood, by humans shall their blood be shed; for in the image of God has God made mankind" (Genesis 9:6).

God's covenant with Noah differed from the original creation story in two ways. First (and great news for those who like barbecue), God told Noah's family they were now free to eat meat. "Just as I gave you the green plants, I now give you everything" (Genesis 9:3; compare to 1:30). Second (and great news even for vegans), God promised never to destroy the world again with a flood. Then He signed this covenant with rainbows. Literally. God said, "Whenever the rainbow appears in the clouds, I will see it and remember the everlasting covenant between God and all living creatures of every kind on the earth" (Genesis 9:16).

Rainbows are signs of God's covenantal love and faithfulness. He saved the world through judgment once. And He will save it through judgment again, when Jesus returns to purify the earth through fire (2 Peter 3:6–13). Meanwhile, take every rainbow as God's bright signature on this world. He loves creation and patiently calls everyone to turn to Him.

125 What is the curse of Ham?

The Bible doesn't sugarcoat its heroes. In the same chapter that God established his covenant with righteous Noah, Noah got drunk and took off his clothes. His son, Ham, saw him lying exposed and told his brothers, Shem and Japheth. These two were more considerate than Ham, backing into the tent and covering up their dad without shaming him or seeing his naked body.

After Noah slept off his stupor and learned what Ham had done, he cursed Ham's son, Canaan. He said Canaan's children would become slaves of Shem's children (Genesis 9:25–27). We're not sure why Noah cursed Canaan for something his father had done, but the story foreshadows how the Canaanites would one day serve Israel in the Promised Land.

Tragically, this vignette has been misread, then wrenched out of context, and finally misapplied by wicked people to justify slavery in America and the genocide of Hutus in Rwanda. These people, with their inexcusably poor reading of the

Bible, claimed God's endorsement for their loathsome injustice. They said the people they were destroying were descendants of Ham, whom God had cursed.

But God did not curse anyone. *Noah* was the one who cursed. And he didn't curse Ham. Noah cursed Ham's son, Canaan, not Ham's other children who eventually settled in Africa. There is no curse of Ham, no biblical reason to enslave or kill millions of Africans. I suspect most of the slave owners throughout history knew this—or at least they would have if they had bothered to carefully read the story in Genesis 9:18–27.

If nothing else, they should have realized that if you think the Bible is telling you to kill or enslave another person, you are probably reading it wrong!

126 What was the tower of Babel?

A climactic symbol of humanity's power and potential for evil.

God told Adam and Eve that their children should spread out until they eventually subdued and ruled the entire creation. After the flood, He reissued the same command to Noah's family (see Genesis 1:28; 9:1, 7). But as Noah's descendants moved east, they decided they had traveled far enough. Rather than obey God and fill the entire earth, they settled down in Shinar, located in modern Iraq. They said, "Come, let us build ourselves a city [later named Babylon], with a tower that reaches to the heavens, so that we may make a name for ourselves; otherwise we will be scattered over the face of the whole earth" (Genesis 11:4).

God was impressed with their cooperation, but He wasn't pleased. "If as one people speaking the same language they have begun to do this," He said, "then nothing they plan to do will be impossible for them" (Genesis 11:6). This is an amazing observation. God understands what ingenuity He instilled in His human image bearers and admitted the sky's the limit. Actually, we've busted through that barrier and are now planning to inhabit other planets!

But God knew sinful people would use their cooperation to defy Him and "make a name" for themselves. So He mercifully confused their language so they couldn't understand each other. Imagine the people's shock when they realized their friends

Nobody knows exactly what the tower of Babel looked like. . .but here's an idea from the 16th-century Dutch painter Pieter Brueghel the Elder.

weren't joking. They really were speaking different languages! "Hand me a brick" was understood as "drink my beer," and the resulting fistfights ground construction to a halt. Angry and confused workers scattered "over the face of the whole earth," as God had commanded (Genesis 11:9).

The variety of human language adds to the beauty and interest of our world. It's also a sign of grace. God confused language so sinful people would struggle to cooperate in defying His authority. Much later, after Jesus had risen from the dead and ascended to heaven, the Spirit of Christ signaled the end of Babel confusion. He filled the followers of Jesus so that those who preached the Gospel could be understood by people in several dialects and languages (Acts 2:1–21). Christians disagree whether this gift of tongues continues today, but all agree it will return in heaven, when "a great multitude that no one could count, from every nation, tribe, people and language," will stand before the throne of God and praise Jesus for our salvation (Revelation 7:9–10).

Until then, technology such as Google Translate is a double-edged sword. Human potential exponentially increases when we immediately understand what everyone else is saying. We can accomplish much good—but because we're sinful, we can also cause great harm. As modern people learn better how to communicate and understand each other, we may reach another Babel moment that requires divine intervention. The Bible indicates that moment may be approaching, for Jesus is coming soon!

127 Why did people in Genesis live so much longer than us?

That's nothing. You should see how long people lived in the Mesopotamian myths. The Sumerian King List includes eight kings who lived a combined 241,000 years. That's some impressive genes! What do you buy a king for his thirty thousandth birthday?

Genesis critiques such fantastic tales with its more realistic lifespans. The first humans were not the demigods of Babylonian lore. But they still lived a long time. Adam died at 930, his son Seth at 912, Noah at 950, and Methuselah holds the age record at 969 (Genesis 5:5, 8, 27; 9:29). People lived such a long time that Noah would have known many people who knew Adam, and Noah himself would have lived long enough to meet Abraham!

We're not sure why the first people lived so long. Perhaps the world was more tropical. Maybe it's because people's bodies were not many generations removed from the original, perfect couple and therefore had fewer genetic mutations, which increase in each successive generation. Or perhaps the fall had not had time to fully unleash its lethal effects, such as the spread of disease. Whatever the proximate cause, we know the ultimate cause for our shortened lifespans was God: He saw the extent of human wickedness and said He would shorten our lifespan to 120 years

(Genesis 6:3). By the time of Moses, average life expectancy had fallen to 70 or 80 years (Psalm 90:10).

Don't be jealous of the first humans who lived nine hundred years. That's nothing. If you are in Jesus, the Last Adam, you will live on this redeemed earth forever. What do you buy a child of the King for his or her gazillionth birthday? Put your faith in Jesus, and you'll find out.

At age 96, this gentleman is 873 years shy of the biblical longevity record—Methuselah's 969 years.

PART 3: ISRAEL

Why the Old Testament Matters Today

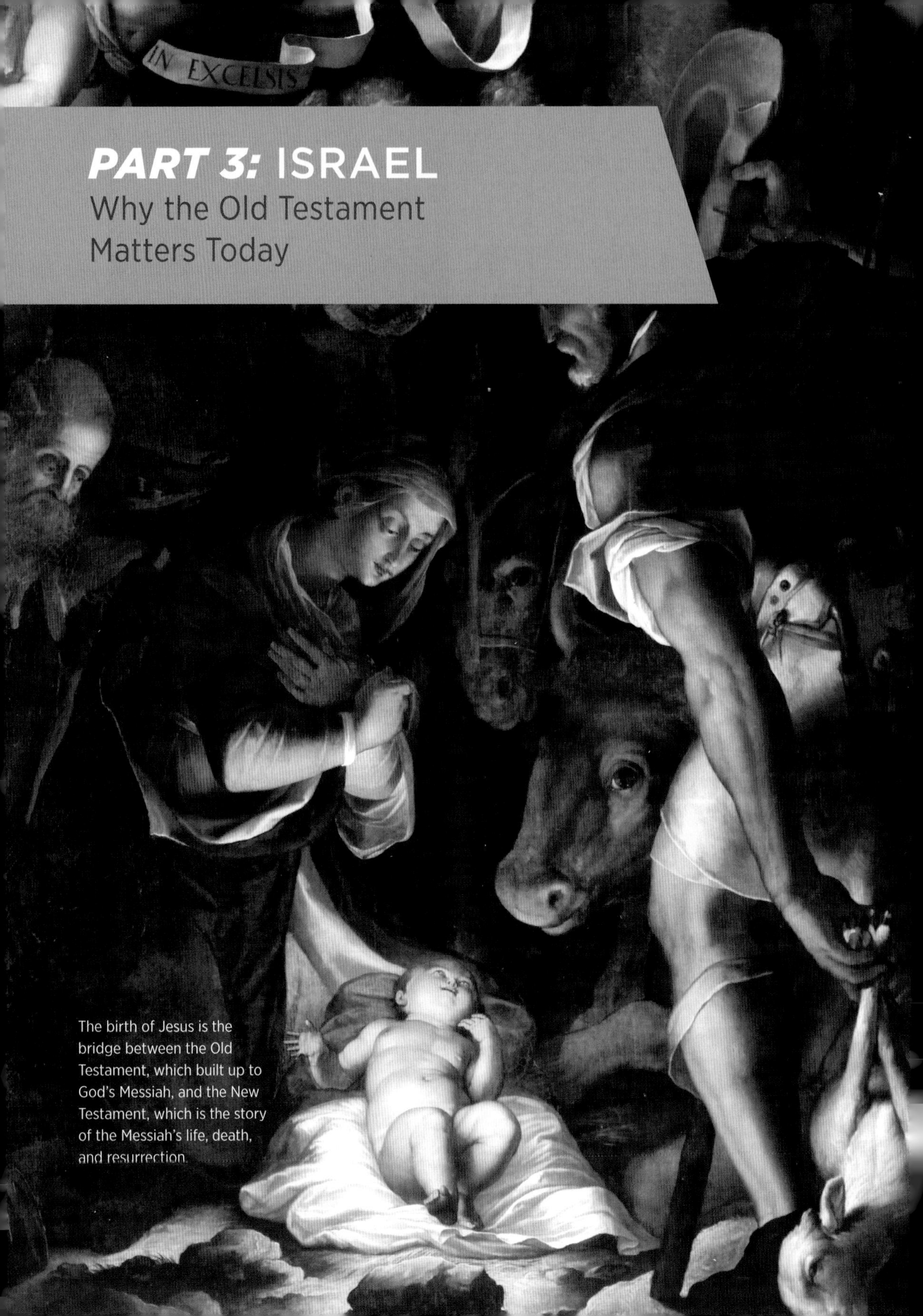

The birth of Jesus is the bridge between the Old Testament, which built up to God's Messiah, and the New Testament, which is the story of the Messiah's life, death, and resurrection.

128 How does the Old Testament relate to the New Testament?

Both testaments describe the same God, the same Savior (Jesus), and the same path of salvation. God's children have always been saved by grace through faith, which subsequently produces the fruit of obedience. Many churches reinforce this unity by reading each Sunday from the Old Testament, the Gospels, and the Epistles. The Gospels fulfill the Old Testament, and the Epistles explain the Gospels. It's the same story.

On the other hand, the testaments do focus on different groups of people—Israel in the Old and the church in the New. They cover different times—before and after Jesus came to earth. God gradually reveals more of Himself and His salvation plan as the story advances.

- In the Old Testament, God emphasized that He was one; in the New Testament, He reveals He is both one and three, the Trinity.
- God promised Old Testament saints that He would send a Messiah; in the New Testament, we learn this Messiah is Jesus, the divine-human Son.
- God gave Old Testament saints the law; Jesus intensified these commands for His New Testament disciples. Not only must they avoid acts of adultery and murder, they must not even harbor the lust and rage that leads to these sins.
- Old Testament saints were forgiven when they sacrificed spotless lambs in the temple; New Testament saints learned these sacrifices only worked because they pointed to the full and final sacrifice of Jesus, the perfect Lamb of God.

Christians agree on these main points, though we may differ on shades of emphasis:

Many churches emphasize the similarities between the testaments. They say Israel is the church of the Old Testament, and the church is the Israel of the New Testament.

The New Covenant, which Jesus established by His death and resurrection, is the continuation of the covenants in the Old Testament (Luke 22:20). So, as Old Testament Israel circumcised infants as a sign of their covenant, the church baptizes infants as a sign of our covenant. And since Israel finds its purpose in the church, the land that God promised to Abraham's children is fulfilled when all God's children inherit the new earth.

Other churches emphasize the differences between the testaments. They say Israel and the church are distinct, so promises made to one do not automatically apply to the other. For instance, the land that God promised Abraham's descendants is specifically for ethnic Jews. God will keep this promise when Jesus returns and gives Israel all of Palestine during His thousand-year reign on earth. Unlike Old Testament covenants that applied to every Israelite, the New Covenant only belongs to genuine followers of Jesus. Since the church is not Israel, it doesn't matter that Israel circumcised infants. The New Covenant is limited to born-again believers, so only those who express faith in Jesus are baptized.

Most churches throughout history leaned toward the similarity side, though the difference angle has recently become popular through what is called "dispensational theology." This emphasis on different dispensations, or time periods in the Old and New Testaments, began among the Plymouth Brethren in nineteenth-century England and continues to influence many American churches. Dispensationalists typically distinguish God's earthly promises made to Israel and His heavenly promises made to the church. The church receives its reward when it is secretly raptured to heaven, leaving Israel behind to suffer through seven years of tribulation before it finally welcomes Jesus, her Messiah, to return for His millennial reign of peace. Dispensational theology lies behind popular books such as *The Purpose-Driven Life* and *Left Behind.* (The latter was made into a movie, which, to no one's surprise, starred Nicholas Cage.)

As Christians continue to discuss the similarities and differences between the testaments, we're finding we agree on most things and all that are important. What unites us is stronger than what might keep us apart.

Abraham, holding a knife, nearly sacrifices his miraculously conceived son, Isaac. A later "son of Abraham," Jesus, would be sacrificed for the sins of the world.

129 What is the Abrahamic Covenant?

God's covenant with Abraham is the starting line of redemption. The fallen world of Genesis 3–11 is full of cursing: the ground is cursed, Cain is cursed, and the whole earth is destroyed by a flood. But in Genesis 12 the language changes. God speaks, and His words drip with blessing. He commands Abram to leave his pagan homeland and travel to the land of Canaan.

There, "I will make you into a great nation, and I will bless you; I will make your name great, and you will be a blessing. I will bless those who bless you, and whoever curses you I will curse; and all peoples on earth will be blessed through you" (Genesis 12:2–3).

God promises Abram three things:

1. ***People.*** Though Abram was seventy-five years old and childless, God promised his descendants would be "a great nation," as many as the stars in the sky (Genesis 15:5). God confirmed His promise by changing Abram's name to Abraham, from "exalted father" to "father of many" (Genesis 17:5).

2. ***Land.*** God told Abraham his children would inherit the land of Canaan, which is roughly where the state of Israel is now, but larger—including the modern areas of western Jordan, southwestern Syria, southern Lebanon, and the Golan Heights. God said, "The whole land of Canaan, where you now reside as a foreigner, I will give as an everlasting possession to you and your descendants after you; and I will be their God" (Genesis 17:8).

3. ***Blessing.*** Most important, God promised to bless "all peoples on earth" through Abraham and his descendants. God kept this promise when He sent Jesus, the Jewish descendant of Abraham, to die and rise again for our sin. Now the whole world can be reconciled to God, through the sacrifice of Abraham's Son.

God foreshadowed this climactic event when He commanded Abraham to sacrifice Isaac, his child of promise. Abraham bound young Isaac, put him on the altar, and raised his knife. But then the angel of the Lord shouted, "Abraham! Abraham! Do not lay a hand on the boy. Do not do anything to him. Now I know that you fear God, because you have not withheld from me your son, your only son" (Genesis 22:11–12).

A relieved Abraham and Isaac were spared that day. Instead, Abraham sacrificed a ram, which together with Isaac pointed toward the perfect Son of God, a lamb without blemish, who would give His life for us.

Every covenant has a sign, something to remember it by. Marriage covenants have wedding rings, Noah's covenant had a rainbow, and Abraham's covenant has circumcision. God told Abraham, "You are to undergo circumcision, and it will be the sign of the covenant between me and you. For the generations to come every male among you who is eight days old must be circumcised. . . . My covenant in your flesh is to be an everlasting covenant" (Genesis 17:11–13).

To this day every religious Jewish family circumcises its baby boys. Cutting off the baby's foreskin symbolizes the cutting away of sin and their hope for Abraham's covenant to be fulfilled. This happened when Jesus died to cut off our sin; it will be consummated when Jesus returns and destroys Satan and evil forever.

130 Who are the descendants of Ishmael, Isaac, Esau, and Jacob?

God promised Abraham and Sarah a son, but they were far too old to have children. Sarah grew impatient waiting for a child that her postmenopausal body would never bear, and she thought she'd help God out by telling Abraham to sleep with her servant, Hagar.

Hagar became pregnant, but that only made Sarah jealous. After Ishmael was born, Sarah pressured Abraham to send this son into the desert with his mother. Consider the irony: the father of our faith was a deadbeat dad!

God did keep His promise to Abraham, and ninety-year-old Sarah miraculously gave birth to a boy named Isaac. He grew up and married Rebekah, who bore him twin sons, Esau and Jacob. Esau came out first and owned the birthright. This ancient honor went to firstborn sons, making them responsible for their families and granting them a double inheritance. The value of a birthright depended on one's family. Abraham's is the most important family in history, so this birthright was priceless. But Esau traded it to his scheming brother, Jacob, for a measly pot of stew.

These four sons and grandsons of Abraham are the heads of great nations. Ishmael became the father of several Arab tribes (Genesis 17:20; 25:12–18). Most Arabs today do not descend from Ishmael, but some do. Muslims say the prophet Mohammed comes from Ishmael's line, and they claim Abraham as their physical and spiritual father.

Esau is the father of the people of Edom, who lived across the Dead Sea from Israel in what today is southwestern Jordan (Genesis 36). While Esau and Jacob were still in Rebekah's womb, God told her they would lead two nations, and "the older will serve the younger" (Genesis 25:23). This prophecy came true when Esau

Modern Jews, here seen celebrating a Bar Mitzvah in Jerusalem, are descendants of Abraham through Isaac and Jacob.

foolishly sold his birthright and then settled across the sea. The descendants of Esau never forgave Jacob (or his descendants) for his treachery, and Edom refused to let Israel pass through its country when Israel left Egypt for the Promised Land (Numbers 20). Edom also participated in Babylon's later plundering of Jerusalem and exile of its inhabitants (Psalm 137:7). God judged them for this, destroying Edom so that the race passed out of existence (Obadiah; Isaiah 34:5–15).

Together with their father and grandfather Abraham, Isaac and Jacob form the chosen line of Israel. Throughout the Old Testament, God identified Himself to Israel as the "God of Abraham, Isaac, and Jacob." Jacob never outgrew his deceitful ways, but God honored his birthright and changed his name to Israel (Genesis 32:27–28).

Jacob's sons became the heads of Israel's twelve tribes. This is the nation through which God kept His promise to Abraham. He would bless the world through the Jews, specifically through their Messiah, Jesus.

131 Why are God's people called Hebrews, Israel, and Jews?

God's Old Testament people go by three different names. Their first name was *Hebrews*, which was used to distinguish themselves from the Egyptians during their stay in Egypt. We're not sure where the name comes from. Perhaps it means descendants of Eber, who was a grandson of Shem and ancestor of Abraham (Genesis 10:21–25). Or it might come from a root word that means "one who has crossed over." Abraham had crossed rivers and boundaries to enter the land of Canaan and was called "Abram the Hebrew" to distinguish him from surrounding ethnic groups (Genesis 14:13). Either way, the name stuck. If you want to read the Old Testament in its original words, the language you must learn is Hebrew.

After the Hebrews left Egypt and returned to Canaan, their preferred name was *children of Israel* (alternately translated "people/sons/men of Israel"). God Himself gave them this name after an all-night wrestling match with their patriarch, Jacob. God appeared in human form—probably an Old Testament appearance of God the Son—and dislocated Jacob's hip. Jacob was in excruciating pain and thereafter would walk with a limp, yet he refused to let go until God blessed him. God refused until Jacob confessed who he was.

God asked, "What is your name?" (Genesis 32:27). After years of deceiving his brother and father, would Jacob cop to what he'd become? Would he name his sin?

He did, saying his name was Jacob, which means "deceiver." God saw Jacob had come to the end of himself, and said, "Your name will no longer be Jacob, but Israel, because you have struggled with God and with humans and have overcome" (Genesis 32:28).

The name *Israel* means "struggle." What an appropriate name for this beleaguered people! Even better, the name also means "God struggles." Through millennia of disobedience, exile, and genocide, the name "Israel" reminds the children of Jacob that God fights on their behalf. Their battle belongs to the Lord.

Israel's final name was *Jews*, which originally derived from Judah, one of Jacob's sons and the premier tribe of Israel. (Both King David and Jesus came from Judah.)

Jacob wrestles the angel of God and earns a new name, Israel, that will be applied to all of his descendants.

When the nation split between the north and south, the ten northern tribes took the name "Israel" and the two southern tribes called themselves "Judah." The northern tribes eventually were exiled and dissolved into surrounding nations, leaving Judah as the catchall term for the surviving followers of Yahweh. A citizen of Judah was called *Yehudi.* The Latin West later shortened the name, replacing the Y with a J to produce *Jew.*

The Jews preferred to call themselves "children of Israel," but their Gentile neighbors often referred to them as *Yehudi*—Jews. The Persians called Mordecai a Jew (Esther 2:5), the Babylonians said Daniel's three friends were Jews (Daniel 3:8,

12), and the Romans called Jesus the "King of the Jews," even though His Jewish opponents used the title "King of Israel" while mocking Him on the cross (Mark 15:2, 32).

Sometimes the Jews also are called *Semites*, a loose term that describes the ancient descendants of Shem and their common family of languages. This term wasn't used until the eighteenth century, and it's an oversimplification, but it generally refers to the inhabitants of the Middle East—both Jew and Arab—and their similar languages.

In sum, Israel is their preferred name, Jew is what others call them, and Hebrew is their first name as well as the name of their language.

132 Are the Jews God's special people?

Yes. Jacob and his children were chosen by God to be His own nation. Not because they were large or mighty, because they weren't. God chose them simply because He loved them (Deuteronomy 7:7–8). Then God stuck with His people through their repeated rebellion and serving of other gods. He did exile them to Babylon but soon relented and brought them home.

God is Team Israel. He didn't give up on the Jews when they killed His Son. His apostles preached the good news about Jesus first to Jews in Jerusalem (Acts 2). But most Jews did not warm up to the good news, as they would have to admit *they* had crucified the Son of God. Unable to accept this message, they attacked the messengers, threatening, beating, and stoning the apostles until finally Paul had enough. He shook the dust off his feet and said from then on he would preach to Gentiles (Acts 13:46–52).

But that was always the plan, starting with the Abrahamic Covenant. God would begin with the children of Abraham, Isaac, and Jacob and then branch out to include everyone else. Jews would always be welcome, and many will return to God and believe in Jesus in the last days (Romans 11:26). But the promise is not exclusively theirs.

All of God's promises to Abraham are fulfilled in the church, which is the spiritual people of God. All except perhaps one. God promised Abraham that his children

An Israeli soldier with the flag of the modern Jewish nation.

would one day inhabit the entire land of Israel. This hasn't happened yet, and dispensational Christians believe God will keep this promise during the millennium, a future thousand years of peace when Jesus will rule the earth from Jerusalem. Even nondispensationalist Christians admit it seems significant that Israel has become a nation again. God may not be finished with the ethnic children of Abraham just yet.

Still, most Jews living in Israel today are nonreligious. They don't pretend to follow God, and so in the most important sense they are not God's people. A Palestinian Christian is God's child in a way these secular Jews are not. God is Team Israel but not blindly so. When discussing Middle Eastern politics, we must not reflexively take Israel's side, assuming they should always get their way because they are God's chosen people. Neither should we overreact and uncritically support Palestine. Sharing God's concern for justice, we must be as impartial as possible while we pray for both Palestinians and Israelis to ultimately find their peace in Jesus.

133 Who is Yahweh?

This is the question of Exodus, the Bible's second book. Moses was tending sheep for his pagan father-in-law in the Midianite wilderness when he noticed a bush that had caught fire but did not burn up. Puzzled, he approached for a closer look. Then God spoke to Moses from the bush.

God said that He was the God of Abraham, Isaac, and Jacob and that He was sending Moses to rescue his people from their slavery in Egypt. Moses had questions—including who exactly this God was. Many "gods" existed in Moses' world. His father-in-law was a priest for some of them. What made this God different? *When the Israelites ask for Your name, what should I tell them?*

God answered, "I AM WHO I AM. This is what you are to say to the Israelites: 'I AM has sent me to you' " (Exodus 3:14). God continued, "This is my name forever, the name you shall call me from generation to generation" (verse 15).

God's name is a verb of being, which means His existence is His essence. God has always existed and always will—His name may also read "I WILL BE WHAT I WILL BE." God cannot kill Himself or go out of existence. He is the unchangeable creator and sustainer of everything else. Whatever exists finds its origin and meaning in Him.

The tetragrammaton—the four-letter name of God that we pronounce as Yahweh—in a church window in Paris.

We're not sure how Moses pronounced the letters that comprise God's name (YHWH), because written Hebrew in his day did not include vowels. By the third century BCE, religious Jews had stopped saying God's name altogether. They had learned from the Babylonian Captivity that God hates idolatry, and they feared that making a mistake when saying God's name would break the command to not "misuse the name of the LORD your God"

(Exodus 20:7). Rather than risk mispronouncing God's personal name, they instead said *Adonai*, the Hebrew term for Lord. Greek-speaking Jews followed suit when they translated the Old Testament into Greek (a version called the Septuagint), replacing YHWH with *kurios*, the Greek word for Lord. Our English Bibles revert back to the Hebrew of the original Old Testament, using "LORD" (in what is called caps and small caps) when translating YHWH and the lowercase "Lord" when referring to Adonai.

One more development: Between the sixth and tenth centuries CE, when Masoretic scribes (Jewish scholars who edited and copied the authoritative text of the Old Testament) inserted vowel points into written Hebrew, they combined the consonants of YHWH with the vowels of Adonai. This created the name *Yahweh*. Latin does not have a Y, so Western Christians substituted a J and pronounced the name *Jehovah*. When we say "Jehovah," we are saying "Yahweh," the personal name of God.

Back to the burning bush. God told Moses to go tell the elders of Israel, "The LORD [Yahweh], the God of your fathers—the God of Abraham, Isaac, and Jacob" was about to "bring you up out of your misery in Egypt into the land of the Canaanites. . .a land flowing with milk and honey" (Exodus 3:16–17). Then Moses and the elders together would meet Pharaoh and demand he let God's people leave.

Pharaoh was unimpressed. He asked, "Who is the LORD [Yahweh], that I should obey him and let Israel go?" (Exodus 5:2). Ten devastating plagues later, Pharaoh had a pretty good idea. That's next.

134 Did God or Pharaoh harden Pharaoh's heart?

This may be hard to accept, but God says plainly that *He* hardened Pharaoh's heart at every stage. From the jump, when God told Moses to deliver His message to the king of Egypt, He said, "I will harden his heart so that he will not let the people go" (Exodus 4:21). Midway through the ten plagues, when a stubborn Pharaoh refused to give in, God told Moses to tell him, "I have raised you up for this very purpose, that I might show you my power and that my name might be proclaimed in all the earth" (Exodus 9:16). And at the end, when a broken Pharaoh finally relented, God said He would harden the king's heart one last time, inciting him to send his army after the Israelites. God would "gain glory for myself through Pharaoh and all his army" when He drowned their pursuing charioteers in the Red Sea (Exodus 14:4).

In the New Testament, God comments on this hardening, saying it's a necessary aspect of His sovereignty (Romans 9:14–26). We can trust our almighty God who holds the hearts of kings in His hands, turning them however He pleases for His glory and fame. No one is unreachable, for God will have mercy on anyone He chooses. And no judgment is wasted, for God's patience in putting up with people like Pharaoh only highlights "the riches of his glory" toward "the objects of his mercy, whom he prepared in advance for glory" (verse 23).

But God's hardening is only half the story. The Bible also says Pharaoh hardened his own heart (see Exodus 8:15, 32; 9:34), which makes him responsible for his sin. He is not a victim. As mere creatures, we cannot comprehend this—but the Bible says both things are true. God is fully sovereign, so Pharaoh's actions are controlled by God. And Pharaoh is a free human agent, so he is responsible for his choices.

Pharaoh defies Moses' God-given commands in a 19th-century fresco from a Viennese church.

Finite creatures can't explain how divine sovereignty and human responsibility coalesce, but we need both to be true. Human responsibility means we can't blame God for our sin. Our choices are on us. Divine sovereignty means we may cry out to God who can save us from our sin. Won't you?

135 What is the Exodus?

The Exodus is the redemptive event of the Old Testament, the paradigm for God's future redemptive acts. God writes a compelling story, and like any good author, includes elements in this first redemption that anticipate what He would later accomplish through Jesus. Several facets of the Exodus story are filled up in the life and work of Christ.

1. ***Out of Egypt.*** Centuries after the Exodus, God reflected on His deliverance and said, "When Israel was a child, I loved him, and out of Egypt I called my son" (Hosea 11:1). Centuries after that, Jesus' parents fled with their baby from the jealous King Herod to the safety of Egypt. They stayed there until Herod died and so added another, climactic layer to the Exodus story, "Out of Egypt I called my son" (Matthew 2:13–15).

2. ***Passover.*** The evening of the Exodus, when God had exhausted Egypt with nine oppressive plagues, He told Israel to prepare for the knockout punch. They should sacrifice a lamb, smear some of its blood on the doorframes of their homes, and eat its meat in a special meal with bitter herbs—symbolizing their hardship in Egypt—and bread without yeast, which symbolized their separation from sin. That night the Lord killed the firstborn son of every person and animal, passing over and sparing the families that had blood on their doorframes (see Exodus 11–12). A millennium later, Jesus was crucified at Passover. He is our Passover Lamb, and those who apply His shed blood to their lives are saved from destruction and for new life in Him.

3. ***God of salvation.*** The name *Yahweh* appears throughout Genesis, but it isn't explained until the Exodus, when God tells Moses to tell the Israelites that "I AM" has sent you (Exodus 3:14). Jesus identified with this God and this salvation. He told His skeptical opponents, "before Abraham was born, I am!" (John 8:58).

4. ***Moses.*** Moses told Israel that someday God would raise up another prophet like himself (Deuteronomy 18:15–19). This new Moses turned out to be Jesus. As Moses went up the mountain to receive the law, so Jesus sat on a mountainside and delivered His commands that intensified and superseded what Moses had given (see Matthew 5). Jesus fulfilled Moses' law by His life, death, and resurrection and so rescued His followers in the most powerful and permanent way.

5. ***Deliverance from bondage.*** This is a big one. Just as Moses led Israel from the bondage of Egypt, so Jesus frees us from the slavery of sin.

6. ***Judgment on unbelievers.*** God's salvation inevitably brings judgment on those who don't believe. Egypt suffered through ten plagues and the deaths of their firstborn sons; today, whoever rejects the salvation offered by God's Son, Jesus, "will not see life, for God's wrath remains on them" (John 3:36).

7. ***Destruction of false gods.*** God's plagues humbled Pharaoh and demonstrated the weakness of his gods. Egyptians worshiped the Nile River and its life-giving waters, so God turned their precious water into blood. They worshiped the frog goddess who assisted in childbirth, so God littered their land with toads. They worshiped the sun, so God smothered them with utter darkness. God didn't merely judge the people who oppressed His children; He humiliated their gods (Exodus 12:12). Jesus also demands our total allegiance. We must deny all competitors, even ourselves, and take up our cross and follow Him (Matthew 16:24).

8. ***Salvation through water.*** Israel wasn't safe from Pharaoh until they passed through the Red Sea. God calls this a kind of baptism, which today is used to initiate believers into the church (1 Corinthians 10:1–2; 12:13).

9. ***Salvation for community.*** The Israelites were not rescued separately but as a group. The Exodus united them into a single, redeemed people. Similarly, Jesus saves us individually but not in isolation. He unites us together in His body, the church.

10. Salvation to an inheritance. The Israelites left Egypt on a journey. They were headed to the Promised Land! We have left the bondage of sin and are also on pilgrimage not to another place but to another time. We are headed toward the return of Jesus, when He will live with us forever here, on this restored earth.

136 Is there historical evidence for the Exodus?

We have evidence from Egypt that someone like the Israelites had lived there as slaves. Paintings in Egyptian tombs depict foreign slaves making bricks, as the Bible says (Exodus 1:11–14; 5:6–21). Archaeologists found a slave house that was divided into four rooms—three parallel rooms butting against a perpendicular room on the end—which was typical for Jewish homes. Also, an ancient papyrus shows a Semitic name for Egypt's Lakes of Pithom, an indication that some Jewish group had lived there long enough to inject words into the Egyptian language. We also know from an Egyptian source that by the late thirteenth century BCE, Israel was living in Canaan. Pharaoh Merneptah commemorated his victories with a victory stele that includes his defeat of a people named Israel around 1219 BCE. This is the earliest extra-biblical mention of Israel.

So we know from sources in Egypt that a people like Israel had lived there and that Israel eventually made it to the Promised Land. We don't have direct archaeological evidence for the journey itself, mostly because the traveling Israelites lived in tents, which don't leave foundations for future archaeologists to discover. Also, three millennia of erosion have swept away much of what would have been there, and it's not always obvious where to dig. Who's going to shovel small holes in a vast desert, looking for what nomads left behind three thousand years ago?

Scholars debate the *timing* of the Exodus—did it occur in 1446/7 BCE or around 1270–60 BCE? They also debate the *size* of the Exodus—did two million Israelites cross the desert or merely tens of thousands? Most English translations say the Exodus contained six hundred thousand men, which with women and children would yield more than two million travelers (Exodus 12:37; 38:25–26). Others say that's a lot of people, and the Hebrew term translated "thousand" might only mean "group" or "clan," which would make a much smaller number.

These discussions will continue among Christians, though some Egyptologists conclude the Exodus is the most widely attested event of the Late Bronze Age.[23] If you doubt the Exodus, you may have to doubt everything else about this period.

137 Why are there so many miracles in the Bible?

Most of us don't experience regular, no-doubt-about-it miracles, so the stories in the Bible may seem suspicious. Did the Red Sea actually part for the Israelites? Did water gush from a rock? Did fire fall from the sky and consume Elijah's sacrifice?

A widow's son returns to life by the intercession of the prophet Elijah.

Really? If the miracles in the Bible are real, shouldn't we experience them too?

Not necessarily. Even in the Bible, miracles don't occur all the time. They appear in clusters, bunched around God's redemptive events. Redemption requires divine intervention, so miracles inevitably happen as God reaches down to save His people. Moses and Jesus performed the most miracles because they were leading God's people from the bondage of Egypt and the slavery of sin. Prophets such as Elijah and Elisha also did miracles, which authenticated their message. The Israelites needed to know the prophets' warnings came from God.

We live between redemptive events—Jesus' first and second comings to earth—so we don't often see miraculous signs and wonders. However, God says that we will see an uptick of miracles in the last days, so expect to encounter more inexplicable events as we approach the return of Christ (Joel 2:28–32; Acts 2:16–21). It may already be happening.

138 How did Israel become a nation?

Jacob's twelve children and their descendants lived a few hundred years in Egypt (Exodus 12:40–41). They shared the same family, language, and culture, but they did not become a united political group—a nation—until the Exodus. As the thirteen North American colonies didn't become the United States until they broke free from Britain, so Jacob's descendants did not become Israel until they were rescued from Egypt.

God brought them straightaway to Mount Sinai, where He declared the covenant that would define them as a nation. God said, "Now if you obey me fully and keep my covenant, then out of all nations you will be my treasured possession. Although the whole earth is mine, you will be for me a kingdom of priests and a holy nation" (Exodus 19:5–6).

This was Israel's Fourth of July, the day it gained independence by declaring its dependence on God. God promised to bring them into the Promised Land and bless them forever—so long as they kept their end of the covenant.

139 What are the Ten Commandments?

Have you heard this one? Moses comes down from Mount Sinai and addresses the children of Israel. "The good news is I got Him down to ten. The bad news is 'don't commit adultery' is still in." The joke is funny because it exaggerates something that feels true: the Ten Commandments seem restrictive. Why does God want to limit our fun?

He doesn't. His commands are for our joy. They are the path to life. David exclaimed, "Oh, how I love your law! I meditate on it all day long. . . . How sweet are your words to my taste, sweeter than honey to my mouth!" (Psalm 119:97, 103). David understood that God's commands give freedom, freedom to know Him and to flourish in life.

When God miraculously delivered Israel from the bondage of Egypt, He asked this grateful people if they would like to become His special nation. They said yes, so God cut the Mosaic Covenant with them, promising to be their God and giving them a constitution to follow. This constitution is the Ten Commandments.

God divides the commands into two parts, or tables: the first four address love for Him and the final six address love for neighbor. Jesus said these two loves are inextricably connected. When asked to choose the greatest command, He couldn't pick just one but had to give two: love God and love your neighbor (Mark 12:28–31). This double love decree is the point of the Ten Commandments. Do you want to love God and others? Keep these commands:

1. "You shall have no other gods before me."

2. "You shall not make for yourself an image" of God or gods.

3. "You shall not misuse the name of the Lord your God."

4. "Remember the Sabbath day by keeping it holy."

5. "Honor your father and your mother."

6. "You shall not murder."

7. "You shall not commit adultery."

8. "You shall not steal."

9. "You shall not give false testimony against your neighbor."

10. "You shall not covet. . .anything that belongs to your neighbor" (Exodus 20:1–17).

With Mount Sinai in the background, Moses shares God's Ten Commandments with the new nation of Israel.

The repeated "You shall not's" sound negative, but they're actually the most positive way to give a command. By marking off the boundary of what we must not do, God opens a wide world for our enjoyment. "Don't murder, steal, or commit adultery" means we and others are free to enjoy life with our spouse and the possessions that God has given us. Everyone wants to live in a world where the Ten Commandments (at least the second table) are followed. The Supreme Court of the United States even has them engraved on its doors and on the wall behind its nine judges.

We all want other people to keep the Ten Commandments, but no one always does. That's why we need Jesus. From the moment God cut His covenant with Israel, He planned for this law to lead us to Him.

140 How does the law relate to grace?

Christians sometimes struggle to reconcile the law with grace, God's rules for life with the freedom we have in Christ. Some say that since we're saved by grace, we shouldn't worry about rules. We're free to live as we please. They suppose God is a soft-hearted pushover who bankrolls their indulgent lifestyle. He doesn't ask for anything and He'll forgive whenever they ask, no questions asked.

Others take the opposite tack. They are so focused on keeping God's law that they crowd out grace. They imagine God as a stern policeman aiming a radar gun at their lives, waiting to catch them being careless so He can pull them over. They forget that God is merciful and that His law gives freedom and life.

Here's how the Bible puts together law and grace, God's rules and His forgiveness:

1. ***God's grace includes His law.*** God loves His people and wants the best for them, so He tells them both how to live and that He will forgive their failure when they repent and turn to Him. His covenant of grace with Israel included the law because God wanted His people to flourish with Him and with each other.

2. ***God's law leads to grace.*** God knew Adam's fall had corrupted all people and that Israel would ultimately reject His law and refuse to do what He said. So God gave the law another purpose: to show people their sin and lead them back to Him. God's law is a mirror that reveals our many blemishes and need for the forgiveness of Christ. When we compare our lives with God's law, we immediately understand that we cannot earn God's acceptance. We throw ourselves on the mercy of the court. If God does not forgive our sin, we are finished.

3. ***God's grace includes His law, again.*** God does forgive and reconcile us to Himself. The law serves its purpose to bring us to God, who saves and empowers us to keep the enhanced law of Christ. God's new covenant with His church contains the law too. Not because our acceptance with God depends on keeping His rules, but because God wants us to enjoy our best possible life. Salvation starts now and necessarily includes obedience to God's law.

God saved us from the bondage of sin so we can live full and free. The highest freedom is not doing anything we want but wanting to do what we should. As a train is only free if it remains on the tracks, so we are only free as we keep our lives on the rails of God's law. A train that leaves its railway and cuts across a field will instantly get stuck. And people who leave God's rules and go their own way will bog down in the muck. The choice to sin may feel free at first, but that choice forms habits that harden into character. We soon realize we can't change who we've become, even if we want to. We have become slaves to sin.

Praise God for His grace that patiently forgives our sin. Grace is essential for our relationship with Him. But don't dismiss the law, which serves grace in two ways. It leads us to God by revealing our sin, and once we're forgiven, graciously shows us the best way to live.

141 Should Christians keep the Sabbath?

The Ten Commandments are repeated in the New Testament. And not just repeated—they are transposed into a higher key. Jesus said it's not enough to not murder. We must not angrily curse another. It's not enough to avoid adultery. We must not lust either.

Each of the Ten Commandments is repeated in the New Testament, except one. Followers of Jesus are not required to keep the Sabbath because its seventh day rest has been filled up in our salvation rest in Him (Colossians 2:16–17; Romans 14:5–6; Hebrews 4:1–11). If you're a Christian, you are not commanded to rest every seventh day.

Observant Jews program elevators to avoid the labor of pushing its buttons on the Sabbath. How does this command apply to Christians?

But why wouldn't you? God gave Israel the Sabbath command immediately after He rescued them from Egypt. Weeks in Egypt were ten days long. Put three together and you get a month.

One week rolled into another, week after week, month after month, and the Hebrew slaves rarely got a break. Imagine their delight when God gave them a new calendar! From now on they would follow a seven-day week, with a Sabbath rest guaranteed every seventh day. What a gift! God demanded they knock off one day each week, a regular reminder they weren't in Egypt anymore.

The Israelites rested one day each week to enjoy life and commemorate their deliverance from Egypt. Their regular rest reminded them their salvation came from God. It was not their doing (Deuteronomy 5:12–15).

We are wise to follow their example. If the Sabbath rest points to our salvation rest in Jesus, then resting every seventh day is a silent witness to our faith in Christ. We won't work every single day because we don't have to. Jesus has come. Our salvation is secure. We rest physically as a sign that we are resting spiritually.

If you're not in the habit of resting every seventh day, ask yourself why. If it's because you're free in Christ and don't have to, then fine. But if it's because you're afraid to stop, you've bitten off more than you can do in six days, or you've got to keep up with the competition, then not fine. *What are you saying?* My significance and security are not settled in Jesus. I've got to keep working, 24/7, to make something of myself. Such constant striving is a sign we don't really believe.

Jesus said it's okay to work on the Sabbath if there is an emergency (Luke 14:5). If someone needs help, give them a hand, even if it's on Sunday. (Christians observe the Sabbath on Sunday—that is, the Lord's Day—because that was the day Jesus arose from the dead.)

Emergencies aside, I've learned to treasure my Sabbath rest. Every seventh day is a guaranteed holiday. I refuse to show up for work. Every Sunday I get to do whatever I want, because I want. I get to be unproductive, on purpose. I aim to do nothing of pragmatic or economic value. I do whatever makes me happy. Read a book, go for a walk, play in the yard, take a nap.

As much as I love my Sabbath rest, every Lord's Day is a test of faith. Do I trust Jesus enough to take a break, worshiping with the church and putting aside my work for an entire day? When I take the day off, not only am I refreshed for the week ahead, but without saying a word, I testify to my salvation in Christ.

The Sabbath is not a duty. It's a gift. Do you feel harried and overcommitted?

Wondering where the years have gone? A Sabbath rest will slow life down long enough for you to linger and savor its many treasures. Your new life doesn't merely begin today. If today is Sunday, your new life *is* today. May it refresh you in the Lord.

This boy in Afghanistan depicts an ancient rule that God gave to Israel: "Do not muzzle an ox while it is treading out the grain" (Deuteronomy 25:4).

142 Why did God give Israel so many meticulous rules?

See "How should I read the Law?" (page 114) for insights on specific rules, such as not eating pork or weaving two kinds of material into the same clothes. I'll try not to repeat what I said there but make a few additional observations.

The greatest command is to love God and your neighbor. This is the point of the law. Every command in the Old Testament is aimed either at loving God or loving neighbor, and often both (Deuteronomy 6:5; Leviticus 19:18; Mark 12:28–31).

This double love command is the foundation for the two tables of the Ten Commandments, which was Israel's constitution. This constitution then supplied the basis for particular case laws. What to do when planting a fruit tree, eating meat, or getting a haircut? Individual laws gave specific directions (Leviticus 19:23–27). The first five books of the Bible contain 613 specific laws. It may not be obvious today, but they all point back to the Ten Commandments, which in turn point to our need to love God and others.

God's very precise rules also taught Israel the concept of holiness. God is holy, set apart from everything else, and His people must be distinctive too. Many of God's rules aimed to keep Israel separate from the idol-worshiping pagans in the land. Israel was God's light, the people through whom He would send the Messiah to save the world. For the sake of the world, Israel needed to keep her light bright until the Messiah came. So God told Israel to defeat their idolatrous neighbors. Don't make friends or let your kids marry theirs, because then your love for God will cool and your mission will fail (Deuteronomy 7:1–6). We know the risk was real, because Israel did let her guard down and had to be destroyed, at least for a while.

God's meticulous laws also taught Israel discipline, which is essential for holiness and a healthy life. Perhaps God's case laws seem over the top because our do-whatever-feels-good culture doesn't appreciate virtue and the discipline it requires. But that says more about us than about Israel's God.

We Christians are not the Jewish nation, so we no longer keep the case laws that applied to ancient Israel. But those 613 laws still teach us discipline, holiness, and principles for loving God and neighbor.

143 Why the Year of Jubilee?

Rest is so important that God demanded even the Sabbaths should have a Sabbath. Every seventh day, people and farm animals must get to rest. Every seventh year, the land must lie fallow and take a break. Every seventh Sabbath year, or fiftieth year, both people and land must celebrate the Sabbath of Sabbaths, or Year of Jubilee.

We're not sure if Israel ever observed this special year. Taking Sabbaths was a test of faith, and Israel was exiled from the Promised Land in part for not trusting God enough to observe this command (2 Chronicles 36:21).

The Year of Jubilee was intended to free Israelite slaves and return the land to its original occupants (Leviticus 25). This was not a form of socialism, as money and possessions other than land were not redistributed. The Israelites could still buy and sell land; they simply calculated the price based on how much time remained until the Year of Jubilee (verses 15–17). The Jubilee did turn the nation of Israel into renters rather than owners. This was the point, to remember the Promised Land belonged to the Lord (verse 13).

The Year of Jubilee provided a safety net and kept the parcels of Promised Land in the tribes and clans who first received it (Leviticus 25:10). A poor Israelite could not squander his family's inheritance. Every fifty years his family would return to their ancestral land and start fresh.

The Year of Jubilee was meant to be a celebration. Israel received an additional year of rest every fifty years to remember that Yahweh was Lord of both time and space. If they could trust Him with their years and with their land, they could trust Him with their lives. But this was the problem: Israel didn't trust God enough to observe His Sabbaths. So God didn't trust them, and He removed them from His land. The proposed jubilee became a curse. That is, until Jesus, who is our Christian Jubilee. He frees us from sin and invites us to rest in Him. Jesus will return to rule with us over all the land of the whole earth.

144 Why did God demand animal sacrifice to forgive sin?

Because God is love. Our triune God is love which is righteousness which is life. If God is these perfections, then the opposite must also be true. The opposite of love is selfishness, the opposite of righteousness is sin, and the opposite of life is death. So selfishness is sin which is death.

God can't ignore that sin is death. He can't brush sin away and pretend it's no big deal. He can't act as if it didn't happen. If selfishness and sin are not death, then

His love and righteousness are not life.

So God has a problem: He loves us and yearns to forgive us, but He must remain faithful to who He is. God's loving and righteous life demands that selfishness and sin bring death. God would violate His character if He were to forgive us without requiring the payment of death. Reality would rupture; the universe would disappear.

Modern people struggle with the idea of sacrificing innocent animals. Perhaps the ancients did too.

There is one solution. Only one.

Our sin requires that someone must die, but happily it doesn't have to be us. God volunteered and sent His only Son to be the atoning sacrifice for our sin (1 John 2:2; 4:10). Jesus' death counts for everyone who puts their faith in Him.

But what about those who lived before the crucifixion of Christ? God commanded them to sacrifice lambs, bulls, and goats as a sign of the ultimate sacrifice who was to come. Old Testament saints didn't understand exactly how their sacrifices worked—could the death of an animal really take away sin?—but they faithfully obeyed. God took their killing of spotless lambs as a foreshadowing of the Lamb of God, and He forgave their sin for Jesus' sake (Hebrews 10:1–10).

It seems terrible to slaughter an innocent little lamb, and that's the point. Our sin is far worse than we imagine. It's responsible for the death of hundreds of thousands of animals. Infinitely worse, it crucified the Son of God. Jesus willingly paid the ultimate price for you because He is God, and God is love.

145 Why don't Jews sacrifice animals today?

A partial answer is that many Jews are secular. In the modern world, being Jewish is more an ethnic identity than a religion. As long as your mother is Jewish, you're a Jew regardless of what you believe or how you live—even if you're an atheist. Many Jews wouldn't offer animal sacrifices because they don't believe in the God of their Bible.

But they couldn't sacrifice even if they wanted to. Animal offerings went away when the place of sacrifice, the temple in Jerusalem, was destroyed. The first time it was razed, by the Babylonians in 586 BCE, demoralized Jews who were scattered throughout the nations regrouped around their sacred Scriptures. They could no longer worship on the Temple Mount in Jerusalem, the one place where God accepted sacrifice, but they could gather in synagogues each Sabbath to read the Scriptures and pray. These weekly meetings were precursors to Christian worship services. Yet today, a Christian visitor to a Jewish synagogue will recognize main elements of the service: Scripture reading, prayer, singing, and a sermon. Synagogue auditoriums even look a lot like a church.

Jews kept their synagogues when they returned from exile and rebuilt the temple. Animal sacrifices were again offered in Jerusalem, but weekly synagogue services remained useful to those living outside the capital. Jews wanted to avoid another exile, and their synagogue gatherings focused their hearts on God's Word and what He required. It's a good thing they kept the synagogues, because when their second temple was destroyed, this time by the Romans in 70 CE, the synagogues again were all they had left.

This remains true today. The temple has not been rebuilt because, in the seventh century, Islam arose and claimed the Temple Mount as the place where Mohammed ascended to heaven. (What are the odds that out of all the patches of ground on earth, a new religion would claim one of its holy spots is the exact same place as another's? The coincidence might make a hardened skeptic reconsider belief in God and a devil who tries to thwart His plans.)

The Temple Mount is the most contested, combustible real estate in the world. Its thirty-seven acres will never be for sale. The nation of Israel controls the space. Israeli police guard the entrances and exits and patrol the site. But Israel cedes religious authority over the Mount to Muslims. Only Muslim prayers are permitted there. Jews and Christians are forbidden to sing, pray, or make any type of religious display. Muslims built the Dome of the Rock on the spot where they believe Mohammed ascended to heaven, near where the temple originally stood. Muslims also built the even holier Al-Aqsa Mosque nearby, on the southern edge of the Mount.

Religious Jews and Muslims continually spar over the Temple Mount. If you visit, you may hear Muslims yelling "Allah Akbar" at Jewish agitators protesting they have the right to be there. These orthodox Jews might one day gain control over the area, destroy the Dome of the Rock, and build a third temple. But not without igniting World War III. Stay tuned.

Lightning is a common metaphor for God's wrath. How does this image relate to the God of love revealed in Jesus?

146 Is the Old Testament God of wrath different from the New Testament Jesus of love?

Some people have a hard time reconciling the God of the Old Testament with Jesus. The Old Testament God seems angry and poised to strike. He sends a flood that drowns nearly everyone, an angel of death that slays the firstborn sons in Egypt, and two bears that maul children for teasing one of His prophets (Genesis 6–8; Exodus 12:23; 2 Kings 2:23–24). On the other hand, Jesus humbly schlepped around Israel, feeding the poor and healing the sick. Are we sure this is the same God?

Yes. Terrifyingly yes. The next time the world sees Jesus, He will not be the meek and mild Messiah. Jesus arose in power and triumphantly ascended to His Father's right hand. He will return in all His glory, trading in His donkey for a stallion. Listen to John's vision of the end:

> *I saw heaven standing open and there before me was a white horse, whose rider is called Faithful and True. With justice he judges and wages war. His eyes are like blazing fire, and on his head are many crowns. He has a name written on him that no one knows but he himself. He is dressed in a robe dipped in blood, and his name is the Word of God. The armies of heaven were following him, riding on white horses and dressed in fine linen, white and clean. Coming out of his mouth is a sharp sword with which to strike down the nations. "He will rule them with an iron scepter." He treads the winepress of the fury of the wrath of God Almighty. On his robe and on his thigh he has this name written:*
>
> *KING OF KINGS AND LORD OF LORDS.*
>
> *. . . Then I saw the beast and the kings of the earth and their armies gathered together to wage war against the rider on the horse and his army. But the beast was captured, and with it the false prophet who had performed the signs on its behalf . . . . The two of them were thrown alive into the fiery lake of burning sulfur. The rest were killed with the sword coming out of the mouth of the rider on the horse, and all the birds gorged themselves on their flesh.*

Revelation 19:11–16, 19–21

The Jesus who comes at the close of Scripture is definitely the same God who appears at the start. Behold the holy and sovereign Lord who powerfully destroys the wicked! If you tremble at this vision of Jesus, you must hide yourself *in* Him. Jesus willingly was destroyed for you so you would not be destroyed by Him. But you must repent of your sin and put all your faith in Him. The only person who can save you from Jesus is Jesus.

147 Did God command Israel to commit genocide?

Genocide is a loaded term. We immediately think of the Jewish Holocaust or Rwanda, where people were killed because of who they were. That is definitely not what is happening in the Old Testament. God never commanded Israel to kill others because of their ethnic identity. Quite the opposite. God is saving people from "every nation, tribe, people and language," and He will fill heaven with their multiethnic praises (Revelation 7:9).

God did command Israel to go to war against the pagan inhabitants of the Promised Land and to fight to win. They were to "destroy them totally. Make no treaty with them, and show them no mercy" (Deuteronomy 7:2). This is hard to read, especially given the religious extremism of our day. Is the Old Testament God no better than ISIS or Al-Qaeda?

Here are several points to keep in mind:

1. ***These people were not innocent. They deserved to die.*** God said so. When Abraham was living in Canaan, God promised his descendants would someday return and take over the land. But they had to wait several hundred years for their conquest, "for the sin of the Amorites has not yet reached its full measure" (Genesis 15:16). Only when the Canaanites' evil became grotesquely indefensible would God tell Israel to take them out.

   What was their sin? Among other things, they sacrificed their babies to idols, casting them into the fire to express their devotion (2 Kings 16:3; 23:10; Leviticus 18:21). God warned Israel not to follow their example and not to tolerate anyone who did. "If the members of the community close their eyes when that man sacrifices one of his children to Molek and if they fail to put him to death, I myself will set my face against him and his family and will cut them off from their people together with all who follow him in prostituting themselves to Molek" (Leviticus 20:4–5).

   Given today's widespread practice of abortion, perhaps the better question is not why did God kill the Canaanites, but why hasn't He killed *us*? Rather than be appalled at their destruction, let's take their demise as God's warning for what we deserve. We are headed for a far worse fate, everlasting suffering in hell, unless we repent and turn to Jesus. God has graciously given us space to repent, but as with the Canaanites, His patience will run out. Don't presume on the grace of God. His conquest of the Canaanites expresses what He thinks of our sin.

2. ***Their defeat was necessary for the world's salvation.*** God promised to make Abraham's children into a great nation that would save the world. Israel would establish a foothold for redemption, preparing the world for the Messiah and showing how God blesses those who are fully devoted to Him.

Abraham's children needed a place to live. God promised them Canaan. They must first go to Egypt, which bought time for the Canaanites' evil to exponentially worsen. Then God delivered Israel from slavery and fought for them as they entered the Promised Land. He said they must not spare the Canaanites, either from pity or fear, but must "completely destroy them." If they made treaties, intermarried, or even ate together, soon enough Israel would be tempted to join their idolatry (Deuteronomy 20:16–17; Exodus 34:11–16). Her light would go out, and God's plan to save the world would seemingly be at risk.

This is exactly what happened. Psalm 106:34–39 laments:

They did not destroy the peoples
as the LORD had commanded them,
but they mingled with the nations
and adopted their customs.
They worshiped their idols,
which became a snare to them.
They sacrificed their sons
and their daughters to false gods.
They shed innocent blood,
the blood of their sons and daughters,
whom they sacrificed to the idols of Canaan,
and the land was desecrated by their blood.

> *They defiled themselves by what they did;*
> *by their deeds they prostituted themselves.*

Because Israel did not kill the idolaters, they killed their own children to appease the idolaters' gods. So God used other idolaters to destroy Israel, leading them into captivity so they would repent and return to Him.

3. ***We are not commanded to kill non-Christians.*** As with other ancient texts, the Bible is full of battles. Even the Bible's prayers—one out of every three psalms—is written within the context of war. God is a Warrior who destroys His enemies and their sin. We must not be offended by this, but neither should we mistakenly assume God is calling *us* to physical violence.

   God's story of salvation has advanced since the Old Testament. Jesus has come, the Light of redemption that God promised the world. As Israel was commanded to cleanse the land by destroying "anything that breathes" (Deuteronomy 20:16), so Jesus cleansed His people, and soon the entire world, with His dying breath. The ultimate sacrifice has been made. Salvation is finished (John 19:30). Followers of Jesus don't make the world holy by killing our non-Christian neighbors. We invite them to die with us to our sin and receive the holiness of Christ.

4. ***Remember other mitigating factors.*** Some scholars soften God's command to kill Canaanites by arguing that many of the cities, such as Jericho, were small military outposts. There wouldn't have been many noncombatants there to be killed. This may be true, though Jericho must have included some women and children. When Jericho's walls fell, the Israelites "destroyed with the sword every living thing in it—men and women, young and old, cattle, sheep and donkeys" (Joshua 6:21).

   More helpful is the point that the Canaanites always had the option to flee. God told Israel to drive the idolaters out of their land, not necessarily exterminate every last one. Even God's fierce command to "destroy them totally. . . show them no mercy" follows His promise to merely "drive out" many nations (Deuteronomy 7:1–2). Elsewhere God promised, "I will send my terror ahead of you and throw into confusion every nation you encounter. I will make all your enemies turn their backs and run" (Exodus 23:27). If the Canaanites had kept running, they would have saved their lives. We know of no instance where Israel chased them out of the land in order to kill them. Once the Canaanites were gone, the land belonged to Israel. As God promised.

Most helpful is remembering the Canaanites always had the option to convert. They could switch sides, repent of their sin and join the Israelite nation. This happened with Rahab, who was spared when Jericho collapsed; Uriah the Hittite, who became a loyal soldier in Israel's army; and Caleb, the courageous spy who, though a former Kenizzite, was given an allotment of the Promised Land "because he followed the LORD, the God of Israel, wholeheartedly" (Hebrews 11:30-31; 2 Samuel 11:6–17; Joshua 14:13–14).

No individual Canaanite needed to die with his or her pagan neighbors. God's salvation is for the whole world, and He invites everyone to repent and follow Him. His invitation stands open until the final moment when justice falls.

148 What does the Bible teach about immigration?

God loves immigrants. He was one—once when Jesus entered our world and again when as an infant He was carried to safety in Egypt.

And God's people have often been immigrants. Abraham migrated to Canaan, Moses to Midian, and the entire company of Israel went to live in Egypt. God said their experience as immigrants should motivate them to care for the outsiders among them. They should be kind to aliens, for "you yourselves know how it feels to be foreigners, because you were foreigners in Egypt" (Exodus 23:9; see also 22:21).

God "loves the foreigner residing among you" (Deuteronomy 10:18), and He told Israel to love them too. "When a foreigner resides among you in your land, do not mistreat them. The foreigner residing among you must be treated as your native-born. Love them as yourself, for you were foreigners in Egypt" (Leviticus 19:33–34).

God told Israel to care for everyone in their community, though He distinguished between Jewish citizens, resident aliens, and foreigners employed either as temporary workers, roaming merchants, or travelers passing through the land.[24] Resident aliens are called *ger* in Hebrew, while mere foreigners are called *nekhar* and *zar*.[25] English translations often muddy this distinction. The Exodus and Leviticus texts above translate *ger* as "foreigner," which isn't precise enough to clarify this point.

The *ger* were foreign, but they were much more. They were legal aliens with many of the same privileges and responsibilities as native Israelites. They could participate fully in the Jewish faith, observing Sabbath, offering sacrifices, and worshiping on the Day of Atonement (Exodus 20:8–11; Leviticus 22:17–19; 16:29–30). They were included in Passover celebrations, from which mere foreigners were pointedly excluded (Exodus 12:43, 48–49).

Resident aliens also were expected to keep the same rules as native-born Israelites and suffered the same consequences when they disobeyed (Numbers 15:15–16;

Both sides of the immigration debate argue with passion. Does the Bible offer guidance on this contested issue?

Leviticus 18:26; 17:8–12). Resident aliens enjoyed the same safety net as the Jewish poor. They were allowed to glean in the fields, picking the grain the harvesters had missed (Leviticus 19:9–10). A poor legal alien must not be charged interest but treated as a fellow Israelite (Leviticus 25:35–37). In sum, resident aliens could be fully incorporated into the community of Israel, whereas mere foreigners were not.[26]

The Bible teaches compassion for all people, because everyone is created in God's image and someday the person in need might be us. The Bible also teaches the importance of boundaries and for governments to rule over their land (Deuteronomy 27:17; Hosea 5:10; Romans 13:1–7). If nations lose their integrity and fall into chaos, everyone loses.

We must love our immigrant neighbors, especially those in desperate need. And we must wisely govern immigration—who and how many are allowed in—or there may not be a "we" left that can love. Don't fall for simplistic, easy solutions: neither "build a wall" nor "open borders." The best course, like many issues in our fallen world, will require warm hearts, soft hands, and a stiff spine. Pray for wisdom, and be kind.

149 What does the Bible teach about homosexuality?

God loves difference. Difference is beautiful. Difference is powerful. Difference is life. The Bible's opening chapter of creation teems with life because it abounds in difference. God created heaven and earth, day and night, morning and evening, land and sea, work and rest, male and female. These complementary halves join forces to produce something larger than themselves. What would our world be like if it was only heaven, only night, only sea, only male, or only female? It wouldn't be at all. We wouldn't exist without both necessary halves for life.

God is for life, so He opposes whatever is anti-life. He loves all people, and He opposes whatever diminishes or frustrates their lives. God invented sex so two people might create new life by joining bodies and souls. This act is only possible between a man and a woman. Two men or two women are unable to have genital union, so they're unable to create life. They cannot aim their love at life, and they

The rainbow, for millennia a reminder of God's promise to Noah, has in recent years become the symbol of the LGBTQIA movement.

understand it is futile to try. Their sexual attempts, though seldom discussed, tend to parody male-female sex and result in degrading both partners.

Because God loves all people and wants the best for their lives, He consistently warns against the sin of homosexual practice. Here's what He says:

Leviticus 18:22; 20:13. Leviticus 18 is an entire chapter that warns Israelite men about all the people (and things) they must not sleep with. Not your mom, not your stepmom, not your sister, not your aunt, not your granddaughter, not an animal. I count twenty things that God says Jewish men must not have sex with. Which begs the question, *How dumb were these guys?* God wanted to make sure His people got the point, so He closed all conceivable loopholes. If He was writing Leviticus 18 today, He would need to add what was previously unthinkable: "not your sexbot, not your laptop, not a child, and not your virtual reality porn star."

Among the twenty or so forbidden items God does cite, He includes other men. "Do not have sexual relations with a man as one does with a woman; that is detestable" (18:22). Our culture still agrees with nearly all that Leviticus 18 says about sex. We agree that we shouldn't sleep with close relatives. Yet we think Leviticus is out of touch for denying sex with someone of the same gender. Why do we accept the other prohibitions of Leviticus but not this one? It seems arbitrary and probably says more about us than about the Bible.

1 Corinthians 6:9. This verse indicates Paul believed the command of Leviticus still applies. Paul read Leviticus 18:22 in the Greek Septuagint, which said a man must not lie in a bed, or *koitēn,* with another man, or *arsenos*. In 1 Corinthians 6:9–10, Paul lists some of the sinners who will not inherit the kingdom of God. He cites thieves, drunks, slanderers, swindlers, and also "men who have sex with men." This phrase translates two Greek words: *arsenokoitai*—literally "male bedders," a term that combines both *arsenos* and *koitēn* from Leviticus 18—and *malakoi*, a term used for the "soft, effeminate" partner who plays the role of the woman in the sexual act. Unlike his Greco-Roman culture, which praised the virility of men who penetrated other men and despised the men who were penetrated, Paul declared that both parties of a homosexual act were wrong.

Paul doesn't fixate on homosexual sin, since he lists other sins that keep people from the kingdom of God. But neither does he ignore it. We must follow his lead, calling out all sin, including sexual sin, so Jesus can save us from it. All unrepentantly immoral people are left outside heaven, looking in (Revelation 22:14–15).

Romans 1:26–27. These verses so strongly oppose homosexual practice that some people call them a "clobber passage." I guess they can be used to yell at sinners, but only by those who don't realize they also are sinners who need Jesus. I'd rather not call any part of the Bible a "clobber passage," because every verse in the Bible is for our good.

In this chapter, Paul lists many sins that deserve the wrath of God. He cites "envy, murder, strife, deceit and malice," along with specific types of people: "gossips, slanderers, God-haters, insolent, arrogant and boastful; they invent ways of doing evil; they disobey their parents" (verses 29–30). None of us are off the hook. But Paul also includes homosexual acts. Some scholars suggest Paul only opposed pedophilia, homosexual acts in which adult men abused young boys. That can't be right, because here Paul mentions lesbian women and men having sex with other men. "Even their women exchanged natural sexual relations for unnatural ones. In the same way the men also abandoned natural relations with women and were inflamed with lust for one another. Men committed shameful acts with other men, and received in themselves the due penalty for their error" (verses 26–27).

Others say Paul wasn't aware of committed, same-sex unions, but this isn't true. His world had them. Despite such attempts, there have been no breakthroughs, either in our understanding of the Greek language or first-century culture, that permit us to evade these clear words. They mean what they say. God opposes homosexual activity because He is for people and He is for life.

Matthew 15:19; 19:4. Some people say it's important that Jesus never spoke against homosexual practice. Actually it's not, because Jesus' silence would only indicate that He agreed with the Old Testament view. If Jesus disagreed with the Jewish consensus on sex, He would have said so. All this is a moot point, because Jesus did allude to homosexual practice. Twice.

In Matthew 15:19, Jesus listed sins and included *porneia*, a plural word that means "sexual immoralities." He had in mind every kind of sexual immorality that the Old Testament mentioned, from fornication to adultery to homosexual practice to bestiality. If Jesus meant to exclude something from this list, He would have said so.

In Matthew 19:4–6, Jesus was asked about divorce. He set His answer in the larger context of God's original plan for creation. Jesus cited Genesis 1:27 and 2:24, which say God intends marriage to be a one-flesh union between a man and a woman. It's not possible for people of the same gender to be married in God's eyes.

I appreciate how difficult this answer may be for some, and there are many practical, pastoral questions that I don't have space to address. Please remember that God is for you, and His Word is for your good. He loves you, and He forgives you and me every time we ask. Every sin is forgivable as long as we agree that it's sin and ask God's forgiveness for Jesus' sake. Don't ever give up, no matter how hopeless you may feel. We may not be delivered from any and all sin in this life—that's why we need Jesus!—but we will be finally healed when Jesus returns.

For those who may not struggle with same-sex attraction, recognize the unique burdens that your brothers and sisters bear. They don't need Jesus anymore than you do, but they do need a family. Include them in your church and family gatherings. Let them know you appreciate them and their contributions to the body of Christ. Let's bear each other's burdens until we make it safely home together.

150 Why do Christians follow the Old Testament's teaching on homosexuality but not its commands about eating bacon and shrimp?

Because the Bible is a story, and not every part of a story applies all the time. As a story advances, some things go with us and some things are left behind.

Consider the story of your life. Why do you brush your teeth every day but not take a nap? Both were commands when you were little, and if you were a good child, you obeyed your parents and did each. Now that you're older, only one still applies. (Of course, live long enough and the naps may come back—not as a command but as something you enjoy.)

When God's people were young, He told them to only sleep with their heterosexual spouses and not to eat bacon and shellfish. The command about sex and marriage continues today and is repeated throughout the Bible. But the commands about bacon and shrimp came with a sell-by date. They were intended to teach Israel the concept of holiness (they must avoid unclean things) and to prevent them from dining with their pagan neighbors and learning their idolatrous ways.

Now that Jesus has come and fulfilled the Old Testament's holiness code, it would be a sin for God's people to avoid bacon-wrapped shrimp, at least on religious grounds. (By the way, *bacon-wrapped shrimp*?) This appetizer seems calculated to flout the Old Testament law, but it's too late for that. If we now refuse any food for religious reasons, we are denying that Jesus has come. The apostle Paul explains, "Therefore do not let anyone judge you by what you eat or drink. . . . These are a shadow of the things that were to come; the reality, however, is found in Christ" (Colossians 2:16–17).

This is the point of Peter's vision in Acts 10. He saw a sheet of unclean animals and heard Jesus say, "Get up, Peter. Kill and eat." Peter responded as a good

Jew: "Surely not, Lord! I have never eaten anything impure or unclean" (verses 13–14). Jesus replied that He had now made this food clean. The vision repeated three times, and then there was a knock on the door. It was messengers from a Gentile named Cornelius, who had been told by an angel to fetch Peter. Peter put two and two together and realized that God was tearing down the wall between Jew and Gentile. Rather than stand apart and admit the few Gentiles who wished to join the Jewish nation, Jewish Christians were now taking Jesus to the Gentiles. No rules or dietary restrictions must stand in their way.

Bacon-wrapped shrimp is doubly not kosher.

We are far along in God's story—perhaps close to the end—and the early rules about bacon and shrimp no longer apply. But it's still a sin to sleep with anyone besides our spouse, because that command is given throughout the story, until the very end. We are all grown up now, so we no longer have to take daily naps or avoid baconnaise (yes, it's a thing). We still, though, must brush our teeth and avoid sexual sin—or suffer the consequences.

151 What does the Bible teach about polygamy?

The Bible teaches that marriage is between one man and one woman. God created one wife for Adam and said their union would be the template for all marriages. "That is why a man leaves his father and mother and is united to his wife, and they become one flesh" (see Genesis 2:20–24).

In the New Testament, Paul says "each man should have sexual relations with his own wife, and each woman with her own husband" (1 Corinthians 7:2). An elder or deacon must be a man who is "faithful to his wife" (1 Timothy 3:2, 12). Even Jesus' Jewish opponents, who tried to trip him on a trick question about a woman with seven husbands, said she married one at a time, remarrying only after each one died (Matthew 22:23–28). Their question is implausible—by the fifth husband, wouldn't these guys have figured out she was bad news and run away?—but it does assume marital monogamy.

And yet. There *are* examples of polygamous marriages in the Old Testament. David, the man after God's own heart, had at least eight wives, and probably more (2 Samuel 5:13; 1 Chronicles 3:1–9). His son, Solomon, took *seven hundred* wives, plus three hundred concubines (1 Kings 11:3). He's like a contestant on *The Bachelor* who gives a rose to all of them, for forty seasons. One thousand women vying for one man's attention? *What could go wrong?*

The Bible simply states the fact of their polygamy. It doesn't say God approved, but neither does it say He came down hard against it. He did warn that a king should "not take many wives, or his heart will be led astray" (Deuteronomy 17:17).

King Solomon of Israel had seven hundred wives. (No, that's not a typo.) They were from neighboring nations and enticed him into idolatry.

"Many" seems more than two or three, so God didn't exactly slam the door on polygamy. Still, there are no examples of happy polygamous marriages in the Bible, and married men, if they were honest, could tell you why!

(It is possible for one woman to have several husbands—a situation called polyandry—but it'd be out of character for most men and women to want this relationship, and it almost never occurs.)

In sum, polygamy seems to be a concession that God made after the fall because of the hardness of human hearts (see Matthew 19:1–10). The Bible makes no similar concession for homosexual practice. The Bible could not be more clear in its opposition. Yet Western culture has blown past that line, gone back and erased it, and then broke the pencil. There will be no more lines. If our culture believes the Bible is okay with gay marriage, there is no principled, biblical way to oppose polygamy. And so we won't. Polygamy is already here and tragically becoming more popular.

152 What does the Old Testament teach about slavery?

Slavery was a fact of life in the ancient world. Every kingdom owned slaves, and Israel was no exception. Its original patriarchs, Abraham, Isaac, and Jacob, all owned slaves, and their wives had female slaves (Genesis 12:16; 16:1; 26:19; 30:3, 43). Slaves were expensive, and most ancient people couldn't afford them. Those who had large flocks and herds, though, needed slaves to look after them. The patriarchs had lots of cattle.

But their children soon acquired an origin story that cut against the practice of slavery. Israel became a nation when God rescued them from slavery in Egypt, and their formative experience forever tempered how they practiced slavery.

First, Israel was forbidden to make slaves of fellow Israelites. If an Israelite became poor and offered to become his Hebrew neighbor's slave, the latter was to respect the former and hire him as a temporary worker—then release him at the Year of Jubilee (Leviticus 25:39-40). God explained His rationale: "Because the Israelites are my servants, whom I brought out of Egypt, they must not be sold as slaves. Do not rule over them ruthlessly, but fear your God" (verses 42–43). The Israelites had been redeemed from slavery. They must never return, especially at the hands of a Jewish brother.

Second, while Israel could take slaves from surrounding nations or the non-Israelites living among them, they still had to treat them with respect, as persons rather than mere property (Leviticus 25:44–46). God told Israelite masters to include slaves in their religious rituals and celebrations and to give them a Sabbath rest, ending each week with a day off (Genesis 17:12–13; Exodus 12:43–44; Deuteronomy 5:14; 12:18; 16:9–12; Leviticus 22:11).

God also commanded protections for slaves, unique in the ancient world. If a slave ran to an Israelite for refuge from a harsh master, the Israelite must allow him to stay. "Do not hand them over to their master. Let them live among you wherever they like and in whatever town they choose. Do not oppress them" (Deuteronomy 23:15–16). God warned Israel not to mistreat their slaves: "Anyone who beats their male or female slave with a rod must be punished if the slave dies as a direct result" (Exodus 21:20).

Slaves in Israel were more than mere property, but they were still property. After warning Israel they would be punished if their slaves died from a beating, God adds, "but they are not to be punished if the slave recovers after a day or two, since the slave is their property" (Exodus 21:21). Ouch! When a bull gores a person, the bull's owner should be killed if he knew his animal was dangerous. But if the bull gores a slave, the owner would merely pay a fine of thirty shekels (Exodus 21:28–32). Ouch again!

What are we to make of this? Slavery was an accepted facet of living in the ancient world. It's what you sometimes did with people you defeated in battle. You didn't want them to regain strength and attack again, so you might take their stuff and themselves as slaves to manage their stuff, which was now yours. It's what you often did with people who had fallen into poverty. You could allow them to starve, but they preferred to become your slaves and live in the security and relative comfort of your home. Slavery provided a safety net, the last refuge for those whose cattle and harvests had woefully underperformed. It could be an act of compassion not oppression.

God didn't eliminate slavery, at least not yet. It was impractical, given the harsh environment of the ancient world. But God did alleviate its abuses. No Israelite could be a slave, and non-Israelite slaves were included in the community and treated with dignity they would not find elsewhere. No one wanted to be a slave, but if you were going to be one, you hoped to be a slave in Israel.

153 What does the New Testament teach about slavery?

While we're on the subject, let's finish what the Bible says about slavery. There is an important difference between the worlds of the Old and the New Testament. Old Testament Israel controlled their society and could freely follow God's highest expressed wishes on any subject. Conversely, the New Testament church lived as moral aliens among a non-Christian population. They did not control their environment, which adds another wrinkle to the New Testament commands on slavery. How much of what we read is God's highest, preferred will (for example, does He want Christians to own or be slaves?), and how much is a concession to a culture that Christians had only begun to influence? That may not always be easy to answer, but it's something to keep in mind as we consider this question.

Slavery was more widespread in New Testament times than in the Old. Scholars estimate that 30 percent of the Roman Empire's population were slaves. Many families owned at least one. Slavery was a vital part of the Roman economy, and most people couldn't imagine a world without it.

Slaves themselves didn't usually revolt because there were so many different kinds, spread over so many occupations and social classes, that they didn't think of themselves as a common group that could unite. The Romans also lacked our modern focus on freedom, so they wouldn't automatically think it was a disaster to be a slave. Slaves were often treated well by their masters, who had an incentive to protect their investment. Some slaves actually found life more difficult once they became free and had to fend for themselves. Former slaves might opt to remain with their masters but now with a paycheck. Those who did leave still had obligations to their former masters (for example, free labor for a period of time) who were now considered their patrons.

We must not read our American practice of slavery back into the New Testament. Slaves taken in war were often mistreated and banished to a cruel life in the mines or on farms, and God warned against this. Paul includes "slave traders" in a list of sinners that God will judge (1 Timothy 1:10). But domestic slaves—those who belonged to a Roman household—were usually treated much better. Their lives were more affluent and secure than the hardscrabble existence of free peasants. Also, unlike our American experience, there wasn't a racial component to slavery. Masters and slaves crossed ethnic boundaries. One race did not enslave another.

Slavery was nobody's ideal destination, but it could provide a way to move up in society. Slaves were often indentured servants who sold themselves to pay off debts, save up money, or learn a skill they could use when they became free. Many household slaves raised the children or ran the family business. Cicero, writing in

Slavery has oppressed many people throughout history. In this colorized engraving from the late 16th century, African slaves process sugar cane on the island of Hispaniola.

the first century BCE, said a typical slave could expect his freedom in seven years and certainly by the age of thirty. Felix, the governor who judged Paul (Acts 24:2), had once been a slave. He climbed the social ladder all the way to the top.

Domestic slavery in the Roman Empire seems similar to America's military. Today young people join the armed forces to get ahead—to pay for school, learn a skill, and retire early. They belong to the military for twenty years. They are told where to live and what to do. But if they stick it out, in twenty years they gain their freedom and a pension for life. Not bad.

Still, I don't want to gloss over slavery in the Roman world. Slaves were owned by their masters, and they ranked lowest in society. There is a reason why, when Paul addresses the members of a Christian household, he starts with husbands and wives, then children, before moving down to slaves. They were on the bottom, without the basic freedoms we take for granted. For instance, slaves were sexually available to their masters. They could not legally resist.

The typical Roman household had slaves, and many Christian converts kept theirs. Even second-century bishops, such as the venerable Polycarp of Smyrna, had household slaves. He was martyred when two of his slaves gave away his location under torture. Given the problems with this institution, why didn't Paul demand that Christian masters free their slaves? Why instead did he command slaves to obey their masters (Colossians 3:22–24; Ephesians 6:5–8)?

Perhaps Paul realized that immediate abolition would hurt many slaves, who'd have no place to live or source of income. It might also damage society and Christian witness. Paul told Christian slaves to serve well so they would "make the teaching about God our Savior attractive" (Titus 2:10). The Romans were suspicious of Christians who claimed Jesus was Lord rather than Caesar. They feared their higher allegiance would overturn the social order and throw the empire into chaos. Could Christians be trusted? Paul wanted his neighbors to be open to the Gospel, and he assured them that far from being troublemakers, Christians made the best citizens. The Romans need not worry that Christian slaves would use their freedom in Christ to demand freedom from their masters. Rather, because Christian slaves knew they were free in Christ, they gladly served their human masters on His behalf. They would take their freedom if they could get it, but they also were content to serve in lesser roles (1 Corinthians 7:17–24).

Paul did not abolish slavery, but he did plant landmines that ultimately blew it up. He leveled the master-slave relationship by telling Christian masters that they were slaves too: "Masters, provide your slaves with what is right and fair, because you know that you also have a Master in heaven" (Colossians 4:1). The pressure was off. The masters didn't have to play lord; they only needed to submit with their slaves to the Lord above.

Paul told masters that their Christian slaves were brothers and sisters. We "are all one in Christ Jesus," whether Jew or Gentile, male or female, slave or free (Galatians 3:28). When a rebellious slave converted under Paul's ministry, Paul sent him back to his master with a letter, the New Testament book of Philemon, urging the master to welcome him "no longer as a slave, but better than a slave, as a dear brother. He is very dear to me but even dearer to you, both as a fellow man and as a brother in the Lord" (Philemon 16). It is hard for one brother to own another. Christian masters will desire to free their Christian slaves, or at least honor them as equals in the Lord, as spiritual freedom inevitably presses toward social and earthly freedom.

Paul also revolutionized the master-slave relationship from the other direction. He relativized the masters by telling Christian slaves their true Master was in heaven. Slaves should "obey your earthly masters in everything," but not for their sake. Instead they should work hard for the Lord, "since you know that you will receive an inheritance from the Lord as a reward. It is the Lord Christ you are serving" (Colossians 3:22–24).

Relativizing their masters actually raised the servants' obedience. Slaves serve their earthly masters best when they are not serving them most. Slaves do their best work when they know the master is watching. Earthly masters are not always around, but their ultimate, heavenly Master is continually watching. So they'd give their best, not to please their earthly masters, but out of "sincerity of heart and reverence for the Lord" (Colossians 3:22).

In sum, Christian masters needed to respect their Christian slaves as brothers—which did prompt many to free their slaves. Until then, Christian slaves were to respect their Christian masters as brothers, which prompted them to serve "even better because their masters are dear to them as fellow believers and are devoted to the welfare of their slaves" (1 Timothy 6:2).

Jesus relativizes and raises everything. If you're a master, you are the slave of Christ. If you're a slave, you are free in Christ. Jesus may not immediately change your circumstances, but He will change you in them. You may be a slave, but you'll never be just a slave again. You serve Jesus, and you're free as anyone can be.

154 Where did Old Testament people go when they died?

They went to Sheol, a sleepy, subterranean world where they existed as faint shadows of their former selves. We're not sure if Sheol is literally underground, but it could be. Samuel's "ghost" was summoned by a witch from beneath the ground, and the ground opened and swallowed Korah's rebellious family down to Sheol (1 Samuel 28:13; Numbers 16:30–34).

The Old Testament typically uses Sheol to describe the destiny of the wicked, but if the righteous prophet Samuel was there, it seems Sheol housed both the righteous and the wicked, though in vastly different areas. Jesus told a story about a rich man who was languishing in Hades, the Greek term for Sheol. He saw Abraham, far away, resting with a beggar the rich man had ignored in life. So "Abraham's side," or perhaps "paradise," is the New Testament name for the comfortable part of Sheol (Luke 16:22; 23:43), and "Hades" is what it calls the suffering realm of the wicked (Matthew 16:18; Luke 10:15; Revelation 20:13–14).

For either the righteous or wicked, Sheol was a dead place. Literally. Not much happened there. Sheol is "the place of silence" (Psalm 115:17). The teacher of Ecclesiastes urged readers to work hard while they're alive, "for in the realm of the dead, where you are going, there is neither working nor planning nor knowledge nor wisdom" (9:10). King Hezekiah thanked the Lord for healing his terminal illness and extending his life, "for the grave cannot praise you, death cannot sing your praise; those who go down to the pit cannot hope for your faithfulness" (Isaiah 38:18).

Old Testament saints hated the thought of dying and going to Sheol, but they

The family of Korah tumbles into Sheol in a 19th-century engraving of Numbers 16:1–33.

realized this was not the end. David praised God "because you will not abandon me to the realm of the dead, nor will you let your faithful one see decay" (Psalm 16:10). Another psalm proclaimed, "God will redeem me from the realm of the dead; he will surely take me to himself" (49:15).

The Old Testament promises the physical resurrection of all people: "Multitudes who sleep in the dust of the earth will awake: some to everlasting life, others to shame and everlasting contempt" (Daniel 12:2). Their "bodies will rise. . .the earth will give birth to her dead" (Isaiah 26:19).

Life isn't over when you die. The life you will have then depends entirely on how you live now. Choose wisely.

155 What is the Davidic Covenant?

God's salvation plan advances through telescoping covenants that make His promises ever more specific. Each succeeding covenant of grace reveals more about how exactly God intends to save the world from Satan's clutches. The Abrahamic Covenant promised to make Abraham's descendants into a vast people that would leverage the land of Canaan to bless the world. The Mosaic Covenant, established with the Ten Commandments at Mount Sinai, formed these people into a nation that would enter the land and show the world how God blessed those devoted to Him.

At least that was the plan. Israel couldn't get its act together. They worshiped a golden calf at the jump—while Moses was on Mount Sinai—thereby breaking the first and second commands as Moses was receiving them. Later they rebelled when they learned there were giants in the land, and they refused to go in and fight. God said, *Fine—you will wander in the wilderness for forty years until the faithless adults die off. Only your children will enter the land.*

The kids didn't do much better. They didn't conquer the whole land, as God had commanded and, just as He warned, they began worshiping the idols of the people they refused to drive out. God sent judges (military leaders such as Gideon and Samson) to lead Israel in battle. And He sent Samuel the prophet to call them to faith and repentance.

Israel muddled along until Samuel was old and about to die. His two sons were no good, and Israel said they'd prefer a king, like other nations. God said, *No, I am your king*. That's what made them special. But Israel said they didn't want to be special. They wanted to be like other nations, "with a king to lead us and to go out before us and fight our battles" (1 Samuel 8:20). God must have thought, *That's kind of My role. What exactly do you think I've been doing?* He warned that a king would seize their land, crops, and children—even their own lives. They'd all become his slaves. But if it's a king you want, a king you shall have.

Israel's first king was Saul. He started out well, but soon his insecurities got the best of him and he spiraled into a jealous rage when his subjects praised David more than him (1 Samuel 18:6–16). Saul died in battle, choosing to fall on his sword after an arrow critically wounded him (1 Samuel 31:1–6). He was succeeded by David, a "man after [God's] own heart" (1 Samuel 13:14). David routed the enemy Philistines and brought peace and prosperity to Israel. At the apex of his success, he decided to honor God by building a temple in Jerusalem.

God was pleased with David's desire but said it wouldn't be right for a warrior—who had killed men fighting God's wars—to build Him a house (1 Chronicles 22:6–10). Instead, God would build David a house:

> *"The LORD declares to you that the LORD himself will establish a house for you: When your days are over and you rest with your ancestors, I will raise up your offspring to succeed you, your own flesh and blood, and I will establish his kingdom. He is the one who will build a house for my Name, and I will establish the throne of his kingdom forever. I will be his father, and he will be my son. When he does wrong, I will punish him with a rod wielded by men, with floggings inflicted by human hands. But my love will never be taken away from him, as I took it away from Saul, whom I removed from before you. Your house and your kingdom will endure forever before me; your throne will be established forever."*
> 2 SAMUEL 7:11–16

This was the next step in God's telescoping promises. His people needed a leader who would rule over them in the land and bless the world. But wait: Wasn't God the only leader they should ever need? Yes, and that's precisely God's point. He

King David is known for many things, including his military prowess, his musical ability, and his adultery with Bathsheba and the murder of her husband. Most importantly, he is the royal ancestor of Jesus.

promised to establish David's dynasty through a son who would rule from Jerusalem. David assumed God meant an immediate son, who turned out to be Solomon. That was part of what God meant but not the most important part. He was looking several centuries ahead, when a "son of David" who was also the Son of God would be born in Bethlehem, David's town. This great great great great (and so on) grandson of David was Jesus, the Jewish Messiah who accomplished all of God's promises to Abraham, Moses, and David. Jesus would bless the world through His life, death, and resurrection and establish His people who would live forever in God's good land.

David was overwhelmed with gratitude. He sputtered, "Who am I, Sovereign LORD, and what is my family, that you have brought me this far? . . . What more can David say to you?" (2 Samuel 7:18–20). David was dumbfounded, and he didn't know the half of it.

156 What was the exile?

David was gobsmacked by God's covenant with him, but it was going to be a long road until the promises were fulfilled. David had managed to unite the twelve tribes around his capital in Jerusalem, and his son Solomon kept everyone in line with his strong hand. But the nation split apart immediately after Solomon died. Ten northern tribes asked Rehoboam, Solomon's son, to lighten their taxes and forced labor. When Rehoboam replied that he was thinking about making their load heavier, they said they were done. They chose Jeroboam as their king in the north and took the name *Israel* to distinguish themselves from the two southern tribes called *Judah* (1 Kings 12:1–16).

Israel had the most people and the better land, but Judah had Jerusalem. This bothered Jeroboam, who figured it would be hard to maintain his people's allegiance if they traveled to the capital of Judah for worship. So he created new centers for worship, at Bethel in the south of Israel and Dan in the north, and put a golden calf in each location. He announced to his people, "It is too much for you to go up to Jerusalem. Here are your gods, Israel, who brought you up out of Egypt" (1 Kings 12:28). He made a mistake. A very big mistake.

Israel slid downhill from there. They survived for two hundred years, from 930–722 BCE, but they repeatedly worshiped other gods and blew off the prophets such as Hosea and Amos, whom God sent to warn of their impending judgment. They would not listen, even when Elijah called down fire from heaven and defeated King Ahab and Queen Jezebel's prophets of Baal. God finally had enough and sent the kingdom of Assyria (today's northern Iraq) to take them out. Assyria marched through Israel on its way to invade Egypt and simply removed Israel from its path. The northern tribes were deported to Assyria and Media (northern Iran), where they intermarried and dissolved into the population, never to be seen again.

Judah didn't wrap herself in glory either. She moseyed down Israel's road of idolatry and injustice, only a tad slower. It took Judah longer to exhaust God's patience, as occasional kings such as Hezekiah and Josiah repented and tried to turn their nation around. But she eventually reached the end of the road.

Assyria's devastation of Israel had also softened Judah, and she fell a hundred or so years later to the rising power of Babylon. Babylon wanted to march on Egypt, and Judah was in the way, so Babylon attacked in three separate campaigns, taking a little bit more each time. In 605 BCE Babylon invaded Judah, in 597 she captured Jerusalem, and in 586, when King Zedekiah foolishly rebelled one last time, Babylon razed and burned the city. The temple was destroyed and, despite what Indiana Jones might believe, the Ark of the Covenant was lost forever. God's presence left Jerusalem and His people scattered from the land. Jerusalem's population fell from 150,000 to 3,000; only the poorest remained (Jeremiah 40:7). The nation and city that were intended to bless the world had become cursed.

The people of Judah languished in exile for seventy years. Unlike Israel, who melded into Mesopotamia, the exiles of Judah preserved their Jewish culture in distinct enclaves. They were prepared when Persia conquered Babylon and permitted all exiled peoples to return to their homelands (Ezra 1:1–6). Persia particularly wanted Judah to resettle her territory, to serve as a buffer state between herself and

The familiar story of Daniel in the lions' den occurred during Judah's exile in Babylon

Egypt. (Why is it always about Egypt?) The books of Esther and Daniel tell Jewish stories of exile, while Ezra and Nehemiah describe their return.

Judah finally was back in the land but not all the way. Only a remnant had returned, and they were not independent. They were a small province named Yehud in the backwater of the Persian Empire, ruled by a governor appointed by the king. Imperial armies were stationed nearby, prepared to pounce at the first sign of trouble.

Judah was back in the land, but it wasn't much better than exile. She was still under the control of foreign powers—Greece, Egypt, Syria, and Rome would successively dominate her politics. She wasn't free to do as she pleased. And Judah was in deeper spiritual exile. What she needed most was to be reconciled to God.

Five centuries later, the resettled Jews still didn't understand this. They yearned for God's promised Messiah, the anointed Deliverer, to come march on Jerusalem, defeat the forces of evil, and fulfill the promises made to Abraham and David. This is exactly what Jesus did. He did it right under their noses, and they missed it. They were looking for a different, merely political messiah.

Jesus did destroy evil in Jerusalem—near the temple and on Passover!—and they still didn't make the connection. Worse, their ignorance combined with pride to prompt them to kill their true Messiah. The Jews handed Jesus over to be crucified (which actually played right into God's hands). The Jews did not understand their deepest exile, so they killed Jesus. And because He died, you and I can be delivered from ours.

157 What is the New Covenant?

Taken as a whole, God's covenants promised to bless His people, and the world through them, if only they would love and obey Him. But they wouldn't. So God said, *Time's up. It's too late to repent and make things right. Babylon is coming, and Judah must not resist.* They should accept their exile as God's righteous judgment.

But just before their impending doom, God offered a glimmer of hope. His people would suffer catastrophe, but on the other side, much later, the nation would return to Him. God's promise builds on His previous covenants, but it was so radically new that He called it a "new covenant." Jeremiah 31:31–34 reports:

> *"The days are coming," declares the* Lord, *"when I will make a new covenant with the people of Israel and with the people of Judah. It will not be like the covenant I made with their ancestors when I took them by the hand to lead them out of Egypt, because they broke my covenant, though I was a husband to them," declares the* Lord.
>
> *"This is the covenant I will make with the people of Israel after that time," declares the* Lord. *"I will put my law in their minds and write it on their hearts. I will be their God, and they will be my people. No longer will they teach their neighbor, or say to one another, 'Know the* Lord,*' because they will all know me, from the least of them to the greatest," declares the* Lord. *"For I will forgive their wickedness and will remember their sins no more."*

God is done messing around. He promises to change His people from the inside, putting His law into their minds so everyone will know Him. He is able to do this because, unlike previous covenants that merely pointed to Jesus, this new covenant is founded directly on Him. Jeremiah 31:31–34 is cited verbatim in Hebrews 8:8–12, which goes on to explain the many ways this New Covenant is better. (Hint: Jesus!) The New Covenant has a better priest: Jesus (7:24); better sacrifice: Jesus (7:27; 9:27–10:4); better temple: heaven, where Jesus offered His sacrifice to

Jesus used the "last supper" with His disciples to describe a "new covenant in my blood" (Luke 22:20).

the Father (8:1–5); better way into God's presence: Jesus (9:8); and better promises: everlasting life and forgiveness in Jesus (8:6; 9:11–15).

Old Testament believers sacrificed animals to temporarily cover their sins, but this was not a long-term solution. Animals could only cover sin, and only for a while. Hebrews 10:4 explains, "It is impossible for the blood of bulls and goats to take away sins." Priests must show up every day, several times each day, to offer sacrifices for the sins of the people.

Then came Jesus, the pure Lamb of God. He kept the law perfectly and offered Himself as the once-for-all sacrifice that doesn't mask sin but deep cleans it. Jesus' sacrifice is complete. Unlike an Old Testament priest, who "day after day. . .stands and performs his religious duties," Jesus, when He "had offered for all time one sacrifice for sins. . .sat down at the right hand of God" (Hebrews 10:11–12). Did you catch that? Jesus *sat down*. His work is finished; our forgiveness is secure. Jesus sits.

Jesus sent the Holy Spirit to write the law on our hearts and empower us to obey, but even when we fail, we are forgiven—because of Jesus. He is what's new about the New Covenant; He is what makes all the other covenants work.

Jesus' sacrifice is why Christians no longer offer up animals. Instead we celebrate the Lord's Supper, when Jesus anticipated His sacrifice by lifting a cup of wine and saying, "This cup is the new covenant in my blood. . .which is poured out for many for the forgiveness of sins" (1 Corinthians 11:25; Matthew 26:28).

158 What happened between the Old and New Testaments?

As the Old Testament ends, a remnant of Jews has returned to Jerusalem. They're slowly rebuilding its walls and temple, which the old men say is a far cry from the glory of Solomon's former temple. So they have a good cry (Ezra 3:12–13). The settlers have started to slide into sin: intermarrying with pagans, ignoring the Sabbath, offering half-hearted worship, and mistreating their neighbors. All the reasons they were exiled in the first place. They're doing them again.

The last chapter of the last prophet of the Old Testament implores the Jews to repent and turn to God. The "great and dreadful day of the LORD" is coming, when God will judge sinners and reward the righteous. Immediately before that day, God will send "the prophet Elijah," whom Jesus would later identify as His predecessor, John the Baptist (Malachi 4:5–6; Matthew 11:13–14). These final sentences of the Old Testament foretell the coming Messiah who will save His people and destroy the wicked.

This promise hung in the air, taunting the Israelites for four hundred years as they muddled along, somewhere between barely making it and unbearable despair. Alexander the Great and his Greek armies defeated the Persians and conquered Judea in 332 BCE. He was kind to the Jews, respecting their laws and inviting many to move to the namesake city he was building in Egypt: Alexandria. For better and worse, his victories imported Greek culture, philosophy, and deities into Israel.

Alexander soon died (323 BCE), and his generals competed for the spoils of his empire. Ptolemy ruled from Egypt and Seleucus from Syria. Over the next century, the Ptolemies in the south and the Seleucids in the north hated each other and often fought. They met in the middle, which happened to be the land of Israel. Back and forth they went, grinding Israel to powder.

Antiochus IV Epiphanes was a major figure in the "intertestamental period," the four hundred years between the close of the Old Testament and the birth of Jesus.

What could be worse than being the battlefield of five major wars? Watching the harsher side win. The Seleucids defeated the Ptolemies and attempted to inject pagan elements of Greek culture into Judaism. When the Jews resisted, Antiochus IV Epiphanes invaded Jerusalem, slaughtering Jews, plundering the temple, burning the Scriptures, and erecting an altar to Jupiter, where he sacrificially offered a pig (170 BCE).

Where was God? Why was He silent?

The Jews responded with apocalyptic writings. These esoteric and symbolic stories, similar to the book of Revelation, encouraged believers to keep on believing that God would win in the end. Sure, life now seems bleak. But keep the big picture in mind. Resist evil and entrust yourself to God. He's got this.

The Jews also responded with guerilla warfare. A line of priests called the Maccabees fought back against Antiochus and won Israel's independence. Their stories are told in 1 and 2 Maccabees, which belong to the Apocrypha. The Maccabees established what is known as the Hasmonean dynasty (it was a family name), which ruled Israel from the middle of the second through the middle of the first century BCE. While better than the Seleucids, the Hasmoneans had too much power. They were both the priests and the kings, the religious and the political. This much concentrated power was bound to corrupt, and it did. By the end of their run, devout Jews were praying for the Messiah to come and topple them.

God heard their prayers but sent Rome instead. In 63 BCE, Pompey defeated Judea, making it part of Rome's ever-widening Mediterranean empire. The Romans replaced the Hasmoneans with the Herodian dynasty, named after its second and most famous king, Herod the Great. Herod was declared procurator, or caretaker of Israel on Rome's behalf. He was a builder, and he was evil.

Ruling from 37–4 BCE, Herod built palaces at Masada, Caesarea Maritima, Herodium, and Jerusalem. To please the Jews, he built an enormous temple that impressed everyone. Jesus' disciples exclaimed, "Look, Teacher! What massive stones! What magnificent buildings!" (Mark 13:1). The smallest stone weighs 2½ tons and the largest 570 tons. It is forty-five feet long, twelve feet high, and fifteen feet deep. Historians are still amazed that Herod's builders set that in place.

Herod was paranoid that his family might try to usurp him—so he killed them. He murdered wives, children, in-laws, anyone who might lay claim to his throne. His subjects joked it was better to be Herod's pig than his son, because out of deference to the Jews, he wouldn't kill his pig.

When he learned from the wise men that a rival king had been born in Bethlehem, Herod was alarmed. He told them to let him know when they found the baby, because secretly he wanted to kill the child. When the wise men did not return to report on the baby Jesus, Herod angrily killed *all* the young boys around Bethlehem just to be sure (Matthew 2).

Some people question this "slaughter of the innocents," saying there's little evidence outside the Bible to support it. But Roman history records that when Herod lay dying soon after this time, he filled a stadium with beloved and important leaders and ordered that they be killed on his passing so someone would mourn at his death. So, yeah, the biblical story of Herod and the wise men is totally believable.

Here's the situation. God had last spoken to Israel over four hundred years earlier, and His final words hinted at the Messiah, who would bring history to its triumphal climax on the Day of the Lord. *Where was He?* Some Jews, known as Zealots, followed the Maccabean plan and fought back with secret, sudden attacks. Others, such as the Pharisees, implored the Jews to purity—perhaps if they kept the law perfectly, they would attract the Messiah's attention. The Essenes demanded even more holiness, and they sequestered themselves into socialist communes on the shore of the Dead Sea. There they maintained ritual purity, copied the Scriptures, and waited for the end of the world, when the Messiah would arise and defeat the "sons of darkness."

Average Jews went to synagogue, observed Sabbath, ate kosher, and remained separate from pagans. They were doing their part. *But where was the Messiah?* Traveling teachers roamed the countryside, promising it would not be long now. Pharisees enforced the rules. Zealots sharpened their knives. Essenes prayed. Herod chewed his nails. Something had to give. It did.

PART 4: JESUS
Who He Is, What He Means

Jesus is the most painted subject in world history. More important than how Jesus looked is who He is.

159 Who is Jesus?

It might seem crazy, but it's true: this is the most important question you can ask. Everything that ultimately matters about your life comes down to your relationship with a Middle Eastern Man you've never seen. Jesus lived two thousand years ago on the opposite side of the world. He inhabited a different culture, spoke a different language. You wouldn't understand Him without a translator. If He lived in America today, He'd be pulled aside by the TSA. Yet nothing matters more than your connection to Him.

Who is Jesus? His best friend, John, wrote his Gospel to answer this question. Near the end he concludes, "Jesus performed many other signs in the presence of his disciples, which are not recorded in this book. But these are written that you may believe that Jesus is the Messiah, the Son of God, and that by believing you may have life in his name" (John 20:30–31).

John says two things about Jesus: He is the Messiah, and He is the Son of God. The term *Messiah* comes from the Hebrew word *mashiach,* which means "anointed one" or "chosen one." In the Old Testament, whenever God chose a prophet, priest, or king, He revealed His selection by having a messenger anoint that person's head with oil. The Greek equivalent of *mashiach* is *christos,* which is what John uses in his Greek-language Gospel. He literally wrote "that you may believe Jesus is *the Christ.*"

Christians typically shorten this phrase to "Jesus Christ," which is not a first and last name—Jesus' parents were not "Mr. and Mrs. Christ"! His name is Jesus, which means "Savior" (Matthew 1:21). His title is "Christ," which comes from the same root as "christen," whereby some churches today anoint babies with oil at their baptism. In Jesus' case, He is the ultimate "Anointed One," the long-awaited Jewish Messiah who would fulfill all the roles of prophet, priest, and king and deliver His people from evil. As Christmas carolers sing, "O little town of Bethlehem. . .the hopes and fears of all the years are met in thee tonight."

When Jesus began His ministry, He stood in His hometown synagogue and read this passage from Isaiah 61: "The Spirit of the Lord is on me, because he has *anointed* (*christened, mashiach*) me to proclaim good news to the poor. . .to set the oppressed free, to proclaim the year of the Lord's favor." Then He said, "Today this scripture is fulfilled in your hearing" (Luke 4:18–19, 21). Translation: *I am your Messiah!* A few chapters later, after Jesus' disciples had heard Him teach and seen His miracles, Jesus asked who they thought He was. Peter answered for the group. We think you are "God's Messiah," literally, *"the Christ of God"* (Luke 9:20).

As Jesus hung on the cross, His enemies mocked Him for His Messianic claims. "He saved others; let him save himself if he is God's Messiah (*"the Christ of God"*), the Chosen One" (Luke 23:35). Ironically, and unknown to them, the reason Jesus did not save Himself was because He is the Messiah. He could not save us from evil unless He remained on the cross and died for our sin. Peter explains that we "were redeemed from the empty way of life. . .with the precious blood of *Christ*, a lamb without blemish or defect. He was *chosen* before the creation of the world, but was revealed in these last times for your sake" (1 Peter 1:18–20, emphasis added).

Anointed. Chosen One. Messiah. The Christ. These titles describe the job Jesus came to do. But who is He? The Son of God. Jesus is the Second Person of the Godhead who came to earth for our salvation. What that means is next.

160 What happened that first Christmas?

Christmas celebrates the birth of Jesus, when the Son of God was born as a baby boy. *How did this happen? What does it mean?* This entire section on Jesus will explore these questions. Here I simply want to say what this birth was by saying what it wasn't.

1. ***Christmas was an addition not a subtraction.*** The Son of God did not lose any part of His deity when He became a man. He did not give up some aspect of His infinite nature in order to squeeze into the cramped confines of a human. The Son of God remained fully divine as much as ever. Without relinquishing any part of who He is, He added a full human nature.

2. ***The Son of God added a human nature not a human person.*** Do you remember the *Men in Black* movies, when aliens came over and possessed human beings?

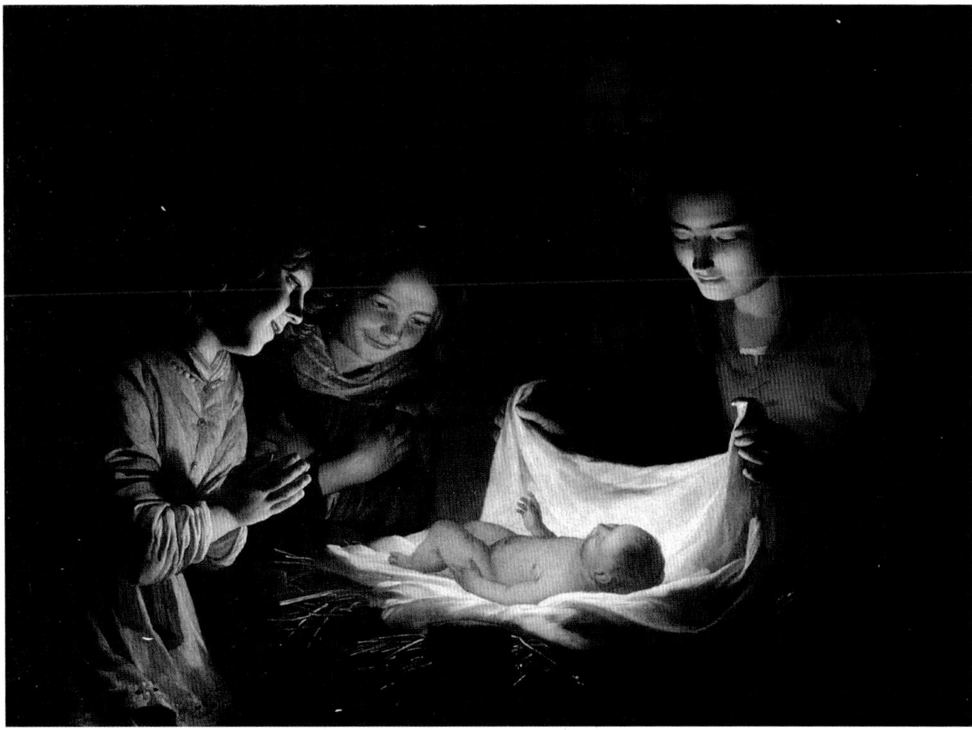

Mary displays the newborn Jesus to young shepherds in the classic Gerard van Honthorst painting of the early 1600s.

That's not what happened that first Christmas. The Son of God did not take over a preexisting human person. He did not add a human person; He added a human nature. This human nature did not exist before His conception but was created at the moment of His conception.

There is only one person in the incarnation (a theological term that describes the embodied, or "in fleshed" Son of God). That one person is the divine Son. The divine Son did not add to Himself a human person. Then there would be two persons in the incarnation. Instead, this one divine Person added a full human nature. At that moment, and not before, the divine Son became Jesus.

3. The human nature that was added is full, neither only a body nor only a soul. John 1:14 declares, "The Word [another name for the divine Son] became flesh and made his dwelling among us." This does not mean that Jesus' human part was only His flesh, so that the Son's deity plugged into Jesus' human body like an astronaut might put on a spacesuit. This would be the ancient heresy of Apollinarianism, popularly known as "God in a bod," which if true would destroy our salvation.

In the fourth century, Gregory of Nazianzus responded to Apollinarius by saying about the Son, "What He has not assumed He has not healed." Jesus must assume every part that you want Him to save. If you want Jesus to save your soul, He must have a human soul. If you want Jesus to save your body, He must have a human body. This was actually the point John 1:14 was making, against other heretics who doubted the divine Son would lower Himself to acquire a human body. John knew Jesus must be fully human to save humans fully, and he announced, "The Word became flesh."

What happened that first Christmas? The person of the divine Son added to His deity a full human nature, both body and soul. For us and for our salvation.

161 Is Jesus divine?

This is the most difficult aspect of Jesus to believe. The Jews in Jesus' day could see He was obviously human. His clothes stunk after a sweaty day schlepping a dusty path. He snorted sometimes when He laughed, got the hiccups and pieces of meat stuck in his teeth, and tooted when He used the bathroom. Could this man also be God?

Many Jewish leaders didn't think so. Once, during a heated argument, the religious leaders picked up stones to hurl at Jesus. They explained, "We are not stoning you for any good work but for blasphemy, because you, a mere man, claim to be God" (John 10:33; see also 5:18). When they finally did kill Him, same thing. The Roman governor asked what crime Jesus had committed, and the Jewish leaders replied, "We have a law, and according to that law he must die, because he claimed to be the Son of God" (John 19:7; see also Matthew 26:63–66).

The Jews did not hand Jesus over to be crucified because they thought He was too kind to sinners. They didn't kill Him because He hung around the wrong kind of people or even because He made them look bad. They killed Jesus because He

Jesus preached His Sermon on the Mount on this northern coast of the Sea of Galilee.

claimed to be God. That sounded like blasphemy, and they had learned from the exile that God really hates that. So they killed the Son of God allegedly on God's behalf.

Modern people also struggle with Jesus' claims to be God. We live in a secular age that doesn't believe much in miracles. Science can explain everything, we're told, using only natural causes and effects. There is no supernatural, so of course Jesus isn't God. He isn't the *metaphysical* Son of God (that is, in reality); He is merely a *moral* son. When Jesus said "I and the Father are one" (John 10:30), all He meant was that He was so devoted to obeying His Father that their wills were intertwined. This modern mistake is similar to the ancient heresy of adoptionism, a second- and third-century idea that Jesus was merely a human who lived so well that God adopted Him into His family. Jesus was just like us, only more so.

A fourth-century minister named Arius tried to split the difference. He said of course Jesus is God, but He's a lesser God than the Father, who alone is God in the highest sense. Jesus is a second-string deity, the first God off the bench. In 325 CE, the Council of Nicea declared Arius's idea out of bounds. The council said the Son is fully equal to the Father because they are the same exact essence.

My favorite story from Nicea is of Saint Nicholas, the bishop of Myra who, because he wore his red bishop's robe as he secretly stuffed gifts into the boots of poor children, became the source of the legend of Santa Claus. The story goes that old Saint Nick was filled with such righteous indignation that he walked across the hall and punched Arius in the face. Of course, Santa Claus should not punch heretics. (Bet you never thought you'd read that sentence!) But Santa would want you to know that Arius's belief that the Son is less than the Father still appears today in two major religious groups.

Mormons often attempt to downplay this fact, as they want to fit in with mainstream Christians. But article one of their church's confession declares, "We believe in God, the Eternal Father, and in His Son, Jesus Christ, and in the Holy Ghost." Notice that only the Father is called "Eternal." Mormons agree with Arius, who said that while the Father has always existed, "there was when the Son was not."

Jehovah's Witnesses are more transparent about their Arianism. Their website claims they follow Jesus' teachings, baptize and pray in Jesus' name, and believe Jesus is the key to salvation and the authoritative Head over every human. That sounds great! However, they add that "we take Jesus at his word when he said: 'The Father is greater than I am.' So we do not worship Jesus, as we do not believe that he is Almighty God."

You can praise Jesus a lot and not praise Him enough. You can list many of the ways that He is better than normal folks. But if you don't also say He is fully God, as fully God as the Father is God, then you have not praised Him enough. You have denied the eternal Trinity and put your salvation at risk (see page 307, "Why must Jesus be both God and man?").

So much for the challenges to Jesus' deity. *Why should you believe He is God?*

Read the Gospel of John, which was written to prove "that Jesus is the Messiah, the Son of God" (John 20:31), and see what you think. You'll see Jesus' claims to be God: seven times He describes Himself with an "I am" phrase (John 6:35, 8:12, 10:9, 10:11, 11:25, 14:6, 15:1) and another time simply says, "I am" (John 8:58), a clear identification with Yahweh (whose name means "I am"). You'll learn how He demonstrated His deity by casting out demons, healing the sick, calming storms, and forgiving sinners. Most of all, He rose from the dead.

A resurrection by itself doesn't prove someone is God. Jesus raised people from the dead, and they weren't God. But He called His own shot. When enemies asked for a sign of His divine authority, Jesus answered, "Destroy this temple, and I will raise it again in three days." They thought He was referring to the Jerusalem temple where they were standing, "but the temple he had spoken of was his body" that was standing before them. "After he was raised from the dead, his disciples recalled what he had said. Then they believed" (John 2:19, 21–22).

As you read John's Gospel, ask the Spirit of God to help you understand and believe His witness. Also check out Hebrews 1:3, Colossians 1:19 and 2:9, and Revelation 1:12–18 and 22:13, which are only some of the Scriptures that claim Jesus is God. "Who is Jesus" is the key to your salvation, so please don't waste another day without investigating this most important question. If you die without answering it, expect to suffer the punishment for your sin in hell (John 3:18, 36). If you answer correctly and put your faith in Jesus, your abundant life starts today—and will continue forever.

162 What is the virgin birth?

The virgin birth starts earlier, with the virgin conception. That is the miracle. Christians believe that Mary became pregnant with Jesus without having had sexual intercourse with a man. The Spirit of God supplied what male sperm typically does, including a Y chromosome. A virgin had never become pregnant before, and it's not happened since. Why do Christians believe this?

1. ***The Bible teaches the virgin conception.*** Twice. Matthew's Gospel begins, "This is how the birth of Jesus the Messiah came about: His mother Mary was pledged to be married to Joseph, but before they came together, she was found to be pregnant through the Holy Spirit." An angel told Joseph not to be afraid to marry Mary, for she had been faithful. Joseph agreed, though "he did not consummate their marriage until she gave birth to a son. And he gave him the name Jesus" (1:18, 25).

   In Luke's Gospel, the angel Gabriel told the unwed Mary that she would have a son. She asked, "How will this be, since I am a virgin?" The angel replied, "The Holy Spirit will come on you, and the power of the Most High will overshadow you. So the holy one to be born will be called the Son of God" (1:34–35).

2. ***The Apostles' Creed teaches the virgin conception.*** This churchwide creed declares what Christians have always believed. It states, "I believe in Jesus Christ, [God's] only Son, our Lord, who was conceived by the Holy Spirit and born of the virgin Mary."

3. ***The virgin conception is a useful test for the deity of Jesus.*** Strictly speaking, the virgin birth wasn't absolutely necessary for Jesus to be God. The Father could have invented some other way to send His Son into our world. But the virgin birth is most fitting, and it's a simple check to see if someone believes Jesus is God.

Told by an angel that she would give birth to God's Son, the unmarried Mary replied, "I am the Lord's servant. May your word to me be fulfilled" (Luke 1:38).

In modern times, progressive Christians often keep the ancient words of the church but fill them with new meaning. For example, William Robertson Smith, a nineteenth-century pastor in Scotland, defended himself against charges that he denied the deity of Jesus. He said, "How can they accuse me of that? I've never denied the deity of any man, let alone Jesus!" Well, maybe that's why.

Traditional Christians realized that when they said Jesus is God, they meant something different than what liberal Christians like Smith meant. How could true believers tell if another person agreed with them or with Smith? They asked about the virgin birth. If someone said, "No, I don't believe it," she was almost certainly a liberal Christian who believed Jesus was merely a larger version of us. If she said, "Yes, I believe," she was most likely an orthodox Christian who believed Jesus is truly God. The virgin birth is not the same thing as saying Jesus is God, but it's the biblical, Christian way to make the point.

4. ***The virgin conception is a fitting way to explain how Jesus was born without sin.*** God could have devised other ways for Jesus to enter our world without sin, but it seems fitting, given Scripture's emphasis that Adam's sin was passed down to his descendants, that Jesus should have been born without a human father (see Romans 5:12–21). Original sin appears, at least in part, to pass from generation to generation through our fathers. The Holy Spirit who conceived Jesus could have protected Jesus from contracting original sin through Joseph, but it seems appropriate to simply remove Joseph from the equation.

   One side note: Roman Catholics and Protestants disagree about Mary's perpetual virginity. Roman Catholics believe Mary and Joseph never had sex, while Protestants say Jesus had younger brothers and sisters (Matthew 13:54–55; Mark 6:3), so they obviously did. But not until after Jesus was born.

163 Is Jesus human?

"Away in a Manger" is sung during every children's Christmas program. It's the perfect carol for toddlers. But have you noticed the second verse? "The cattle are lowing, the poor Baby wakes, but little Lord Jesus, no crying He makes." *What?* Baby Jesus doesn't cry? Is this baby human?

If liberal Christians doubt Jesus' deity, conservatives sometimes struggle with His humanity. We may imagine a stained-glass Jesus floating through life, a few inches off the ground. His face shimmers with heaven's glow; every sentence is hailed by angelic choirs in triumphant crescendo.

We rightly say Jesus is God. But then we assume He was too important to play sports or card games. He was too serious to attend parties. The Gospels only mention them because they were unusual. If we're not careful, this uptight view of Jesus

The resurrected, flesh-and-blood Jesus invites "Doubting Thomas" to touch His wounded hands and side. On a previous visit the resurrected Christ had told His disciples, "A ghost does not have flesh and bones, as you see I have" (Luke 24:39).

can slide into heresy. Not just any heresy, but the first heresy that challenged the early church.

The Gnostics were overly spiritual thinkers who believed the physical world was bad—so they taught the Son of God wouldn't dirty Himself by taking a human body. They said Jesus only *seemed* to be human. The name for this heresy is *docetism*, which comes from the Greek word *dokeō,* which means to seem or appear. Jesus only appeared to be human. He was really a divine phantom.

The early church hated docetism because it ruined our salvation. Jesus must be fully human if we are to be fully saved. John had a Gnostic teacher named Cerinthus in mind when he wrote "the Word became flesh" (John 1:14). Jesus must have our flesh to save our flesh. John once encountered Cerinthus in a Roman bath. He immediately ran outside with his disciples saying, "Let us fly, lest even the bath-house fall down, because Cerinthus, the enemy of the truth, is within." Apparently John didn't mind taking baths in public, just not with heretics. Not a bad rule! Likewise, Polycarp, the second-century bishop of Smyrna, encountered a docetic teacher named Marcion. When Marcion asked if Polycarp knew who he was, Polycarp replied, "I do recognize you, the firstborn of Satan."[27]

Satan is a switch-hitter. He can tempt us into caring only for the material world, and he can tempt us into despising it. Both extremes make a mess of our Christian faith. Jesus is more than human—He transcends the physical world—but He is not less than human. Contrary to what some say, the Son of God did not pass through Mary like water through a pipe, taking nothing from her. No! Jesus is fully human, even now. He has His mother's eyes.

The Gospels affirm Jesus' full humanity. Luke says, "the child grew and became strong," and "Jesus grew in wisdom and stature, and in favor with God and man" (2:40, 52). As other humans, Jesus grew tired (John 4:6), became hungry (Luke 4:2), and claimed there was at least one thing He didn't know (Mark 13:32).

Jesus remained human after His resurrection. He appeared to His disciples, who "were startled and frightened, thinking they saw a ghost." Jesus told them to "touch me and see; a ghost does not have flesh and bones, as you see I have." When "they still did not believe it because of joy and amazement, he asked them, 'Do you have anything here to eat?' They gave him a piece of broiled fish, and he took it and ate it in their presence" (Luke 24:37, 39, 41–43). What a pathetic scene! That morning Jesus had defeated Satan, sin, and death when He rose from the grave. Now He is finishing history's greatest day by demonstrating He has the life skills of a toddler. "Look, I'm chewing! I'm swallowing! See, it's going down!"

I'm glad Jesus humbly accommodated His disciples, because this moment suggests the incarnation was not a one-off. The Son of God did not temporarily become human. Even after His resurrection and ascension, He remains one of us! The Son loved us enough to become who we are so we might become like Him. For the sake of our salvation, this Christmas let the Baby cry!

164 Could Jesus sin?

Let's begin with a warning, which I will then foolishly ignore. Here's the warning: never directly answer a question like this. Jesus possessed a divine and human nature, and any answer you can give will inevitably minimize one or the other. If you say Jesus couldn't sin, how is He human? If you say He could, how is He divine?

The Council of Chalcedon (451 CE) wisely drew a circle around the person of Jesus, saying we must not confuse or change His two natures, and we must not divide or separate them. These "four fences of Chalcedon" are entirely negative—they say what we can't say. The minute we attempt to say something positive, we're bound to topple one of these fences. We'll either confuse or change Jesus' two natures, or we'll divide or separate them. So don't try to answer questions about Jesus directly; it's much safer to speak indirectly, saying what is out of bounds rather than what is in play.

Here's me imprudently ignoring my own advice: if I were to attempt to answer this question, I would say Jesus *could* sin but He never *would.* Jesus *could* sin because He possessed powers that enabled Him to do things. If He did these things in the wrong contexts or for the wrong reasons, it would be sin. Jesus had arms and hands that could flip over tables. He used this power to righteously chase moneychangers out of the temple. Good. But what if He had used this power after dinner at your house? Not great. If Jesus is coming to dinner, use paper plates!

Jesus asked John for baptism, normally an indication that a person has turned from sin to follow God. But Jesus didn't sin.

Jesus possessed powers that *could* be used to sin, but His perfect divine and human wills meant He never *would.*

This is an ironclad moral inability. Jesus was never going to sin. No way, no how. Sin was morally impossible for Him.

Does this make His temptations less real? No. It makes them more real. Jesus would never sin, which means He felt the full force of His temptations. You and I rarely feel the brunt of our temptations because we give in too early. Jesus outlasted every temptation every time. He fought His temptations to the bitter end, until the clock ran out.

What do you think? Should I have followed my own advice? Does my answer minimize Jesus' deity or humanity, or does it give full weight to both? How would you answer the question? (Be careful. It's a trap!)

165 Why must Jesus be both God and man?

We humans have a problem: our sin owes a debt to God that we can never repay. We can't make up for our rebellion, because any good act that we might do for God is something we already owe Him. We can't earn extra credit. Worse, we continually sin against God, so our debt daily grows larger.

There is only one possible solution. It's such a longshot that no human would ever have thought of it: What if a substitute paid our debt? That person would have to be human like us in order to stand in our place. If He wasn't human, His perfect life and sacrifice could not count for us. He would also have to be God, in order to avoid being corrupted by Adam's sin and guilty Himself. As God His payment would have infinite value, enough to pay for the sins of the whole world.

That was our only shot. It has a name: Jesus.

166 Does Jesus suffer from a split personality?

The incarnation proves that humanity is compatible with deity. Our finite, created natures are fit to be joined with the infinite, divine nature. But it's impossible for us finite creatures to comprehend how this works.

How can one person be both God and man? Because He is God, Jesus knows all things. Because He is human, He admits He doesn't (Mark 13:32). Because He is God, Jesus possesses all power and fills the universe with His presence. Because He is human, the baby Jesus cried softly in His mother's arms and pooped in His swaddling clothes.

You might expect Jesus to suffer from what psychologists call multipersonality dissociative disorder, but the Gospels consistently present Jesus as a unified subject. The Jewish leaders and some of His siblings did wonder if He was crazy, but only because He claimed to be God (Mark 3:21; John 10:19). According to the DSM, the psychologist's Bible, they understandably thought He suffered from delusions of grandeur.

The church cannot explain how deity and humanity coexist in Jesus' one person, but it has laid down some ground rules for talking about this "hypostatic union." In the fourth and fifth centuries, the churches of Antioch (Syria) and Alexandria (Egypt) opposed each other's understanding of Jesus. Antioch emphasized Jesus' two natures, which leaned toward dividing Him into two persons. Alexandria emphasized Jesus' one person, which leaned toward merging His two natures. Each city overplayed its hand and was helpfully corrected by church councils.

Antioch went first. Its leader, Nestorius, said Jesus joined His two natures like a marriage unites two distinct wills. The church thought this analogy was problematic because a marriage involves not only two wills but two people. Was Nestorius saying Jesus was two people? The Council of Ephesus (431 CE) said Nestorius's view was out of bounds. We cannot divide Jesus' two natures as he seemed to do.

Alexandria was happy to see its rival smacked down, then promptly went off the cliff in the other direction. Its bishop, Cyril, liked to say Jesus possessed "one nature after the union" of the divine Son and human embryo. The Council of Ephesus indicated this was heretical because it doesn't keep Jesus' two natures distinct. But Cyril continued preaching about "the one incarnate nature of the Word."

After he died, an elderly but influential monk named Eutyches stumbled into this minefield. He staunchly supported the Alexandrian view and said Jesus' humanity had been swallowed up by His divinity, as a "drop of wine in the ocean of his deity." What happened next is made for a Hollywood movie. There was a double-cross, a lethal beating, and Egyptian armed monks (you read that right). Also, an emperor was providentially thrown from his horse and died. Cut to the chase, and the Council of Chalcedon (451 CE) restored order, declaring Eutyches's view out of bounds.

Chalcedon established the ground rules that have guided the church since. Against Alexandria's distortion, the council said Jesus' two natures are "without confusion, without change." Against Antioch's mistake, the council said Jesus' two natures are "without division, without separation."

These "four fences of Chalcedon" are essential for understanding Jesus and preserving our salvation. Against Nestorius, how could Jesus save us if He is two persons? Which person is doing what and when? How can Jesus stand in for us if He Himself is divided? Against Eutyches, how could Jesus save us if His two natures are blended together, a kind of Jesus smoothie? Both natures might be diluted, especially His humanity, which would likely be overwhelmed by His infinite deity. Remember the principle of Gregory of Nazianzus: "What he has not assumed he has not healed." Jesus is fully God and fully man—two natures that are distinct but not separate—so we can be saved.

167 Does it matter that Jesus is real?

Progressive Christians attempt to reconcile their Christian faith with the modern, secular world. When it comes to Jesus, they often suggest His *principles* matter more than His *person*. Just as we are inspired by the *Rocky* movies (at least the first two) even though we know they aren't true, so we can be changed by the stories of Jesus, some say, even if they didn't happen. Jesus' life inspires us to love others, His death teaches the power of sacrifice, and His resurrection encourages us to hope. This remains true even if much of Jesus' story is false.

Progressive Christians who make these moves think they are saving the Christian faith. God says they are losing it. The Christian faith does have wise principles—the book of Proverbs is full of them—but it is primarily not about those. At bottom, the Christian faith is about the person of Jesus. Unlike Rocky, this person must be real and His stories must be true. If Jesus is not risen from the dead, there is

The front of the modern Church of the Annunciation in Nazareth, Israel. The Latin carving above the main door reads, "The Word was made flesh and dwelt among us." In an ancient chapel inside, the altar reads, "The Word was made flesh here."

no hope. Life loses all meaning. Paul attests, "If the dead are not raised, 'Let us eat and drink, for tomorrow we die.' " But if Jesus came out of His grave, then we will too. So we can "stand firm," giving ourselves "fully to the work of the Lord, because you know that your labor in the Lord is not in vain" (1 Corinthians 15:32, 58).

The Christian faith is a historical faith. It's about what God has done in time and space. These acts of God arise from His will. He chose to do what He did. Which means He could have chosen to do something else. None of God's acts are absolutely necessary, so they can't be proven. The Christian faith isn't like a math problem, which smart people can work out with certainty if they have enough time. There is lots of evidence for the Christian faith, but we shouldn't expect to prove it to all people at all times. That's not how history works.

The Christian faith is a historical faith, which means it's flesh-and-blood real. You can visit Israel today and see the valley where David fought Goliath, the lake where Peter and John fished, and the remains of the temple steps where Jesus walked. The Bible includes names, dates, and places you can look up. There's a reason Pontius Pilate made it into the Apostles' Creed. That Jesus "suffered under Pontius Pilate" underscores this isn't a fairy tale. It happened.

The Christian faith is a historical faith, which means it's particular. What happens in time and space is very specific. This, not that. Jesus was born in Bethlehem and raised in Nazareth. If you visit Nazareth today, you can visit the Church of the Annunciation that commemorates the angel's appearance to Mary. In the chapel beneath the church is an altar with this inscription: "The Word was made flesh here." Here, not there. Here, for everywhere. God became flesh in our time and space to provide salvation for people of all times and space. It's real, or it's nothing.

168 When was Jesus born?

Jesus is safe from identity theft. For the obvious reason that no one would believe you are Him and for the technicality that no one knows His birthday.

We don't know the year Jesus was born. You might think BCE and CE mean Jesus was born in year zero. But there isn't a year zero. The year leading up to Jesus' birth would be 1 BCE, and the year starting with His birth would be 1 CE. If our calendar is right, Jesus was born in 1 CE. But it isn't quite right. In 525 CE, a monk and member of the Roman curia (administrators that govern the church) named Dionysius Exiguus pegged Jesus' birth at 1 CE. This date was popularized by Venerable Bede in his eighth-century book *The Ecclesiastical History of the English People*, and it became the default view of European Christians.

However, many scholars now suspect Jesus was born between 6 and 4 BCE. Why? Because King Herod, who tried to kill the two-year-old child (Matthew 2:1–18), probably died in 4 BCE. Other scholars note we're not sure when Herod died, as 4 BCE is based largely on the historian Josephus, and there are issues with his dates. We do know John the Baptist began his ministry "in the fifteenth year of the reign of Tiberius Caesar" (Luke 3:1), which we believe was 29 CE, give or take a year. Shortly thereafter, Jesus "began his ministry" when he "was about thirty years old" (Luke 3:23). Counting backward from John's ministry, Jesus may

A Roman coin depicting Tiberius Caesar. By measuring events in Jesus' life against this ruler's reign, the date of the first Christmas is estimated at 2–3 BCE.

have been born between 3 BCE and 2 CE, with a 2–3 BCE time frame becoming increasingly popular.

We don't know the year, and we don't know the *day* Jesus was born. There are two theories why the church chose to celebrate Jesus' birthday on December 25. The popular view is that fourth-century Christians, emboldened by imperial support for their faith, co-opted a pagan feast day. Romans celebrated December 25 as the feast of "the Unconquered Sun" to commemorate the time when bleak midwinter days began to lengthen. From then until the middle of summer, each day would have more sunlight than the last. The parallel between the invincible sun and the resurrected Son may have been irresistible, and Christians may have taken over December 25 to popularize their faith and make it more accessible to their pagan neighbors.

However, the Christmas link to the pagan feast day is not mentioned until the twelfth century, and there is evidence that Christians were celebrating December 25 already in the third century, long before Christians rose to power and began co-opting pagan holidays. This leads some scholars to suggest that perhaps December 25 has more connection to Judaism than paganism.

The Babylonian Talmud states that the bookends of the world, both creation and redemption, should occur at the same time of year. A rabbi explains, "In [the month of] Nisan the world was created; in Nisan the Patriarchs were born; . . .and in Nisan they [our ancestors] will be redeemed in time to come." Placing creation and redemption in the same month was a Jewish way of integrating the story of the world.

The early church adopted this bookend idea and applied it to individuals. The church assumed the date a saint was martyred was also the date on which he or she was conceived. It was a satisfying way to integrate the story of their lives. Applied to Jesus, Tertullian wrote around 200 CE that Jesus was crucified on Nisan 14. This corresponds to March 25 on the Roman solar calendar. If Jesus was conceived on March 25, He would have been born approximately nine months later, on December 25.

The Eastern church didn't use the Jewish calendar, so instead of using Nisan 14, they used the fourteenth day of their first spring month, which is April 6 in our calendar. If Jesus was conceived on April 6, He was born nine months later, on January 6. Armenians still celebrate Jesus' birthday on January 6. This is an important date to other Christians, who celebrate January 6 as the Feast of Epiphany, when the wise men visited the two-year-old Jesus. If you're counting, the period between December 25 and January 6 are the twelve days of Christmas.[28]

Ultimately we don't know the day Jesus was born because His birthday didn't matter much to the first Christians. They were less interested in His birth than in His death and resurrection. The church has always celebrated Easter more than Christmas—what Jesus came to do more than His arrival. We are right to protect the "real meaning of Christmas" from secular encroachment. But if Christians did steal Christmas from the pagans, it may only be fair that they steal it back. Far worse is losing Easter. Our danger isn't Santa Claus, it's the Easter Bunny.

169 Why didn't Jesus come sooner or later?

We cannot say for sure why Jesus came when He did, as God is free to act whenever He wants. But we can see why it made sense for Jesus to be born when He was. The world was ready.

Religion was ready. The Jews had centuries of learning from the law how great was their sin and need for a Savior. It was time for the Savior to come. Paul writes, "When the set time had fully come, God sent his Son, born of a woman, born under the law, to redeem those under the law, that we might receive adoption to sonship" (Galatians 4:4–5).

Philosophy was ready. Socrates, Plato, Aristotle, and their protégés had pondered the meaning of life for four hundred years. They expressed many truths about moderation and morality, but they couldn't explain the good life because they didn't have room for God. Plato thought God was an abstract ideal (the highest form, called the Good); Aristotle supposed He was a nonexistent, theoretical postulate (the Unmoved Mover); Epicurus was a materialist who didn't believe in an afterlife; and stoicism said "deity" was a pantheistic, rational force that inhabited human minds. No one believed God was a real, separate being. By the time of Christ, the Epicureans were content to avoid pain, the stoics to remain calm, and both "spent their time doing nothing but talking about and listening to the latest ideas" (Acts 17:21).

The first Christians told Greeks and Jews that the culmination of both their philosophy and religion was Jesus. Jesus is the Logos, the Word that orders our wisest thoughts and instructs us how to live (John 1:1–5). Jesus is the Lamb who fulfills centuries of Jewish sacrifice (Hebrews 10:1–14). Any good Jew or Greek should join the church, God's "third race" that completes their religious and philosophical paths.

Language was ready. Greek philosophy developed the Greek language until it could handle sophisticated conversations about God, then Alexander the Great's conquests spread that language and culture throughout the Eastern Mediterranean world. The first Christians wrote their sacred Scriptures and explained their religion in this advanced, Greek language, thereby communicating with literate people throughout the Mediterranean region.

Technology was ready and not too advanced. Have you wondered how Christianity might be different if Jesus had come to earth during the age of radio or television? What if we had audio of Jesus' preaching or video of His healings, death, or resurrection? How might these recordings change the Christian faith, and maybe not for the better? Consider how easily digital recordings can be altered and how fast technology changes. If Jesus had ministered during the 1970s, perhaps our memories of Him would be stored on eight-track cassettes! Good luck accessing that.

All things considered, it's good that our faith is stored in a Book. Books promote thought and reward study. They discourage idolatry and fixation on outward appearance. If we had a picture of Jesus and knew exactly how He looked, wouldn't we obsess over those people who most looked like Him and give less attention to those who didn't?

Travel was ready. The Greeks united the Mediterranean with their language and culture; the Romans came immediately after and united this Greek world into their peaceful empire. The first Christians could travel safely and quickly throughout the Mediterranean, telling the good news of Jesus as they went. On the Day of Pentecost, when the Holy Spirit descended from heaven and started the church, Peter spoke to visitors in Jerusalem from present-day Rome, Crete,

The Appian Way near Rome, an example of the advancing transportation systems available when Jesus came to earth.

Turkey, Syria, Iraq, Saudi Arabia, Egypt, and Libya (Acts 2:9–11). Thanks to the *pax romana* (peace of Rome), these new Christians could swiftly bring the Gospel to their homelands. The greatest missionary was Paul, and because he was a Roman citizen, he decided to take the Gospel to the furthest reaches of the Roman Empire. He would try for Spain (Romans 15:24)!

God did not have to send Jesus when He did, but it's easy to see why He did. The "time had fully come."

This star marks the traditional spot of Jesus' birth, in the grotto of the Church of the Nativity in Bethlehem.

170 What do we know about Jesus' early years?

The Gospels don't say much about Jesus' early life. They begin with His birth then generally skip over thirty years to the start of His ministry. Even then, the Gospels focus most on the last week before Jesus' death. To paraphrase theologian Martin Kähler, the Gospels are "passion narratives with extended introductions." They say less about Jesus' birth and three-year ministry and almost nothing about His childhood and adolescence.

Luke mentions one incident when Jesus was twelve. He had gone with His parents to Jerusalem for Passover. As Joseph and Mary were returning home, they realized Jesus wasn't with them. Retracing their steps, they found Jesus in the temple courts, hanging out with the religious teachers, "listening to them and asking them questions. Everyone who heard him was amazed at his understanding and his answers" (Luke 2:46–47). Twenty years later, some of these same leaders would confront Jesus in the same place, at the same festival, and call for His death.

Besides this episode, Luke summarizes Jesus' childhood in two sentences: "The child grew and became strong; he was filled with wisdom, and the grace of God was on him. . . . And Jesus grew in wisdom and stature, and in favor with God and man" (Luke 2:40, 52).

The Bible's lack of information about Jesus' childhood tempted others to fill the void. *The Infancy Gospel of Thomas* describes a five-year-old Jesus crafting clay into sparrows that came to life and flew away; turning a rushing stream into pools of clean water, then pronouncing death on a child who had taken a stick and destroyed His pools; speaking a word that killed a child who had bumped into Him; correcting His father who was understandably nervous about how flippantly He used His powers; raising a playmate from the dead so he could testify that Jesus had not pushed him off the roof, and so on. If these stories sound more like Bart Simpson than Jesus, it's because they are told by a heretical Gnostic sect. Christians have always known about this second-century "Gospel" and have never taken it seriously.

We do not know much about Jesus' early years, but it's important to remember that He had them. Jesus did not show up on earth, die for our sins, and return to heaven. He lived a normal, human life for thirty-some years. Keep this in mind when you're tempted to minimize an ordinary, earthly life. How can you justify mowing the lawn, washing your car, playing sports, or doing a hobby when people need the Lord? I appreciate the question. But remember the Lord Himself spent most of His life as a normal human. Only the last ten percent—and it was an important three years!—was devoted to preaching the Gospel and establishing the kingdom of God. Ninety percent of Jesus' life was spent working alongside His father, resting on the Sabbath, and doing whatever good Jews normally did.

171 Why was Jesus baptized?

That's what John the Baptist wanted to know. God had sent John to open for Jesus, warming up the crowds by warning them to repent of their sins—and baptizing those who did.

Baptisms, or ritual washings, are staples of many religions. They symbolize cleansing from sin and renewal for the life ahead. Some devout Jews in John's day baptized themselves often if not daily. They walked down steps into a ritual bath, or *mikvah*, immersed their entire body, then walked back out. So the Jews understood what John was doing. Many went out to him, and "confessing their sins, they were baptized by him in the Jordan River" (Matthew 3:6).

John didn't understand why Jesus came too. He didn't have sin to repent from. He didn't need a fresh start. So John asked: "I need to be baptized by you, and do you come to me?" Jesus answered, "Let it be so now; it is proper for us to do this to fulfill all righteousness" (Matthew 3:14–15).

An excavated mikvah—or ritual bath—from the Essene community near the Dead Sea. This pool was filled with water, and devout Jews of Jesus' day would descend the stairs for a purifying dip.

Fulfill all righteousness? What did Jesus mean? Well, righteousness is obedience to God's commands, and the Father had commanded His Son to save His people from their sin. Jesus saves us by becoming our substitute; His life and death in our place, counting for us. To count in our place, He must be in our place. He must identify with us, expressing solidarity with us and our condition. He who had never sinned and could never sin must join us in our plight. The holy Jesus was humbly baptized to identify with us sinners.

In so doing, He put Satan and his demons on notice: Jesus had come to rescue us from the bottom up. And that rescue starts now. The entire Godhead gathered in conspicuous presence to mark this beginning of Jesus' ministry. As Jesus walked out of the Jordan River, "he saw the Spirit of God descending like a dove and alighting on him. And a voice from heaven said, 'This is my Son, whom I love; with him I am well pleased' " (Matthew 3:16–17).

God was calling His shot: *Hey Satan, what you got? Game on!*

172 Why did Satan tempt Jesus?

Jesus did not ease into His battle with Satan. Neither wasted time coming for the other. Immediately after the baptism that began His ministry, "Jesus was led by the Spirit into the wilderness to be tempted by the devil" (Matthew 4:1).

Satan tempted Jesus to snuff out God's salvation before it had a chance to begin. Temptation had worked before. Easily. Satan had tempted both Adam and Israel to rebel against God. Their failure could only be fixed by Jesus, the Last Adam and the True Israelite. Would He fare any better?

Jesus intended to find out. He purposefully retraced Adam's steps to correct his errors. The First Adam sinned inside Eden and was kicked out into the wilderness; the Last Adam went out into the desert to defeat sin and lead His people back to paradise. The First Adam caved to a sin that was easily avoidable: *You may enjoy the fruit of every tree in the garden except one.* The Last Adam renounced a sin that caused His body to tremble with desire: *After 40 days of fasting, why not make a little bread?* Adam and Eve lost their lives when they ate a fruit they thought would make them like God. Jesus, who is God, retained His deity when He refused to eat what would keep Him alive.

Jesus also purposefully retraced the steps of Israel. In Deuteronomy 8:2, Moses told the Israelites that God had led them in the wilderness for forty years "to humble and test you in order to know what was in your heart, whether or not you would keep his commands." Jesus recognized the link between Israel's forty years of testing and His forty days of fasting, and He likely spent His forty days meditating on the book of Deuteronomy—especially chapters six through eight. His temptation was a crucial turning point in salvation history: unlike Israel, who had failed as God's people in the wilderness, Jesus went to the wilderness to prove the true Son of God, or "true Israel," was now here. Deuteronomy 6–8 must have weighed heavily upon Jesus, for when He turned to God's Word to defeat Satan's temptations, it was this section He cited.

In Matthew's Gospel, Satan's first temptation urged Jesus to prove He was the Son of God by turning stones into bread. *Congratulations on Your forty-day fast! You did it! Why not celebrate with some bread?* But Jesus remembered Israel's rebellion in the wilderness. They had complained about God's daily gift of manna that miraculously appeared on the ground each morning. It "was like coriander seed and looked like resin," and "tasted like something made with olive oil" (Numbers 11:7–8). The manna was enough to sustain Israel, but they wanted more variety in their menu. They longed for meat, fish, and the vegetables they ate when they were slaves in Egypt. They grumbled against God and His leader, Moses. Jesus remembered their sin and declared He would remain content with whatever His Father chose to provide. He quoted Deuteronomy 8:3, "Man does not live on bread alone but on every word that comes from the mouth of the LORD."

Satan was perplexed by Jesus' biblical answer. Tempting a child of God had never been this difficult. Adam and Eve? They had immediately gone for the fruit. Israel? A couple weeks of manna and they'd had it. Jesus seemed more knowledgeable, more godly than the others. Fine, then. . .Satan would test Jesus at His strength.

The devil created a temptation out of Jesus' piety, using His spiritual commitment against Him. Satan took Jesus to the temple, where, in keeping with the mood of the place, he began to quote Scripture. *If You are the Son of God, jump off*

Satan tempted Jesus in this rugged Judean desert.

this temple. God promises to send His angels to catch You. (See Psalm 91:11–12.) *Don't You believe?*

Many godly people would have felt pressured to jump. *I'll show you I believe! Geronimo!* But Jesus replied with Deuteronomy 6:16: "Do not put the LORD your God to the test." Jesus had too much faith to jump. He knew His Father would protect Him, and He didn't need to jump to prove it. Faith isn't about getting ourselves in trouble and waiting for God to bail us out. Faith simply claims God's promises and obeys His commands. Jesus didn't have a promise or command from God to jump, so it wouldn't be faith if He did. It would be foolish, and it would be sin. God tests us; we don't test God. He already knows He's good.

Satan realized he wasn't going to trick Jesus into sinning. Neither physical nor spiritual desire would deceive Him. Okay, then. Satan decided to make a clean, straightforward offer. No gimmicks, just the hard truth, right down the middle. Satan took Jesus "to a very high mountain and showed him all the kingdoms of the world and their splendor. 'All this I will give you,' he said, 'if you will bow down and worship me'" (Matthew 4:8–9). *Look, Jesus. I know why You're here. You've come to take back the world. I'll give it to You right now for a song. All I'm asking for is a little gratitude. Tip Your hat. Bow Your knee. Thank me for sparing You what Your Father has in store.*

But Jesus was too grounded in Deuteronomy 6–8 to fall for this one. He knew Israel's history was riddled with cutting corners, taking the easy way out. The people shrank in fear when they learned the land they were supposed to conquer was inhabited by giants. Some of the pagan people were never driven out, and soon Israel was worshiping their idols. Jesus remembered Israel's sad history as His eye ran up a mental page of Deuteronomy 6. How did the chapter begin? It was the whole point of Deuteronomy: "Hear, O Israel: The LORD our God, the LORD is one. Love the LORD your God with all your heart and with all your soul and with all your strength" (6:4–5). So with the confidence of holy Scripture and knowing full well what it would cost Him, Jesus replied with the words of Deuteronomy 6:13. "Away from me, Satan! For it is written: 'Worship the Lord your God, and serve him only'" (Matthew 4:10). This is the pivotal moment of Jesus' ministry. This is the moment when all creation held its breath.

Three years later Jesus would face what the Gospel writers present as His ultimate test. In the garden of Gethsemane, on the cusp of the godforsaken night ahead, Jesus involuntarily sweat what Luke described as drops of blood (22:44). How did Jesus find the resolve to forge ahead? He found it here, in His final temptation. Long before that dark night of Gethsemane, Jesus had been offered the easy way out and passed. He refused to accomplish redemption on the cheap. He knew that acquiring the entire world meant nothing if the deal meant selling out to Satan. He would not save His own skin. He committed to the cross.

Dying on the cross would be the most difficult thing anyone has ever done, but there was never any doubt what Jesus would do. He had decided years before, in His first go-around with the devil, that He would choose the cross. He had already died in His temptations. Now He only had to go through with it.

Not that it was easy. Looking down the road to the cross knocked the wind out of Jesus. Angels came and ministered to Him, preparing Him for the painful path ahead (Matthew 4:11).

173 Why did Jesus preach?

After His baptism, Jesus "withdrew to Galilee," where He "began to preach, 'Repent, for the kingdom of heaven has come near' " (Matthew 4:12, 17). Jesus preached to announce His arrival. Israel's long-awaited King was here. Deliverance was at hand. "Repent and believe the good news!" (Mark 1:14–15).

Jesus preaches His "sermon on the mount" in a painting from India.

Jesus preached sermons and told parables to instruct His followers how to flourish under His benevolent rule. Israel knew to "Love the LORD your God with all your heart and with all your soul and with all your strength" (Deuteronomy 6:5). Jesus applied this to Himself. He was this God, so those who loved God must "deny themselves and take up their cross and follow me" (Matthew 16:24). If you want to enjoy the benefits of Jesus' kingdom, you've got to submit to the King.

Israel knew to "love your neighbor as yourself" (Leviticus 19:18). Jesus applied this to His kingdom, saying His followers must humbly serve others. Don't aim for power or the top rung in the administrative flow chart. "Instead, whoever wants to become great among you must be your servant, and whoever wants to be first must be your slave—just as the Son of Man did not come to be served, but to serve, and to give his life as a ransom for many." In the pecking order of Christ's kingdom, "the last will be first, and the first will be last" (Matthew 20:26–28, 16).

Jesus' preaching and healing ministry drew a crowd. Once, when healed admirers begged Him to stay, Jesus said, "I must proclaim the good news of the kingdom of God to the other towns also, because that is why I was sent" (Luke 4:43). He didn't get far. Seventy percent of Jesus' ministry occurred on the northwest corner of the Sea of Galilee. He focused His efforts on Bethsaida, Capernaum, and Chorazin, three villages that formed a triangle whose points are only three miles apart.

What an amazing strategy! The Son of God invested His life in such a small area, and most of its inhabitants ultimately rejected Him. Jesus denounced all three villages by name because they had seen His miracles and yet "did not repent": "Woe to you, Chorazin! Woe to you, Bethsaida! . . . And you, Capernaum" (Matthew 11:20–21, 23). Jesus said these villages would receive a harsher judgment than wicked Sodom for they had rejected the revelation of God in the flesh.

And yet. Jesus stuck to the plan, and somehow it worked. Large crowds came "from all over Judea, from Jerusalem, and from the coastal region around Tyre and Sidon." They came "to hear him and to be healed of their diseases" (Luke 6:17–18). But for the most part, Jesus entrusted His kingdom to the common, country folk around the Sea of Galilee. For three years, He mentored His twelve disciples—the leaders of which were uneducated fishermen—then marched with them on Jerusalem for the climactic battle.

Within the week, Jesus was dead. All seemed lost. But He arose from the dead and ascended to heaven, where He rules the world from the throne of His father, David (thereby fulfilling more of the promise that God made to David and Israel; 2 Samuel 7:8–16). Our sovereign Lord sent the Holy Spirit to empower us to preach this saving good news of the kingdom throughout the world (Acts 2:29–41). No one need wallow in the misery of sin and death. Jesus has come. The kingdom is here. Turn from your sin, and believe the good news!

Jesus restored Lazarus to life after His friend had been dead for four days. According to John 11:45, many people who saw the miracle "believed in him."

174 Why did Jesus do miracles?

Jesus' miracles were a vital part of announcing His kingdom. The kingdom of God is a realm of peace, wholeness, and delight; Jesus cast out demons and healed the sick to demonstrate the King had arrived.

Jesus' miracles were obvious signs that He was the Messiah. Peter told his fellow Israelites that "Jesus of Nazareth was a man accredited by God to you by miracles, wonders and signs, which God did among you through him, as you yourselves know" (Acts 2:22; see also Hebrews 2:4). Jesus' miracles proved He was God, as long as you read them correctly—through the prophecies of the Old Testament. What you see depends on what you're looking for and where you're looking from. Different people looked at Jesus' miracles and came away with wildly different conclusions.

Jesus' disciples believed He was the Messiah, and every miracle confirmed God was with Him. Jesus' religious opponents agreed Jesus had supernatural power, but they believed it came from Satan. Every miracle Jesus performed only proved in their minds how powerfully evil He was. He must be demon-possessed (John 7:20; 8:48–52)! Jesus' brothers suspected He was going insane. *What kind of person thinks He is God?* They tried to grab Him and bring Him home, "for they said, 'He is out of his mind' " (Mark 3:21).

Jesus used logic to disprove His opponents' wrong interpretations. He said it was foolish to suppose His power to exorcise demons came from the devil. "How can Satan drive out Satan? If a kingdom is divided against itself, that kingdom cannot stand" (Mark 3:23–24). Why would Satan attack himself?

Ultimately Jesus knew He couldn't prove He was the Messiah to those who refused to be convinced. They had to start with faith. He said, "Anyone who chooses to do the will of God will find out whether my teaching comes from God" (John 7:17). Commit to obey God, and then you will learn the truth about Jesus.

We must also look at Jesus' miracles through the eyes of faith. When a discouraged and imprisoned John the Baptist wondered why Jesus hadn't yet overthrown the Jewish and Roman leaders, he sent a message to Jesus: "Are you the one who is to come, or should we expect someone else?" (Matthew 11:3). Jesus wasn't offended by John's doubt. He told the messenger to "go back and report to John what you hear and see: The blind receive sight, the lame walk, those who have leprosy are cleansed, the deaf hear, the dead are raised, and the good news is proclaimed to the poor" (11:4–5).

Jesus was citing Messianic prophecies in Isaiah (35:5–6; 61:1–3) and claiming they applied to Him. Jesus' assault on the powers in Jerusalem may have been slower than John wanted, but Jesus' miracles are precisely what the Old Testament said the Messiah would do. Everything is right on schedule. Oh, and one more thing: tell John, "Blessed is anyone who does not stumble on account of me" (Matthew 11:6).

Don't be offended by the slow, steady growth of the kingdom. Jesus has established His kingdom by His preaching and miracles, and He will consummate this kingdom when He returns. Believe Him when He says He is God, that "I am in the Father and the Father is in me; or at least believe on the evidence of the works themselves" (John 14:11).

175 What is the unpardonable sin?

Jesus was in a heated argument with the teachers of the law. They said He was casting out demons by the power of Satan. Jesus said that made no sense. Why would Satan attack Satan? Then He added this zinger: "Truly I tell you, people can be forgiven all their sins and every slander they utter, but whoever blasphemes against the Holy Spirit will never be forgiven; they are guilty of an eternal sin" (Mark 3:28–29).

There's a sin that can never be forgiven? What if you accidentally commit it? And what if you accidentally commit it when you're older, after faithfully serving Jesus for most of your life? If you're a little obsessive-compulsive, you might be tempted to do it now, just to get it over with.

I've got good news: you cannot accidentally commit the unpardonable sin. You cannot commit it at all.

As Jesus heals a demon-possessed man, Jewish religious leaders accuse Him of conducting exorcisms in the power of Satan.

The unpardonable sin is blasphemy against the Holy Spirit. It should have been obvious to any observer that Jesus relied on the Spirit's power to cast out demons. But the Jewish leaders were so bent on opposing Jesus, they claimed He was using the power of Satan. Jesus replied it's bad enough when they slander Him. That can be forgiven. But He will not stand by and allow them to speak "against the Holy Spirit." Jesus has the Spirit's back. This sin "will not be forgiven, either in this age or in the age to come" (Matthew 12:32).

Blasphemy against the Spirit is the deliberate and malicious rejection of His power in Jesus. You cannot commit this sin today because Jesus is not standing before you, casting out demons in the unmistakable power of the Spirit. You don't blaspheme the Spirit when you are suspicious of someone's claim to heal or disagree with their "word from the Lord." You don't blaspheme the Spirit when you disobey the prompting you sensed was from Him. You only blaspheme the Spirit if, when you see Jesus perform miracles, you willfully, maliciously, and repeatedly attribute them to Satan. You've not yet seen Jesus in the flesh, so this is one sin you cannot commit.

Any sin you can imagine doing can be forgiven—even sins you haven't thought of yet. The only unpardonable sin is the sin of not asking for pardon. Don't waste time fretting that your sin is unforgivable. Repent, and run to Jesus.

176 Why did Jesus avoid publicity?

Jesus traveled among the villages in Galilee, proclaiming the arrival of His kingdom in word and deed. So why did Jesus sometimes tell the people He had healed not to tell anyone else? Didn't He want publicity?

Sort of. Too much of a good thing can be bad, so Jesus tried to tamp down the excitement about His miracles. We can understand why when we read of healed people joyfully disobeying His order. People who are suddenly cured of debilitating diseases are not going to stay quiet, and "as a result, Jesus could no longer enter a town openly but stayed outside in lonely places" (Mark 1:45). When Jesus did sneak into town, crowds quickly gathered at the house "so that he and his disciples were not even able to eat" (Mark 3:20).

The excitement surrounding Jesus threatened His mission. Jesus needed to invest deeply in His small band of disciples. He couldn't do that when He was continually pressed by enthusiastic throngs. So Jesus told His disciples, "Come with me by yourselves to a quiet place and get some rest" (Mark 6:31). At least once when He "passed through Galilee[,] Jesus did not want anyone to know where they were, because he was teaching his disciples" (Mark 9:30–31).

The excitement surrounding Jesus threatened His message. He realized that most people pursued Him around the countryside because they wanted to catch another miracle. Jesus was the Greatest Show in Galilee. Who would want to miss that?

But Jesus knew that His full salvation would not be understood until after He died on the cross for our sin. He must not let immediate, temporary healings distract from His ultimate, permanent healing. Salvation must not be replaced by spectacle. If the crowds grew too large too soon, they might force a confrontation with Rome before Jesus had prepared His disciples with the true meaning of His ministry. So Jesus thinned the crowds by saying mysterious and controversial things, like His followers must eat His flesh and drink His blood (John 6:26, 53–56).

It worked. Many would-be "disciples turned back and no longer followed him." Jesus turned to the twelve that remained, asking, "You do not want to leave too, do you?" Peter spoke for the group. They might not have liked this morbid turn in His message either, but where were they going to go? Jesus alone had "the words of eternal life." *Besides,* Peter added, *we're starting to get it.* "We have come to believe and to know that you are the Holy One of God" (John 6:66–69).

Mission accomplished.

177 Was Jesus a pacifist?

In His Sermon on the Mount, Jesus said, "Blessed are the peacemakers, for they will be called children of God" (Matthew 5:9). Later in the sermon, He told His followers to "not resist an evil person. If anyone slaps you on the right cheek, turn to them the other cheek also" (5:39). These commands, combined with Jesus' own example of not resisting the evil powers that nailed Him to the cross, lead many Christians to conclude that those who follow Jesus should practice nonviolence. They believe it is always wrong for Christians to use physical force that may injure another, whether in the military, the criminal justice system, or even in self-defense.

This view is compelling. We should imitate our loving, countercultural Lord. Besides, who wants to argue for violence? Who is for war? And yet there are reasons to believe Jesus does not command pacifism.

1. ***Jesus' commands don't demand nonviolence.*** When Jesus said don't resist an evil person, He didn't mean we shouldn't protect ourselves. After all, the devil is an

Though Jesus could have called "twelve legions of angels" to get out of His arrest (Matthew 26:53), He allowed Himself to be falsely accused, beaten, and crucified. Did Jesus refuse to fight back because He is a pacifist?

evil person, and God tells us to resist him (James 4:7).

Jesus isn't arguing against self-defense but retaliation. The Old Testament limited the damage that victims could collect from those who hurt them. Victims must not seek revenge but allow the law courts to exact commensurate justice, taking only an "eye for eye" and "tooth for tooth" (Leviticus 24:20). Jesus reinforces the point about nonretaliation and seems to take it further. Rather than an eye for an eye and a tooth for a tooth, Jesus' followers should not seek revenge either individually or through the courts.

What about turning the other cheek? Most people are right-handed, so to be struck on the right cheek means you were hit with the back of the hand rather than a punch to the face. A back-handed slap is more of an insult than an assault. It's how a superior might show his disdain for a subordinate. It's not how an aggressor would try to knock you out.

So Jesus is not telling us to never act in self-defense or protect those He has entrusted to us. Parents are responsible to God to defend their children. And though Jesus didn't want His disciples to fight His arrest and crucifixion, He did tell them to take along a sword for their travels, presumably for self-protection (Luke 22:36–38, 49–51).

Jesus *is* saying that when someone insults you, don't insult them back. You won't persuade them; you'll only escalate the war of words (see Twitter!).

2. ***Jesus Himself commits acts of violence.*** In His first coming, Jesus nonviolently submitted to the powers that crucified Him. But He will return on a white stallion, leading the armies of heaven and wielding "a sharp sword with which to strike down the nations" (Revelation 19:15). He will throw the devil and his followers "into the lake of burning sulfur," where "they will be tormented day and night for ever and ever" (Revelation 20:10). Not exactly the model of pacifism.

   How could it be? Commands, and the authority behind them, always carry the implicit threat of force. Children obey their parents because Mom and Dad are bigger. Citizens obey the police, who can whisk people off to jail. Employees obey their bosses, who have the authority to fire people. For God to govern our world, He must back up His commands with consequences for disobedience. A world without the threat of hell would be chaos.

3. ***Christians seem permitted to serve in government and the military.*** This is a point of contention. Christian pacifists agree that government is necessary to maintain order, but they disagree that Christians should serve in roles that require the use of physical force.

   However, when soldiers asked John the Baptist what they should do to show repentance, he didn't tell them to quit the military or police force. Instead, he said, "Don't extort money and don't accuse people falsely—be content with your pay" (Luke 3:14). Christianity's first Gentile convert was a Roman centurion who commanded one hundred soldiers in the Italian Regiment. Cornelius's conversion was a momentous turning point in the history of the church, as it opened the nations to the Gospel. Yet there is no hint that Cornelius left his post in the military (see Acts 10). Likewise, Paul led some soldiers of the

Praetorian Guard to Christ. These were the empire's elite troops, and they apparently were not told to leave their employ. Paul brags that their presence in the palace meant that some "who belong to Caesar's household" also belong to Jesus (Philippians 1:13; 4:22).[29]

There are some professions that a Christian could not in good conscience perform. But neither police nor the military seem to be among them. Martin Luther explained that a Christian may serve in government so long as his motives are pure. He will not use violence from anger or revenge but will stop evil with force as an act of love—both to the victim and the perpetrator. It's not loving to allow someone to be abused, and it's not loving to allow someone to abuse. God has established governments as His servants, "agents of wrath to bring punishment on the wrongdoer" (Romans 13:4). The God who created this civil authority may also call His children to serve in it for the common good.

178 Was Jesus a feminist?

This is a loaded question and means different things to different people. Let's start with the simplest and most important meaning of the question: Did Jesus believe women were equal in value to men? Absolutely. Jesus honored women in ways that jarred His patriarchal world.

He struck up a conversation with a Samaritan woman with a past. Jews didn't talk to Samaritans, and men didn't talk to women, especially alone. Yet Jesus engaged this woman in personal banter, asking increasingly probing questions about her marital history. His disciples were surprised by the attention He gave her (John 4:1–27).

Jesus defended a sinful woman who anointed His feet with perfume and washed them with her tears. At dinner. Hosted by an uptight, religious leader who despised the woman, as well as Jesus for allowing her to touch Him. Jesus told the man He could learn a thing or two from her tender caresses (Luke 7:36–50).

He was also touched by a desperately ill and unclean woman as He jostled through a crowd. Jesus stopped everyone and called on the woman to show herself. When she came forward and fell at His feet, trembling in fear and gratitude, He spoke kindly: "Daughter, your faith has healed you. Go in peace" (Luke 8:48).

Jesus had female disciples. The inner circle of twelve were men, but Jesus was also followed by "some women who had been cured of evil spirits and diseases," women who supported Him financially from "out of their own means" (Luke 8:2–3). He encouraged a friend named Mary to sit as His feet as a disciple; when her sister grumbled that Mary wasn't helping enough with the women's work of preparing dinner, Jesus told Martha to leave her alone. "Mary has chosen what is better, and it will not be taken away from her" (Luke 10:42).

Jesus treats women better than anyone and any culture ever has.

Jesus compared God to a woman who had lost one of her silver coins and swept the house searching for it. God is like that woman, urgently seeking every lost sinner. She will not give up until she finds him (Luke 15:8–10).

When Jesus rose from the dead, guess who He looked for first? Not Peter, James, or John, His closest three disciples, but Mary Magdalene, a woman from whom He had cast out seven demons. The resurrected Christ lingered by the tomb, knowing that Mary and the other women disciples would be coming to anoint His body with spices to mask the stench of its decay. Mary mistook Him for the gardener and asked where He had moved the body. Jesus said, "Mary." That's right. He announced His resurrection to the world by saying the name of a woman (see John 20:11–16).

Mary melted in Jesus' arms. She clung to Him, afraid to lose Him again. But Jesus told her and the other women to go tell His male disciples that He had risen from the dead. The disciples didn't believe the women because a resurrection is unbelievable—and because the reporters were women. A woman's word was inadmissible in first-century Jewish courts. But Jesus valued women and their word, and He trusted them with the message that brings hope to the world (Matthew 28:1–10; Luke 24:11).

Jesus seems to believe in male headship—His twelve disciples were men, and He did not disagree with Scripture's depiction of men's and women's roles in the temple and in the home. If you find that distasteful, remember that no one has done more to elevate women than Jesus, and no book more than the Bible. Paul's epistles countered the tendency of Roman men to dominate their wives. He commanded husbands to sacrificially love their wives, as Jesus gave His life for the church (Ephesians 5:25–33). The early Christians rescued infant girls who were left outside and exposed to die just because they were girls.

What religion has a higher view of women? Do women flourish better in Islam, Hinduism, Buddhism, or Christianity? Where else are women treated with the dignity they deserve? You might think women fare better in nonreligious circles, until you consider the logical end of the sexual revolution. When everyone asserts their right to be and do whatever they wish, no one is safe—especially women. Radical individualism inspired sexual freedom, which produced radical feminism, which inevitably led to the transgender movement. Now the very meaning of a woman—including her hard-won rights and even her safety—is at risk.

It's true that Christians have not always treated women well. We are fallen people who commit both willful sins and foolish mistakes. Whether from malice or ignorance, we have not always lived up to the high standards of our Lord. And yet, Christianity is history's leading supporter of female dignity and equality. This may partly explain why most churches attract more women than men. If you rounded up all the people in the world, the person most likely to be a Christian is a woman of color. Women vote with their feet—they run to the Lord who loves them.

179 Was Jesus a socialist?

Some people suggest Jesus was the original socialist because He was kind and shared with others. They say the early church caught His vision when "they sold property and possessions to give to anyone who had need" (Acts 2:45). Isn't this what Karl Marx meant by his slogan "From each according to his ability, to each according to his needs"?

But socialism means more than sharing. It amounts to *forced sharing.* Socialism places ultimate power in the government, which plans the economy, owns all property, and redistributes wealth. A socialist government takes money from one person and gives it to another. This may be a form of "sharing the wealth," but it's not voluntary. And it doesn't work.

Socialism tends to destroy wealth. In the history of the world, no one has ever washed a rental car. The car doesn't belong to them, so they don't care. If you want people to protect and develop resources, you must give them ownership of the resources and the freedom to creatively deploy them as they see fit. This happens best in a capitalistic economy.

Capitalism isn't perfect, but it is remarkably effective at creating wealth. Most

On the anniversary of the Bolshevik Revolution, a Russian man places a portrait of Jesus with Vladimir Lenin.

people have been miserably poor for most of human history. Until two hundred years ago, that is, when the wealth and productivity of many nations suddenly jumped. Economists call this capitalism's "hockey stick effect," because if you're charting productivity, the line suddenly shoots straight up, like the tall handle of a hockey stick. Modern capitalism unleashed innovation that generated so much wealth that now even the poor in developed countries have microwaves, air conditioning, and cell phones.

Few of us want to live in a purely capitalist or socialist economy. We need capitalism to generate wealth and taxes to provide a safety net for those in need. We may debate the right mix—who should be taxed and how much—but no one should doubt our need for some taxes and a whole lot of freedom.

Jesus supported freedom and the ownership of private property, so He could not be a socialist. He said freedom was the reason He came. "If the Son sets you free, you will be free indeed" (John 8:36). He was referring to spiritual freedom, but wouldn't it be strange for Jesus to champion freedom in one realm and take it away in another? If Jesus is for spiritual freedom, He is for social, political, and economic freedom too. Jesus also defended the Ten Commandments, which protect private property by commanding "You shall not steal" and "You shall not covet" (Exodus 20:15, 17).

Personal freedom and ownership of property are proof the early church was not practicing socialism either. The new believers were not forced to share their wealth. No central authority seized their land. They sold their land freely with joy and generosity. When Peter confronted Ananias, who lied about how much of the profit he was sharing with the church, Peter asked, "Didn't it belong to you before it was sold? And after it was sold, wasn't the money at your disposal?" (Acts 5:4). "God loves a cheerful giver," and it's hard to be cheerful and generous when you're giving "under compulsion" (2 Corinthians 9:7).

Most importantly, Jesus warns against the greed that tempts both socialists and capitalists. Someone once yelled from the crowd, "Teacher, tell my brother to divide the inheritance with me" (Luke 12:13). Jesus didn't do what socialists recommend, analyzing the situation so He could redistribute the wealth and make sure the brothers were square. Neither did He praise the brother who may have schemed his way to more than his share. Instead, Jesus warned, "Be on your guard against all kinds of greed; life does not consist in an abundance of possessions" (12:15). Then He told a parable about a rich man who built bigger barns rather than freely share his wealth with others. God called him a fool and took his life (12:16–21).

Greedy capitalists like this rich man want to keep what they have, while greedy socialists want to take what others have. Both are selfish, foolish ways to live. Watch out for greed on the right and on the left. Defend freedom in order to generate wealth and to generously give it away.

180 Was Jesus married?

No.

181 Was Jesus a racist?

This is less ridiculous than the last question. Unlike the entirely unsubstantiated rumors about Jesus' love life, spread by scholars, novelists, and filmmakers who do not believe the Bible, there is a Bible story about Jesus that makes us wince.

Jesus was looking for some alone time with His disciples in the northern, non-Jewish region of Tyre and Sidon. A Phoenician woman heard He was there, and she cried out to Him to heal her demon-possessed daughter. Loudly, repeatedly. Jesus ignored her pleas, until the disciples begged Him to do something. Heal her daughter. Send her away. Make the noise stop!

Jesus seemed to agree with His disciples' disdain. He said, "I was sent only to the lost sheep of Israel." At this point in God's redemption story, Jesus was focusing on the Jews. The mission to the Gentiles wouldn't begin until Jesus ascended to heaven and sent the Holy Spirit. But still. . .have a little compassion, Jesus! This mother is in anguish!

The woman noticed Jesus and the disciples talking about her. She had His attention! She thrust herself forward and knelt at His feet. "Lord, help me!"

Jesus appears to get nasty. " 'First let the children eat all they want,' he told her, 'for it is not right to take the children's bread and toss it to the dogs.' "

The woman brushed aside Jesus' attack. She would show how dogged she was! "Even the dogs eat the crumbs that fall from their master's table."

Jesus was impressed. He said, "Woman, you have great faith! Your request is granted." And her daughter was healed at that moment. (See the whole story in Matthew 15:21–28; Mark 7:24–30.)

This is the only time anyone defeated Jesus in an argument. What are we to make of it?

Jesus let this compassionate mother get the best of Him. He *wanted* her to win not only to help her but also to show His disciples that, while they were presently focusing on Israel, the time would soon come when the good news would spread to the Gentiles they despised. Perhaps Peter remembered this Phoenician woman when later he pondered his vision of sheets filled with unclean food (Acts 10).

Jesus could tell that this woman would not go away quietly. She had already made herself a nuisance. She had nothing to lose by pushing further. So Jesus baited her. He said His blessings were not for her. His food was for the children of Israel not their pet dogs.

This sounds harsh, but Jesus actually softened the metaphor in a way that both she and His disciples would appreciate. Jews despised Gentiles who worshiped many gods, comparing them to wild dogs that scavenged for scraps of truth. Jesus didn't call her a wild stray but a *kynarion,* or "little dog." This woman was more like a puppy, a household pet that enjoyed the family's affection and lay under the table while they ate.

Jesus may have smiled when He said it, because she saw He had given her an opening. And she took it: *If we are lying beneath the table, we can eat the crumbs that fall.* Jesus was proud of her, and He raised her up in triumph. "Woman, you have great faith! Your request is granted" (Matthew 15:28).

Jesus lived in a racist world. Most Jews, including those closest to Jesus, thought they were better than Gentiles, who were scarcely above animals. Jesus reached down to the depths of this racism so He could lift them out. He used their racist image, modified it in a positive direction, and "lost" the argument to show them a better way.

How badly does Jesus hate racism? He'll throw the argument if that's what it takes to get rid of it.

182 How does the cross save us?

Jesus' death on the cross, followed by His resurrection, is the climax of history. Nothing more important has ever happened. Nor can it. As you might guess, something so important may be doing more than one thing. In this case, the death of Jesus accomplished at least four things.

It's easy to remember all four when you use the cross itself as a memory device. The arms of the cross point in four directions: downward, upward, and then outward in two ways, both left and right. Each direction represents a reason why Jesus died.

You'll find crosses everywhere, quiet reminders of Jesus' sacrificial death.

1. ***The cross points down, toward Satan.*** The main reason Jesus died was to defeat sin, death, and Satan. John writes, "The reason the Son of God appeared was to destroy the devil's work" (1 John 3:8). Hebrews 2:14–15 adds that the Son of God became human "so that by his death he might break the power of him who holds the power of death—that is, the devil—and free those who all their lives

were held in slavery by their fear of death." Paul says Jesus didn't merely defeat Satan and his demons, He humiliated them. "And having disarmed the powers and authorities, he made a public spectacle of them, triumphing over them by the cross" (Colossians 2:15).

This explanation for the cross is called *Christus Victor* (Latin for "Christ is the Victor"). Satan had gained the upper hand when he tempted Adam and Eve to rebel against God. He had ruined God's world, and there wasn't much God could do about it. His own words had said humans must die if they sinned.

But God had a plan. He sent Jesus to conquer sin, death, and Satan. But how? This requires the cross's second direction.

2. ***The cross points up, toward God.*** The big picture, the main *why* of the cross is Christus Victor. The substance, the main *how* of the cross is called *penal substitution*. How did Jesus defeat sin, death, and Satan? By bearing our punishment in our place. Jesus endured the holy wrath of God against sin so we could be forgiven.

Satan thought he had God in a corner. God could not forgive sinners without violating His own righteous character. He could not win—God must lose either Himself or the humans He loved. But Satan failed to factor in the unrelenting love of God. John writes, "This is love: not that we loved God, but that he loved us and sent his Son as an atoning sacrifice for our sins" (1 John 4:10).

Jesus satisfied God's holy character when He died in our place, the innocent for the guilty. Paul explains, "God made him who had no sin to be sin for us, so that in him we might become the righteousness of God" (2 Corinthians 5:21). Jesus' substitutionary death was foreshadowed by Israel's animal sacrifices. Old Testament priests sprinkled the blood of lambs on the lid of the Ark of the Covenant. Every year, on the Day of Atonement, the priest entered the Holy of Holies and drenched this "Mercy Seat" with blood. Jesus is the Lamb of God. He is our Mercy Seat, "the atoning sacrifice for our sins" (1 John 2:2).

We are saved from the clutches of sin, death, and Satan when we put our faith in Jesus and what He did for us. We simply turn from our sin and tell Jesus that we want His life, death, and resurrection to count for us. Paul writes, "God presented Christ as a sacrifice of atonement, through the shedding of his blood—to be received by faith." In this way God can both "be just and the one who justifies those who have faith in Jesus" (Romans 3:25–26).

I hope you have done this. I hope you are doing this. Nothing matters more than putting your faith in Jesus. *What then?* This requires the cross's final directions.

3. ***The cross points out, toward us.*** The horizontal arms of the cross point in opposite directions, but they amount to much the same thing. Both directions emphasize how Jesus' death serves as our example for loving others. They differ in that one stresses Jesus is God while the other focuses on His humanity.

The "moral influence" view says Jesus' death demonstrates how much God loves us. Paul says, "God demonstrates his own love for us in this: While we were still sinners, Christ died for us" (Romans 5:8). And John applies this act of love to us: "This is how we know what love is: Jesus Christ laid down his life for us. And we ought to lay down our lives for our brothers and sisters" (1 John 3:16; see also 4:7–12).

The "moral example" view makes a similar point from the opposite direction. We must imitate Jesus' example, but this time focusing on His human rather than divine nature. Peter says we are called to love our enemies, "because Christ suffered for you, leaving you an example, that you should follow in his steps. . . . When they hurled their insults at him, he did not retaliate; when he suffered, he made no threats. Instead, he entrusted himself to him who judges justly" (1 Peter 2:21–23).

If you have been rescued by Jesus' loving sacrifice, you will want to imitate Him, trusting your Father and loving others as God loves you.

Putting it all together, Christus Victor is the big picture, penal substitution is the substance, and moral influence and example are the application. CV answers *why*, PS answers *how*, and MI and E answer *so what*—how should I live now?

Or, to use a baking analogy, CV is the cake, PS is the ingredients, and MI and E are the icing. The cake is the thing, but you can't have a cake without flour and sugar. And any cake worth eating has icing. We must not make icing the main thing, as progressive churches often do, but it is important.

Why did Jesus die? To defeat sin, death, and Satan by bearing God's wrath in our place, leaving us an example of love and faith to follow.

183 Is the cross divine child abuse?

Of the four main reasons why Jesus died, the most controversial is penal substitution. Modern people are offended that a loving God has wrath that must be satisfied. They forgive people who wrong them without demanding a sacrifice. Why can't God? They also wonder why a supposedly loving Father would sacrifice His innocent Son for sinful others. If this happened in our town, we'd call Child Protective Services. Isn't this divine child abuse?

In response, remember that our triune God is one. Father, Son, and Spirit are the same exact divine essence. God didn't sacrifice someone else for our sins. He gave Himself.

It's equally true that the trinity is three and that Father, Son, and Spirit are distinct persons. Viewed this way, the Father did send His innocent Son to die for our sins. How is that okay?

Rather than be offended at the radical step God took to save us, we should take His radical step as a reading on our sin. How bad are we if the death of Jesus was required for our salvation?

Think about it: if a desperate situation calls for extreme measures, then an extreme measure is a sign you're in a desperate situation. If a police car flashes its lights behind me, my wife will turn to me and say in her disapproving voice, "What did you do?" If a convoy of police cars surrounds our car and a television helicopter circles overhead, my wife would get a bit more accusatory. *What did you do?* If a fighter jet joins the chase, machine gunning the pavement toward our car, she's going to scream like a lady in an action movie. *WHAT DID YOU DO?*

Consider what God did to save us. He did not hand us a brochure as if we were merely uninformed. He did not stage an intervention as if we were simply stubborn. God answered our need with the cross. If the death of the Son of God was necessary for you and me to be saved, *What did we do?* I hate to admit it, but I deserve hell. There's no other way to make sense of the cross.

We know that God believes the cross was necessary, because Jesus asked. In Gethsemane, He sweat blood as He braced Himself for the cross. In horror, Jesus asked His Father if there was any other way. Heaven responded with silence; there was no other way (Luke 22:42–44). As I explained in "Why did God demand animal sacrifice to forgive sin?" God's loving, righteous nature that is life requires that its opposite also be true. Selfishness is sin that must produce death. (I'm not saying sin is necessary, only that it necessarily kills.)

God isn't free to shrug off our sin or give us a mulligan. If He did, reality would rupture. The universe would disintegrate. Everything would collapse into a void. So the price must be paid. The shocking beauty of the Gospel is that God stepped forward to pay it. He sent His Son to bear the unfathomable cost of our sin because that's the only way He could preserve His justice and forgive us (Romans 3:25–26).

And that's the only way we can forgive others. Have you noticed? There is no free lunch. Not in economics nor in the criminal justice system. Someone always pays. If I get a government grant, someone else was taxed to pay for it. If the criminal gets off on a technicality, his victim must suffer the injustice.

There's also no free lunch in forgiveness. The only reason we can forgive others without demanding payment is because Someone already paid. We don't need a kill because Someone already died. Let's stop the silly talk, asking why God can't forgive like us—we are not more magnanimous than God because we forgive without demanding a sacrifice. When we forgive—truly forgive—we are merely passing on the payment Jesus made. If I didn't know Jesus, if I hadn't received His forgiveness, I doubt I would—I doubt I could—ever forgive another.

One more thing: it's ironic that opponents of penal substitution say it promotes divine child abuse, because penal substitution is the only way the cross *isn't* that! Unless Jesus is bearing the Father's wrath in my place, I cannot tell you why Jesus died. No one can. Throw out penal substitution, and you have God the Father requiring the death of His Son for no reason. Who's got the real case of divine child abuse now?

You and I do not know better than God. He believes the cross was the only way to save us from the hell we deserve. Don't be offended by the depth of God's love. Let its terrible extremes flood you with horror for the hell you deserve then fill you with gratitude for His amazing grace.

Jesus was buried in—and arose from—a Jerusalem tomb like this.

184 How does Jesus' resurrection save us?

Which is more important, the cross or the resurrection? That's a trick question. Both are equally important. We need both the death and resurrection of Jesus to be saved.

We may mistakenly assume we were saved entirely by the cross. Our sins were forgiven the moment Jesus died. If He had not risen from the dead, we would still be forgiven, we just wouldn't know it for sure. God raised Jesus to give us this assurance. The resurrection of Jesus is God's greatest miracle. It's proof the cross "took."

Paul says it's so much more. In Romans 4:25, he writes that Jesus "was delivered over to death for our sins and was raised to life for our justification." *Justification* is a theological term that means our righteous standing before God. *Jesus was raised for our acceptance with God.* Paul says it again in 1 Corinthians 15:17: "If Christ has not been raised, your faith is futile; you are still in your sins." No resurrection, no forgiveness.

Here's why: the innocent Son of God bore the guilt of the world when He died on the cross. All of our vile, disgusting sins were placed on Him. Even though He had never sinned, Jesus was declared guilty by God the Father, and so He died. If Jesus had remained dead, He would have remained guilty. So would you; so would I.

But the Father raised Jesus from the dead, vindicating Him and releasing Him from that guilt. Now all of us who put our faith in Jesus are justified, accepted by God as if we were His righteous Son.

Jesus died in our place as our substitute. He was raised as our representative to establish our place. Both are essential. We are saved by both the horrific crucifixion of Good Friday and the triumphant resurrection of Easter morning. But we are living on this side of the resurrection. We must not get stuck on Good Friday, wandering around the cross like a donkey tied to a post, trying to feel sorry for Jesus. Christians are not morose—we remember Jesus' agonizing death then raise a fist of triumph. We're Easter Christians, and we live in the victory that Jesus won for us.

185 How do we know Jesus rose from the dead?

The resurrection of Jesus is the foundation of the Christian faith and its most remarkable claim. We believe—and have staked our lives—on the historical fact that our crucified Lord bodily arose from the grave.

We don't merely believe that Jesus' spirit somehow lingers when we gather to remember Him. He doesn't "live on" because we feel Him smiling down on us whenever we feed the hungry or give to the poor. Our faith isn't built on the sappy sentimentality you might find in a Hallmark condolence card.

We believe in hard facts. At sunrise of the third day after His excruciating crucifixion, a bolt of supernatural power jolted Jesus' corpse to life. His blood-crusted eyelids fluttered awake. Sunlight flooded the tomb through the hole where the door used to be. He heard the voice of angels outside and multiple thuds hitting the ground. He smiled and used His arms to push apart the tightly wound strips that bound Him. He rolled over and sat up, rubbed the sleep from His eyes. Then

He stood up, stretched, folded the cloth that had been wrapped around His head, and walked out of the tomb. He grinned as He stepped over and around the unconscious guards. They were posted to prevent grave robbers. They weren't prepared for an inside job.

Why do Christians believe this story? We have three main reasons.

1. ***We believe in Jesus' bodily resurrection because of the missing body.*** The Christian faith would be the easiest thing to disprove. All anyone would have to do, all anyone had to do, was produce the body of Jesus. No one ever did.

   This is compelling evidence because all of Jesus' opponents had powerful reasons to find His body. His resurrection was a disaster for the Romans. They had just crucified Jesus for causing unrest in this corner of the empire. If word about His resurrection spread, imagine the chaos! His followers might claim Jesus is Lord, not Caesar. The Roman Empire might even fall. The Romans never produced a body, so the disciples did make that claim—and Christians did more or less take over the empire.

   Jesus' resurrection was a more immediate disaster for the Jewish leaders. His crucifixion had proved Jesus was cursed by God (Deuteronomy 21:23; Galatians 3:13). If word about His resurrection spread, many people might believe He actually is the Son of God and not the blasphemer the Jewish leaders had alleged. But the Jews could not produce the body, so they bribed the Roman guards to say His disciples had stolen it during the night, while they slept (Matthew 28:11–15).

   These guards had the most pressing need to find the body, because falling asleep on the job was a capital offense. Under normal circumstances, they might be killed. *How bad must the truth be when your best defense is you deserve to die? If that's the story you're going with, what are you hiding?*

2. ***We believe in Jesus' bodily resurrection because of the witnesses.*** No one saw the moment that Jesus' body quivered to life. But hundreds of people saw Him afterward.

   The first people were women. This is compelling evidence today because it wasn't then. Female testimony was inadmissible in Jewish court, so first-century

Jews would not make women their lead testimony. But all four Gospels agree. Women were the first people to find the empty tomb and the first people to see Jesus. Why would the Gospels include this allegedly weak testimony unless it was true? These women saw their Lord.

So did the disciples. They couldn't believe their eyes and assumed they must be seeing Jesus' ghost. But He insisted, "Look at my hands and my feet. It is I myself! Touch me and see; a ghost does not have flesh and bones, as you see I have" (Luke 24:39). He then ate some broiled fish to prove it was Him in the flesh. Paul adds that Jesus also "appeared to more than five hundred of the brothers and sisters at the same time, most of whom are still living" (1 Corinthians 15:6). Paul's point was that Jesus' resurrection appearances were "not done in a corner" (Acts 26:26). If first-century seekers wanted to investigate further, there were many witnesses they could talk to.

The testimony of the twelve apostles is compelling because each one, except

Luke reports that the resurrected Jesus appeared to His apostles "and gave many convincing proofs that he was alive" (Acts 1:3).

for John and Judas, was martyred for their faith in the resurrected Christ. Ten men chose painful death rather than recant their story. If they had stolen the body as the compromised guards claimed, wouldn't one of them have come clean before the nail was struck or the match lit? Most people don't give their lives for what they know is a lie. The disciples were so convinced they had seen and touched their risen Lord that they chose to be stoned, burned, impaled, and crucified for Him.

3. ***We believe in Jesus' bodily resurrection because of the Bible.*** You might object that all of this evidence for the resurrection comes from the Bible. So ultimately the question of the resurrection comes down to whether or not we believe the Bible. I think that's right. It's why this book includes several questions on the historical truthfulness of the Bible.

I won't repeat that material here but simply say that the Bible is the most compelling reason to believe Jesus rose from the dead. At least Jesus thought so. On the afternoon of His resurrection, Jesus encountered two disciples on the road from Jerusalem to Emmaus. They were sadly discussing Jesus' crucifixion and the early reports that something had happened at the tomb. No one knew where the body of Jesus was. The disciples didn't know what to make of it.

Jesus did not say, "Hey guys, it's Me! Look at the evidence!" Instead, He told them they would understand the day's news if they knew their Bible better: "And beginning with Moses and all the Prophets, he explained to them what was said in all the Scriptures concerning himself" (Luke 24:27). Jesus did the same thing later that day when He appeared to the rest of the disciples. He began with "Look at my hands and my feet" (verse 39), then finished their time by opening their minds "so they could understand the Scriptures" (verse 45). He explained from the Bible why the Messiah had to suffer and rise from the dead to provide forgiveness of sins. Then He reminded them, "You are witnesses of these things" (verse 48).

Don't feel bad that your knowledge of the resurrection comes from one source. That source is the Bible, so you can scarcely do better. If Jesus was standing before you right now, He would say, "Look! Touch me and see!" Then He would open your Bible and show you what it says about Him.

You have a Bible, don't you? Then you don't have to wait. Why not read it, asking the Spirit of Jesus to help you see what it says about Him?

186 What was Jesus doing between His death and resurrection?

Jesus died at 3:00 on the Friday afternoon of Passover and rose from the dead at sunrise on Sunday morning. What was Jesus doing during the intervening day and a half? His body was taken down and placed in a tomb. Where was His spirit?

The Apostles' Creed says Jesus "descended into hell." This line may not be in the Creed's earliest versions, and it can be taken in various ways. The early church understood it to mean that Jesus descended to the place of the dead. Everyone who died before Jesus' resurrection went to the lower regions beneath the earth, variously called *inferna* (Latin), *hades* (Greek), or *sheol* (Hebrew). So "descended into hell" simply means Jesus died.

Some later theologians, such as John Calvin and the Heidelberg Catechism, interpreted this phrase to describe Jesus' spiritual agony as He suffered on the cross. The traditional Roman Catholic view follows Thomas Aquinas, who said Jesus went to *limbus patrum* ("the father's limbo"), to free Old Testament saints and lead them to heaven. Lutherans believe Jesus descended to hell to announce His victory over Satan. Although they differed on what did happen, no one thought the Apostles' Creed was saying Jesus suffered for three days in the furnace of hell.

The Bible says Jesus' spirit may have preached to other spirits in prison. Jesus "was put to death in the body but made alive in the Spirit. After being made alive, he went and made proclamation to the imprisoned spirits—to those who were disobedient long ago when God waited patiently in the days of Noah while the ark was being built" (1 Peter 3:18–20). The church has traditionally interpreted this to mean Jesus went to hell to proclaim His victory to humans and/or angels who had sinned grievously before the Flood.

Maybe, but this is a difficult passage that can be understood in other ways. Perhaps it means that a preincarnate Jesus preached through Noah to his wicked generation. Or that the people who listened to Jesus' earthly ministry were as obstinate as the sinners of Noah's day. Or that Jesus' resurrection triumphs over the most extreme powers of evil, represented by these "imprisoned spirits." We just don't know. It wouldn't be wise to build too high on this unclear foundation.

What was the spirit of Jesus doing before His resurrection? Perhaps He was merely resting with other dead saints in the presence of His Father, until the dawn that burst open the first day of the new creation.

187 Why did other people rise from the dead with Jesus?

Strange things happened in Jerusalem when Jesus breathed His last. Matthew writes, "At that moment the curtain of the temple was torn in two from top to bottom. The

Sarcophagi in a building at the foot of the Mount of Olives.

earth shook, the rocks split and the tombs broke open. The bodies of many holy people who had died were raised to life. They came out of the tombs after Jesus' resurrection and went into the holy city and appeared to many people" (27:51–53).

These events were signs that a new epoch had arrived. The ground had shifted, literally. The earthquake ripped in half the temple's sixty-foot-high and thirty-foot-wide curtain made of seventy-two twisted plaits of twenty-four threads each. This thick, impenetrable barrier blocked the entrance to the Holy of Holies. God split this massive curtain to visually show that we may now approach Him through Jesus, whose sacrifice brings us safely into the presence of God (Hebrews 10:19–22).

What about the other, stranger sign? How weird that the earthquake broke open tombs, and saints from ages past arose and entered Jerusalem! This was not the zombie apocalypse. These saints were resurrected to full life; they were not merely undead, resuscitated corpses. Remember also that first-century Jewish tombs were not underground. Jews washed and wrapped their dead, anointed their bodies with spices, and placed them in tombs. After twelve months, they returned to collect the bones, which they placed in ossuaries, or bone boxes. This gruesome task—who wants to enter a tomb and collect Grandma's bones?—gives us a picture of how this resurrection occurred. Resurrected saints were not crawling out of holes in the ground. Rather their bones rattled together, added muscle, organs, and skin, then popped off the lids of their ossuary boxes (consider the imagery of Ezekiel 37:1–14).

We don't know much about this strange event. How many resurrected saints were there? Were they from a certain era or from all ages past? How long did they stay in Jerusalem? What did they tell the people they appeared to? What happened to them afterward? Did they climb back into their bone boxes (doubtful), or did they ascend to heaven like Jesus (probable)?

We don't know the details, but we can guess the meaning and purpose of this sign. First, it combined with the other wonders to prove that Jesus is someone special. Matthew notes, "When the centurion and those with him who were guarding Jesus saw the earthquake and all that had happened, they were terrified, and exclaimed, 'Surely he was the Son of God!' " (27:54).

Second, the odd, elongated timeframe—the graves open when Jesus dies, but the saints don't leave their tombs until after Jesus' resurrection—may be Matthew's way of tying together Jesus' death and resurrection. Good Friday and Easter morning are essential bookends of the same event. There is no Christian faith without both.

Third, the saints' resurrection is an early return on the promise of Jesus' resurrection. Easter morning was the dawn of a new age. Life had conquered death. We no longer need to fear death, because we know that all who die in Christ will rise with Him. It happened before, when Jesus arose, and it will happen again, when Jesus returns for us. Jesus is "the firstfruits" of our resurrection, a sign of coming attractions (1 Corinthians 15:20). We know this because for some lucky saints, He's already cashed in.

188 What was Jesus doing between his resurrection and ascension?

The resurrected Christ did not return to heaven right away. He lingered for forty days, appearing now and again to His disciples to prove He was alive and instruct them about the kingdom of God (Acts 1:3).

There was a lot for the disciples to process. They were triumphant. Jesus is alive! He has conquered sin and death forever! But the curtain had not yet come down. Jesus was not now sitting on David's throne in Jerusalem, as they had expected. Instead, the intermittently appearing Jesus seemed to be preparing them for the road ahead. The climactic battle had been won, but the war wasn't over. A new phase was about to begin.

The forty days between Jesus' resurrection and ascension are God's way of letting us know this was an important transitional time. Many significant periods in Scripture come in packs of forty. It rained forty days and forty nights during Noah's Flood. Moses went up to meet with God on Mount Sinai for forty days. He spent forty years in Egypt, forty years in the Midianite desert, then forty years wandering with Israel in the wilderness. Israel spied out the land for forty days, Nineveh was given forty days to repent, and Jesus fasted and was tempted forty days.

So now, Jesus spent forty days in this time between. He wasn't yet in heaven, but He wasn't exactly on earth either. He wouldn't leave until His followers were ready for the next phase, the coming of the Holy Spirit that would detonate God's explosive plan for world evangelization. Jesus appeared to His disciples and "gave many convincing proofs that he was alive" (Acts 1:3). He invited doubters to touch His pierced side and believe (John 20:27). He reconciled with Peter, who had denied Him, and gave him a path to prove his love: "Feed my sheep" (John 21:15–19). And He explained how His life, death, and resurrection were the fulfillment of Israel's

The resurrected Jesus tells Peter to "feed my sheep" (John 21:15–19).

story. All the pieces fell into place for the disciples; they finally realized why Jesus had to die and rise again and why they were now being sent to preach forgiveness in His name to all people (Luke 24:45–49).

If you are a follower of Jesus, you are an extension of this ministry. What Jesus was preparing His disciples for is now being accomplished through you.

189 Why did Jesus return to heaven?

Forty days after Jesus rose from the dead to conquer sin, death, and Satan, He ascended to heaven for His coronation. Jesus now sits enthroned at the right hand of His Father, the rightful ruler over the kings of the earth (Revelation 1:5).

We were not present for the ceremony, but a biblical hymn announces what occurred. "God exalted him to the highest place and gave him the name that is above every name, that at the name of Jesus every knee should bow, in heaven and on earth and under the earth, and every tongue acknowledge that Jesus Christ is Lord, to the glory of God the Father" (Philippians 2:9–11).

Jesus' coronation fulfills Old Testament dreams for the Messiah. Daniel saw "one like a son of man, coming with the clouds of heaven. He approached the Ancient of Days and was led into his presence. He was given authority, glory and sovereign power; all nations and peoples of every language worshiped him. His dominion is an everlasting dominion that will not pass away, and his kingdom is one that will never be destroyed" (Daniel 7:13–14).

Jesus' coronation dashes the dreams of His challengers. Roman emperors rarely claimed to be gods while they were alive, and the few who did (Caligula, Nero, and Domitian) ended badly. Roman emperors were said to become gods sometime after their deaths, and the proof was witnesses who came forward to say they had seen the deceased emperor ascend to heaven.

The Acts of the Apostles wags its finger at such ridiculous claims. Dead Caesars are not Lord. Jesus is Lord, and He proved it by rising from the dead and ascending to heaven (Acts 1:9).

The first half of Acts demonstrates Jesus' authority over Jewish kings. He is the Jews' true Lord and Messiah (2:36). Herod might think he is king, and his flattering subjects might shout that he speaks with "the voice of a god, not of a man." But immediately "an angel of the Lord struck him down, and he was eaten by worms and died." Not, "he died and was eaten by worms." Being eaten by worms was the cause of his death (Acts 12:21–23). Don't mess with our enthroned Lord!

Jesus returns to heaven in an event called "the Ascension."

The second half of Acts demonstrates Jesus' authority over Roman kings. Caesar might think he is king, and flattering subjects might pretend to honor and obey him. But the book of Acts ends with Paul sailing right into Rome. For two years, "with all boldness and without hindrance," Paul "proclaimed the kingdom of God and taught about the Lord Jesus Christ" (28:30–31). Paul proclaimed Jesus was Lord right under Caesar's nose and won many disciples. Don't mess with our enthroned Lord!

190 What is Jesus doing in heaven?

The Son's incarnation and ministry on our behalf is not over. Jesus remains one of us—He is fully human—and He remains fully engaged for us. While on earth, Jesus fulfilled Israel's three highest offices. He was the consummate prophet, priest, and king rolled into one. He still is.

Our ascended Lord is our King. He is king over the world and head of His church (Colossians 1:18). There is nothing Jesus cares more about than His people in His church. When Stephen was about to be stoned for his faith in Christ, he looked into heaven and saw "the Son of Man standing at the right hand of God" (Acts 7:56). Why was Jesus standing? At His coronation He sat down at His Father's right hand (2:34). But Jesus cares about Stephen's ordeal, and He stands to cheer him on and to welcome him into heaven.

Our ascended Lord is our Prophet. He went to heaven in order to send the Holy Spirit, who inspired the apostles to write sacred Scripture that continues to guide and teach us today (John 15:26; 16:13–15). The Bible reveals more about Jesus than even His disciples knew, before His ascension.

Jesus prayed often when He was on earth. He continues to pray for us in heaven.

Our ascended Lord is our Priest. He mediates between His Father and us in both directions. Jesus intercedes on our behalf before the Father. When Satan accuses us before God, Jesus raises a nail-scarred hand and shushes him. Satan can't get traction with our crucified, enthroned Lord pleading our case (Hebrews 7:25; 9:24).

Jesus also conveys His Father's forgiveness to us. Peter said, "God exalted him to his own right hand as Prince and Savior that he might bring Israel to repentance and forgive their sins" (Acts 5:31). Jesus' enthronement means He has the authority to forgive sin. There is no higher court of appeal. If the crucified, ascended Lord declares you are forgiven, then you are forgiven. There is nothing anyone can do about it.

With Jesus as our enthroned priest, Hebrews says we may "draw near to

God with a sincere heart and with the full assurance that faith brings." We will "hold unswervingly to the hope we profess" and "consider how we may spur one another on toward love and good deeds, not giving up meeting together. . .but encouraging one another" (10:22–25).

Do you believe Jesus has been crowned as Lord? Then keep the faith, and get to church.

191 What is a disciple?

Jesus' final instructions to His followers was to "go and make disciples of all nations" (Matthew 28:19). The Greek word for disciple, *mathētēs,* means learner. Not only intellectually, as when a student takes a class from a teacher, but broad, holistic learning. Disciples don't have mere teachers; they have masters. They listen and live with these masters until they learn to be like them.

The word *disciple* is almost entirely missing from the Old Testament. In the Septuagint, the early Greek translation of the Old Testament, the term *mathētēs* does not appear. In the original Hebrew, there's only one instance when a prophet mentions his disciples (Isaiah 8:16). The prophets often had apprentices, but they did not usually call them "disciples" (1 Samuel 19:20; 2 Kings 4:1, 38; 9:1). Perhaps God wanted the prophets in training to focus on His Word, not the leaders who delivered that Word.

Then a leader appeared who *was* the Word. Jesus did not merely pass along God's revelation; He was the revelation. Jesus did not ask people to be His students; He called them to be His disciples. He told Peter and Andrew to drop their fishing nets and, "Come, follow me" (Mark 1:17). He walked by Matthew sitting in his tax collector's booth and said the same (Mark 2:14). These three belonged to Jesus' inner core of twelve disciples, but there were others. A larger entourage, including women patrons who supported Jesus, followed Him from village to village (Luke 8:1–3).

Jesus invested three years in His disciples, teaching and modeling the kingdom of God—then commanded them to keep the chain going. Just before He returned to heaven, Jesus told them to make new disciples, "baptizing them in the name of the Father and of the Son and of the Holy Spirit, and teaching them to obey everything I have commanded you" (Matthew 28:19–20).

Jesus did not tell His disciples to make converts—He isn't satisfied with merely asking someone to believe in Him. Jesus wants *disciples*. This requires baptism into a church, because a disciple is signing up for a new life in Christ and with His people. Disciples do life together. This requires "teaching them to obey everything," because disciples don't pick and choose which parts they're willing to do. Disciples gather regularly with other disciples as a church to be instructed by God's Word and unleashed back into the world, where they call others to follow Jesus too.

192 What is an apostle?

The familiar imagery of the Last Supper includes Jesus' twelve apostles ("sent ones"), who originally began as disciples ("learners").

We're all called to be disciples, but none of us are apostles. Only a handful of men ever were. Jesus "called his disciples to him and chose twelve of them, whom he also designated apostles," to be His key leaders (Luke 6:13). Three of these—Peter, James, and John—formed an inner core, with Peter being the top apostle of them all.

The apostles were personally selected by Jesus to be the original leaders of the church. God says the church is "built on the foundation of the apostles and prophets, with Christ Jesus himself as the chief cornerstone" (Ephesians 2:20). Apostles are no longer necessary because the foundation of the church has been laid. Apostles are no longer possible because the founding of the church has passed. There can be only one beginning.

The term *apostle* means "messenger" or "sent one." Jesus sent His apostles on kingdom missions throughout Galilee. Then, before He ascended to heaven, Jesus sent them on their final—and our ongoing—mission throughout the world. He told them to "go and make disciples of all nations" (Matthew 28:19), sharing His good news beginning in Jerusalem, then "in all Judea and Samaria," and finally "to the ends of the earth" (Acts 1:8).

The Bible tells their story in the Acts of the Apostles. The first part, chapters 1–12, describes Peter's mission to the Jews in Jerusalem and Judea. The second part, chapters 13–28, describes Paul's mission to the Gentiles and "the ends of the earth."

Paul was not one of the original apostles. He met Jesus later, on the road to Damascus. At that time known as Saul, he was heading there to imprison Jesus' followers when Jesus intervened. A "light from heaven flashed around him" (Acts 9:3), blinding and knocking Saul to the ground. Jesus asked why Saul was persecuting Him and announced, "Get up and go into the city, and you will be told what you must do" (9:6). In Damascus, God instructed a disciple named Ananias to help Saul, saying that he would "proclaim my name to the Gentiles and their kings" (9:15). Paul later reflected on this commission and concluded that he too was an apostle, though "one abnormally born." He came after the others, and was "the least of the apostles. . .because I persecuted the church of God" (1 Corinthians 15:8–9).

The apostles lived up to their name as "sent ones" and spread the good news about Jesus throughout the world. Paul covered the length of the Roman Empire, perhaps making it all the way to Spain. We know that Peter preached in Rome and John in Turkey. It's hard to tell truth from legend, but it's believed that James son of Alphaeus went to Syria; Andrew to Georgia, Bulgaria, Ukraine, Russia, Greece, and Romania; Matthew to Iran and Ethiopia; Philip to Turkey and North Africa;

Judas Thaddeus to Syria, Turkey, Georgia, Iraq, and Iran; Simon the Zealot to Lebanon and Iran; Bartholomew to Georgia, Iraq, Iran, Pakistan, Afghanistan, and India; and Thomas to Iran, Afghanistan, and India.

All but one of these apostles were martyred for their faith—and John was exiled to an inhospitable island. Some were stabbed or beheaded, others were stoned, one was burned, and two were crucified. They died so that you and I could hear about Jesus. They gave their lives so our lives might be saved.

Jesus said some people wouldn't follow Him because they loved money too much. It would be easier for a camel to pass through the eye of a needle than for a rich man to be saved (Mark 10:25).

193 Why didn't everyone follow Jesus?

Because of sin. This is the number one reason people didn't follow Jesus. We all want to play God; to do what we want when we want. We've got plans, and we won't take orders from anyone, even if He is Jesus.

A rich young ruler asked Jesus what he must do to live forever. Jesus replied with an ultimatum that struck at his idol. "Go, sell everything you have and give to the poor, and you will have treasure in heaven. Then come, follow me" (Mark 10:21). The man "went away sad, because he had great wealth" (verse 22). Jesus was sad too and commented that following Him isn't merely hard—it's impossible unless God changes sinful hearts.

There were other less important yet real reasons for not following Jesus. People turned away because of His claims and His challenges.

Because of His claims. Think about someone you admire. You love his kindness, stories, and all around good humor. He always picks you up; he never has a bad day. He's one of your best friends.

What if he started dropping hints that he was God? Wouldn't that change your relationship? Wouldn't you encourage him to seek counseling, and if he refused, wouldn't you stop returning his texts?

Jesus' outrageous claims didn't make it easy for people to follow Him. He either was the God He claimed to be, or He was a psychopath. No one could listen to Jesus' claims and offer a lukewarm, "Meh." You either pitied Him because He was a lunatic, fought Him because He was a devious liar, or worshipped Him because He was Lord. There was no other option. Jesus made sure of that.

Jesus began His ministry in His hometown of Nazareth. Everyone liked Him and "spoke well of him." They "were amazed at the gracious words that came from his lips"—until Jesus said He was the Chosen One, the long-awaited Messiah who would rescue Israel and bring salvation to the world. They scratched their heads. "Isn't this Joseph's son?" they asked (Luke 4:22). Don't we know His family? Isn't He one of us? "And they took offense at him" (Mark 6:3).

Because of His challenges. Jesus didn't merely claim to be the Messiah; He blamed those who did not believe. It was their fault. They should know better.

Think again about your friend who claims to be God. Wouldn't your friendship be considerably more strained if he criticized you for not believing? You might get mad.

You can appreciate Jesus' townsfolk. They "were furious" (Luke 4:28) when He told them "no prophet is accepted in his hometown" (verse 24), so God often sends His prophets to faraway, non-Jewish people. They "drove him out of the town, and took him to the brow of the hill on which the town was built, in order to throw him off the cliff." But Jesus "walked right through the crowd and went on his way" (verses 29–30).

Because His claims were true.

194 Why did the Roman leaders hate Jesus?

They didn't. But only because they didn't perceive Jesus as much of a threat. He seemed to be a traveling preacher of love who wore on the nerves of the Jewish leaders. As long as Jesus remained a Jewish squabble, there was little reason for Rome to be concerned. He wasn't their problem.

So the Jews tried to make Jesus the Romans' problem. Jewish leaders believed Jesus must die because He had committed the blasphemy of saying He was God. They knew Rome wouldn't care about their theological tiffs, so they told Pilate, the Roman governor, that Jesus was leading a revolution. "He opposes payment of taxes to Caesar and claims to be Messiah, a king" (Luke 23:2).

Pilate yawned. "Are you the king of the Jews?" he asked (Luke 23:3). Jesus said that He was. Pilate didn't care. He told the Jewish leaders, "I find no basis for a charge against this man" (verse 4).

The remains of the imperial temple in Ephesus, built when the brutal emperor Domitian exiled the apostle John from that city (mid-90s CE).

The Jews insisted. *You don't understand.* "He stirs up the people all over Judea by his teaching. He started in Galilee and has come all the way here" (Luke 23:5).

The Jews thought they'd grab Pilate's attention with "He stirs up the people," but all he heard was *Galilee.* Huh? *Say, that's the jurisdiction of Herod Antipas* (son of the wicked and long-deceased Herod the Great). *He's in Jerusalem for Passover, and I bet he'd love to see You.* So Pilate sent Jesus to Herod.

"When Herod saw Jesus, he was greatly pleased, because for a long time he had been wanting to see him. From what he had heard about him, he hoped to see him perform a sign of some sort" (Luke 23:8).

Do you see how ridiculous this is? Jesus and the Jews were locked in a life-and-death struggle. The Jews were burning with righteous indignation as Jesus was preparing to die for our sins. And Herod only wanted a show. *Do a trick, Jesus!* The government could not have taken Jesus more lightly. Too lightly, it turns out.

Jesus refused to entertain Herod. He wouldn't even speak. So "Herod and his soldiers ridiculed and mocked him" (Luke 23:11). They dressed Him in a royal robe and sent Him back to Pilate.

Pilate gathered the Jews and reviewed their charge that Jesus "was inciting the people to rebellion" (Luke 23:14). He announced that neither he nor Herod had found this to be true, so he would simply flog Jesus for good measure and release Him.

The crowd was incensed. They screamed that Jesus must die because He claimed to be the Son of God (John 19:7). This grabbed Pilate's attention. Jesus had been eerily calm during these trials. He had said little, suffering jeers and humiliation in silence. Maybe He wasn't of this world.

Pilate took Jesus inside his palace for a private meeting. "Where do you come from?" he asked (John 19:9). Jesus did not answer, and Pilate became alarmed. "Do you refuse to speak to me? Don't you realize I have power either to free you or to crucify you?" (verse 10). Jesus replied that Pilate's power came from God, and one day he would answer for what he was about to do (verse 11).

"From then on, Pilate tried to set Jesus free, but the Jewish leaders kept shouting, 'If you let this man go, you are no friend of Caesar. Anyone who claims to be a king opposes Caesar' " (John 19:12).

The Jews made Jesus into Pilate's problem. If he released Jesus, they would tell Caesar, and Pilate might get in trouble with Rome. If Pilate killed Jesus, he'd get in trouble with God, at least for violating his conscience and crucifying an innocent man. And possibly for killing God's Son. Who should Pilate please? He chose Rome.

And so was fulfilled the prophecy made by Simeon, the old man who held the infant Jesus and said, "This child is destined to cause the falling and rising of many in Israel, and to be a sign that will be spoken against, so that the thoughts of many hearts will be revealed" (Luke 2:34–35).

Jesus was a larger threat than Rome knew. As with Pilate, our response to Jesus reveals what is in our hearts. Don't be a coward. Don't cave to the crowd. Choose Him.

195 Why did the Jewish leaders hate Jesus?

Not all of them did. Joseph of Arimathea and Nicodemus were members of the Sanhedrin, the Jewish ruling council, and they secretly followed Jesus. They had such devotion that they boldly stepped forward and asked Pilate's permission to take Jesus' body down from the cross (John 19:38–40; 3:1–2; Mark 15:43). Their faith had been crucified, yet they continued to love and serve Jesus, even when all seemed lost. Their obedience in the teeth of despair is an underappreciated part of the Christian story: if Jesus' body had been left to be eaten by birds and jackals, He would "see decay" (Acts 2:27), and the resurrection, as it unfolded in Scripture, would have been impossible.

By the end of Jesus' ministry, most Jewish leaders shouted for His death. They had overlearned the lesson of the Babylonian exile. God had decimated their country for worshiping other gods, and they determined not to make that mistake again. So when a very human Jesus appeared and claimed He was God, they assumed He was guilty of blasphemy (Matthew 26:63–66; John 10:33).

Their hatred for Jesus was also personal. Jesus' most vitriolic opponents were the Pharisees, a group of devout teachers who enforced adherence to Jewish law. If disobedience brought exile, and if obedience might inspire God to send the Messiah,

Pharisees hassle Jesus after His disciples pluck heads of grain for a snack on the Sabbath. This was one of their gentler interactions with Jesus.

then the Pharisees would make Israel obey. They would teach the Jews what God expected and shame them when they failed.

Jesus said the Pharisees' focus on outward conformity turned them into hypocrites. They emphasized tithes, ritual washings, and picayune rules but neglected the more important attitudes of the heart. They appeared good, "like whitewashed tombs, which look beautiful on the outside"—but on the inside "are full of the bones of the dead and everything unclean" (Matthew 23:27). They were nothing but snakes, a "brood of vipers!" (verse 33). They zealously made converts to their legalistic ways, only to "make them twice as much a child of hell as you are" (verse 15).

Well! The Pharisees were Israel's most respected religious leaders. The Jewish people admired them, giving them seats of honor at banquets and greeting them with "Rabbi" ("Teacher") when they saw them about town (Luke 23:6–7). Jesus' criticism was tantamount to calling the pope a hypocrite or the Dalai Lama a fraud. Even if you thought it, you wouldn't say it. It just wasn't done.

Like the pope or the Dalai Lama, the Pharisees had a lot to lose. They were jealous of Jesus, who was drawing ever-larger crowds when He spoke. This country bumpkin was eroding their status and authority! How humiliating! They would not go down without a fight, so they dressed their jealousy in pious fears about blasphemy and schemed with the chief priests "to arrest Jesus secretly and kill him" (Matthew 26:4). It was just what Jesus said these snakes would do (26:2).

196 Why did Jesus speak kindly to sinners and harshly to religious leaders?

It's a story not found in the earliest biblical manuscripts, yet many scholars believe it happened. The Pharisees caught a woman in the act of committing adultery, brought her to Jesus, and asked if He agreed with the Old Testament Law that she should be stoned. Jesus didn't answer the question directly but said, "Let any one of you who is without sin be the first to throw a stone at her" (John 8:7). As the Pharisees slunk away, leaving Jesus alone with the woman, He said to her, "Then neither do I condemn you. Go now and leave your life of sin" (8:11).

Jesus' kindness to this immoral woman is a far cry from His angry denunciation of Israel's religious leaders. He called the Pharisees every name except what their mammas gave them. Why the difference?

Contrary to popular opinion, Jesus wasn't tough on the Pharisees because He dislikes religious people. Some critics, perhaps trying to excuse their own sinful behavior, use Jesus' words against the Pharisees to warn those who desire to read the Bible and do what it says. "Watch out," they say. "Remember that Jesus saved His harshest words for those who were most religious." As if Jesus has a soft spot in His heart for sin.

Jesus greets the short tax collector Zacchaeus, who'd climbed a tree so he could see the Lord. Religious leaders soon complained that Jesus had invited Himself into the home of a "sinner" (Luke 19:1–10).

Jesus does have a soft spot for sinners, and that explains the difference. Jesus told the Pharisees that He was the Great Physician who had come to heal the sick. "I have not come to call the righteous, but sinners to repentance" (Luke 5:32).

This means everyone, though not everyone realized they were sick. Jesus rode the Pharisees hard because He had to cut through layers of hypocrisy and self-righteousness to uncover their sin. This was a painful process, and most Pharisees fought Him for every inch. They didn't want to be exposed. Who does? But without confession, there can be no forgiveness.

The diagnosis was much easier with broken, unchaste women. No one had to convince them they were sinners. Everyone knew it, so there was no use pretending. Jesus didn't even bring it up. When a woman with a reputation for having "lived a sinful life" (Luke 7:37) anointed Jesus' feet with perfume and her tears, He accepted her public demonstration of devotion and declared, "Your sins are forgiven. . . . Your faith has saved you; go in peace" (Luke 7:48, 50).

Do you want Jesus to speak softly to you? Confess your sins. Admit you are sick, trust the Doctor, and you will be healed.

197 How does Jesus' life, death, and resurrection count for me?

Jesus lived on earth a long time ago in (for many of us) a faraway place. How does what He did then and there count for us here and now? By faith. Faith is a time traveler. And a space eraser. Faith leaps over two thousand years and a couple of continents and unites us to Jesus. When we tell God that we are turning from sin and putting all our trust in Jesus, He responds by uniting us with His Son. All the righteousness that Jesus earned by His perfect life, substitutionary death, and triumphant resurrection counts for us.

By ourselves, we are sinners who deserve hell. But we are not by ourselves. If we just believe, we are in Christ. God could not have made our choice clearer: "Whoever believes in the Son has eternal life, but whoever rejects the Son will not see life, for God's wrath remains on them" (John 3:36).

A member of New Guinea's Korowai tribe, believed to have been unaware of any other people groups until the 1970s.

198 What about people who've never heard of Jesus?

God sent His Son into the world so that "whoever believes in him shall not perish but have eternal life. . . . Whoever believes in him is not condemned, but whoever does not believe stands condemned already because they have not believed in the name of God's one and only Son" (John 3:16, 18).

Whoever does not believe stands condemned. But what if they don't believe because they've never heard about Jesus? What if it's not their fault?

This is a painful question, but God doesn't shrink from answering it. There are people who tragically live and die without hearing the good news about Jesus—but none are innocent. Everyone sinfully suppresses something they know about God.

Paul opens his letter to the Romans by explaining that all people are guilty before God, and so all people need Jesus. His conclusion comes in Romans 3:23—"all have sinned and fall short of the glory of God." He proves this in chapter one, which describes why all Gentiles have sinned; and in chapter two, which explains why all Jews have sinned. Since everyone is either a Gentile or Jew, Paul concludes that all have sinned and need salvation.

Romans 1 demonstrates how every Gentile is guilty before God. Even those who don't have access to God's special revelation—they have never seen a Bible or heard about Jesus—still know something about God. They know His "eternal power and divine nature," which is obvious to all people "since the creation of the world," so that "people are without excuse" (1:20). Every sunrise, rain shower, and starry night reveals some aspect of God's nature. No one can live in God's world and claim they don't know He exists. At least they can't come up with an excuse that God will accept.

Although everyone knows something about God's existence and power, they "suppress the truth by their wickedness" (1:18). No one, left to themselves, worships God as they know Him to be. We all are sons of the fallen Adam, and we invariably distort and push down our knowledge of God so we might live as we please. Paul concludes that both "Jews and Gentiles alike are all under the power of sin. As it is written: 'There is no one righteous, not even one; there is no one who understands; there is no one who seeks God'" (3:9–11).

Everyone is born in sin. Everyone needs to be born again. How does that happen? Jesus told Nicodemus that people are born again when they believe in the Son of God (John 3:16–18). Paul agrees: "Everyone who calls on the name of the Lord will be saved" (Romans 10:13). But then Paul asks, "How, then, can they call on the one they have not believed in? And how can they believe in the one of whom they have not heard? And how can they hear without someone preaching to them? And how can anyone preach unless they are sent? As it is written: 'How beautiful are the feet of those who bring good news!' " (Romans 10:14–15).

Paul's words inspired the modern missionary movement. If everyone is a sinner and Jesus is the only Savior, and if no one can trust Jesus as Savior unless they know about Him, then we need to go throughout the world and tell people about Jesus!

What happens to those who have never heard? Going forward, let's do our best to not find out. Let's invest prayer, time, and money into making this a moot point. Let's do all we can to spread the good news about Him.

The death of children is a terrible aspect of our fallen world.

199 What happens to babies who die?

The previous question addressed the destiny of those who haven't heard about Jesus. They tragically do not have sufficient knowledge to be saved, yet they know enough about God from nature to be held accountable. But what about children whose minds are not developed enough to understand and believe? What happens to them should they die?

I am a father and desire someday to be a grandfather, so I understand this question is every parent's nightmare. No question is more urgent to grieving parents; we need a biblical answer that is both honest and hopeful.

Honesty requires me to tell you there is no slam-dunk Bible verse that promises every child who dies before a certain age goes to heaven. There is no Scripture, and I think I know why. If God had promised this, wouldn't well-intentioned Christians kill Muslim or Buddhist babies? Wouldn't some be tempted to kill their own children? Why risk eternity in hell? Snuff out their lives now, before they grow old enough to reject Jesus. You see that God's hands are tied. He could not promise that our babies are in heaven without unleashing hell on earth.

We do have compelling reasons to hope. Jesus loves our children more than we do. More than anyone ever could. His disciples rebuked parents for bringing their "little children to Jesus for him to place his hands on them and pray for them" (Matthew 19:13). Jesus rebuked the rebukers: "Let the little children come to me, and do not hinder them, for the kingdom of heaven belongs to such as these" (verse 14). If you grew up in church, you probably know the song "Red and yellow, black and white, they are precious in His sight; Jesus loves the little children of the world." We may sing those lines in our tears, inserting our child's name into the song. Jesus loves our little one even now.

The Bible says there is something special about the child of a believing parent. Peter told the crowd gathered on Pentecost that the promise of the Spirit "is for you and your children. . .for all whom the Lord our God will call" (Acts 2:39). Paul said God considers a child of a believing parent to be set apart from other kids. "For the unbelieving husband has been sanctified through his wife, and the unbelieving wife has been sanctified through her believing husband. Otherwise your children would be unclean, but as it is, they are holy" (1 Corinthians 7:14).

The seventeenth-century Synod of Dort was a conservative gathering of Calvinist theologians, so it wasn't prone to sentimental fluff. These were not the kind of folks who made up stuff just to make us feel better. Yet this synod declared that Christian parents who lose a child "ought not to doubt" their child was taken to heaven. That seems pitch perfect. We can't claim a Bible verse, but given all that Scripture says about our holy and loving God, we shouldn't doubt that we'll see our child again.

The Jesus who wept at Lazarus' tomb also weeps with us in our grief (John 11:35). Entrust your baby into the arms of your Savior. He will do what is loving and right.

PART 5: THE CHURCH

How the New Testament Affects Our World

You could say Jesus' church is found at the intersection of earth and heaven.

200 How does Christianity relate to Judaism?

Judaism gave birth to Christianity. The Christian faith is all about Jesus, and Jesus is a Jew. More importantly, Jesus is the fulfillment of Judaism. He is the King of the Jews, their long-awaited Messiah who delivered the promised kingdom and is returning soon to consummate it.

All Old Testament prophecies are finally fulfilled in Jesus. He is the everlasting peace that God promised His people. Every Old Testament law is fulfilled in Jesus. He is our righteousness, keeping the law perfectly on our behalf, then calling us to an even higher obedience by His Spirit. The Old Testament priestly system is fulfilled in Jesus. He is our great High Priest and sacrificial Lamb. Every slaughtered lamb, bull, and goat points to His once-and-for-all sacrifice.

The first Christians told the story of Jesus in synagogues, proclaiming to their Jewish audiences that Jesus is the One they had been waiting for. Paul explained in a synagogue in southern Turkey, "The people of Jerusalem and their rulers did not recognize Jesus, yet in condemning him they fulfilled the words of the prophets that are read every Sabbath" (Acts 13:27). Paul noted that the Jews had handed Jesus over to be crucified, then announced, "We tell you the good news: What God promised our ancestors he has fulfilled for us, their children, by raising up Jesus" (verses 32–33). Paul then quoted from the Psalms and prophets to show *how* those promises are fulfilled in Jesus.

Most Jews do not believe Jesus is their Messiah. Those who do are known as "messianic" Jews.

Paul's sermon made sense, and the

Jews invited Paul and his companion Barnabas to return the following week to say more. "Many of the Jews" converted to Jesus and "on the next Sabbath almost the whole city gathered to hear the word of the Lord" (Acts 13:43–44). But the Jewish leaders became jealous, and "they began to contradict what Paul was saying and heaped abuse on him" (verse 45). Paul and Barnabas, however, didn't back down. They declared, "We had to speak the word of God to you first." The Jews were God's original people, and they deserved first crack at the good news. But "since you reject it and do not consider yourselves worthy of eternal life, we now turn to the Gentiles" (verse 46).

From that moment on, Christianity began to separate from its Jewish mother. That story is next.

201 How did Christianity separate from Judaism?

The first Christians didn't leave Judaism. They were pushed out. Because the first Christians were Jews, they initially remained in the synagogue. They longed to maintain their spiritual heritage and tight-knit bonds with their Jewish families and friends. Judaism also enjoyed legal protection. As long as Christians could claim they were Jews, they would not be persecuted by Rome. So the Christians argued to stay in while the Jews kept kicking them out. "They're not us," the Jews told the Romans. "Sic 'em!"

This anti-Christian animosity drove a wedge between Jews and Christians. You can only get shut out so many times before you begin to think maybe you don't belong. When Rome crushed Jewish uprisings in 70 and 135 CE, Christians wondered if they even wanted to belong. Judaism might not be the safe harbor it once was.

Meanwhile, Christian missionary efforts to the Gentiles had borne fruit. Synagogues contained a significant amount of Gentile "God-fearers," pious men who admired Judaism but feared the pain of circumcision. When Jewish Christians offered salvation without surgery, these God-fearers entered in droves (Acts 10:1–2; 11:19–21; 13:26). As more Gentiles joined the faith, Christianity became increasingly Greek and less Jewish. Christians showed their independence from Judaism by changing their fast days from Monday and Thursday to Wednesday and Friday and replacing the Jewish Sabbath and Passover with the Christian Lord's Day and Easter.

By the beginning of the second century, Christians were less concerned to prove they were "true Israel" and more apt to argue they were a "third race." Their primary identity was "neither Jew nor Gentile" (Galatians 3:28), yet they were the fulfillment of both Jewish religion and Gentile (or Greek) philosophy. If you pursued God like a Jew or wisdom like a Greek, then you must come to Jesus, the Son of God and the Wisdom of God.

Christianity's debt to Judaism can never be repaid, but as missionaries explained Jesus to Gentile audiences, they began to rely more on Greek philosophical categories. This was a double-edged sword: Greek concepts proved helpful for describing the Trinity and the two natures of Jesus, yet the Greeks' low view of the physical world tended to pull Christianity in Gnostic, subhuman directions.

Christian independence from Judaism continued as Jesus' followers expanded the church far beyond its Jewish beginnings. The third-century church father

A fresco of the twelve apostles. Tradition says they spread the Gospel far beyond Israel, in Gentile areas such as Syria, Persia, north Africa, and India.

Origen noted that Judaism had become Christianity's "little sister." Judaism had remained an ethnic religion, while Christianity had designs on the empire. Early in the fourth century, the Roman emperor Constantine declared himself a Christian. By the end of that century, Christianity was the official religion of the empire. For better or worse, the once persecuted sect was now in charge. Judaism's child had become a man.

202 What is "the church"?

The church is the people of God. The word *church* translates the Greek term *ekklesia,* which means "assembly." In the Old Testament, "the day of the assembly" was God's name for the time He gathered Israel on Mount Sinai and declared that He would be their God (Deuteronomy 4:10, 9:10, 18:16). Israel left Sinai with instructions for building the tabernacle, which God's Spirit would fill when Israel stopped to rest and assembled around it. The traveling tabernacle was later superseded by the stationary temple, which itself was replaced by the church. Now "we are the temple of the living God," for God's Spirit dwells among us (2 Corinthians 6:16; 1 Corinthians 3:16).[30]

The church began on the Jewish feast of Pentecost, fifty days after Jesus rose from the dead and ten days after He ascended to heaven. The apostles had assembled in Jerusalem, when "suddenly a sound like the blowing of a violent wind came from heaven and filled the whole house where they were sitting. They saw what seemed to be tongues of fire that separated and came to rest on each of them" (Acts 2:2–3). The promised Holy Spirit had arrived.

The Spirit empowered the apostles with the gift of tongues (the ability to speak other languages) so they could proclaim Jesus to all the Jewish foreigners who had gathered in Jerusalem for the feast. Three thousand Jews believed and were baptized in the ritual *mikveh* baths outside the temple. Pious Jews dipped there before entering the temple; the apostles now repurposed the baths for entering the church.

And never looked back. The church exploded from Jerusalem, establishing assemblies of Jesus in most people groups throughout the world. If you belong to a church, even a humble one in the middle of nowhere, this is your story. You are part of the greatest movement of God in the history of the world.

Besides the people and temple of God, the church is also the body and bride of Christ (Ephesians 5:25–32; Romans 12:4–8; Colossians 1:24; 1 Corinthians 12:12–27). Being "the body of Christ" doesn't mean—as many Christians have claimed over the years—that we are Jesus' hands and feet. We aren't Jesus. But we are the world's access to Jesus. Do you want to meet Him? Get to church.

As the bride of Christ, we are Jesus' true love. No church is perfect, including our own. (How could it be, if we are there?) We may not like our church's music, preaching, or friendliness, but we must be careful how we talk about it: whatever we say about Jesus' bride implicates Him. Most guys aren't happy when we trash their girl. *Dude! What do you see in her?* There's going to be a fight.

So be cautious when criticizing the church, even if you're only sharing concerns from love. Jesus' bride can always improve, but she's worth fighting for—because Jesus thinks she's worth dying for. He will marry her (Revelation 19:7).

"The church" is not a building. It's the gathering of believers in Jesus.

203 Why should I join a church?

Here's a better question: *Why wouldn't you?* Would you win the lottery and not cash the ticket? Would you decline a Nobel Prize if it were offered? It's more outrageous to say you love Jesus and not join His church. It may not be possible.

If Jesus is the head and the church is His body, how can we claim we're joined to Him if we're not joined to His body? Those who try are bound to pull a muscle. Third-century church father Cyprian said, "Outside the church there is no salvation." If you want to unite with the Savior, you must belong to what belongs to Him. As contemporary theologian Beyoncé explains, "If you like it, then you shoulda put a ring on it." Don't just live with Jesus. Marry Him! Join His bride.

The church implemented membership on its first day. When Peter preached his Pentecost sermon, "those who accepted his message were baptized, and about three thousand were added to their number that day" (Acts 2:41). These first Christians assembled often to pray, study the Bible, and encourage one another, "and the Lord added to their number daily those who were being saved" (Acts 2:47).

Membership has its privileges. Our lives now have the greatest possible meaning, for we "are the body of Christ, and each one of you is a part of it" (1 Corinthians 12:27). We may only be a pinky toe, but the tiniest digit on the body of Christ trumps the head on anything else. Even the toes have the priceless opportunity to gather with the body of Christ, to unite with Jesus under the presiding presence of His Spirit.

Membership also has responsibilities. We commit to meeting regularly so we might "spur one another on toward love and good deeds" (Hebrews 10:24). And we hold each other accountable. When a professing Christian committed salacious sexual acts and refused to repent, Paul instructed the church to "expel the wicked person from among you" (1 Corinthians 5:13). The fact that this man could be expelled means the church practiced membership. And she wanted him back. Paul commanded, "when you are assembled. . .and the power of our Lord Jesus is present, hand this man over to Satan for the destruction of the flesh, so that his spirit may be saved on the day of the Lord" (1 Corinthians 5:4–5).

Any church is free to join, because Jesus paid the entrance fee "with his own blood" (Acts 20:28). Jesus loves the church enough to pay the ultimate price, and He asks you to give your life to it too. Jesus said His church is assaulting Satan, "and the gates of Hades will not overcome it" (Matthew 16:18). If death and hell cannot stop the church, can there be a safer place to invest your life? If you love Jesus, you will.

There are literally millions of churches you could join. But do you really have to?

204 Isn't it enough to belong to the universal church?

Perhaps you understand why those who love Jesus must belong to His body. But why should we join our local Methodist or Presbyterian church? Isn't it enough to belong to the worldwide church? Why must we join any particular one?

Because our local church is how we access the church universal. The universal church is more than the sum of each local church, but it is not less. Paul told the church located in Corinth, "Now you are the body of Christ" (1 Corinthians 12:27). He didn't say, "You are *one part* of the body of Christ," but "You *are* the body of Christ." The whole universal church is present at the gathering of each local church. Our church may seem small and insignificant, but we assemble in the Spirit of Christ, who unites us to the entirety of His church in heaven and on earth.

God explains what happens in your local church each Sunday: "You have come to Mount Zion, to the city of the living God, the heavenly Jerusalem. You have come to thousands upon thousands of angels in joyful assembly, to the church of the firstborn, whose names are written in heaven. You have come to God, the Judge of all, to the spirits of the righteous made perfect, to Jesus the mediator of a new covenant, and to the sprinkled blood that speaks a better word than the blood of Abel" (Hebrews 12:22–24). Since this invisible reality is happening in your church, "let us be thankful, and so worship God acceptably with reverence and awe, for our 'God is a consuming fire' " (verses 28–29).

The first step to worshiping God is showing up. Too many Christians are hopeless romantics: we love the idea of church, just not ours. We see its flaws, so we don't join or we don't stay. We move on, looking for our ecclesiastical soul mate. We'd do better to follow the advice of Pastor Eugene Peterson, who advised Christians, "Go to the nearest smallest church and commit yourself to being there for six months. If it doesn't work out, find somewhere else. But don't look for programs, don't look for entertainment, and don't look for a great preacher. A Christian congregation is not a glamorous place, not a romantic place."[31]

But it's the one place you're guaranteed to find Jesus and have the opportunity to unite with Him. Do you believe in Jesus and His church? Then believe in yours.

205 What is a sacrament?

Churches worship differently in various cultures, but some customs are universal. Every true church that has ever existed teaches the Bible, prays, and practices the sacraments. The first two are obvious, but why the sacraments?

We do them because Jesus told us to. Less formal churches call them "ordinances" for this reason. Jesus ordained baptism when He commanded us to "go and make disciples of all nations, baptizing them in the name of the Father and of the Son and of the Holy Spirit" (Matthew 28:19). He ordained the Lord's Supper when He took bread and the cup and told His disciples to eat and drink in His memory (Matthew 26:26–28; 1 Corinthians 11:23–26).

Some churches add a third ordinance—foot washing—because Jesus washed His disciples' feet and told them to do the same for each other (John 13:14). Others say Jesus only meant to leave His disciples with an illustration of selfless love. He didn't intend to create a mandatory element of Christian worship.

Roman Catholics have seven sacraments. Besides baptism and the Lord's Supper, they add confirmation, penance, ordination (to a religious vocation), marriage, and last rites. Most Protestants say there are only two, as only baptism and the Lord's Supper are clearly ordained by our Lord.

Jesus told us to observe the sacraments because we are physical creatures who need tangible expressions of His love. Sacraments are external signs that seal our faith. They nourish, strengthen, and confirm our faith by making the Gospel individual and concrete. It's one thing to hear the preacher tell an audience that God loves them and salvation is available to all. It's another thing altogether to be immersed in water and come up dripping. To hold the bread and the cup and hear, "The body of Christ, broken for you. The blood of Christ, shed for you."

These personal, tangible signs of grace impress upon our hearts that the story of Jesus and the work of the Spirit are real. Jesus really died and rose again, and the Spirit is really uniting us to Him and His church. We receive baptism, we take the bread and the cup, and we believe.

206 What is baptism?

Baptism is the rite of initiation that marks our entrance into the church. Churches differ on what baptism does, who should receive it, and how much water should be used, but all agree it announces our membership in the body of Christ.

1. ***What baptism does.*** Following are the main church positions, from those who say baptism does the most to those who think it does the least.

Roman Catholics believe the waters of baptism supernaturally impart spiritual life that makes every recipient a born-again Christian. Baptism automatically saves, whether or not the recipients believe. Lutherans say it's the Word proclaimed in baptism—not the water—that imparts spiritual life and only to those who receive it in faith. Reformed churches say baptism does not save the recipients, but it does mark them as God's covenant children. They will be raised in church, surrounded with many opportunities to believe in Jesus and be saved. Baptists and many less formal, "low church" evangelicals (also known as "Bible" churches) typically say God is not doing anything in baptism. He is merely a spectator. Baptism is our pledge of allegiance, our public testimony that we are born again.

The last view is closest to my own, though I have learned from the others that God must be doing something in baptism. He is impressing upon my heart and announcing to the world that I am His child, and He is uniting me to His church. As His child, I commit to the daily rhythm of dying to sin and rising to life depicted in my baptism. As a member of His church, I commit to joining and serving the local body that baptized me.

2. ***Who should receive it.*** Every church baptizes those who believe in Jesus, but Roman Catholics, Lutherans, and the Reformed also baptize infants. They have different reasons, whether for salvation or merely a sign of the covenant, but they agree that whatever grace is present in baptism should not be denied to children.

Baptist and Bible churches emphasize our need to believe in Jesus, and since babies do not show signs of faith (how much does an infant know?), they should not be baptized until they are old enough to profess faith in Jesus.

3. ***How baptism is performed.*** Here Baptist and Bible churches seem to have a clear edge. They immerse believers from head to toe, which is the best picture of our dying and rising with Christ. We go under the water to signify our death to sin and are lifted out of the water to represent our new life in Christ.

Other churches tend to sprinkle water on the baptized, because often they are infants and it seems cruel to dunk a baby. (Though medieval Christians sometimes did. Apparently infants instinctively close their esophagus so they won't drown. Still, it's not a good look.) Mennonites split the difference. They don't fully immerse and they don't lightly sprinkle. They pour water over the believer's head.

Churches may disagree about baptism's mode and meaning, but all true churches agree that baptism must include some amount of water and the trinitarian words, "I baptize you in the name of the Father, of the Son, and of the Holy Spirit." The most conservative Reformed or Lutheran church accepts a Roman Catholic baptism, because as long as baptism is performed in the threefold name, it counts.

A joyful river baptism in Cork, Ireland.

Baptism should also be done only once. When we repeat a rite of initiation, we risk doubts about when our new phase began. Consider marriage: we may renew our vows with our spouse, but we don't have another wedding. If we marry them again, we may wonder, *When were we married, the first time or now?* In the same way, the more times we are baptized, the less certain we'll be which one was real. When exactly did we join the church and begin our new walk with Christ?

I appreciate that people who were baptized as infants may want to receive baptism as believers, now that they know what they're doing. This seems permissible, though we should definitely stop at two. It's not a good idea to be baptized a third time, even if your tour bus is parked by the Jordan River and everyone else is doing it. Rites of initiation should only be done once. The more we do them, the more we water down our entrance into the faith.

207 What is the Lord's Supper?

Our salvation rests on sacrifice. Jews slaughtered animals daily in the temple so they could meet with God. Now Jesus has come and done away with our need to kill innocent lambs. He is the Lamb of God who takes away the sin of the world. Though we no longer slaughter animals, we still depend on a sacrifice—our salvation rests on Jesus' sacrificial death, which we remember by eating the bread and drinking the cup of the Lord's Supper (1 Corinthians 11:23–26).

The Lord's Supper is also called *communion* because it connects us to Jesus and others in the church (1 Corinthians 10:16–17); *Eucharist* (a Greek word for thanksgiving) because we give thanks for Jesus' sacrifice just as He gave thanks when He took the cup (1 Corinthians 10:16, Mark 14:23); and *Mass* because the last word of the Roman Catholic supper was *missa,* which means "Go, you are dismissed."

Christians disagree about what belongs in the cup. Roman Catholics and Lutherans insist it must be wine. Baptists and Bible churches prefer grape juice, and Reformed churches go either way.

More importantly, Christians disagree about how Jesus is present at His supper. Roman Catholics say the bread and wine turn into the body and blood of Jesus; Lutherans say the bread and wine remain the same yet Jesus is really present "in, with, and under" them; the Reformed say Jesus is present at the table spiritually; and Baptists and Bible churches say Jesus is present in the church, as He is whenever we gather.

These differing beliefs on Christ's presence produce different beliefs about what happens in the Lord's Supper. The real presence of Christ leads Roman Catholics and Lutherans to say that forgiveness of sin comes through the Lord's Supper—to everyone who receives it if you're Roman Catholic, to everyone who has faith if

Bread and wine (or, for many churches, grape juice) portray Jesus' body and blood in the "Lord's Supper."

you're Lutheran. The lesser, merely spiritual presence of Christ prompts Reformed Christians to say something less: salvation does not come through the supper, but the bread and cup do enable us to commune with Jesus in a uniquely powerful way. The Holy Spirit lifts our hearts to heaven, where we fellowship with our ascended Lord. Baptists and Bible churches typically say even less. Jesus is not present in the supper in any special way; we are merely remembering His sacrifice on our behalf.

Whatever your church believes, it's important to celebrate the Lord's Supper often. Old Testament saints would not imagine appearing before God without a sacrifice, and we should not regularly worship God without commemorating Christ's. When we take the Lord's Supper, we touch the palpable proof of God's love. We commune with our risen and ascended Lord, perhaps more than we know.

208 Why are there so many different churches?

Because we're free. We weren't always. During the religious wars of the Reformation, Roman Catholics, Lutherans, and Reformed Christians battled to impose their views on the people living in their regions. Citizens were forced to adopt the religious flavor of their government or move to a territory that agreed with them.

By the middle of the seventeenth century, Christians were exhausted from the fighting. Especially the Anabaptists, who, because they were pacifists, did not have a fighting chance. All they could do was run away.

Weary Europeans decided it would be better to permit people to follow their consciences, which naturally gave rise to different kinds of churches. Denominations are a good thing. It means I may not agree with your brand of Christianity, but I won't kill you for it. Or even make you move.

When you drive past a Pentecostal, Methodist, or Brethren church (or any other kind), thank God that you live in a country that allows people to worship as they see fit. We tried the alternative. It wasn't good.

209 What are the different churches?

Following is a quick sketch. For other details, see the sidebars "Western Church, Eastern Church" (page 57) and "Roman Catholic Church, Protestant Church" (page 55).

The church is mainly divided between East and West. The Eastern Orthodox Church includes the Greek Orthodox, Russian Orthodox, Ukrainian Orthodox, and other regional Orthodox churches that are in fellowship with the Patriarch of Constantinople. The patriarch doesn't govern the Eastern Church like a pope; he is merely a bishop who is "first among equals." The Eastern Church suffered a major split in 2018, when the Patriarch recognized the Ukrainian Church as an independent church, separate from Moscow. This angered the Russian Church, which broke ties with the Patriarch and all churches in fellowship with him.

This is the largest rift in Orthodoxy since the East officially split from the West in 1054. East and West spoke different languages, had different interests, and often competed for power, so they rarely got along. The final straw came when the West inserted the word *filioque* ("and the Son") into the Nicene Creed, claiming that the Spirit proceeds both from the Father *and the Son*. The East said the Spirit proceeds from the Father only. He might also come *through* the Son or *by* the Son, but not *from* the Son. So the East excommunicated the West, a breach that stands to this day.

Martin Luther (1483–1546) was a key figure in the Reformation, which led to the many varieties of Protestant churches.

The West began dividing during the sixteenth-century Reformation. The Roman Catholic Church evicted Martin Luther, who was forced to start a new, Lutheran church. John Calvin and

Ulrich Zwingli also left the Roman Church and became leading figures of the Reformed Church. Zwingli's church soon evicted some of its members for practicing believer's baptism. They were called Anabaptists because they believed they should be baptized *ana,* or again, this time as believers. These three Reformation churches all taught the Bible is our final authority and that we're saved by grace through faith—though the persecuted Anabaptists sometimes insisted that salvation also required suffering.

Each denomination broke with Rome a little bit more. Lutherans agreed with Rome that baptism saves and that Jesus is really present in the Lord's Supper—but they said it's the Word that accompanies baptism that brings new life, and the presence of Jesus in the supper does not replace the bread and wine. The Reformed went further, asserting that baptism is a sign of the covenant rather than the means of salvation and that Jesus is spiritually rather than physically present in the Lord's Supper. Anabaptists took the Reformation to its furthest extreme, insisting that the sacraments are merely ordinances because they are a human rather than divine work. Baptism is the believer's testimony that he or she is born again and the Lord's Supper is our remembrance of Jesus. Jesus is not uniquely present or performing a special work in either case.

Lutherans dominated Germany and Scandinavia. Luther's death unleashed thirty years of debate within the church, until they reached consensus and compiled their doctrinal statements into *The Book of Concord.* (If you come across a college or publishing house with Concordia in its name, it's bound to be Lutheran.) The Reformed began in Switzerland, then spread to the Netherlands and the British Isles. Consequently, these churches exist today in two main groups: the Dutch Reformed, who follow the Belgic Confession, Heidelberg Catechism, and the Canons of Dort; and the Scottish Presbyterians, who hold to the Westminster Confession and Catechisms. The Anabaptists fled for safety mostly to Moravia, England, and the Netherlands, where they laid the foundation for future Mennonite and Brethren churches.

So much for the continent of Europe. Across the channel, sixteenth-century

England started its own church, and for a bad reason. King Henry VIII wanted to divorce his wife, who happened to be the aunt of the Holy Roman Emperor. The pope feared the emperor's armies and told Henry he couldn't have a divorce. So Henry started his own Church of England (the Anglican Church), which promptly granted his divorce.

It's not surprising that a church that began for an entirely pragmatic reason would struggle with doctrinal clarity. From the beginning, the Anglican Church was a broad tent that attempted to hold together Christians who were sympathetic to Roman Catholicism with those who had strong Protestant convictions. Both sides fought for the soul of the church. In the seventeenth century, a reform movement attempted to purify the church from its Roman Catholicism. These "Puritans" ultimately failed and were evicted from the church. Some became Baptists while others came to America and started Congregational churches.

Despite its inauspicious start, the Anglican Church has spun off the world's largest denominations. John Wesley was an Anglican preacher who emphasized the need for every Christian to commit to Jesus and a life of holiness. This offended the staid sensibilities of his fellow pastors, who told him to keep his revivals out of their parishes. But Wesley refused to stay in his lane. He went around the pastors to start new, Methodist churches.

Methodists and Baptists caught fire during America's Great Awakenings of the eighteenth and nineteenth centuries. These revivals emphasized conversion and personal piety, which were right in their wheelhouse. Baptists dominated America's southern states while circuit-riding preachers spread Methodism on the western frontier. By the first quarter of the nineteenth century, one out of every forty Americans was a Methodist.

Early in the twentieth century, Methodism and its accompanying Holiness groups birthed the burgeoning Pentecostal movement. Pentecostals and their charismatic cousins now comprise 27 percent of all Christians and 8 percent of the world's population.[32] Not bad for a church whose roots run back to England and a king who wanted a divorce.

210 Why are there hypocrites in church?

Of course there are hypocrites in church. Where else would you find them? Churches will always attract hypocrites because something precious is there.

Hypocrites only fake what's desirable. You never hear, "Is Jack a child molester?" "No, he's just pretending." "Did Susan embezzle the money?" "No, she only made it look like she did." No one pretends to be a gossip, racist, or pompous windbag. We're only tempted to fake what is good.

No one hates hypocrisy more than Jesus, because it blocks many from coming to Him. Jesus lashed out at His religious opponents: "Woe to you, teachers of the law and Pharisees, you hypocrites! You shut the door of the kingdom of heaven in people's faces. You yourselves do not enter, nor will you let those enter who are trying to. Woe to you, teachers of the law and Pharisees, you hypocrites! You travel over land and sea to win a single convert, and when you have succeeded, you make them twice as much a child of hell as you are" (Matthew 23:13–15).

Hypocrites will be punished in hell. But what should you do when you find them? Take their presence as a sign that you're in the vicinity of something precious. Something so valuable that some people are willing to fake it. You can let someone's proud pretense keep you from Jesus, or you can push past the posers and grasp the precious Person they're only pretending to know.

Don't let the hypocrites win. Use their falsehood as an alert to the real thing. They are inadvertently, clumsily pointing toward Jesus. Slip past them and into His arms.

211 Why don't Christians love like Jesus?

Because we are sinners. We are forgiven and covered with the righteousness of Christ, but we continually mess up. That's why we need Jesus. Christians are the last people who should ever claim to be perfect. If we loved like Jesus, we wouldn't need His sacrificial death on our behalf. We Christians never outgrow our dependence on the cross.

Christians certainly *should* love like Jesus—but Jesus Himself was misunderstood and ultimately crucified.

So when people say we don't love like Jesus, we assume there is some truth in the charge. We want to humbly listen and ask forgiveness for our unloving words, attitudes, or actions. But we also realize that everyone is a sinner, and sometimes people may wrongly accuse us of sins we didn't commit.

For instance, conventional wisdom in the West says we must approve of everyone's gender and sexual choices. If a man declares he is a woman or wants to marry another man, we must applaud his courage to "live his truth." But God says He made us as male and female and that marriage is a covenant between one man and one woman (Genesis 1:27; 2:23–24). We aren't able to change this—it's how God made the world.

We should humbly listen to others' stories. And we must speak God's truth as kindly as we know how, explaining that His rules are from love and for our good. Some may say this is harsh and unloving, but we disagree. God wants the best for everyone, so He calls us to share His loving law with others. Then we can all thrive in His world.

Ultimately Christians can't take responsibility for what others hear. We can only own what we say and do. If we conclude that we have lovingly presented God's Word, we won't repent simply because others are offended. We'll remember that we follow Jesus, the most loving Person who ever lived—and He was crucified.

Jesus' death proves it's possible for love to be misunderstood. The cross is history's greatest act of love, and it was misunderstood at the time. No one who saw Jesus die thought they were witnessing an act of love. Jesus' enemies thought His death proved He was a damned blasphemer; Jesus' friends thought it meant the mission was over.

Jesus had failed, epically. His mission could not have turned out worse.

No one who saw Jesus die understood what was actually happening. That Jesus was dying to save the world because He loved the world. If Jesus' love was misunderstood and we are called to follow Jesus, we shouldn't be surprised when our love is misunderstood too.

Why don't Christians love like Jesus? Often we don't because we're sinners who desperately need Jesus. But sometimes we do. And because everyone else is a sinner too, they may not realize that we *are* loving like Jesus. And they might mistreat us as they did Him.

212 How can I tell if a church is good?

Jesus is full of grace and truth, and a church that follows Jesus will exude both (John 1:14). A healthy church is a place for friends and a place to learn. It loves people well and teaches sound doctrine, for grace without truth isn't grace and truth without grace isn't the truth. You've likely found a good church when you can't wait for Sunday, and you look for ways to connect with your church friends throughout the week.

A healthy church unites us to Jesus through His Word. Everything depends on this. A good church will read, explain, and apply the Bible to life. It will encourage attenders to commit to Jesus by receiving baptism and joining the church. It will sing joyfully and reverently, celebrating the Lord's Supper often and devoting itself to prayer.

A healthy church purposefully worships Jesus and encourages us to love and pray for each other and serve in our community. It equips us on Sunday to enter the world on Monday. A good church explains that we don't merely have family, friends, neighbors, and jobs; we have divine callings. Each of our relationships is an important way that we serve Jesus. When we do our callings well, we may have opportunities to witness for Jesus and invite others to church, where they can learn about Jesus and join His body.

Since every church consists of forgiven sinners, none of them will be perfect.

But rather than flit between churches, going to this one for its children's ministry, that one for its youth program, and another for its adult small groups (and finally concluding your career with whichever church charters buses to Branson), it's best to stay where you are. To paraphrase John F. Kennedy, "Ask not what your church can do for you, but what you might do for your church." Your church needs you, especially if you see room for improvement. Plug in, and see if you can't make a difference. There may come a time when you must leave this church and go to another one—especially if it is fudging on grace or truth—but that should be a last resort.

Do you yearn to love the risen Christ? He feels your love when you serve His imperfect, blemished body. Your church may be flawed, but it's your opportunity to love Jesus.

213 Who are the leaders of a church?

It depends on the church. Roman Catholic churches follow the Pope, the Bishop of Rome, who rules over regional bishops and local church priests and deacons. This top-down approach is called an Episcopalian form of government because ultimate authority lies in the *episcopoi,* or bishops. It's also found in the Anglican Church and those churches that arose from Anglicanism, such as Methodists and (surprise!) Episcopalians. The latter are Americans who dropped their Anglican name after the Revolutionary War, when it was no longer popular to swear allegiance to the British king.

The opposite of Episcopalianism is Congregationalism, which is a bottom-up approach found in Baptist, nondenominational, and (surprise!) Congregational churches. Here authority lies with the members of each local church. They typically hold annual business meetings to approve the budget, call pastors, vote on elders and deacons, and dispute—I'm sorry, *amicably discuss*—what to do about the carpet in the nursery.

A centrist position is Presbyterianism. Here authority lies in the middle, between the General Assembly (if you're Scottish) or Synod (if you're Dutch) at the top and the leaders of each local church, called the Session for the Scots and Consistory

Leaders known as cardinals gather in Rome, world headquarters of the Roman Catholic Church. Protestant churches are led by pastors and elders who often are chosen by their own congregations.

for the Dutch. Churches in the same region unite to form a Presbytery (Scots) or Classis (Dutch). This meeting of area churches holds the final authority to ordain and call pastors and decide doctrinal and ministerial issues. If you're a progressive pastor in a conservative presbytery or a conservative pastor in a progressive classis, you might want to change to a more hospitable region.

Within each local Protestant church, the two main offices are either pastor and deacon (Acts 20:28; 1 Peter 5:2) or elder and deacon (Acts 14:23; 15:2–6; 20:17; Titus 1:5; James 5:14; 1 Timothy 3:8–13; Philippians 1:1). The office of elder includes both lay and teaching elders. Lay elders are church members who are elected but not employed by the church. Teaching elders are often vocationally trained and are the equivalent of pastors.

Here's the main practical difference: if your church has elders, the pastors or teaching elders share authority with the lay elders. If your church does not have elders, the pastors tend to have the final say. Unless, as is common in Baptist churches, the deacons function as elders—then all bets are off. Deacons originally arose to be *diakonoi,* or servants of the congregation's physical needs (Acts 6:1–7). That's still their most appropriate, biblical purpose, though some churches use deacons as governing boards.

I wouldn't leave a church over its form of government. The worst system can work if the people are godly, and the best system will fail if the people are not. Wise systems tend to have a clear division of labor (who does what) and accountability (who is responsible to whom) and involve all stakeholders at the appropriate level. Whatever your form of church government, it's wise to regularly ask, *When is the last time someone said no to the people in authority and got away with it?* If it's been awhile, you might have a problem. Perhaps not with your form of government, but at least with the people leading it.

214 Can women be elders or pastors?

This controversial question has fine Christians on both sides. Complementarians believe men and women have different but complementary roles, while egalitarians believe their roles may be the same.

The church has traditionally been complementarian, reserving the leadership offices of elder and pastor for men because the Bible teaches male headship. This does not mean that every man is the head of every woman, but that men should lead in the home and church.

Regarding the home, Paul says "the husband is the head of the wife as Christ is the head of the church, his body, of which he is the Savior. Now as the church submits to Christ, so also wives should submit to their husbands in everything" (Ephesians 5:23–24).

Regarding the church, Paul says "the head of every man is Christ, and the head of the woman is man, and the head of Christ is God" (1 Corinthians 11:3). He adds, "I do not permit a woman to teach or to assume authority over a man; she must be quiet. For Adam was formed first, then Eve" (1 Timothy 2:12–13).

Paul grounds his argument in Adam and Eve, which supports the traditional Christian idea that male headship is built into creation. Women naturally nurture and follow men who naturally lead, provide, and protect. This created difference is evident in dating, the marriage proposal, the bride's taking of her husband's name, and even the act of sex (the man leads and the woman receives). There's a reason we praise a man for physically defending his wife and lose all respect for the man when the roles are reversed. It's not merely because men are stronger and taller, though that is a telling sign about God's intentions for His world.

In the last fifty years, women have made long overdue strides in Western society, and their progress has coincided with a reevaluation of their roles in the home and church. Egalitarians concede Paul told men to lead, but that was because he was writing in a patriarchal culture in which women were less educated and more dependent on men. He would support women pastors if he were writing today.

Egalitarians say this is a matter of justice—it's just the right thing to do. They also claim the Gospel is at stake. Paul says we "are all one in Christ Jesus," so "there is neither Jew nor Gentile, neither slave nor free, nor is there male and female" (Galatians 3:28). If we deny women the same leadership opportunities as men, we are denying their full equality in Christ. And we needlessly offend our enlightened neighbors, who won't become Christians if it means returning to the Dark Ages.

The arguments continue back and forth but ultimately come down to where you believe the Bible puts male headship: Does it belong in creation, as an important foundation for the world God made? Or did it arise after the fall, as Adam and Eve fought for dominance? Complementarians affirm male headship as a vital part of God's creational design while egalitarians strive to eliminate it as a stubbornly sticky consequence of sin.

It may seem unfortunate, but every church will choose a side. You either will ordain women as elders and pastors or you won't. If you're a convinced complementarian, you may find you need to leave your egalitarian church for one that supports this important value. If you're a convinced egalitarian, you may need to do the same, in reverse. In either case, leave with friendships intact and prayers for God's continued blessing on the church. We may no longer worship together each week, but we still belong to the one body of Christ. He who unites us remains infinitely more precious than what temporarily divides.

215 Do I need a priest?

In the Old Testament, Israel's priests mediated between God and His people. They represented God to the people and the people to God, offering sacrifices to close the gap and bring both sides together.

The Roman Catholic Church continued this tradition. Its priests mediated between God and the church through the reenactment of Christ's sacrifice in the Mass. When the priest said the words, "*Hoc est corpus meum*" ("This is my body"), from which we get the magician's phrase *hocus pocus,* the bread and wine transformed into the body and blood of Jesus. The gap was closed again.

In the sixteenth century, Martin Luther raised important objections to the Mass. He said it had become a human work. A priest says something to make Jesus appear, then sacramentally resacrifices Him to infuse grace into the onlookers.

And they *were* onlookers. By Luther's day, the Mass had become a spectator sport. Only the priest was allowed to eat and drink the elements. Laypeople were given the bread on Easter but never the wine, because what would happen if they spilled Jesus' blood?

Luther realized the Mass, though ostensibly centered on Jesus, had become an end around Him. Rather than revel in Jesus for our salvation, the church had turned His sacrifice into a human work and normal believers into second-class Christians. Laypeople could not approach God directly; they had to go through a priest, who was called by God for this task.

Luther found the answer in Hebrews: Jesus is our high priest and final sacrifice who tore open the veil guarding the Holy of Holies. We are now free to approach

God boldly, entering "the Most Holy Place by the blood of Jesus" (10:19). We don't need a priest to mediate between us and God. Every believer is his or her own priest.

But this does not mean that we don't need the church. Just the opposite. Luther's "priesthood of all believers" taught that each Christian is empowered to represent God to the others and the others to God. We perform our mediating role by praying for our friends and by proclaiming God's Word and promise of forgiveness to them. Luther didn't need a priest to access God's forgiveness, yet he yearned for a friend to hear his confession and pronounce, "You are forgiven. Go in peace and sin no more." Luther wrote, "I will allow no man to take private confession away from me, and I would not give it up for all the treasures of the world, since I know what comfort and strength it has given me."[33]

We priests not only speak for Christ to others in the church. As the church, we also represent Christ to the world. We "are a chosen people, a royal priesthood, a holy nation, God's special possession, that you may declare the praises of him who called you out of darkness into his wonderful light" (1 Peter 2:9). Luther said those ordained to the priesthood are not the only ones with a divine calling—they are not more spiritual than cobblers and blacksmiths. God has called every Christian to love and represent Him by serving their neighbor in their various professions. Our callings may differ, but one is not better than another. When we help others for Jesus' sake, we are not merely giving them a hand—we are acting as priests, fulfilling our calling "to be a kingdom and priests to serve our God, and [we] will reign on the earth" (Revelation 5:10).

A fresco of Israel's first high priest, Aaron. Do God's people still need priests today?

Beautiful scenery and the cars we drive to see it in are examples of God's "common grace." His "special grace" involves Jesus, the Holy Spirit, the Bible, and the church.

216 What is grace?

Grace is God's undeserved gifts that start, sustain, and save our lives. Everything that we are and everything that we do depends on these gifts.

God's grace comes in two main varieties: common and special. Common grace is given to all people because they belong to creation. Our existence is a gift of this grace. None of us were asked if we wanted to be born. We didn't get a vote. Yet here we are, because God wanted us.

The God who made us continues to sustain us. His common grace supplies natural gifts: He sends rain and sunshine to grow wheat, peaches, and beefsteak tomatoes. He provides oxygen for our lungs and water to quench our thirst—and rinse off the day's grime. Every sunrise and fresh season is an undeserved gift from our Creator, who "made the moon to mark the seasons, and the sun knows when to go down. . . . How many are your works, LORD! In wisdom you made them all" (Psalm 104:19, 24).

Common grace also supplies cultural gifts. God equips any and all people—Christians and non-Christians alike—to develop the raw materials of creation into cars, computers, baseballs, and sonnets. We enjoy indoor plumbing, air conditioning, and guacamole because God gifted and inspired someone to create them. We bow our heads before each meal, understanding our taco salad and strawberry pie are tasty slices of God's undeserved gifts.

Common grace also enables moral good. People are not as wicked as they could be because God's Spirit holds sin back. Common grace prompts drivers to put down their cell phones, enemies to put down their weapons, and potential shoplifters to put back the merchandise before leaving the store.

Finally, common grace inspires civic good. When neighbors bring chain saws to clean up our fallen elm, when friends check in to see how we're doing, when a tall stranger grasps the package of paper towels that lies beyond our reach, we thank them—and we thank God, who motivated such kindness.

Praise God for His common grace! We could not live one moment without it. But common grace has never saved anyone from hell. For that we need God's special grace, His undeserved gifts of redemption that are showered on those who believe in His Son.

Special grace is *Jesus*, the One who lived, died, and rose again for us; the *Bible*, which informs us about Jesus and God's gift of salvation; the *church*, which uses the Bible, baptism, the Lord's Supper, worship, prayer, and fellowship to unite us to Jesus; and the *Holy Spirit*, who employs all these to bring us to the end of ourselves and faith in Jesus. Special grace is these gifts, and it's also the change these gifts make in us: the Spirit of God uses the Word of God among the people of God to transform our hearts so that we joyfully desire to trust and follow Jesus.

If you love Jesus and have committed your life to Him, you have received God's greatest gift. Paul explains, "It is by grace you have been saved, through faith—and this is not from yourselves, it is the gift of God" (Ephesians 2:8). There is only one appropriate response to this priceless gift. It may not seem like much, but it says everything. *Thanks.*

Jesus saves people *from* sin and *to* a fruitful life: "I am the vine; you are the branches. If you remain in me and I in you, you will bear much fruit" (John 15:5).

217 What is salvation?

God sent His Son to save us *from* something and *for* something. The angel told Joseph to name Mary's Son "Jesus," which means "Yahweh saves." Saves from what? The angel explained, "you are to give him the name Jesus, because he will save his people from their sins" (Matthew 1:21). Jesus entered our world to save us from sin and its harm—injustice, hatred, violence, despair, disease, death, and everlasting damnation in hell. That is a lot to be saved from! If that is all Jesus did, who could complain?

But Jesus didn't merely save us *from* sin, He saved us *for* something—more precisely, He saved us for Someone. He saved us for Himself. On the night Jesus died, He talked to His Father about His disciples, saying, "Now this is eternal life: that they know you, the only true God, and Jesus Christ, whom you have sent" (John 17:3). Jesus told His disciples that He is the one true vine and they are the branches; they will only live and bear fruit as they remain in Him (John 15:1–9).

Salvation means union with Christ. When we put our faith in Jesus, and when we demonstrate that faith by receiving baptism and joining His body, we are united with Christ. This is a mysterious, organic union. As branches are distinct from the vine but not separate, so it is difficult to say exactly where our life ends and Jesus' begins. This is a personal union. Jesus' description of His vine and our branches abounds in pronouns: I, you, me. "If you remain in me and I in you, you will bear much fruit" (John 15:5). And this is a vital union. Jesus is the only "true vine" (John 15:1). He is not an add-on to an already full life. Union with Christ is the only way to truly live. We're either living or dying, depending on our connection to Jesus.

If we are in Christ, all that He accomplished by His obedient life counts for us. Why are we adopted? Because we are one with God's natural born Son. Why are we justified? Because we are one with Christ, so His righteousness is credited to us. Why are we sanctified? Because we are one with God's Holy Son, and His Spirit indwells us. Why will we persevere to the end? Because we are one with Christ. Jesus said on that last day, "You will realize that I am in my Father, and you are in me, and I am in you" (John 14:20). It's unimaginable that the Father would ever lose His Son. The same love that binds together the Triune God also grips us.

Union with Christ is not automatic. No one is born in this glorious condition. The angel said Jesus "will save his people from their sins." Not everyone; only *His people.* How do we become His people? Through conversion. That's next.

218 What is faith?

Conversion is our turning from sin to Jesus. It's one turn, but it can be described from two directions. The turn from sin is repentance, and the turn to Jesus is faith.

Faith means to trust, rely, or depend on. We express faith in Jesus when we put our full weight on Him. We push all of our chips to the center of the table. If faith is a roulette wheel, we ignore the black and the red and put all our money on brown (Jesus is a Middle Eastern Man). If Jesus is not God, if He did not rise from the dead, then we are toast. We have no backup plan.

This all-or-nothing allegiance requires knowledge. Knowledge isn't enough by itself, as even demons know some facts about God and tremble (James 2:19)—but it's impossible to have faith without it. We cannot give ourselves to someone or something we do not know. Paul explains, "Faith comes from hearing the message, and the message is heard through the word about Christ" (Romans 10:17).

Conversion is our turning; it's something we must do. But it's really God's turning, because He is the One who makes it happen. The Holy Spirit turns our hearts toward Jesus as we commit to what the Scriptures say about Him. This commitment opens our minds to take in more knowledge, which we then rely on, which stretches our minds to receive more truth, which we then obey, and so on. Unless interrupted by distrust and disobedience, this virtuous cycle spirals forever upward.

Do you want to be a person of faith? Start with what you know about Jesus. Give yourself to that. You will then discover more. Submit to that. If it's a promise, claim it. If it's a command, obey it. And you're on your way.

219 What is repentance?

Conversion is our turning from sin to Jesus. Both aspects of the turn are required. If we try to turn to Jesus without turning from sin, we will throw out our back.

It's impossible to claim Jesus as Savior without turning from sin, because sin is the thing He saves us from. Jesus is our Savior, and He's also our Lord. Jesus is called "Lord" 747 times in the New Testament and 92 times in Acts. Acts calls Him "Savior" only twice (Acts 5:31; 13:23).

Repentance does not mean we must clean up our act for Jesus to accept us. Jesus takes us as we are, though He loves us too much to allow us to stay that way. Repentance does not mean we won't struggle with pride, lust, and greed, but it means we're committed to the fight. We won't make peace with sin, excusing it as "guilty pleasures" or "just the way I am." We won't use Jesus' forgiveness as cover to sin more. Repentance means we begin to think, feel, and act toward sin the way God thinks, feels, and acts toward sin. We recognize that our sin is evil, we hate our attraction to it, and we determine with God's help to keep fighting.

This is easier to do when we suffer significant loss. A close friend lay dying from

Repentance takes sins "like scarlet" and makes them "white as snow" (Isaiah 1:18).

a dissected aorta, a genetic defect he inherited from his father. I pondered this as I stood by his hospital bed, staring at the machines and tubes hooked to his bloated body. Why was he dying? Because of a genetic defect. Why do such defects exist? Because of the fall. I saw clearly then: *I hate sin!* Sin will one day rob me of everyone and everything I ever cared about. I will die alone, with only Jesus to carry me home. Sin is not my friend. It is not something to dabble in, to see how much pleasure I can squeeze out before I get caught. Sin is my sworn enemy. I will not be entertained by it again.

One last encouragement: the better we get at repentance the more we'll find to repent from. An artist's eye and a musician's ear become more discriminating as they improve. Shades and sounds that once seemed fine no longer do. So it is with saints. The closer we grow to Jesus, the larger the gap between us will seem. That's a good sign.

I now wince at aspects of my personality that I used to enjoy. What I once thought was confidence I now see as pride. What I once thought was funny I now see as mean. What I once thought was fiscal responsibility I now see as selfishness. Do you feel like you're getting worse as you grow in Christ? That may be a sign you're getting better. You're growing closer to Jesus, and the sin that once brought pleasure now brings pain. That's great! The first step of repentance is to recognize our sin. Confess it, and receive your Father's forgiveness.

220 What does it mean to be born again?

No one is born a Christian. We are born into this world naturally from the union of our parents' egg and sperm. We are born again supernaturally when the Holy Spirit uses the Word of Christ to create new, spiritual life within us.

Jesus explained to an interested Pharisee named Nicodemus, "Very truly I tell you, no one can see the kingdom of God unless they are born again" (John 3:3). Nicodemus asked how that was possible, and Jesus said it's something only the Holy Spirit can do: "Flesh gives birth to flesh, but the Spirit gives birth to spirit" (verse 6). Nicodemus pressed further: "How can this be?" (verse 9).

Jesus answered with the most famous verse in the Bible. You've seen John 3:16 written on highway overpasses and signs held high during televised field goal attempts. "For God so loved the world that he gave his one and only Son, that whoever believes in him shall not perish but have eternal life."

The Spirit of Christ uses the Word of Christ to stir spiritually dead people to put their faith in Christ. The apostle Paul explains, "As for you, you were dead in your transgressions and sins. . . . But because of his great love for us, God, who is rich in mercy, made us alive with Christ even when we were dead in transgressions—it is by grace you have been saved" (Ephesians 2:1, 4–5). Elsewhere he adds that God "saved us, not because of righteous things we had done, but because of his mercy. He saved

The Jewish leader Nicodemus is curious about Jesus and visits at night. He is confused by Jesus' statement, "You must be born again" (John 3:7).

us through the washing of rebirth and renewal by the Holy Spirit" (Titus 3:5).

Being born again (also called regeneration) is the everlasting difference between Christians and non-Christians. The difference is not, as some say, that one person said "the sinner's prayer" and another didn't. The difference is not saying the magic words, "Jesus come into my heart." The difference is regeneration. Our prayer of faith matters because it is our response to the Word of God, and the Word is what the Spirit uses to create our new spiritual life. The Spirit doesn't zap people—"You're saved!" and "You're saved!" like Oprah handing out car keys. The Spirit uses the Word to save us, and the Word requires our response of faith. This is why we invite lost sinners to pray and receive Christ.

When they do and are born again, the new life started in them is an early shoot of the life that will transform the whole world. God declares, "Therefore, if anyone is in Christ, the new creation has come: The old has gone, the new is here!" (2 Corinthians 5:17). Someday, Jesus will return to regenerate the entire planet (Matthew 19:28). That same power can transform you now. Come to Christ.

221 What is adoption?

Adoption is a most precious, identity-altering aspect of our salvation. What would happen if, as you gathered with family this Thanksgiving, your mom let slip that you were adopted? Wouldn't this news shake you to your core? Wouldn't you wonder who you are?

If you're a Christian, I've got news for you: you *are* adopted! God has only one natural-born Son; the rest of us got into the family by adoption. This news should transform our identity. Who are we? John exclaims, "See what great love the Father has lavished on us, that we should be called children of God! And that is what we are!" (1 John 3:1).

Our adoption means:

1. ***God wants us.*** We applaud benefactors who build orphanages and schools in poor countries. Their generosity is all we could expect. But occasionally a donor does more. He not only starts an orphanage for neglected children, he adopts one of them. He gives her his name; he identifies with her and brings her into his home.

   It would be enough for God to save us from sin, death, and hell. Who could complain? But God doesn't merely want to help us, He wants us! He adopts us into His family, gives us His name, and forever binds Himself to us. Want proof that you are loved? God has adopted you. He is your Father.

2. ***We are heirs of God.*** We are adopted to "sonship through Jesus Christ" (Ephesians 1:5). Sonship may sound sexist, but it's radically inclusive. In the first century, only sons inherited their father's possessions. Not so in God's family. Here both sons and daughters have the right of sonship. We all are "heirs of God and co-heirs with Christ" (Romans 8:17).

   Heirs stand to receive all that their father owns. What belongs to our Father? Everything. Our entire world belongs to God, and one day it will belong to us.

Jesus promised the meek "will inherit the earth" (Matthew 5:5). That's not a metaphor. Because God adopted us, we will live forever with His Son on this restored earth.

3. ***We should extend grace to others.*** No one deserves to be adopted. We belong to God's family solely by His grace. Let's remember that the next time we lose patience with an annoying or arrogant person. We must offer others the grace that God lavished on us.

4. ***We can relax.*** There's an important difference between a son and a slave. A slave works partially from fear, knowing that a string of mistakes could cost his job. A son serves freely. He knows a bad day won't eliminate his position; his dad might dismiss a slave, but he won't disown his son. A son is free to give his best without fear of the consequences.

5. ***We should try our best.*** Adoption explains why a son will give his best. Adoption brings together justification (our legal status as righteous before God) and sanctification (our continued moral improvement). Adoption clarifies why both justification and sanctification are required, and in that order.

   Adoption explains why justification is necessary and must come first. My children are allowed to contact me anytime, anywhere. Other children may not. My child may come into my bedroom at 2 a.m. and complain that he cannot sleep. If the neighbor kid does this, I'll yell, "Get out of my room! Go tell your own mom!" You don't get to act like my child unless you are my child. Likewise, we aren't allowed to pretend we're God's children unless we really are. We become God's children when He adopts, regenerates, and justifies us—forgives and accepts us as righteous for Jesus' sake. Justification must come first.

   Adoption illumines why sanctification is necessary and must come after. A child who is adopted should act like it. How strange if an adopted child stays in his room, never coming down for family meals, never going on family vacations, and never appearing in family photos. What kind of child is this?

Adoption clarifies why justification must come first and why sanctification must come after. God changed our identity when He adopted us, and He expects us to live into our new status. Sanctification is our daily growth in Christ. We become more like what we already are, the children of God.

222 What is prayer?

Prayer is talking to God. God speaks to us when we read the Bible, and we speak to God when we pray. It's best to begin and perhaps end our day with Bible reading and prayer. This is how we cultivate our relationship with God.

If you think about it, prayer is the one thing we do with God. Can you imagine having a car you never drive or a house you never live in? What good are they? Why have something you never use? In the same way, why have a God if we never pray? What's the point?

God wants us to pray because He wants a relationship with us. This is a challenge, because our relationship could not be more lopsided. Have you seen a twelve-year-old girl at a boy band concert? She meets her heartthrob at the rope line, and all she can do is scream. The rock star tries to help by asking some basic questions. What is your name? Where are you from? What's your favorite song? The girl can only squeal with delight. At least he tried.

God's relationship with us is infinitely more lopsided. He knows we're at risk of being overwhelmed by His majesty, so He asks us to pray. Nothing flowery, nothing worthy of being bronzed or engraved in marble. He just wants to hear from us. He wants us to find our voice, to be an authentic partner in this relationship.

Our prayers don't have to be long. They can be short because our God is real. The prophets of Baal shouted all day to their god. They danced, cried, and slashed their bodies. He never replied. Elijah simply said, "Answer me, LORD, answer me, so these people will know that you, LORD, are God, and that you are turning their hearts back again" (1 Kings 18:37). Then fire fell from the sky.

Jesus isn't a fan of long prayers. He specifically warns against them. "When you

Prayer is simply talking to God—such as Peter's desperately quick, "Lord, save me!" (Matthew 14:22–33).

pray," He said, "do not keep on babbling like pagans, for they think they will be heard because of their many words. Do not be like them, for your Father knows what you need before you ask him" (Matthew 6:7–8). Instead, Jesus proposed the Lord's Prayer, which is only four sentences long:

> *"Our Father in heaven, hallowed be your name, your kingdom come, your will be done, on earth as it is in heaven. Give us today our daily bread. And forgive us our debts, as we also have forgiven our debtors. And lead us not into temptation, but deliver us from the evil one."*
>
> MATTHEW 6:9–13

How often we pray matters more than how long we pray. God tells us to "pray continually" (1 Thessalonians 5:17). This doesn't mean we do nothing but pray (how would we eat, sleep, or read the Bible?), but that we do everything in a spirit of prayer, aware that we are living before the face of God, and ready to express whatever joys or burdens are on our minds.

Most Christians feel guilty about how much they pray. No one thinks they pray enough or well enough. Maybe we're missing the point. Prayer isn't a competition or a duty. It's our privilege to talk with God, to find our voice in this most lopsided relationship.

God knows it's lopsided, so He's not looking for us to amaze Him with our spiritual vocabulary. We may simply pray a psalm or the Lord's Prayer, then add our own words. What we say matters less than that it comes from our heart. Tell God whatever's on your mind. He wants to hear your voice.

223 Can good works save me?

If you owed someone one hundred dollars, you'd confidently assure them you'd pay them back. One thousand dollars might be a struggle. But if you saved and took a second job, you'd eventually be debt-free. One million dollars? That might seem hopeless. Why bother? What if you owed someone an infinite amount of money, so that no matter how much you repaid them, you never took one step toward closing the gap?

We have rebelled against an infinite God, so we owe Him an infinite amount of justice. Our debt is unending and grows larger each day. We can't begin to close the gap not only because the debt is infinite but also because any righteous act that we might do is something God already requires. We can't earn extra credit with God. There's no going above and beyond.

This terrible predicament terrorized Martin Luther. He was a sixteenth-century monk who desperately tried to earn merit by saying prayers, fasting for days, going without sleep, and sleeping without covers. He said, "I was a good monk, and I kept the rule of my order so strictly that I may say that if ever a monk got to heaven by his monkery, it was I."[34]

Yet he realized it wasn't enough. He dragged his burdened conscience to his priest and confessed his sins for hours. His exasperated priest finally exclaimed, "Look here, if you expect Christ to forgive you, come in with something to forgive—patricide, blasphemy, adultery—instead of all these peccadilloes." When Luther wouldn't leave him alone, the priest tried a gentler approach, "Man, God is not angry with you. You are angry with God. Don't you know that God commands you to hope?"[35]

But Luther knew he never did his absolute best, so how could he be righteous? He explained, "Yet my conscience would never give me assurance, but I was always doubting and said, 'You did not perform that correctly. You were not contrite enough. You left that out of your confession.' "[36] Luther conceded, "I was myself more than once driven to the very abyss of despair so that I wished I had never been created. Love God? I hated him!"[37] Luther trembled before God's impossibly high standard and nearly lost his mind.

Then one day he was poring over the apostle Paul's words: "I am not ashamed of the gospel, because it is the power of God that brings salvation to everyone who believes: first to the Jew, then to the Gentile. For in the gospel the righteousness of God is revealed—a righteousness that is by faith from first to last, just as it is written, 'The righteous will live by faith'" (Romans 1:16–17). Luther understood how God's righteousness condemns. How could Paul also say it saves?

Then the answer came to him: God's righteousness is not merely His unattainable holiness. It is the righteousness of Christ, earned by His perfect life and put in escrow by His death on our behalf, a line of credit that can be tapped when we unite with Him by faith. Luther now read Romans 1:17, "The one who is declared righteous by faith, shall live." He announced, "I felt myself to be reborn and to have gone through open doors into paradise. The whole of Scripture took on a new meaning, and whereas before the 'justice of God' had filled me with hate, now it became to me inexpressibly sweet in greater love."[38]

Luther's discovery is what Protestants call "justification by faith alone." Justification is our just (or righteous) standing before God. How is that possible for sinners like us? Only by faith in Jesus. Luther called this the "joyous exchange." When we unite with Jesus by faith, we share the same balance sheet. Our guilt and shame are put on Jesus and His righteousness is credited to us. What a trade! When God looks at us, He sees our sin but no longer takes it into account. He considers us to be as holy as His Son.

Here's the point and the most important question of your life: What is your basis, your ground, your reason for God to accept you? When God asks how sinners like us can possibly live with Him, what answer can we give? There is only one thing to say, as short as it is strong: *Jesus.*

That's it. Not Jesus plus our good efforts. Not Jesus plus we went to church. Not Jesus plus we recycled. Not Jesus plus anything. If we add to Jesus, we always take away. We say Jesus isn't enough. We need something more. If Jesus is the only Savior, that's a dangerous, damnable thing to say.

Good works can save me as long as they're not mine. Good works have saved me because I've put my faith in Jesus. His righteous life now counts for me. It can count for you too. All you have to do is ask.

A girl in Thailand opens a Christmas gift box prepared by the Christian ministry Samaritan's Purse.

224 Why should I do good works?

Have you ever wondered, *If God forgives me no matter what I do, what does it matter what I do? Why not sin away? It's covered!*

God raises and answers this question through the inspired words of Paul. "Shall we go on sinning so that grace may increase? By no means! We are those who have died to sin; how can we live in it any longer?" (Romans 6:1–2). We were buried with Jesus "through baptism into death in order that, just as Christ was raised from the dead through the glory of the Father, we too may live a new life" (verse 4).

God saves us by faith without our works, but He saves us by faith "to do good works" (Ephesians 2:10). The order here is everything. We don't do good works to earn God's acceptance. We do good works because we are accepted.

But what's the motivation? Paul explains, "The grace of God. . .teaches us to say

'No' to ungodliness and worldly passions, and to live self-controlled, upright and godly lives" (Titus 2:11–12). How does grace do that? It makes sense that grace would provide a blank check. Do whatever you want because you can always tell God you're sorry and be forgiven. How does grace prompt the opposite—self-control and holiness?

Like this: grace is God's loving response to our sin. Only forgiven sinners can begin to fathom God's bottomless grace. The more we appreciate God's grace, the more our hearts will overflow with gratitude. The Greek term for grace is *charis,* and its word for gratitude is *eucharistia.* (See *charis* right in the middle?) The Greek word for gratitude is mostly grace. This is fitting, as thanksgiving is our automatic response to grace. We instinctively give thanks for the kindness we've received and look for heartfelt ways to express our appreciation.

If we're lacking good works, it's because we're not thankful. Why aren't we thankful? Because we don't appreciate the depth of God's grace. Why aren't we moved by grace? Because we don't grasp the weight of our sin. We don't think we're all that bad.

The key to pleasing Jesus isn't to try harder but to know better. Only if we understand how depraved we really are can we begin to comprehend grace. Once we understand these two things—our sin and God's grace—we will naturally respond with gratitude. And gratitude always seeks to please its benefactor. Always.

Jesus' salvation is free, but we'll resist taking advantage when we remember why. Some things are free because they're worthless, like a box of videotapes or floppy disks. Other things are free because they're priceless, such as the love of a mother for her child. How much is that worth? It's impossible to say. Any value you would place on it, regardless of how high, would immediately cheapen it.

What kind of free is the love of Christ? God tells us. "You know that it was not with perishable things such as silver or gold that you were redeemed from the empty way of life handed down to you from your ancestors, but with the precious blood of Christ, a lamb without blemish or defect" (1 Peter 1:18–19).

Our salvation is free because it cost Jesus' life. No greater price was ever paid, or could be paid, for anything. Our salvation is so expensive, it can't be anything but free. Is your heart filling with gratitude? That's your motivation to please God.

225 Does God want my money?

Absolutely. He wants all of us, including our cash. That doesn't mean He wants us to give all our money to the church or even to the poor. We're allowed to have nice things. God commands us "to be generous and willing to share," because we've put our "hope in God, who richly provides us with everything for our enjoyment" (1 Timothy 6:17–18).

We must do both things simultaneously: enjoy God's gifts and share them with others. These aren't as opposed as you might think. The reason we eagerly give to others is because God has given to us, and we know there's more where that came from. Paul says we should give cheerfully, knowing "God is able to bless you abundantly, so that in all things at all times, having all that you need, you will abound in every good work" (2 Corinthians 9:8). Our generosity is a straightforward gauge of our confidence in God.

Jesus explains in a parable about three servants who were given money by their master to invest. One used his five bags of gold to earn five more. The second used his two bags of gold to gain two more. "But the man who had received one bag went off, dug a hole in the ground and hid his master's money." When the master returned, he praised the five- and two-bag servants. He said to each, "Well done, good and faithful servant! You have been faithful with a few things; I will put you in charge of many things. Come and share your master's happiness!" The servant who refused to invest his one bag blamed the master. "I knew that you are a hard man. . . so I was afraid and went out and hid your gold in the ground." The master was not impressed. *If you knew I was a hard man,* he replied, *you should at least have put the money in the bank, so I'd collect a little interest.* Calling the third man a "wicked, lazy servant," the master snatched his one bag and said, "Throw that worthless servant outside, into the darkness, where there will be weeping and gnashing of teeth." (See the whole story in Matthew 25:14–30).

Weeping and gnashing of teeth are images of hell. Why is hell the consequence of not investing what God has given us? Because it reveals a hardened heart of selfish fear. We don't trust God enough to risk investing what He has entrusted to us. We play not to lose rather than to win. We want to keep whatever we have even though we know we can't. We will die, and we'll leave our money for someone else. So it's not exactly our money. It comes from God; we're merely managing it for a while.

Why not steward it strategically? At bottom, money is a vote. When we buy a car, jeans, or movie ticket, we signal the producers to make more of what we bought. If we pay for trashy films or shoddy microwaves, we support a coarsening, disposable culture. If we purchase quality books and free-range eggs, we will get more of the same.

This is why it's not a great idea to give away all our money or fall deeply into debt. When we run out of money, we run out of votes. We no longer have a say in what our economy produces.

What should we vote for? Start with Jesus. Financially vote for His church and other ministries that support His kingdom. Vote for your family, those people God has entrusted to your care. Vote for other people, especially the poor who could use a hand-up. You can also vote for your favorite football team and mint chocolate chip ice cream. I do!

Jesus commends a poor widow who gave what she could (Mark 12:41–44).

Every dollar expresses our values. Jesus said, "Where your treasure is, there your heart will be also" (Matthew 6:21). Open your checkbook, credit card statement, or your receipts from the past month. What are your purchases voting for? How do they express your confidence in God?

"Does God want to take away my fun?" The question has plagued humanity since the serpent tempted Eve.

226 Does God want to take away my fun?

A variation of this question ignited all that's wrong in the world. The serpent told Eve the only reason God said not to eat from the tree of the knowledge of good and evil was He wanted to keep her down. How silly! God had created Eve and every animal and tree in the garden. He had given her the man of her dreams, who loved and cherished her. He created sex so she could embrace and share that love. How could she possibly think God was against her?

This question lies at the bottom of what's wrong in our lives. We don't believe God is for us, so we strike out on our own. The old hymn had it right: *Trust and obey, for there's no other way, to be happy in Jesus, but to trust and obey.* When we trust God is on our side, we'll happily do what He says.

So let's work on that trust. Think about it: God didn't make a bland world of black and white. He created our world in dazzling color, with zesty flavors and soothing aromas. God invented roses, mountains, and dolphins. He built every pleasure receptacle in our bodies, then flooded our zone with triggers. Every wholesome pleasure we enjoy comes from God. It was His idea first. God came up with chocolate, cheese, and wine. That was Him. How could we possibly think God is against fun?

Yet sometimes we suppose that's the purpose of God's law. He wants us to love Him most, so He gives us rules to make our lives on earth a little less enjoyable. Do you see how silly that sounds?

When my children were small, I had a rule they didn't understand. We lived on a busy street, and I showed them a crack in the driveway they were not allowed to cross. Ever, for any reason. They couldn't comprehend the gravity of my rule. That was okay, as long as they trusted me. As long as they believed I had good reasons, that I was on their side.

It's no different now with me and God. I can't comprehend the depth behind every rule. That's okay, as long as I trust Him, just like I needed my toddlers to trust me. If I trust, I will obey.

And that obedience will lead to heightened joy. Unlimited freedom is not fun. Not for long. Structure, discipline, and obedience deliver the highest joys. My children now participate in their high school's marching band. They're number one in our state because they follow directions well. They drill for hours, endlessly repeating the formations and movements of their program. It's hard and sometimes boring, but what a payoff! The kids exult in their accomplishment. They've created something together that's larger than anything they could have done alone or without the firm hand of their director. A marching band that tells its musicians to saunter onto the field and do whatever they want isn't much of a band. And it definitely won't march. It won't even be fun.

We can trust God is for us. He is our Creator, so He knows what brings us joy. And He's our Father, so He loves and wants that for us. He gave us Jesus, whose death on the cross is the clinching proof that God is on our side.

Life in a fallen world won't always be fun. We will suffer because of other people or events beyond our control. This doesn't mean God is against us. He will use all of our painful experiences to bring us to glory (Romans 8:28–30). Praising Jesus in glory will be more than fun, but it will not be less. So go ahead, crank the music, order a milkshake, go to the beach. Do whatever wholesome activity brings you pleasure. This is your Father's world. He made it for you.

227 What is a normal Christian life?

A normal Christian cherishes the body of Christ, the Word of God, and prayer. Healthy Christians join and serve in a local church and make time each day to read the Bible and talk to their Father. Many choose to start each day with God.

In most other ways, a normal Christian life is, well, normal. Paul commands Christians "to make it your ambition to lead a quiet life: You should mind your own business and work with your hands, just as we told you, so that your daily life may win the respect of outsiders and so that you will not be dependent on anybody" (1 Thessalonians 4:11–12). Christians work in typical jobs, wear ordinary clothes, and eat in average restaurants, when they can't find a Chick-fil-A. They do mostly what other people do but hopefully with a higher motivation and spirit.

Here's what I mean: Christians don't merely have jobs or professions. We have callings. Paul explains, "You, my brothers and sisters, were called to be free. But do not use your freedom to indulge the flesh; rather, serve one another humbly in love" (Galatians 5:13).

The medieval church taught that only monks, nuns, and priests were called by God. Farmers, bakers, and maids had lesser jobs that God didn't much care about. The sixteenth-century Reformation changed this attitude forever. Martin Luther, John Calvin, and other Reformers taught that Jesus levels the playing field of spirituality. One profession does not earn more God points than another. We're all called by Jesus to "serve one another humbly in love."

What are your callings? Mine are church member, husband, father, son, brother, professor, author, preacher, neighbor, citizen, and so on. God has given me these opportunities to serve those He wants me to care for. When I mow the lawn, grade a paper, and finish this sentence, I'm not just doing my job, I'm answering God's call on my life.

Every corner of everyday life is an avenue for spiritual service. Paul encourages slaves, "Whatever you do, work at it with all your heart, as working for the Lord, not for human masters, since you know that you will receive an inheritance from the Lord as a reward. It is the Lord Christ you are serving" (Colossians 3:23–24). We're not merely serving our spouse, child, boss, or client. We're serving Jesus by serving them. Even if we're a slave.

Do your best in all your callings for the Lord Jesus. Some callings may give way to others as you move through the day or seasons of life. This morning I put aside my calling as author—I'm writing this sentence several hours later than planned—because a child needed me. My calling as father trumps my calling to finish this book. Both count. Each will receive Christ's reward or chastisement. Do what God has called you to do, do it with all your heart, and do it in the order of its importance. Then go to bed.

228 What are spiritual gifts?

When we are saved by Jesus and born again, the Holy Spirit equips us with special abilities to serve the body of Christ so that together we might make disciples within the church and throughout our world.

These spiritual gifts are:

1. ***Intended to benefit others.*** Our spiritual gifts are not for us, so we should probably get over them. We sometimes take spiritual gift inventories and online quizzes, crossing our fingers for a "platform gift" such as teaching or leadership.

Billy Graham (1918–2018) had the spiritual gift of evangelism. Christians are variously gifted to teach, lead, serve, and give, among other things.

We groan when we get mercy, service, or helps. *Guess I'm a nobody, a behind-the-scenes kind of person.*

We might do better to put the tests away, look around our church, and ask whom can we serve. Don't worry if their need is not in your wheelhouse. Do whatever needs doing. Do it until someone better comes along. If you happen to excel in this area, others will notice and ask you to keep doing it. This is your spiritual gift. Great! Keep using it, and remain willing to serve in other areas too, whatever your church needs.

2. ***Usually related to our natural abilities.*** If you'd rather die than speak in public, there's a good chance the Spirit will not give you the gift of teaching. If you are an office manager or run a tight ship at home, you might have the spiritual gift of leadership or administration. If you volunteered in the community before you came to Jesus, you might have the gift of service now. God has transformed stutterers into powerful preachers and narcissists into angels of mercy, but a good place to start for finding your gift is what you're good at and what you enjoy doing.

3. ***Not necessarily limited to the biblical lists.*** The spiritual gifts are mentioned in 1 Corinthians 12:4–11, 28; Romans 12:6–8; Ephesians 4:11; and 1 Peter 4:11. They include apostleship, prophecy, teaching, evangelism, administration, leadership, helps, serving, encouragement, giving, mercy, faith, working miracles, healing, tongues, interpretation of tongues, word of knowledge, word of wisdom, and evangelism.

   This list may not include every possible gift. If you have an ability that serves others in your church, this is your spiritual gift, even if it's not mentioned in the Bible. Piano accompaniment and maintaining the church website may fall under the headings of helps, service, or leadership, or you might consider them spiritual gifts in their own right. Who cares what you call them, as long as you use them to serve Jesus' body.

4. ***Not necessarily forever.*** Some gifts in the biblical lists may not continue today. Christians disagree about whether the "sign gifts" of prophecy and speaking in tongues still exist. They called attention to the new faith as it was starting out, but now that we have God's completed Word in the Bible, do we need to receive new revelation from God? Others believe that tongues and prophecy cultivate passionate intimacy with God. Most Christians agree the sign gifts of healing and miracles have disappeared. God still performs miracles in answer to our prayers, but He no longer seems to heal the lame and sick through people gifted with that power, as He used Peter and Paul (Acts 3:1–10; 19:11–12).

5. ***Distributed throughout each local church.*** All Christians have at least one spiritual gift, though no one has them all. The Spirit spreads the gifts around so we will depend on and serve each other. No one is equipped to go it alone, just that person and God. We may assume that Jesus has equipped each local body with the gifts it needs. That means *you.* Serve confidently, filling whatever role is needed, believing the Spirit will supply the grace and power to love His people well.

229 What is "speaking in tongues"?

The gift of tongues announced the arrival of the Holy Spirit and the birthday of the church. On Pentecost, ten days after Jesus returned to heaven, the Holy Spirit filled the apostles so they spoke fluently in the languages of the foreign Jews gathered in Jerusalem. This gift accelerated the spread of the Gospel. Three thousand Jews converted and took the message of Jesus back to their countries (see Acts 2:1–41).

The gift of tongues continued, marking the advance of the church. When the first Gentiles converted to the faith, they too were enabled to speak in languages they hadn't studied. The apostle Peter took this as proof that they had received the Spirit, and he baptized them into the church (Acts 10:44–48).

At least one church continued speaking in tongues long after their church had been established. The Corinthians used the gift during worship, which concerned Paul. He said it was good to speak in tongues—he spoke in tongues himself—but he suspected they were doing it to impress others, and he feared it was disrupting their worship. One person said this, another said that, and no one understood either. Paul admonished them to only speak in tongues when an interpreter was present, so everyone could understand what God was saying through them. . .and visitors wouldn't think they were crazy (1 Corinthians 14).

The necessity of an interpreter implies that the tongues in Corinth differed from the tongues spoken on Pentecost, when everyone understood without help. Perhaps the gift had changed into an unknown prayer language that someone could speak to God alone, or in the church if another was able to interpret.

Christians disagree about whether the gift of tongues continues today. Pentecostal and charismatic Christians say it obviously does, and they enthusiastically speak in tongues both in church and in their private time with God. They testify that the gift draws them into intimacy with God, as their spirit connects with God's Spirit at a depth they do not understand and cannot rationally express. Some go further and say the gift is a necessary sign of being filled with the Spirit. This can have unintended consequences: it might encourage believers to pretend they have the gift and discourage those who know they don't. Are they second-class Christians because they don't speak in tongues?

Some Christians note these problems and believe that tongues, while essential for the founding and advance of the early church, are no longer needed today. We have the completed Word of God, something not yet available in Corinth, so we do not need to receive and interpret extrabiblical messages from God. The Bible is sufficient for life and godliness.

It seems best for non-Pentecostal, noncharismatic Christians to be open to the gift of tongues yet discerning. The Bible does not say that tongues have ceased, and the gift apparently blesses many. At the same time, there are excesses to watch out for. The chaotic every-man-for-himself confusion in Corinth may still occur today. Not everyone who claims the gift actually has the gift. On the other hand, God says He will pour out His Spirit "in the last days," and the explosive spread of the Pentecostal church may be evidence of this (Acts 2:17). On the other, other hand, how helpful can tongues be if the Corinthian church known for them was also known for outrageous sin, pride, and divisions? Tongues can distract from the main business of the Christian life, which is normal, everyday faithful obedience. For these reasons, we should remain open to the gift—even praying whether God wants us to have it—while evaluating claims to the gift with careful discernment.

230 Does God choose some people to be saved and others to be lost?

God loves and wants to save everyone. He flings opens the gates of heaven and scans the horizon, watching for His prodigals to come home. He could send Jesus back now to judge the earth, but He has lovingly decided to give us more time, "not wanting anyone to perish, but everyone to come to repentance" (2 Peter 3:9). The Bible ends with God's plea to all: " 'Come!' Let the one who is thirsty come; and let the one who wishes take the free gift of the water of life" (Revelation 22:17).

God urges us all to come, but none will come on their own. We are depraved sinners who, left to ourselves, will always choose ourselves over God. Every single time, unless God changes our hearts to make us want Him. So God does. How humble is God? Although He is the most beautiful being there ever could be, He knows that's not enough to win our hearts. He gently yet powerfully draws us to Himself, opening our blind eyes so we see His beauty and desire Him as we should.

God loved us before we were born. Before the dawn of creation's first day, He decided to save us. Paul writes, "He chose us in [Jesus] before the creation of the world to be holy and blameless in his sight. In love he predestined us for adoption to sonship through Jesus Christ, in accordance with his pleasure and will—to the praise of his glorious grace, which he has freely given us in the One he loves" (Ephesians 1:4–6; see also Acts 13:48; 1 Thessalonians 1:4–5).

The ultimate reason that God chose us is "his pleasure and will." We can't go

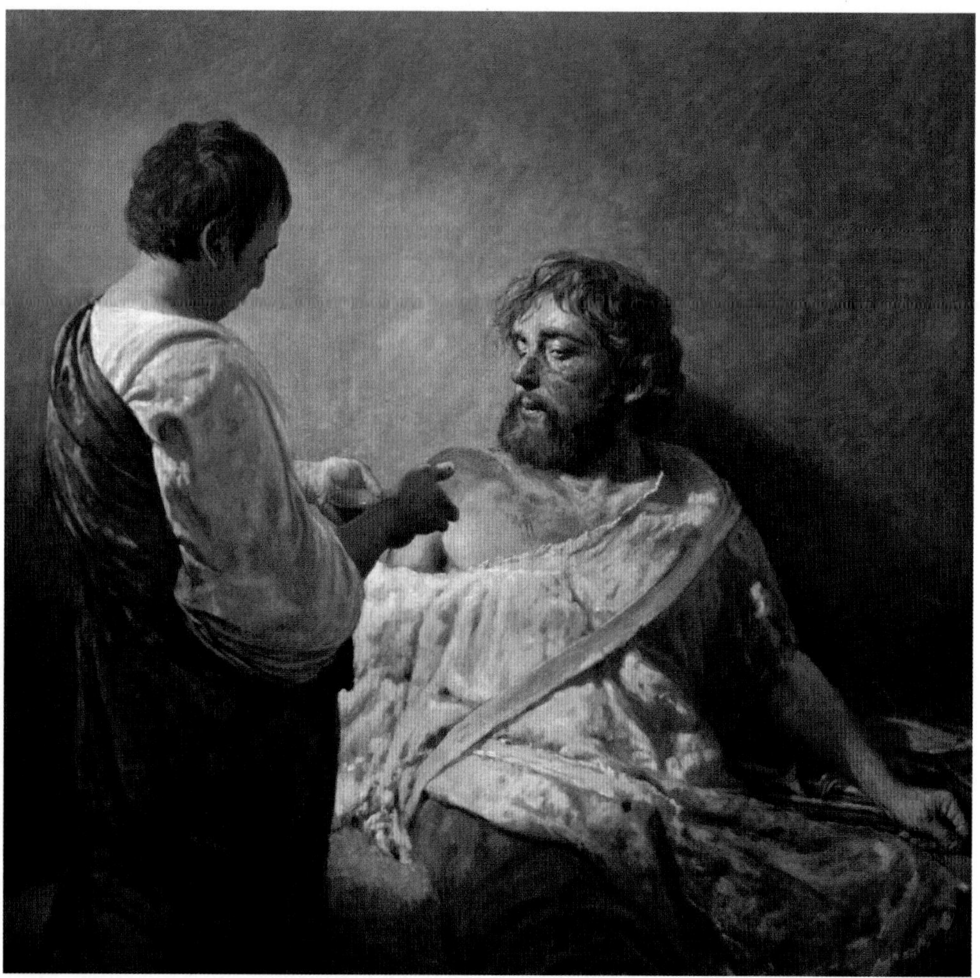

Jacob convinces his hungry older brother, Esau, to give up his birthright in exchange for a bowl of soup. What did God mean when He said, "Jacob I loved, but Esau I hated" (Romans 9:13)?

beyond God's will and say *why* He wanted us. He wanted us because He wanted us. He didn't choose us because we were special. We are special because He chose us.

This bright line of God's love raises a dark question that's impossible to answer: If God powerfully changed our hearts so we would love Him, why doesn't He do that for everyone? Paul asked this question in Romans 9–11. *Why did God choose Jacob but not Esau?* The apostle said it's not because God is unjust or unloving, because God is love and always does what is right. Paul wrestled with this question for three chapters, finally concluding that finite creatures will never comprehend the ways of God. He exclaimed, "Oh, the depth of the riches of the wisdom and knowledge of God! How unsearchable his judgments, and his paths beyond tracing out!" (Romans 11:33).

If that's the best Paul could do writing inspired Scripture, you and I are not going to solve this question. But we can say this:

1. God never blocks anyone from coming to Him. He pleads and waits, even now, for lost sinners to come home.

2. God's election is hidden in His sovereign mystery. Do not try to find yourself in God's eternal decree, asking whether or not God chose you. You have no access to God's secret will, so there's no point in asking the question. It does you no good. Focus instead on what God has commanded. Turn from your sin and put your faith in Jesus. Do this, and you may assume you are chosen by God, for you would not choose Him if He hadn't first chosen you.

3. Like crossword puzzles and M. Night Shyamalan movies, election is best understood after the fact. If we lead with election, examining God's choice before we are saved, we inevitably ask the unproductive and paralyzing question, *Am I elect?* But if we wait until after we have repented and put our faith in Jesus, we can look back on our salvation and ask, *What just happened? What changed that I believe?* And we'll be encouraged to learn of God's sovereign choice.

4. God's election has two main benefits. First, it humbles us because we realize God prefers to choose the weak and foolish people to shame the wise and strong. We did nothing to win Him over. He loved us because He loved us (1 Corinthians 1:26–31). Second, election comforts us. We realize that our salvation lies in the sovereign grip of God. The One who chose us before time began will keep us all the way to the end. Those God "predestined, he also called; those he called, he also justified; those he justified, he also glorified" (Romans 8:30). We can rest in God's powerful love.

231 How do we reconcile God's sovereignty and human freedom?

We finite creatures cannot comprehend how this works, but Scripture teaches both that God sovereignly rules over our choices and that we remain genuinely free. The Sabeans and Chaldeans freely stole Job's flocks and herds, yet their theft was part of God's plan to test Job (see Job 1:13–17).

The king of Assyria boasted of his plundering exploits. He invaded other nations and toppled their kings. "As one reaches into a nest, so my hand reached for the wealth of the nations; as people gather abandoned eggs, so I gathered all the countries; not one flapped a wing, or opened its mouth to chirp" (Isaiah 10:14). But then God spoke: "Does the ax raise itself above the person who swings it, or the saw boast against the one who uses it?" (verse 15). The king was freely terrorizing others, yet he was merely a tool in God's hand. God gripped the handle of the king's will, swinging him this way and that, yet without violating his free choice. The king did what he wanted, and God would punish him for it.

The most poignant example is the death of Jesus. Peter explained to his Jerusalem audience why Jesus died: "This man was handed over to you by God's deliberate plan and foreknowledge; and you, with the help of wicked men, put him to death by nailing him to the cross" (Acts 2:23). In this single verse, Peter combines both truths. *Why did Jesus die? It was God's plan, and you did it. God determined that Jesus must die to save the world, but you are not off the hook. You must answer to God for nailing His Son to the cross.*

We cannot comprehend how God's sovereignty and human freedom interface, but we need both to be true. Human freedom gives meaning and responsibility to our choices. We're not merely playing out a predetermined plan. We have options. The future is open. Events could go this way or that.

This may surprise you, but our freedom itself is grounded in divine sovereignty. If God was not sovereign, nothing would be fixed. Everything would be random and up for grabs. How could anyone meaningfully choose in that environment? We can't choose responsibly unless we can reasonably predict the outcome of our choices. Our world must be firm enough for us to choose freely. Only a sovereign God guarantees that.

Besides grounding human freedom, divine sovereignty supplies lockdown security for life. God firmly controls the free choices of his creatures. He is never surprised by what happens to us. He saw it coming and promises to hold us close through the whole ordeal. If God was God at the cross, He remains God in whatever comes our way. So we pray.

Our prayers assume both human freedom and divine sovereignty. Human freedom means the future is open, so God's actions can make a difference. Divine sovereignty means God isn't limited by our freedom; He can override our free choices without violating them. I can't explain how He does it, but I assume He can every time I ask for a safe journey home, a successful interview, or a new friend. In each case I'm assuming God can guarantee what free people freely do, without compromising their freedom.

We cannot comprehend the mystery of God. We can only praise Him for His inscrutable power that both makes human freedom possible and rules every decision. "The lot is cast into the lap, but its every decision is from the LORD" (Proverbs 16:33).

232 How should Christians relate to their government?

God tells us to do two things for our political leaders: pray and obey. Christians pray for "kings and all those in authority, that we may live peaceful and quiet lives in all godliness and holiness" (1 Timothy 2:2). And we submit "for the Lord's sake to every human authority: whether to the emperor, as the supreme authority, or to governors, who are sent by him to punish those who do wrong and to commend those who do right" (1 Peter 2:13–14).

We pray and obey even when the government is far from perfect. The apostle Paul wrote to Christians in Rome when their emperor was an evil madman. Nero would later set fire to Rome and blame the Christians, using them as human torches to light his gardens. He would decapitate Paul. Yet Paul told Christians that

When the apostle Paul wrote, "Let everyone be subject to the governing authorities, for there is no authority except that which God has established" (Romans 13:1), the governing authority was the vicious Emperor Nero.

even wicked government is established by God and deserves our taxes, submission, and obedience. He included this ironic line, "For rulers hold no terror for those who do right, but for those who do wrong" (Romans 13:3). This is true most of the time, but not always—as Paul would soon find out. Even so, we serve God by obeying the authorities that He has sovereignly placed over us.

With one big exception. We must disobey any government that demands we disobey God. When Jewish leaders commanded the apostles to stop teaching about Jesus, they answered, "We must obey God rather than human beings!" (Acts 5:29). When Roman emperors demanded that Christians pinch a bit of incense and say "Caesar is Lord," true followers of Christ refused, and many were martyred. They took comfort from the book of Revelation. There Jesus appeared to John, who had been exiled by the emperor, and declared that He alone is "the ruler of the kings of the earth" (Revelation 1:5). Every prince, president, and prime minister reports to King Jesus.

This big exception kicks up smaller questions. What if your government isn't demanding you disobey God, but it has passed laws that oppress others and remove some of their human rights? We may respond within the political system, peacefully protesting unjust laws and voting and lobbying for something better.

What if your government is not a democratic republic that gives citizens the right to vote? Then there's little we can do within the political system. We may choose a combination of bravely enduring the unjust situation, supporting those who bear its brunt, and publicly defying the laws and suffering the legal consequences. All three were used by America's civil rights movement, which finally won black people the right to vote. All three are currently employed by Chinese Christians with not much political success yet.

Regardless of the outcome, the one thing Scripture seems to forbid is revolution against one's government. *I'm looking at you, America.* Yes, the American Revolution may have been an act of disobedience against God (British theologian John Wesley thought so). But now that it happened, America has a new government, and it would be wrong for Christian citizens to rebel against it. Rebellion leads to civil war and chaos. If there is one thing worse than a bad government, that is no government at all. Your government may be wicked and incompetent—if it's wicked, let's hope it's incompetent!—yet in many ways we take for granted it is God's common grace upon your life.

PART 6: THE END
Where Things Are Ultimately Headed

Many once feared that nuclear weapons would destroy the earth; now, the concern is climate change. What does the Bible say?

233 How will the world end?

It won't. The Bible never says our world will end. This age will end but not the world itself. Scripture speaks only of one world, or *cosmos,* that has more than one age, or *aiōn.* Jesus said that anyone who sins against the Holy Spirit "will not be forgiven, either in this age or in the age to come" (Matthew 12:32). There is this fallen age, and there is the "age to come," when Jesus returns and restores all things.

It's fitting that Jesus would do this. God created a beautiful world that pulsated with love, joy, and peace. Adam's fall ruined this good world, and God wants it back. He won't obliterate our world, as if Satan and sin were too strong for Him to overcome. Everything God created was good, everything has been ravaged by evil, and everything must be redeemed. Satan wins nothing in the end. The end will come for him, not for our Father's world.

234 When will this age end?

The disciples asked Jesus this question. Point blank. "Tell us," they said, "when will this happen, and what will be the sign of your coming and of the end of the age?" (Matthew 24:3). Jesus said He wasn't sure. "But about that day or hour no one knows, not even the angels in heaven, nor the Son, but only the Father" (verse 36).

Still, Jesus did give us some signs to watch for. As we approach the end, "Nation will rise against nation, and kingdom against kingdom. There will be famines and earthquakes in various places" (Matthew 24:7). Many of Jesus' followers will be hated, persecuted, and put to death. Others will turn away and deceive "many people. Because of the increase of wickedness, the love of most will grow cold" (verses 11–12). But God's true children will persevere. They will proclaim the "gospel of the kingdom" throughout "the whole world as a testimony to all nations, and then the end will come" (verse 14).

Jesus prophesied that the temple in Jerusalem would suffer an "abomination that causes desolation" (Matthew 24:15). Christians believe this occurred in 70 CE, when the Romans destroyed the temple. Dispensational Christians believe this will

Jews pray at the Western Wall, all that's left of the Jerusalem temple of Jesus' day.

happen yet again during a future tribulation—a time of "great distress, unequaled from the beginning of the world until now" (verse 21), when the Antichrist breaks his covenant with Israel. Either way, Jesus warned of terrible trials during the end times. "If those days had not been cut short, no one would survive" (verse 22).

Despite these ominous signs, Jesus predicted that life near the end will seem normal for many people. As in the days of Noah, when "people were eating and drinking, marrying and given in marriage, up to the day Noah entered the ark. . . that is how it will be at the coming of the Son of Man" (Matthew 24:37–39). Most people will be caught unprepared.

Since no one knows when Jesus will return—and since it might be today—Jesus said we must watch. We must always "be ready, because the Son of Man will come at an hour when you do not expect him" (Matthew 24:44). Have you thought that Jesus might return right now? No? That's reason to think it might happen in the next moment. May Jesus catch us with our eyes on the sky.

235 What is the millennium?

The millennium is a thousand years of peace that may or may not occur before the Last Judgment and the redemption of all things. All Christians should agree that our story ends in the golden age of the new heavens and new earth. Will there also be a lesser, "silver age" immediately prior?

Premillennial Christians say yes. They believe Jesus will return *pre-*, or before, the millennium, because that's what a straightforward reading of Revelation 20:1–10 seems to say. Immediately before His ascension, Jesus shocked His disciples by telling them the Messiah would come twice. He wouldn't consummate the kingdom just then; He'd return at a later date (Acts 1:6–8). Did Jesus have one more surprise? Three chapters before the Bible ends, John received a vision from Jesus that implies His return will also have two parts. Before He consummates all things on the new earth, Jesus will bind Satan and physically reign with His followers on the earth for one thousand years. After the millennium is over, Satan will be released to deceive people one last time. He will gather a massive army to march on Jerusalem, fire will fall from heaven and consume them, and Satan will be thrown forever into the lake of burning sulfur.

Other Christians disagree with this view. They notice the book of Revelation is apocalyptic literature, so they say it should not be read literally. Besides, a straightforward reading of chapter twenty raises puzzling questions: How is Satan able to rustle up a massive army after Jesus has reigned for one thousand years? Wouldn't this humiliate Jesus? How could our loving Savior be that unpopular?

These Christians say Revelation 20 describes our present age. The millennium occurs now through Jesus' spiritual reign. He has bound Satan, though not entirely. Like a desperate MacGyver tied to a chair, Satan is able to bounce around, freeing his fingers enough to inflict some damage upon his enemies.

Since the 1930s, these Christians have divided into two camps. The majority are called *amillennialists.* This name is misleading because it implies they don't believe in a millennium; a better name might be *nowmillennialists,* for they believe in a spiritual millennium that is happening now. The smaller group is called *postmillennialists* because they believe Jesus will return *post-*, or after, an indefinite period of peace. They believe the millennium may have already begun, as Gospel preaching slowly but surely improves human society. Our world will continue to improve until Jesus returns to top it off.

In brief, premillennialists believe Jesus will physically reign on earth in the future. Amillennialists believe Jesus is spiritually reigning over the church now. Postmillennialists believe Jesus is spiritually reigning over the earth through the church, some now and much more as time goes on.

You can tell which view you favor by how you read the day's news. If you notice the negative stories and believe the world is getting worse, as it must before Jesus returns, you're probably premillennial. If you are struck by what's positive—especially stories of revival and Christian witness—you might be postmillennial. If you suspect it's a wash, the good and bad stories roughly canceling each other, you're likely amillennial.

None of the views are perfect. Each view has interpretative problems: premillennialism puts a lot of weight on one apocalyptic passage, while amillennialism and postmillennialism struggle to make sense of Revelation 20—Satan is simultaneously bound and not bound? The first resurrection of Revelation 20:4–5 isn't physical? Aren't resurrections always physical?

Each view must fudge on some part of biblical prophecy. Scripture teaches that Jesus' return is *imminent* (it could happen at any moment) and *unified* (He comes once) and that *events must still occur* (for example, Matthew 24:14 says the Gospel must be preached throughout the whole world). Postmillennialism fudges on imminence; it believes the world must progress further before Jesus returns, so He is not coming today. Amillennialism fudges on events that must still occur; it rightly believes Jesus could come back today but struggles to explain how that's possible if the Gospel must first be preached to all people groups. Premillennialism reconciles imminence and events that must still occur by separating Jesus' return into two parts. They say His heavenly rapture of the church is imminent, but He won't touch down on earth until the events described in Matthew 24. This distinction sounds promising, except the separation between rapture and return raises questions about the unity of Jesus' coming. How is it a single event if it has two parts?

The challenges to each view prompt many Christians to joke they are *panmillennialists.* They aren't sure about the specifics; they're just confident it will all pan out. This isn't bad, actually. Whichever view we prefer, we shouldn't be shocked if it turns out we were wrong. And that's okay, because the millennium is one of the least important aspects of our Christian hope. What matters far more, and what the Bible is clear about, is the return of Christ, the resurrection of the dead, the last judgment, heaven and hell, and everlasting joy for the redeemed on this restored earth.

236 What is the rapture?

The rapture is a relatively new idea, developed by dispensational premillennialists in nineteenth-century Britain (see "How does the Old Testament relate to the New Testament?" on page 233). Critics say it amounts to a cosmic dog whistle, when Jesus secretly and instantaneously calls His followers up to heaven. Planes will crash as Christian pilots are whisked away. Cars will run off the road. Steaming plates carried by raptured waitresses will clatter to the ground. An unconverted child in a Christian family will be left behind.

This was my biggest fear in second grade. I'd walk home from school, and finding no one there, worry that I had missed the rapture. I searched until I found a neighbor who I was reasonably sure was a Christian. *Phew!* Mischievous church campers sometimes staged the rapture, dropping clothes in piles as if their raptured bodies had quickly shed them. A poor child returning to his cabin would, at least for a moment, question his salvation.

The key biblical passage for the rapture is 1 Thessalonians 4:13–18. Jesus will return from heaven and raise His followers who have died. "After that, we who are still alive and are left will be caught up together with them in the clouds to meet the Lord in the air. And so we will be with the Lord forever" (verse 17). Theologically, the rapture may also solve how Jesus' return can be imminent and yet won't happen until the whole world hears the Gospel. The rapture can happen at any moment, but Jesus won't physically return to stay until the Gospel is preached to all nations.

Why have a rapture? Dispensationalists say the rapture removes the church from the world as God turns His attention back to the nation of Israel. Most dispensationalists believe the rapture will happen at the start of the tribulation, a seven-year period in which God uses the Antichrist to judge Israel for their long history of disobedience. Others believe the rapture will occur in the middle of the tribulation, before the worst suffering begins. Still others say the rapture won't happen until the tribulation's end. These nondispensational, or historic premillennialists, believe thc tribulation isn't targeting Israel but is bringing God's wrath upon the entire world. God hasn't promised to remove His people from the world's suffering, only to preserve us through it. When the seven years of tribulation end, the church will rise to meet Jesus in the air and welcome Him back to planet Earth.

The previous answer said the question of the millennium is relatively unimportant. The tribulation matters less. Christians hope for the three R's: the *return* of Christ, the *resurrection* of the body, and the *restoration* of all things. These promises are solid and last forever. In view of this promised future, does it really matter if there is a seven-year tribulation and if the church is raptured at the start, in the middle, or not until the end?

237 What is Israel's role in the end times?

It depends who you ask. Dispensationalists believe the nation of Israel will be God's focus at the end of our age. The tribulation will punish Israel and bring many Jews to Christ, and the millennium will finally deliver to Israel the whole land of Palestine that God promised Abraham's children.

Historic (nondispensational) premillennialists say Israel will have a special place in the millennium, but it will be spiritual rather than physical. Israel will find its fulfillment in the church, as many Jews are converted during the millennium.

Amillennialists and postmillennialists typically don't have a special role for Israel. All of God's promises made to His Old Testament people are now fulfilled in the New Testament church. However, Israel became a nation again in 1949, and it continues to be the world's focus, the most volatile hotspot on earth. Perhaps God isn't through with this nation yet? He does promise that in the end "all Israel will be saved" (Romans 11:26). Some amillennialists and postmillennialists concede this

Israeli soldiers in a quiet moment. There have been many unquiet moments since modern Israel became a nation in 1949.

may imply a blessed future for ethnic Israel, though it's unclear what this blessing involves and whether it requires a tribulation or millennium to make it happen.

The question of Israel inspires us to read the Bible with one eye on international news, yet we should be humble about our interpretation of current events. Watch out for anyone who declares confidently what this event or that person means. We can't be sure. . .but it sure is interesting.

238 Who is the Antichrist?

Satan will become increasingly manic as his doom nears. He will terrorize God's people with a great tribulation—a "time of distress such as has not happened from the beginning of nations" (Daniel 12:1). He will tempt many Christians to throw away their faith (Matthew 24:10–12), and he will raise a rival imposter to Jesus. This Antichrist will impress the world when he performs miracles and recovers from an apparently fatal wound. Everyone will worship him, except for the people of God, whom the Antichrist will attack for forty-two months (Revelation 13:1–8).

Who are these people of God? Dispensational Christians say they aren't the church, which will be raptured at the beginning of the tribulation. They are Israel, whom God will discipline during the tribulation to turn their hearts back to Him. Daniel prophesied:

> *"The people of the ruler who will come will destroy the city and the sanctuary. The end will come like a flood: War will continue until the end, and desolations have been decreed. He will confirm a covenant with many for one 'seven.' In the middle of the 'seven' he will put an end to sacrifice and offering. And at the temple he will set up an abomination that causes desolation, until the end that is decreed is poured out on him."*
>
> DANIEL 9:26–27

In an early 16th-century painting, Satan whispers into the ear of the Antichrist, who looks remarkably like Jesus.

Dispensationalists interpret this prophecy as saying the Antichrist will appear at the start of the tribulation as a friend of Israel. He will make a covenant with the nation for seven years then break it halfway through. He will desecrate Israel's rebuilt temple by setting "himself up in God's temple, proclaiming himself to be God" (2 Thessalonians 2:4). The Antichrist will "wage war against God's holy people" for three and a half years, until Jesus returns and hurls him "alive into the fiery lake of burning sulfur" (Revelation 13:7; 19:20).

Covenant theologians believe Israel's role has folded into the church, so Israel as a nation is not the focus of the end times. The Antichrist will attack the followers of Jesus, whether they be Jew or Gentile, during the final tribulation. But Daniel prophesied about "an abomination that causes desolation" in the temple. Doesn't this imply a renewed focus on Israel?

Covenant theologians say this abomination occurred first in 163 BCE, when Antiochus Epiphanes dedicated the temple to Zeus and erected a pagan altar upon which he sacrificed unclean pigs. It occurred again in 70 CE, when the Romans destroyed the temple and insisted that everyone worship the emperor. It will also be fulfilled spiritually in the future as the Antichrist poses as God and attacks the church. This future fulfillment need not be a physical act in a literal temple. Setting "himself up in God's temple, proclaiming himself to be God" may only be a figurative way to describe the Antichrist's blasphemy.

Whether we believe the Antichrist will attack Israel or the church, we should be careful in guessing his identity. The early church thought he was Nero. (Some covenant theologians agree—they aren't looking for a future Antichrist.) The Reformers thought he was the pope. World War II–era Christians believed he was Hitler or Stalin. When I was a child, the best guess was Henry Kissinger. (Apparently, we had run out of major league villains!) These conjectures are not entirely wrong, as some of these figures would count as antichrists—they oppose Jesus and all that He loves and represents (1 John 2:18). But none turned out to be *the* Antichrist. Our speculation only sensationalized their limited powers and frightened children like me.

Let's not give the Antichrist too much credit. He is "doomed to destruction" (2 Thessalonians 2:3). Jesus will easily take care of him. Run to Jesus, and He will take care of you.

239 What's the significance of 666?

John's vision of the last days includes a false prophet, "a second beast" that will compel all people to worship the Antichrist, or "first beast." He will force everyone "to receive a mark on their right hands or on their foreheads, so that they could not buy or sell unless they had the mark, which is the name of the beast or the number of its name.

This calls for wisdom. Let the person who has insight calculate the number of the beast, for it is the number of a man. That number is 666" (Revelation 13:16–18).

Apocalyptic writings use symbolic numbers to hide key points from enemies who might happen to read them. The number 666 is a riddle, known to the initiated but concealed from first-century Roman officials. It's such a good riddle that today we're not entirely sure what it means.

The number might represent an evil, ineffective parody of the true God. Revelation uses the number seven to connote divine completeness. There are seven blessings, seven angels, seven churches, seven spirits of God, seven golden lampstands, seven seals, seven trumpets, and so on. God is triune, so the number that best represents Him would be three sevens, or 777. Perhaps 666 refers to the evil trinity of Satan, the Antichrist, and his false prophet, and how their strength is dramatically inferior to the powerful blessedness of God. They can't match His excellence, but repeatedly come up one digit short. They fail and fail and fail again.

Or 666 could mean someone else. John's invitation to calculate the number led many in church history to investigate what the numbers spell. Hebrew and Greek letters have numerical values, which can be added together to create numbers. And numbers can be reverse engineered to spell words. In this case, the Hebrew letters that spell Nero Caesar add up to 666. An alternate Hebrew spelling of Nero Caesar adds up to 616. Some manuscripts of Revelation say the beast's number is 616, indicating they agreed it meant Nero but used the variant spelling. (616 happens to be my area code, so for selfish reasons I'm going with the more traditional 666!)

If 666 refers to Nero, the first Roman emperor to persecute Christians, then God is telling us that the final Antichrist will be an evil ruler, in the trajectory of the man who beheaded Paul and crucified Peter. The Roman Empire that harassed the first Christians has never entirely gone away. It morphed into the countries of Europe and migrated across the Atlantic Ocean to America. Twenty-first-century Christians in the West are beginning to see how governments could use technology and public pressure to make it hard for them to "buy or sell" unless they capitulate and worship the beast.

I understand the temptation to take "the mark of the beast," but remember how the story ends. The angel of God promises:

The altar of the imperial temple in Pergamum, where Roman citizens pledged loyalty to the empire by pinching a bit of incense and saying, "Caesar is Lord."

> *"If anyone worships the beast and its image and receives its mark on their forehead or on their hand, they, too, will drink the wine of God's fury, which has been poured full strength into the cup of his wrath. They will be tormented with burning sulfur in the presence of the holy angels and of the Lamb. And the smoke of their torment will rise for ever and ever. There will be no rest day or night for those who worship the beast and its image, or for anyone who receives the mark of its name."*
> REVELATION 14:9–11

God knows it won't be easy. "This calls for patient endurance on the part of the people of God who keep his commands and remain faithful to Jesus" (Revelation 14:12). But faithfulness is worth it, an infinity of times over. Don't sell Jesus for the right to buy and sell. Fear no man, even the Antichrist. All he can do is kill you. Instead, "be afraid of the One who can destroy both soul and body in hell" (Matthew 10:28). He is your Father, and He loves you more than you'll ever know. Stay faithful to the end, and you will rise to shine forever in His love.

240 What is Armageddon?

Armageddon is both the name and location of earth's last battle. Last at least for this age—premillennialists believe Satan's final defeat will occur one thousand years later, at the end of the millennium. As this age nears its climax, demons will disperse throughout the world to round up armies "for the battle on the great day of God Almighty. . . . Then they gathered the kings together to the place that in Hebrew is called Armageddon" (Revelation 16:14, 16).

Armageddon is literally *Har Megiddo* in Hebrew, which means "Hill of Megiddo." This prominent hilltop overlooks the vast plain of Megiddo, which lies in the Jezreel Valley in northern Israel, along an important trade route from Egypt to Syria. Today this plain is traversed by Highway 66—one six shy of a bleak coincidence and home to the world's most unfortunately placed truck stop. (Who thought *that* was a good idea?) In Bible times, Megiddo's strategic location made it the site of key battles, so it's fitting that history's final showdown would occur there.

Or not. While it's possible, perhaps likely, that the armies of the world will gather there to be destroyed by Jesus, it's also possible that Armageddon is symbolic of God's final conflict with evil. Or both. Jesus will effortlessly defeat Satan, his demons, and his armies wherever and however He encounters them. That's the point of Armageddon.

An archaeological site at ancient Megiddo, the area of biblical Armageddon.

241 What is the Last Judgment?

At the end of this age, after God decimates Satan's armies and hurls the devil into the fires of hell, He will summon every one of us to appear before Him (Romans 14:10). John writes:

> *Then I saw a great white throne and him who was seated on it. The earth and the heavens fled from his presence, and there was no place for them. And I saw the dead, great and small, standing before the throne, and books were opened. Another book was opened, which is the book of life. The dead were judged according to what they had done as recorded in the books. . . . Anyone whose name was not found written in the book of life was thrown into the lake of fire.*
>
> REVELATION 20:11–12, 15

Heaven and earth will recede, leaving us fully exposed. No place to hide. Every secret made known (Luke 12:2–3; Romans 2:16; 1 Corinthians 4:5). We will see clearly in that moment—nothing will be more obvious—that our sins deserve hell. Everyone who goes to hell will know that God is right to send them there. They have no defense.

Our only hope of surviving God's judgment is Jesus. If we put our faith in Him, God will credit Jesus' righteousness to us. He will count us as holy as His beloved Son (Romans 3:21–26; Philippians 3:9). Remarkably, He will then reward us for every good thing, no matter how small, that we ever did (Mark 9:41). What euphoria! We will stand before God's throne, having escaped the hell we deserve. *And* we'll receive God's rewards for our obedient service. This could not have gone better, especially considering the stakes.

The last judgment, though terrifying, means that Christians can relax. Yes, we will be fully exposed, but we'll also be fully embraced. We will never feel more known or loved. The God who sees straight through us, who understands our motives better than we understand ourselves, will call us His sons and daughters. Our judgment will feel like home.

The last judgment means we can also relax with others. If there was no day of reckoning, we might be tempted to take matters into our own hands. The ones who hurt us must pay; we can't let them get away with it. The last judgment guarantees they won't. There's no room in God's world for vigilante justice. Paul writes, "Do not take revenge, my dear friends, but leave room for God's wrath, for it is written: 'It is mine to avenge; I will repay,' says the Lord" (Romans 12:19).

The last judgment will be our vindication. We may suffer now for obeying the Bible. Friends and family may not understand. They may say we're foolish or perhaps wicked and curl their lips in scorn. The last judgment will clear our name. God will announce to the world that yes indeed, we were on the right side of history. Come, Lord Jesus!

242 What are our rewards?

Jesus promises to reward our good works (Matthew 5:11–12; Luke 6:35) and suggests that some Christians will receive more than others (Luke 19:11–27; see also 1 Corinthians 3:14–15). But He doesn't explicitly say what these rewards are.

Perhaps they are increased responsibilities in the next age. Jesus told a parable in which a master praised a servant for stewarding his master's gifts. He said, "Well done, good and faithful servant! You have been faithful with a few things; I will put you in charge of many things. Come and share your master's happiness!" (Matthew 25:21). Your station in life may seem low. No matter. Serve Jesus well, and you will be given a larger role in the life to come.

The Bible often describes our rewards as crowns. The apostle Paul disciplined himself to win "a crown that will last forever" (1 Corinthians 9:25). He anticipated receiving "the crown of righteousness, which the Lord, the righteous Judge, will award to me on that day" (2 Timothy 4:8). Those who persevere in their faith will receive a crown of life (James 1:12), and pastors who shepherd well "will receive the crown of glory that will never fade away" (1 Peter 5:4).

When John got a peek into heaven, he saw the people of God praising their Lord and laying their crowns before His throne (Revelation 4:10–11). Which raises the question: What's the point of earning rewards if we're going to give them back?

A laurel wreath at Olympia, Greece, birthplace of the Olympic games. The apostle Paul contrasted this "crown that will not last" with the Christian's enduring rewards (1 Corinthians 9:25).

Maybe that is the point. When someone important invites us to dinner, it's good manners to bring a gift. Especially if that person is a king or queen. What if that person is God, and the dinner is the climax of history? The consummation of all things is the "wedding supper of the Lamb," when Jesus marries His church (see Revelation 19:7–9). If we're going to the party, we're going to want to bring a gift.

But what could we give the God who owns everything? What could we give, period? We leave this life with nothing, so we'll show up to the wedding supper with nothing. Unless God saw our predicament long before we did and has already taken care of it. He promises to fill our obedient hands with rewards so we won't be embarrassed at heaven's epic celebration. We'll have something valuable to bring our King.

243 What is hell?

Hell is the place of final punishment for Satan, demons, and those humans who did not repent and trust Jesus for the forgiveness of their sin. The Bible describes hell as a "lake of fire" infested with worms that feast on human flesh (Revelation 20:14–15; Isaiah 66:24). This may not be literal, because the reality is much worse. God describes the terror of hell with images that we can barely grasp. Fire, darkness, worms, and gnashing of teeth. Jesus pointed to the Valley of Hinnom, just south of Jerusalem, an ancient place of child sacrifice and perhaps a smoldering garbage dump in His day, and said hell was like that (Matthew 5:22; 10:28; 18:9; 2 Chronicles 28:3).

He was reaching for words. There are no pictures to portray the horrors of hell. A July afternoon is not "hot as hell." Divorce is not "hard as hell." Root canals do not "hurt like hell." Nothing we can suffer in this life comes close to the agonies of hell. Not even slavery or the Holocaust. Jesus said if our hand or foot causes us to sin, it'd be better to cut it off than to suffer in hell forever; if our eye causes us to sin, it would be better to gouge it out than suffer forever in hell (Mark 9:43–49). Hell must never be a punchline. We should only speak about it with tears.

Like everything connected to the fall, hell is a mystery that cannot be explained. If we could explain hell, it wouldn't be so bad. Hell is irrational. It's not supposed to make sense.

But we can speak a few truths about hell. God does not hold anyone in hell against their will. The Christian apologist C. S. Lewis said hell is locked from the inside. Everyone in hell desperately wishes they were someplace else, yet they are unwilling to do the one thing that might free them—repent of their sin and follow Jesus as Lord. No one turns to Jesus unless the Holy Spirit draws them, and the Spirit is not doing this work in hell. To cite Lewis again, those in heaven say to God, "Your will be done," while God says to those in hell, "Your will be done."

Hell is a mystery, but there's a biblical logic to it. It's difficult to dismiss the biblical teaching about hell without minimizing our sin. If you don't believe in hell, it's nearly certain that you don't think we deserve it. We're not *that* bad. But now you've

This image of a California wildfire hints at Scripture's awful depiction of hell as a "lake of fire."

raised insurmountable questions about the cross. If we don't deserve hell, why did Jesus die? We can't say, which raises questions about Jesus. If He was not suffering the hell we deserve, does He need to be both man and God? You know, a man to take our place and God so His sacrifice would be perfect and sufficient to cover the sins of everyone. Maybe Jesus was only a man who died because—well, what can we say? There isn't a compelling reason left for the central event of our faith.

You see, the Bible is not a smorgasbord. We can't walk up to the Bible buffet and take an extra helping of grace but skip the justice. Load up on love and hold the wrath. The Bible is like a sweater—yank hard enough on one strand, and the whole thing unravels. Hell is the most terrible teaching in the whole Bible, yet if we pull it out, the death of Jesus makes no sense.

The cross reminds us that God does not inflict upon anyone anything that He has not already suffered. Jesus suffered the terrors of hell when He wailed from the cross, "My God, my God, why have you forsaken me?" (Matthew 27:46). We can't explain why God allows people to remain in hell. Why doesn't He change the hearts of the damned so they will love Him? Yet we know that God has allowed hell to get to Him. Something unimaginably horrific happened in that dreadful moment. Something Jesus braced for and sweat blood anticipating, yet it still crushed His soul.

Jesus went to hell so you don't have to. Hell is so unnecessary! God has graciously kept you alive this long so you can turn to Him and believe in His Son. He has given you this moment. Use it. Repent of your sin. Do it right now. Tell Jesus you are sorry for living for yourself. You believe in Him and His death on your behalf, and from this moment on you will strive, with the Spirit's help, to live for Him. Tell someone else what you have done so they can avoid hell too!

244 Where is hell?

The Bible doesn't say. Medieval Christians thought hell might be in the center of the earth. Fiery volcanoes erupted from there and Aristotle's philosophy indicated it should be there. His "chain of being" posited higher, spiritual essences in heaven and lesser, material objects on earth. The heaviest, densest matter—what one would expect to find in hell—would invariably sink to the furthest depths, all the way to the center of our round planet.

The New Testament suggests that Hades, a place of punishment for the wicked, is underground. Jesus warned unbelievers in Capernaum that they "will go down to Hades" (Luke 10:15). *Hades* is the Greek term that translates the Hebrew word *Sheol,* and the Old Testament said that was underground (Numbers 16:31–34; 1 Samuel 28:13–15).

But Hades is not the final hell. It's a fiery holding cell for the damned who die without believing in Christ. It's where they go until the resurrection and the last judgment, when they and Hades itself will be "thrown into the lake of fire" (Revelation 20:14).

Where is this lake of fire? We can't say, except that it must lie outside of this good creation. God promises to redeem all things, and that wouldn't be possible if a part of His world contained those who are unredeemed (Colossians 1:20). Hell is outside of our universe—perhaps in the suffocating emptiness of a black hole?—where no light exists and no light can escape. Hell is for humans who, because they turned their backs on the true human, Jesus Christ, disintegrated into wretched parodies of who they were meant to be. They lost everything, forever. And so needlessly! If you haven't already, repent of your sin and put your faith in Jesus. Do it now, before it's too late.

245 Does hell last forever?

Some Christians suggest hell lasts forever, but not the humans who are sent there. They believe some people will suffer more and longer than others, but no one will suffer forever. After a period of punishment that God deems sufficient, He will declare that sinners have atoned for their sins and mercifully allow them to go out of existence.

This view, called annihilationism or conditional immortality (only believers in Jesus live forever), notices that Scripture often says that hell's fire, smoke, and worms last forever. It doesn't necessarily say that those in hell will exist forever (Isaiah 66:24; Matthew 3:12; 25:41; Revelation 14:11).

I understand why Christians would want to believe this. Who can fathom the fierce and unrelenting wrath of God? One friend told me it's unthinkable. I agreed. That's the point. That's why God urges us to believe in His Son and to tell others to do the same.

While I'm sympathetic to the annihilationists' concerns, two Scripture passages seem to straightforwardly say that those in hell are forever conscious. John says the devil, the beast, and the false prophet will be thrown into the lake of fire, where "they will be tormented day and night for ever and ever" (Revelation 20:10). These are creatures, and the latter two seem to be humans who will endure everlasting, conscious punishment. And John clearly has humans in mind in Revelation 14:10–11, where he says the people who receive the mark of the beast "will be tormented with burning sulfur. . . . And the smoke of their torment will rise for ever and ever. There will be no rest day or night for those who worship the beast."

Annihilationism does not deny hell, but it does minimize it. Annihilationists believe that no finite person deserves infinite punishment. Is this true? If our sin is against an infinite God, then it's possible, even likely, that the punishment of our sin is more than we can ever repay. We cannot atone for what we have done.

And what would be the point of the fire, smoke, and worms lasting forever if no one is left to experience them? Why did Jesus warn so often and urgently about hell if He knew the suffering wasn't permanent? Hell would still be terrible, but the stakes would be dramatically lower.

We must never minimize what's at risk in this life. Those without Jesus face unending torment. Not torture, as if they were subjected to something they didn't deserve, but endless, agonizing torment.

Why wouldn't this awareness rob the redeemed of their joy? If we are with Jesus and a loved one isn't, how would this not ruin our happiness? We can't explain this because we're talking about the mystery of evil, but God has promised to "wipe every tear from [our] eyes" (Revelation 21:4). This implies that some of us will show up with tears, tears that must be wiped away. And will be.

246 What is heaven?

Heaven is the throne room of God, where the Father, Son, and Spirit most directly reveal themselves to the angels and saints who have departed this life. Jesus ascended to heaven after His resurrection, to rule the earth from His Father's right hand. We who believe in Jesus will follow Him there when we die. We will worship Jesus with multitudes of redeemed people "from every nation, tribe, people and language," shouting, "Salvation belongs to our God, who sits on the throne, and to the Lamb" (Revelation 7:9–10). We will never be more alive. Yet we won't be fully satisfied.

There is no suffering in heaven, but there is impatience. The martyred saints inject a plea with their praise: "How long, Sovereign Lord, holy and true, until you judge the inhabitants of the earth and avenge our blood?" (Revelation 6:10). How long until You return, resurrect our bodies, restore all things, and show the world that we were right all along? God gave each of them a white robe, symbolizing their

The Bible's descriptions of heaven imply much more substance than the popular conception of fluffy white clouds.

righteous victory, and told them to "wait a little longer" (verse 11).

Praise God that we who die in Christ go to heaven. And praise God that heaven is not the end. As wonderful as it will be to worship our Lord as a disembodied soul, there is one thing better—to live with Jesus as a whole person, in our resurrected body, on this redeemed earth. When we die, we will praise Jesus for bringing us to heaven. And we will praise Him for what happens next.

247 What happens after heaven?

Christians call heaven our "intermediate state" because it is where we temporarily live between this life and the next. When we go to heaven, we are "home with the Lord" (2 Corinthians 5:8). We will worship God there, and that's all we know for sure. The Bible says nothing more about heaven because taking us to heaven is not God's goal. His ultimate plan is not to snatch us out of this world but to come to this world and save it.

Remember, Christians hope for the three R's: the *return* of Christ, the *resurrection* of our bodies, and the *restoration* of all things. We believe that Jesus will return—gloriously, physically, and triumphantly—to rule this earth that He took back from Satan. Heaven, the throne room of God, will become a place on earth. That might happen today, so we look to the skies and pray the next-to-last sentence of Scripture, "Come, Lord Jesus!" (Revelation 22:20).

When Jesus comes, He will raise our dead bodies. Your body is not just the shell for the real you, the temporary residence of your soul. Your soul can exist independently of your body, as it must in heaven. But it won't stay that way for long. The Christian hope is not that our souls go to heaven, but that Jesus will bring back our souls with Him, resurrect our bodies, and put us back together. We will live forever with Jesus as whole people, body and soul, on the earth He designed for us.

When Jesus comes, He will restore all things (Acts 3:21; Colossians 1:20; Ephesians 1:10). Everything that sin has broken, His grace will restore. God created this world good, Satan ruined it through Adam's fall, and God wants it all back. He will send King Jesus not to obliterate our fallen world but to fix and rule over it. Heaven sings the Hallelujah Chorus: "The kingdom of the world has become the kingdom of our Lord and of his Messiah, and he will reign for ever and ever" (Revelation 11:15). Jesus will reign forever here, over His whole wide world.

248 What is the new earth?

God promises our final home will be "a new heaven and a new earth" (2 Peter 3:13; Revelation 21:1–5). *Heaven* here means sky, where airplanes fly. "In the beginning God created the heavens and the earth" (Genesis 1:1); in the end He will recreate "new heavens and a new earth" (Isaiah 65:17). Creation, then new creation.

The phrase "new earth" means our final destination is both *new* and *earth*. What is different about the new earth, and what remains the same? The apostle Peter gives us a clue: "But in keeping with his promise we are looking forward to a new heaven and a new earth, where righteousness dwells" (2 Peter 3:13). The one new aspect that Peter sees is righteousness. Unlike this fallen age that has been ravaged

The lakes and mountains of Colorado kindle our longing for God's promised new earth.

by evil and injustice, the new earth will be inhabited by righteousness.

Righteousness describes actions rather than things. What we do not what we are. We might say someone has a "righteous hand," but only because she uses it to do righteous acts. Hands aren't righteous by themselves. Neither are trees or tomatoes. And definitely not kale! Only actions can be righteous. Here's the point: when Peter looks ahead to the new earth, he does not see new things but new, righteous actions, and the peace and justice that flow from them. The new earth seems to be this earth—with its mountains, rivers, forests, and animals—that's been fixed.

God says as much when He thunders from His throne, "I am making everything new!" (Revelation 21:5). Notice God does not say, "I am making new things," but "I am making all things new." God is not replacing our things with other things; He is taking the things that are already here and restoring them. The new earth is this earth, redeemed from the ravages of sin.

This means our everlasting choice is not between heaven and hell. It's between hell and here. Would you like to live forever here, on the earth that has been fully restored? Then repent of your sin—the sin that is destroying you and damning you to hell—turn from that sin and throw all your weight on Jesus, the God who came to earth to cross out our sin and save the planet.

If you believe in and follow Jesus, stop what you're doing and look around. All that you see will one day be yours, when you return to reign with Jesus. He said, "Blessed are the meek, for they will inherit the earth" (Matthew 5:5). He meant you.

249 What will we do on the new earth?

We will worship Jesus, the God who gave His life to rescue us from hell and live with us forever. Nothing will be more satisfying than praising our Lord and Savior with millions of other redeemed people. We were made for this.

And we were made for more. Jesus is the center of the new earth, yet there's also a circumference. Adam and Eve walked with God in Eden, and they also made time for other activities. They tilled the garden, named and played with the animals, and enjoyed each other's company, if you know what I mean. Likewise, on the new earth we will exult in the worship of Jesus, and we'll also have time—literally forever—to enjoy the best this redeemed world can offer.

Do you enjoy oranges, strawberries, and peaches? Every fruit you've ever eaten has come from cursed soil. Imagine the luscious flavors of the new earth! And what about colors? How brilliantly will blue pop and red sizzle when the haze of sin is removed? Do you enjoy music, sports, technology, and travel? You will have forever to see this world, engineer new computers, craft recipes, play games, snuggle with lions, and shoot the breeze with thousands of your new best friends. If you like being human and you enjoy living here, you're going to love the new earth.

You can scrap your bucket list. It's not true that you only go around once. If you're a Christian, you're coming back, and you'll have forever to do in the next life what you didn't get to this time around.

Redemption restores creation. All of it. The only good of creation that won't

Peace will reign on the new earth—even between what are now predators and prey.

appear on the new earth is marriage (Matthew 22:30). Because of the fall, people die and divorce, and their spouses remarry. Some people, through no fault of their own, have had multiple husbands or wives. If marriage were to exist on the new earth, who would these people be married to? The fall has so scrambled marriage that God can't restore one marriage without violating another. So marriage as we know it now won't exist then.

But marriage won't exactly go away—it will be fulfilled in a higher key. God says that marriage now is a shadow of the deeper union between Jesus and His church (Ephesians 5:32). On the new earth, we'll all be married to Jesus, and we'll remember whom we had married in this life. We won't enjoy less intimacy with them; we'll simply enjoy more, nonsexual intimacy with others.

Redemption restores creation, all of it, so animals will exist peacefully on the new earth: "The wolf and the lamb will feed together, and the lion will eat straw like the ox" (Isaiah 65:25). If animals no longer eat each other, does that mean we can't eat them either? Maybe the wolf won't bite the lamb, but might we?

No. Killing an animal and eating it would disrupt the peace of God's restored creation. He promises "no more death or mourning or crying or pain, for the old order of things has passed away" (Revelation 21:4). This certainly applies to humans, but it's not limited to us. Before you lament your last barbecue, remember that we're already developing plant-based imitation meat. The redeemed chefs on the new earth could easily perfect the recipe—if they had to and if we'd care. We'll likely be so thrilled with the succulent fruit from the tree of life that we won't hanker for anything else (Revelation 22:2).

We don't know all that we'll do on the new earth, but the pictures of Scripture indicate it will be much like our present experience—just with all of its sin and suffering removed. This perfect life will be yours if you give your life to Jesus.

250 How is the end better than the beginning?

God does not merely restore creation. He consummates it, taking our world to the higher place it was always intended to go. The end of our world is better than its beginning in at least five ways.

1. ***Immanuel.*** God walked with Adam and Eve in Eden, then He left. He came and left, came and left. In the end, God is coming to stay. When heaven descends to earth, He will say, "Look! God's dwelling place is now among the people, and he will dwell with them. They will be his people, and God himself will be with them and be their God" (Revelation 21:3). The Bible ends with God fulfilling the promise of His name, Immanuel. He is "God with us," here and forever more.

2. ***Spiritual bodies.*** God says our resurrection bodies will be "spiritual" (see 1 Corinthians 15:42–49). This doesn't mean they won't also be physical, because Jesus' resurrection body remained physical, and His body is the pattern for ours. Our resurrection bodies won't be less than physical, but they will be more. Unlike our present bodies, which are one accident or virus away from death, our spiritual bodies will be indestructible. I'm saving cliff diving, bungee jumping, and parachuting for the next life. Do what you want now, but I won't jump off things until I have my resurrection body!

3. ***Higher culture.*** The Bible's story begins in a garden and ends in a city (Revelation 21:2). What's the difference between a garden and a city? Humans. We take the raw materials of nature and build bridges, parks, and cafés. Humans have made stunning technological and cultural breakthroughs in the last century. Consider what we'll achieve when we have unlimited time to study, experiment, and improvise without the handicap of sin. If you enjoy finely tuned engines, engrossing novels, and the perfect cup of coffee, you're going to love the new earth.

4. ***Glorification.*** Adam and Eve were created good but with the possibility of sin. Which they did. On the new earth, we will be much better off for we'll be perfected and confirmed in righteousness. We will have the absolute assurance that God will not allow us to mess this up. What peace of mind! (Romans 8:30).

5. ***Grace.*** There is one way the end is better not *despite* our fall but *because* of it. Adam and Eve knew God was good, but they could not have guessed His bottomless, extravagant grace. Only forgiven sinners can begin to understand the depths of God's love. Angels have never received grace, and they stand on tiptoe trying to see what you and I commonly thank God for (1 Peter 1:12).

Redemption restores creation with three exceptions. As the last question explained, marriage is the one good of creation that will not be renewed on the new earth. There also are two—and only two—effects of the fall that will never be fixed. Isaiah says when wolves and lambs are feeding together and lions have become vegetarians, yet "dust will be the serpent's food" (65:25). The snake was cursed in Eden, and that curse will never lift. Also, Jesus still bears the scars of His cross even in His resurrection body (John 20:27).

These two traces of the fall will forever remind us of the greatest story ever told. The story of the Bible, the story of our lives. At some point we will have lived on the new earth for a gazillion years. But we'll never get full of ourselves, thinking that somehow we deserve this. Every time we see a snake slithering in the dirt, we'll remember the depths of our sin. Every time we see Jesus' scars, we'll remember the deeper reach of His love. And we'll praise His bottomless grace.

Are you in Christ?

This book answers two hundred fifty questions about God and His Word. Now God has one for you. It's the most important question you will ever be asked: *Are you in Jesus?* Nothing matters if you're not; everything will be well if you are.

God loves you. He created you to live forever with Him here, on this restored earth. He so much wants to live with you that He sent His Son to die for you. Will you receive Jesus? Will you turn from your sin and tell Him you believe and want to follow Him?

The Bible ends with God's invitation: "The Spirit and the bride say, 'Come!' And let the one who hears say, 'Come!' Let the one who is thirsty come; and let the one who wishes take the free gift of the water of life" (Revelation 22:17).

Are you thirsty for a meaningful life? Do you fear everlasting torment in hell? You can live forever with the God who died for you. Come home.

Acknowledgments

This book was the vision of Paul Muckley. Paul is a college friend who pitched this idea and then diligently located the pictures and edited my text. I don't quite know how to express how delightful it has been to work with Paul. His professional competence is exceeded only by his energy and humble kindness. He is one of the very good ones.

This book was supported by my dear wife, Julie, whose loving home gave me the space over the past year to complete it. Avery, Landon, and Alayna are preparing to launch into life, leaving us with the love we've built. It hurts to say goodbye, but I like what we've got.

This book was cheered by Harvey Alley. Each time I wrote a book, he would look at me and say, "What this book needs is pictures." His wife would roll her eyes and say, "Oh, Harv." Jan died of cancer several years ago, and Harvey passed away last month, still living with enthusiasm at age 94. He was pleased that I finally took his advice, and I am pleased to include a few of his achingly beautiful photos (see p. 379, 399, and 404).

I dedicate this book to Harvey and Jan Alley, for their love for Jesus, their family, and the many outsiders who found two friends on the inside who saw them and served them.

–Michael Wittmer

Endnotes

1 Paul D. Wegner, *The Journey from Texts to Translations* (Grand Rapids: Baker Academic, 1999), 30.

2 This statement of the Bible's theme comes from Doug Wilson.

3 Crossway Publishers, "The Origins of the Red-Letter Bible," March 23, 2006. Online: https://www.crossway.org/articles/red-letter-origin/

4 Verlyn D. Verbrugge and Keith R. Krell, *Paul & Money* (Grand Rapids: Zondervan, 2015), 100-2.

5 Josephus, *Contra Apion* 1.8 §42, in *Josephus in Nine Volumes; Volume 1: The Life Against Apion*, trans. H. St. J. Thackeray (Cambridge: Harvard University Press, 1976), 179–81.

6 J. Stevenson, ed., *A New Eusebius* (Grand Rapids: Baker Academic, 2013), 130–31.

7 *The Gospel According to Thomas*, trans. A. Guillaumont, et al. (New York: Harper & Brothers, 1959), 56–57.

8 F. G. Kenyon, *Our Bible and the Ancient Manuscripts*, rev. A. W. Adams (New York: Harper & Brothers, 1958), 78–79.

9 Craig L. Blomberg, *Can We Still Believe the Bible?* (Grand Rapids: Brazos Press, 2014), 35–36; J. Ed Komoszewski, M. James Sawyer, and Daniel B. Wallace, *Reinventing Jesus* (Grand Rapids: Kregel, 2006), 71–72.

10 Tacitus, *Annals*, xv. 44. This translation is from *Tacitus: The Annals of Imperial Rome*, trans. Michael Grant (Baltimore: Penguin Books, 1956), 354.

11 Flavius Josephus, *Antiquities*, 18:3:3. This version, with its later Christian insertions edited out, is derived from Edwin Yamauchi, "Jesus Outside the New Testament: What Is the Evidence?" in *Jesus Under Fire: Modern Scholarship Reinvents the Historical Jesus*, ed. by Michael J. Wilkins and J. P. Moreland (Grand Rapids: Zondervan, 1995), 212–14.

12 Mortimer J. Adler and Charles Van Doren, *How to Read a Book* (New York: Simon & Schuster, 1940; 1972), 341–43 (emphasis theirs).

13 Søren Kierkegaard, "The matter is quite simple," *Journals and Papers* 2872 (X3 A 34 n.d., 1850), as quoted in Stephen Backhouse, *Kierkegaard: A Single Life* (Grand Rapids: Zondervan, 2016), 172.

14 John Calvin, *Institutes of the Christian Religion*, I.7.4, ed. John T. McNeill, trans. Ford Lewis Battles (Philadelphia: The Westminster Press, 1960), 78–79. Subsequent quotes in this question are from I.7.4 and I.8.1.

15 Anselm, "Proslogion," chapter 8, in *Anselm of Canterbury: The Major Works*, ed. Brian Davies (New York: Oxford University Press, 1998), 91.

16 The Eastern church says the Spirit proceeds only from the Father. The Western church, at the Council of Toledo in 589, added that the Spirit proceeds also from the Son. This *filioque* ("and the Son") clause, which the West inserted into the Nicene Creed, is the main doctrinal reason the Eastern Church split from the West in 1054.

17 Basil of Caesarea, *Epistle* CLIX.2, in J. Stevenson, ed., *Creeds, Councils, and Controversies* (1966; revised 1989; Grand Rapids: Baker Academic, 2012), 97.

18 For instance, C. John Collins, *Reading Genesis Well* (Grand Rapids: Zondervan, 2018) and J. B. Stump, ed., *Four Views on Creation, Evolution, and Intelligent Design* (Grand Rapids: Zondervan, 2017).

19 Ken Ham, "Young-Earth Creationism," in *Four Views on Creation, Evolution, and Intelligent Design*, 29. The four views presented here are summarized in this book.

20 Calvin, Institutes 1.14.7, trans. Ford Lewis Battles (Philadelphia: The Westminster Press, 1960), 167.

21 This is a hypothetical scenario. God's hands don't slip, so the Godhead was never in danger of rupture. Nevertheless, the harrowing peril was real, as expressed by Jesus' bewildered cry of despair.

22 Many Reformed Christians believe God's first covenant was a "covenant of works" made with Adam and Eve, promising obedience if they obeyed and death if they did not (Westminster Confession 7.2). While this accurately depicts God's relationship with Adam and Eve, the Bible does not say this arrangement was a covenant.

23 See James Hoffmeier, *Ancient Israel in Sinai* (New York: Oxford University Press, 2011) and Manfred Bietak, "Exodus Evidence: An Egyptologist Looks at Biblical History," *Biblical Archaeology Review* 42:3 (May/June, 2016): 31–37.

24 God also gave instructions regarding slaves, who could come from either foreigners or resident aliens but not fellow Israelites (Leviticus 25:44–46 says *ger* may become slaves; see note 25).

25 Sometimes these terms overlap, but in legal contexts *ger* is often used to distinguish resident aliens from native Israelites on one hand and mere foreigners (*nekhar* and *zar*) on the other.

26 This essay is indebted to James K. Hoffmeier, *The Immigration Crisis* (Wheaton: Crossway, 2009).

27 Both quotes in this paragraph are found in Irenaeus, Against Heresies III.4, in J. Stevenson, ed. *A New Eusebius*, rev. W. H. C. Frend (London: SPCK, 1987), 116.

28 The material on December 25 relies on Andrew McGowan, "How December 25 Became Christmas" Bible Review 18:6 (December 2002), 46–48, 57–58.

29 This may not be the whole story. Roman soldiers structured their day and campaigns around expressions of loyalty to the "genius of the emperor" and other gods. Many early Christians believed they must not do this, and it may be that Cornelius and the converts of Caesar's household decided they could not stay. This seems plausible, though the Bible doesn't say.

30 This paragraph is indebted to Jim Samra, *The Gift of Church* (Grand Rapids: Zondervan, 2010).

31 Jonathan Merritt, "Faithful to the end: An interview with Eugene Peterson," *Religion News Service*, September 27, 2013. Online: https://religionnews.com/2013/09/27/faithful-end-interview-eugene-peterson/.

32 "Christian Movements and Denominations," Pew Research Center. Online: https://www.pewforum .org/2011/12/19/global-christianity-movements-and-denominations/.

33 Martin Luther, "Eight Sermons at Wittenberg: The Eighth Sermon, March 16, 1522," in *Luther's Works* 51, ed. John W. Doberstein and Helmut T. Lehmann (Philadelphia: Muhlenberg Press, 1959), 98.

34 Roland H. Bainton, *Here I Stand* (New York: Abingdon-Cokesbury Press, 1950), 45.

35 Bainton, *Here I Stand*, 54.

36 Martin Luther, "Lectures on Galatians (1535)," in *Luther's Works* 27, ed. Lewis W. Spitz and Helmut T. Lehmann (Philadelphia: Muhlenberg, 1960), 13.

37 Bainton, *Here I Stand*, 59.

38 Bainton, *Here I Stand*, 65.

Art Credits

16 S: Dew scientartist / 19 Flickr: NYC Wanderer / 20 S: Farres / 20–21 Bette Dickinson / 24 S: Renata Sedmakova / 26: Barbour Publishing, Inc. / 27: Michael E. Wittmer / 28 S: Renata Sedmakova / 30: S: John Theodor / 32 S: Buradaki / 34 S: Renata Sedmakova / 37 S: Max Maximov / 38 S: Adam Jan Figel / 40 S: Joyfuldesigns / 43 S: Everett—Art / 44 S: Renata Sedmakova / 47 S: Keep Smiling Photography / 48 S: Francois Arseneault / 53 S: ChameleonsEye / 55 S: Boris Strojko / 58 S: TalyaPhoto / 59 S: M. Bonotto / 61 S: Arkady Mazor / 64 S: Michael E. Wittmer / 67 S: Renata Sedmakova / 70 S: Marco Peretto / 73 S: Seth Aronstam / 75 S: ChameleonsEye / 77 S: PhotoFires / 79 S: Jorisvo / 83 Michael E. Wittmer / 84 S: Everett—Art / 86 S: Artur Bogacki / 91 S: Nancy Bauer / 94 S: Igal Shkolnik / 96 W: Oren Rozen / 97 Michael E. Wittmer / 99 S: Lincoln Rogers / 102 S. Everett Historical / 104 S: Cecil Bo Dzwowa / 107 S: Nancy Bauer / 108 S: Sean M. Smith / 110 S: guruXOX / 113 W: Google Art Project / 114 S: Chadin0 / 117 S: Renata Sedmakova / 119 S: Perlphoto / 123 S: Dwi Yulianto / 125 S: Nicku / 128 S: Pullia / 131 S: Zwiebackesser / 132 S: Martin Charles Hatch / 134 S: Renata Sedmakova / 136 S: Renata Sedmakova / 138 S: Fotoaway / 139 Michael E. Wittmer / 141 S: Renata Sedmakova / 143 S: Alex Segre / 147 S: James Kirkikis / 149 S: Pixelheadphoto/Digitalskillet / 151 S: Gorodenkoff / 153 S: Georgios Kollidas / 154 S: Pmmrd / 157 NASA / 160 S: Fausto Renda / 163 S: Dipak Shelare / 167 W: Tretyakov Gallery / 171 S: Renata Sedmakova / 175 S: Vieriu Adrian / 179 S: Uncle Leo / 183 W: Osama Shukir Muhammad Amin / 187 S: Paula Cobleigh / 188 S: Everett—Art / 190 S: Renata Sedmakova / 192 S: IvashStudio / 193 S: Tuomas Kallio / 196 S: Everett—Art / 198 S: Sean Pavone / 199 S: Crazystocker / 201 Ashley Wittmer / 203 S: Wead / 204 S: Magnus Binnerstam / 206 S: Zvonimir Atletic / 208 W: Tiberioclaudio99 / 210 W: Luc Viatour (lucnix.be) / 214 S: Anthony Correia / 216 S: Renata Sedmakova / 217 S: Ruskpp / 218 S: Hurricanehank / 220 W: Daderot / 222 W: Rama / 225 S: Albert Russ / 226 S: TTstudio / 229 S: Jorisvo / 231 S: Valentina Razumova / 232 S: Zvonimir Atletic / 235 S: Renata Sedmakova / 238 S: Chameleons-Eye / 240 S: Nicku / 242 S: Max Zalevsky / 243 S: Jorisvo / 245 S: Renata Sedmakova / 249 W: Wellcome Images / 252 S: Jorisvo / 254 S: Tonya Jaure / 256 S: Jono Photography / 259 S: Erik Lam / 261 S: Den Rozhnovsky / 267 S: Diego G. Diaz / 269 S: Ink Drop / 273 S: Andrey Starostin / 274 W: Affresco / 278 S: Everett Historical / 282 W: Gustave Dore / 285 S: QQ7 / 287 S: Everett—Art / 289 S: Yuri Turkov / 291 W: José Luiz Bernardes Ribeiro / 294 S: Paulius Bacinskas / 297 W: Google Art Project / 299 Michael E. Wittmer / 302 S: Bogdan Vasilescu / 304 S: Nancy Bauer / 306 S: Renata Sedmakova / 310 S: Dale Primov / 312 S: Eduardo Estellez / 315 S: Matremors / 316 Michael E. Wittmer / 318 Michael E. Wittmer / 321 S: GotovyyStock / 323 S: Zvonimir Atletic / 325 S: Renata Sedmakova / 327 S: Ruskpp / 330 S: Jorisvo / 333 S: Renata Sedmakova / 335 S: Alexey Borodin / 339 S: FooTToo / 344 S: Mick Harper / 347 S: Adam Jan Figel / 350 Michael E. Wittmer / 353 S: Renata Sedmakova / 355 S: Renata Sedmakova / 356 S: Keith McIntyre / 358 S: Renata Sedmakova / 360 S: Katiekk / 362 Michael E. Wittmer / 365 S: Ruskpp / 366 S: Stig Alenas / 368 S: Gudkov Andrey / 370 S: Anne Kitzman / 372 S: Beeline Aerial / 373 S: A. Katz / 375 S: Renata Sedmakova / 377 S: John Wollwerth / 379: Harvey Alley / 383 S: Tyson Ross / 385 S: Mark Zhyhman / 387 Michael E. Wittmer / 391 S: Renata Sedmakova / 394 S: Paolo Bona / 398 S: Renata Sedmakova / 399 Harvey Alley / 401 S: Andrew Hagen / 404 Harvey Alley / 406 W: Toby Hudson / 410 S: Renata Sedmakova / 414 S: MIA Studio / 417 S: Freedom Studio / 418 S: Ivan Yohan / 422 S: Anthony Correia / 426 W: Andrey Mironov / 430 S: Antony McAulay / 432 S: Vadim Petrakov / 434 Michael E. Wittmer / 439 S: ChameleonsEye / 440 S: Pieruschka / 443 Michael E. Wittmer / 444 S: Tokar / 448 S: Ververidis Vasilis / 450 S: Erin Donalson / 454 S: Bouybin / 456 Michael E. Wittmer / 458 S: Iakov Filimonov, Eric Isselee

S: Shutterstock / W: WikiMedia